The Northeast

The Midwest
and the Great Plains

The South

alexander

This, as citizens, we all inherit.
This is ours, to love and live upon,
and use wisely down all the generations of the future.

Reader's Digest

AMERICA
THE
BEAUTIFUL

THE READER'S DIGEST ASSOCIATION, INC.

Pleasantville, New York   Montreal

The acknowledgments that appear on pages 351-52 are
hereby made a part of this copyright page.

Library of Congress Catalog Card Number 73-103727
ISBN 0-89577-003-2

Printed in the United States of America

Seventh Printing, March 1979

CONTENTS

Part I

EMERALD FORESTS, GRANITE COASTS

Maine New Hampshire Vermont
Massachusetts Rhode Island Connecticut
New York Pennsylvania New Jersey

THE NATURAL LOOK OF NEW ENGLAND

LOUISE DICKINSON RICH

Although New England is the smallest regional division of the nation, it has greater geographical variety than any other area its size in the country, perhaps in the world. To the south, sandy beaches are washed by a warm and lazy sea, while to the north, along the coast of Maine, a tremendous icy surf constantly assaults great granite ledges. In between are New Hampshire's pebble and shingle beaches. This long coastline is deeply indented by quiet basins like Buzzards Bay, wide estuaries such as that of the Kennebec, safe harbors large and small, narrow inlets, hidden coves—as well as the only true fjord on the Atlantic coast, Somes Sound. Balancing these indentations are countless capes, peninsulas and promontories ranging in character from Cape Cod's crooked arm and the gentle swell of Cape Ann to the forbidding crags of Schoodic Point.

Offshore lie hundreds of islands, some of them —Nantucket, Mount Desert and Vinalhaven— large enough to support whole villages. Others are less than an acre, too small to support anything except a little coarse salt grass, some barnacles and blue mussels, and a few gulls and terns. Many of the medium-size islands are inhabited by man, but many more are not and never have been. They rise from the sea, changed only by the slow, inexorable agencies of wind and weather, time and tide from what they were on the day of their creation.

Interior New England varies as much as the shoreline does. Vermont, most of New Hampshire and part of Maine are mountainous. Much of this area is heavily forested. Western Massachusetts is folded into quiet hills. Between the uplands and

Spruce trees crowd down to the rocky shore of a cove on Maine's Mount Desert Island, site of Acadia National Park. Compressed by the weight of glaciers for thousands of years, the New England coast is now very slowly rebounding.

the sea lies a plain, a piedmont broken occasionally by salt marshes and freshwater swamps. Here the towns are surrounded by open meadows, orchards and airy groves. All over New England lie thousands of lakes and ponds, shallow and warm on the southern plain, incredibly deep and cold in the mountains. Some, like Moosehead, are large enough to be dangerous at times, and some are so tiny that they are little more than big springholes. Many of the rivers of New England—the Connecticut, the Androscoggin, the Penobscot—rise in mountain lakes and snarl down steep gorges to the lowlands where they become broad and placid as they meander to the sea.

There are moors and heaths in New England, and natural caves, underground streams, even a small desert, all within a day's driving distance of one another. None of these features is the largest or smallest, the highest or deepest in the world. In New England almost nothing except the variety rates a superlative—that and the beauty. But, barring a geyser or an active volcano, New England does have a sample, in sample size, of a large number of geographical attributes.

Variety is not restricted to the terrain. The climate is as diversified as the land and, due to many factors, is almost unpredictable. The paths of storms change unaccountably as they approach New England, or cold fronts that should have stayed in Canada creep south. Great banks of fog steal silently in from the ocean, blotting out everything. Blizzards howl down from the north, deep snow blankets the country, and the mercury plunges to well below zero; or a heat wave sweeps in from the Midwest, and the thermometer registers over ninety for days and nights on end. Hurricanes roar destructively up the Atlantic into New England; a three-day nor'easter brings a drenching rain; or a dry west wind prevails for weeks, parching the land. But betweentimes come days when the weather is absolutely perfect, blue and diamond clear, cool as a young leaf in the shade, warm as new milk in the sun.

The contradictory nature of New England arises not from spells cast by the Salem witches but from its geologic history and peculiar position on the face of the globe. Twenty thousand or so years ago the great polar ice cap, with its center over Hudson Bay, extended south to a line roughly determined by Nantucket, Block Island and Long Island. At its thin edge, it was probably over 1000 feet deep. This enormous weight caused the crust of the earth to fault along the line of the islands, so that the entire area of New England was depressed several hundred feet. The shore and many of the lower hills sank beneath the sea, which crept up the river valleys, encircled the higher elevations and lapped against the bases of what had been inland mountains.

Eventually the glacier retreated, the enormous pressure was relieved, and the resilient crust of the earth rose toward its former position. That it was only partly successful in regaining the lost altitude is shown by marine fossils at the 200-foot level on Mount Desert and Isle au Haut, Maine. The damage was too great for complete recovery. The result was what geologists call a drowned coastline: a coastline bordered by a continental shelf that was once a coastal plain, ringed by islands that were once hilltops and indented by bays and estuaries that were once mountain valleys.

Other things took place as the glacier melted. The millions of tons of boulders and gravel that it had pushed before it in its advance were left stranded to form ridges of land called terminal moraines. These formed the basic structure of what would become a sweetly rolling countryside. Other deposits dammed rivers, making large lakes. One of these was Lake Hitchcock, which extended 160 miles to the north from what is now Middletown, Connecticut. When the dam finally broke and the imprisoned water rushed forth, it carved the broad and beautiful Connecticut Valley the length of New England, between the Green and the White Mountains. Other riverbeds, such as that of the Narragansett, were washed out by the melted ice water that streamed from under the glacier; and as the land continued to rise, bodies of water were trapped in low-lying areas. One of these was a large inland sea between Plymouth, Massachusetts, and Newport, Rhode Island, which through drainage and evaporation shrank to become Hockamock Swamp, one of the few large swamps in New England.

At last this chaotic period came to an end. The ice retreated far to the north, and the land became stabilized at about its present level. The framework of New England had been formed. It needed only time and the patient, stubborn work of the lichens and mosses, then the grasses and weeds, finally the shrubs and trees, to clothe the barren rocks and lifeless sand and silt for the shelter and support of animal life; to create the New England of today.

The weather of New England needs as much explaining as the topography. Lying halfway between the equator and the North Pole, the region should have a typical north-temperate climate.

Moreover, New England is bordered on the south and east by the Atlantic Ocean, which ought—one would suppose—to exert the modifying effect on climate that is commonly, and for the most part correctly, attributed to large bodies of water. One would also suppose that the wall of mountains to the north and west would divert storms originating in those directions and provide shelter for the area.

None of these things works the way it should, however. While some storms are diverted to the sea by the mountains along the valleys of the Hudson and the St. Lawrence, others that should follow that course unaccountably soar over the wall. Instead of stabilizing the climate, the Atlantic compounds confusion. The warm Gulf Stream sweeping north and the frigid Labrador Current flowing south meet just off the New England coast at a point referred to by Down East lobstermen as "the fog factory," the place where fog is made by the confluence of waters of very different temperatures. Furthermore, neither ocean current is irrevocably committed to a fixed course. They whip back and forth slightly, and the air and water temperatures alongshore faithfully reflect these deviations.

Weather can change fast in New England. "If you don't like it," say New Englanders, "wait a minute." And it's true that following a brief, sharp thunderstorm the mercury sometimes drops as much as forty degrees in as many minutes; and that you can go to bed in a solid freeze and wake up to a balmy spring morning. In short, the region that, according to the rules, should have four well-defined seasons of about equal length has instead a hodgepodge climate. It is often possible to pick roses at Christmastime on Cape Cod and to ski on Mount Washington on the Fourth of July.

Not surprisingly, the weather preoccupies the thoughts of New Englanders, especially in the country. A city visitor to rural Maine once told me of a conversation he'd had with a local farmer soon after World War II. He'd been going to Maine regularly for a long time until Pearl Harbor. Then wartime pressures forced him to skip his annual vacation for several years. Finally, the hostilities having ended, he was able to return. He found his farming friend busy in the hayfield and, thinking of the beaches of Normandy and Iwo Jima and food rationing and the atom bomb and the surrender of Japan, he said, "Well, a lot has happened since I last saw you."

"I guess *so!*" the man of the soil told him with

feeling. "There was the hurricane and then that Thanksgiving blizzard two years ago, and the big floods the following spring, and the drought this past summer. Plenty has happened since you were here last!"

My friend thought this was amusing, but I am enough of a countrywoman myself to agree with the country point of view. Wars and rumors of war, political upheavals and scientific revolutions are important, of course, but they're rather superficial, too. The weather is man's original, implacable enemy; the one he cannot defeat but can only outwit; the one that will still be lying in wait when all the others have abandoned their strategies and laid down their arms. Concern about the weather legitimately comes before other concerns; and only those who have never lived close to the land are apt to find it amusing or to consider talk about the weather the last conversational ditch.

I listen to weather broadcasts not to find out about future weather where I am, but to check up on present weather in places in which I have lived and which I know well and love. I like to know that, though I'm basking in the warm autumn sun on Cape Cod, there are snow flurries in the mountains and the summit of Mount Washington reported a depth of four inches at dawn. "From Eastport to Block Island," the forecaster might say, "light southerly winds prevail, and the visibility is good except for patches of fog off the Bay of Fundy."

This to me is sheerest poetry, and like all good poetry it evokes emotions once experienced, now recalled in tranquillity. I know just what it's like this morning in the mountains. The crimson and gold of maple and birch are powdered with white, and the peak to the south glimmers ghostly against a gray sky. Briefly but truly I feel again the anxious urgency of all the tasks that must be finished before winter closes in. I know, too, what it's like Down East today. A slow surf is breaking on the reefs and islands, sending up fountains of spray, and the frost-touched grass on the heath is bronze in the sun. The lobster boats are all out, skirting the patches of fog or plunging boldly through them; and everybody in the village is brisk and busy, happy that it's a good hauling day.

That's what the weather reports do for me. They transport me quickly all over New England, like a housewife inspecting the familiar rooms of her home. If there is dust on the picture frames, she wants to know about it; and if there are abnormally high tides at Race Point, Massachusetts, so do I.

MAINE'S BAXTER STATE PARK

Baxter State Park, a spectacular wilderness area in the heart of Maine, is a monument to its donor, the late Percival P. Baxter, former governor and conservationist. The Maine legislature, in accepting the nearly 200,700-acre gift, accepted also the condition that it "forever be left in its natural wild state, forever be kept as a sanctuary for wild beasts and birds." Both park and access roads are protected from "improvements," lest overuse destroy the very features—scenery, wildlife, a peaceful refuge for contemplation and understanding—that visitors come to enjoy. One of the road signs bears an identification and a warning to motorists: "This is the Sourdnahunk Tote-Road. It is winding and narrow and is to remain as a wild forest tote-road. It is not a parkway or a boulevard." The park includes several lakes and mountains, but mile-high (almost—5267 feet) Katahdin is its principal feature and the highest point in Maine. The mountain is also the northern terminus of the Appalachian Trail.

A summer sunrise gilds the ring of peaks that make up Mount Katahdin in this view of the south slope across Togue Pond. The first rays of sunlight to strike the United States each day fall on Katahdin. Topping the mountain is Baxter Peak; on the right, the Knife Edge, a mile-long ridge that in places is less than three feet wide—and 1500 feet almost straight down on both sides—circles east and then north to South Peak and Pamola.

14

A NOTCH IN NEW HAMPSHIRE

FREEMAN TILDEN

Wherever the forces of nature have sculptured rock shapes, people have exulted in finding likenesses. A bishop's miter, an old-fashioned sugarloaf, an Indian with feathered headdress, a baby's shoe—the variety is interminable. Occasionally a similarity is seen by many people and agreed upon; more often the imagination suffers a severe sprain.

Of all the rocks that have dared to be so imitative, it is safe to say that one is preeminent; one alone is nationally and even internationally famous. This one is the chief—but far from the only—outstanding feature of Franconia Notch State Park, New Hampshire. It is the Great Stone Face, otherwise known as the Old Man of the Mountain. Nobody has ever questioned this resemblance to a human face. From the time it was first seen by white men, probably somewhere between 1800 and 1810, when a road through the notch was being cleared, up to the present moment when a cloud of visitors are gazing up at it, it has been unquestionably a face. As to *whose* face—that is something else. A legend has it that one of the discoverers nudged his companion and exclaimed, "Look! There's Jefferson!" Another early viewer thought it was the very image of Benjamin Franklin. And so on.

No doubt it was Nathaniel Hawthorne who gave the Old Man the first push toward world fame. His *Great Stone Face* is a sort of lay sermon in short-story form. There is some doubt as to whether Hawthorne had actually seen the rock when he wrote. And if you reread the story, in *Twice-Told Tales*, you may wonder exactly what the author meant. But what a piece of unconscious advertising it was!

Periodically, crews of workmen ascend to Cannon Mountain in the hope of keeping the Old Man from disintegrating. About 1915 a climbing parson named Guy Roberts called attention to the danger of a rockfall that would destroy the face, so the state anchored the projections of the ledge. But erosion, coupled with the pull of gravity, constantly threatens the granite blocks. An impassioned legislator once stated that the face must be preserved, even at the cost of $1 million. "It is worth that, and more, to the state," he proclaimed. The legislator was right. The Old Man is an intrinsic part of the Granite State. It is the inheritance of every child born to the cultural and spiritual resources of New Hampshire.

It is rather amusing to note that Charles Hitchcock, the geologist who surveyed New Hampshire in 1870, studied the Stone Face carefully and wrote that "the pieces are liable to fall at any time." He noted: "The profile is made of three jutting masses of rock (an ordinary granite quite friable from decomposition) in different vertical lines; one piece making the forehead, the second piece making the nose and upper lip, and the third the chin.

"I would advise any persons who are anxious to see the Profile to hasten to the spot, for fear of being disappointed," warned Professor Hitchcock. You might grin at this prediction, made a hundred years ago. The chances are that the Old Man with the stony visage will be with us a long time; yet . . . well, one never knows . . . perhaps you should get to Franconia Notch and see him soon.

Since geologists are not overly sentimental about rocks that resemble other things, it is significant that, besides Hitchcock, a much earlier state geologist, Charles T. Jackson, was also at great pains to make the Old Man known. Perhaps because he felt that the face might not exist much longer, Hitchcock devoted a whole page in his report to a line drawing indicating what the profile was like and how it appeared when one shifted from the straight line of observation either to the left or to the right. Jackson, after stating that it was held to be "one of the greatest natural curiosities of the State," became less expansive: "It is a proper subject for romantic legends, but there is no proof that it has been known more than forty or fifty years [he was writing this in 1840] by white men, nor does it seem to have been specially observed by Indians." But the visage no doubt *was* well known to the Indians. It may have had religious significance, in which case they didn't talk about it. Possibly they merely commented that it looked like one of their sachems.

Jutting from the sheer east cliff of Cannon Mountain, the Great Stone Face looms over Franconia Notch. The forty-foot-high visage, also called the Old Man of the Mountain, is recognizable only from Profile Lake, 1200 feet below.

Franconia Notch is a deep defile that lies between the Kinsman Range on one side and the Franconians on the other. Rugged as the surroundings are, nothing could be more lovely and inspiring than the view from the Old Man observation point. There the towering mountain, rising a sharp 1200 feet, is mirrored in Profile Lake at its foot; Echo Lake, a little farther on, is another bit of limpid perfection. Of still another silver blue sheet of water, nestling in the side of the mountain itself, Charles Dudley Warner said years ago that it is "a mirror for the sky and the clouds and the sailing hawks."

Almost as widely known as the Great Stone Face is the Flume, reputedly discovered by a ninety-three-year-old woman looking for a place to fish. Along the flank of Mount Liberty for 800 feet the visitor may make his way up a cleft in the mother rock, by means of a boardwalk, with vertical walls rising seventy feet above his head. Though in times of freshet the stream at the bottom of the chasm roars impetuously through it, the side walls do not give the impression that rushing water could have been the scouring agent that created the Flume. Jackson thought it was clearly a fracture that had been deepened but not widened very much. When he first saw it, and for many years afterward, another phenomenon was connected with it that can no longer be seen.

Pictures taken in the Flume before 1883 show a huge boulder wedged between the walls of the cleft. After the glaciation theory of Louis Agassiz had finally been accepted by the scientific world, no geologist could doubt how the boulder got there. But, though the receding ice that invaded New Hampshire left boulders aplenty strewn upon the denuded surface of the land, it was rare chance that deposited one of these into the narrow Flume in such a manner that it remained securely wedged in the upper part.

Securely wedged? It would appear so, since the boulder must have been in the Flume between 10,000 and 12,000 years. Thousands had walked beneath it with the assurance that it wouldn't drop. But nothing in nature endures. In June 1883, following several days' rain which ended with a cloudburst, the Flume became a thundering raceway. The guests in the Flume House, which had recently opened for the season, heard the roaring,

and some thought they heard a mighty blast. When it became possible once more to get near the gorge, it was seen that the great erratic had fallen from its perch. As Dr. Hitchcock said of the Great Stone Face, it had been "getting ready to fall anytime"—anytime, that is, the last few thousand years. Apparently it was smashed into small pieces, for it has never been found. The same storm added two new waterfalls to the Flume.

Millions of people have made the ascent to the top of Cannon Mountain in the enclosed cablecar. From the observation platform on the 4200-foot crest one looks down upon the valley floor and around at the folded, forested peaks of the White Mountains. Far below these folks who take the easy way to the sky will be hundreds of happy campers in the beautifully kept campground called Lafayette. Here is a recreation building with showers and laundry and comfort rooms; and when the tent sites are filled—and they are very quickly during the season—the considerate rangers will try to find a temporary place for your tent somewhere nearby. Here, too, the desire of people to get back to nature is markedly apparent. No matter how rapidly the facilities of the camping parks are increased, they continue to fall behind the demand.

Lafayette is, naturally, a favorite with campers. This is a region of trails that lead not only through wonders of natural history but through marvels of human occupation and pioneering as well. For, one remembers, this was tourist country when the territories of the United States west of the Mississippi were still unmapped, and when great Yellowstone, for example, was known only by tall tales that nobody believed.

A little off the highway in the notch is an enormous, oddly shaped boulder set down by the ice at such an angle that under one side of it a dozen people could easily take shelter. There is a somber story connected with that boulder—known as Boise Rock. Once in the early days, when the road through the notch was not much more than a trail, a lone horseman was making his way in the gloom of a cloudy day. The impending blizzard struck around him at a point near this rock; he had the wit to realize that he could not go on. The temperature was dropping rapidly; even if he could find shelter under the rock, he might not survive the cold. Boise made a fast decision. He killed his horse, skinned it, dragged the still-warm hide into the shelter of the glacial boulder and wrapped himself in it. When a search party found him, the traveler was alive but tightly frozen in!

The vertical walls of seventy-foot-high Flume Gorge are made of Conway granite (like the nearby Old Man of the Mountain). Above the tumbling waters, lush mosses and ferns flourish in deep fractures about 200 million years old.

WHITE MOUNTAIN NATIONAL FOREST

Spanning northern New Hampshire and extending into Maine, the 716,000-acre White Mountain National Forest includes what many consider the ruggedest scenery east of the Rockies. The forest's most imposing group of mountains, the Presidential Range, is dominated by the massive, barren summit of Mount Washington, which at 6288 feet is the Northeast's loftiest peak.

In this aerial view over Mount Washington's southern slope, glacier-carved Tuckerman Ravine, one of the most formidable ski runs on the continent, falls away to the lower left. Forty miles to the south portions of Lake Winnipesaukee and Squam Lake gleam near the horizon.

THE WEATHERED PEAKS OF VERMONT

ROCKWELL STEPHENS

One bright day a young couple from Holland, visiting the town of Windsor, read the sign "Birthplace of Vermont" and turned to their host. "Who was Mr. Vermont?" they asked. Their smiles grew as their host explained. "Of course—*monts verts*—green mountains, naturally. One would have to name the state for its mountains."

Few states have a more dominant geographic feature than the Green Mountains. But despite the legend that the Reverend Samuel Peters, standing on the summit of Pisgah (now Killington Peak) in 1763, christened the wilderness below him "Verdmont," the mountains did not officially name the land until the Constitutional Convention met in Windsor in 1777 and created the independent state of Vermont.

No poetic imagination was required to give the Green Mountains their name. From the time of Samuel de Champlain's first sight of their peaks and valleys in 1609 the term must have been so generally used that Ethan Allen's irregulars came naturally by their designation as the Green Mountain Boys. For the mountains *are* green, their slopes and all but a few of their highest summits covered with the dark evergreen of fir, pine and hemlock and the lighter shades of maple, birch and beech. Even the upland pastures and valley sides, rocky as they were when the first settlers broke the shell of the wilderness to find and cultivate its soils, make a pattern in harmony with the forest. In the southern two thirds of the area the Green Mountain National Forest incorporates more than 260,000 acres, including abandoned orchards. One Forest Service project involves caring for apple trees—the deer love the fruit.

These are old mountains—"mature" in the geologist's term—and the forces that shaped the

The apple blossoms of May fill Vermont's air with a lingering sweetness. Orchards, pastures dotted with dandelions, woods and rolling fields surround South Strafford in the valley of the Connecticut River in east central Vermont.

Autumn turns the sugar maples and other hardwoods near
East Barnard, Vermont, to brilliant shades of yellow, orange
and scarlet. Known also as rock maples, sugar maples are as
useful for their strong, fine-grained wood as for their syrup.

land so many thousands of years ago have long since tempered their assaults, to leave a heritage of soil for all growing things.

Common usage often refers to all of Vermont's up-ended geography as the Green Mountains, but the name properly applies only to the major mass running the full 159-mile length of the state a little west of its center, trending in a somewhat northeasterly direction, and consisting of three roughly parallel ranges. The longest and the central one of the three is the Main Range, which includes the highest peaks.

The separate Taconic Mountains frame the west side of the Valley of Vermont, with the Main Range on the east. Lying in the north portion of the Taconics are the great formations that produce nearly half of the nation's marble, first quarried commercially in 1785. Proctor is now the center of the industry and the site of what is said to be the world's largest marble exhibit and museum. West of the marble formations are beds that produce more slate than any other source except Pennsylvania. The industry is concentrated around Poultney, near the New York border.

There are some 420 named mountains in the Green Mountain ranges or occurring as isolated peaks, and many more without names. Eighty rise to more than 3000 feet, twenty-one top 3500, seven in the Main Range go over 4000. These are Mount Mansfield, 4393, and in descending order Killington, Mount Ellen, Camel's Hump, Cutts Peak, Mount Abraham and Lincoln Peak.

East of the mountains lies a plateaulike region extending the length of the state and cut into an irregular pattern of hill and valley by streams hurrying to the Connecticut River. Though the predominant ridges run north and south, glacier, wind and water have combined to mix the hills and valleys to such an extent that it is a direction-wise traveler indeed who knows which way he is heading on many of the winding roads that make the region a favorite of the shun-pike explorer. The ridges run 1200 to 1800 feet in elevation, often commanding views of the high peaks to the west and the White Mountains to the east.

The 600 square miles of the Northeast Province (as the geologists call it) or Northeast Kingdom (as Vermonters know it) add to the mountain inventory. This thinly populated region includes

As dusk in Vermont ends a cold January day, a sunset afterglow paints snow-covered Mount Mansfield and surrounding peaks an eerie pink, forecasting bone-chilling temperatures by morning—in this instance twenty degrees below zero.

27

some 130 high hills or mountains, with at least eight over 2500 feet. They are not properly a part of the Green Mountains, but an extension of the White Mountains of New Hampshire.

By geologic time the Green Mountains and the Taconics are the oldest of the long Appalachian chain, which extends from Alabama to the Gaspé Peninsula and the Gulf of St. Lawrence. What we see now are only the roots of a one-time truly alpine range.

The stuff of which the mountains were made may have come from Archean times, perhaps 2.5 billion years ago. But their present form is a product of repeated folding and upthrust extending into more recent periods in the long geologic scale and culminating in their shaping during the last Ice Age, when a great glacier began the work of erosion that is still going on.

This vast ice sheet, thousands of feet thick and extending southward almost to Philadelphia, was the giant bulldozer that planed off the summits and gouged lakes and ponds, dammed the flow of some streams with its debris and created others. Its great weight bore down the earth's crust to change the course of Lake Champlain's waters and turn them northward through the Richelieu River into the St. Lawrence, rather than south through the Hudson Valley. The marks of its passage are to be seen everywhere in this region—in grooves and scratches on the rocks of Mount Mansfield's summit, in huge boulders strewn erratically on pasturelands.

The mountains remained a barrier even after the development of the turnpikes and plank roads of the mid-1800s. Only three roads had been pushed across the state by 1800. Early travel was hazardous at best. The state in 1852 lost one of its leading citizens when ex-governor Richard Skinner was thrown from his carriage and killed while crossing the mountains.

Today's good roads have eliminated the spine of the mountains as a barrier and made exploration by car easy and rewarding. With the aid of a map one can plot routes back and forth over the crest line or through the notches, or, to add a touch of uncertainty and excitement to the game, put maps away and follow the compass east or west as roads and terrain permit. Practitioners of this art, the true aficionados of exploring, will use a geological survey map as an auxiliary, but half the fun is speculating whether a dwindling road will vanish in a pasture or reassert itself as a highway a few miles farther on. Practical considerations eliminate most of the graveled town and county secondary roads

from the usual maps, but an inquiry to the Highway Department in Montpelier will bring detailed sheets for each county, to permit exploration of the backcountry with some degree of certainty. Remote as one may feel while thus exploring, a major state or federal road is actually never very distant; in fact, 80 percent of the entire area of the state is no more than thirty miles from an interchange on Vermont's interstate routes 89 and 91.

There is no consensus among Vermont enthusiasts on "best" areas for exploration. Many of the dozen or more trans-mountain routes bring the westbound motorist to a crest that reveals in one sudden, breathtaking instant the sweep of the Green Mountains and beyond them the waters of Lake Champlain and the peaks of the Adirondacks. Others, notably the passage through Smugglers Notch at Mount Mansfield, lead up ever-narrowing valleys closely flanked by mountainsides rising more than 1000 feet above the road. Many lead into mountain masses that seem to offer no loophole, and one wonders through which fold the road builders chose to thread the highway.

Vermont Route 100 might well be called the Green Mountain Highway, for it closely follows the east side of the Main Range the full length of the state. From it one may turn at any intersection signposted to a settlement on the west side of the divide and find rich reward in the passage. On the west side of the range U.S. Route 7 performs somewhat the same function, though it swings west away from the mountains in its northern section.

But the best prescription for those who would savor the mountain wilderness more intimately is to hike the Long Trail. This "Footpath Through the Wilderness" is the project of the Green Mountain Club, which since its founding in 1910 has cut and marked 255 miles of trail from the Massachusetts line to Canada. It follows the ridge of the Main Range, dropping occasionally along valley streams, and traverses forty peaks over 3000 feet, including the four highest. There are a hundred side trails totaling 175 miles in length. More than sixty shelters are strategically placed to permit trips of varying length each day. Some are lean-to structures with bunks for six; others are huts containing a stove and bunks for eight to twelve. The club, with headquarters in Rutland, is administered through a number of sections, each responsible for continuous maintenance of its portion of the trail. In the Green Mountain National Forest maintenance is carried on by the U.S. Forest Service, and other sections are covered by affiliated groups.

The Long Trail is joined by the Appalachian

Trail on its course from Maine to Georgia near Sherburne Pass over Mendon Mountain, east of Rutland. The two run together to the Massachusetts line. The Appalachian Trail comes in from the east, crossing the Connecticut at Hanover, New Hampshire. Like the Long Trail it is well marked and easily picked up from intersecting highways.

The Green Mountains have a character of their own. Their contours and summits, rounded by age and softened by the dense growth of their forests, have none of the savagery of younger mountain masses, with their sharp peaks and naked rocks. Grim as the tasks of settlement were, the pioneers nevertheless found a friendly land rich in timber for their homes, minerals for their forges and fertile soil for crops and pastures.

Today it is not only the peaks and valleys of the mountains but the shared intimacy of people and their land that gives the country its special quality. The merino sheep that produced quick fortunes in the mid-1800s have gone, and the dairy cattle of the old upland, hillside farms are now increasingly concentrated in larger units in the valleys. But their pastures still make landscape patterns that only the Green Mountains afford.

The forests have reproduced themselves in generous measure, and for more than fifty years Vermonters have been concerned that they shall remain an ever-increasing asset. Besides the acreage in the Green Mountain National Forest, there are over 96,000 acres in state forests and parks under the continuous care of trained foresters. (Vermont was first in the nation to provide a trained forester for every county.)

The Green Mountains are a working wilderness, and the people of the area are united in their determination that the mountains' assets shall not be exploited at the cost of commercial and industrial blight, or the development of the region as a 9000-square-mile tourist trap of the sort that has destroyed so much of the nation's heritage of natural beauty. For this land of hill and mountain, some 160 miles long and 36 to 86 miles wide, is an island all but surrounded by a megalopolis of perhaps a quarter of the nation's population, and accessible to more than 70 million people by a long day's drive or a few hours' jet flight.

The "Welcome to Vermont" sign is still out, freshly painted and larger than ever before. But the forces of conservation and planning are now marshaled in full recognition that prompt action for both long- and short-term goals is urgently necessary if the future is to see the Green Mountains unspoiled.

AMERICA'S PRICELESS SEASHORE

DON WHARTON

Cape Cod is unique. A peninsula that stands farther out to sea than any other portion of our Atlantic coast, it was created, geologists say, by mile-high glaciers, which dropped deposits here in the last Ice Age—about 11,000 years ago. It was then molded for more than a hundred centuries by winds, waves, tides and currents. You can see mile after mile of original glacial deposits sliced by the elements into clean-sloping cliffs. Layers, some as distinct as in a cake, show the advances and retreats of the ice. You can even pick up pebbles brought by glaciers from the Laurentian Mountains in Canada.

After reaching out thirty-five miles into the Atlantic, Cape Cod narrows and curves abruptly to the north for thirty-five miles more. It was named in 1602 by an English navigator who found fabulous quantities of codfish in the local waters. In 1614, six years before the Pilgrims arrived, Capt. John Smith described the Cape succinctly: "Made by the main sea on the one side, and a great bay on the other, in the form of a sickle."

This "sickle" fairly reeks with history. At Follins Pond there is evidence that Norsemen visited the Cape 1100 years ago, and Indians were living here at least 2000 years before that. Here, and not at Plymouth Rock across the bay, the Pilgrims first came ashore, first drank New World fresh water, first glimpsed the Indians. While their ship lay in the harbor inside the Cape's hook, they drew up the Mayflower Compact.

But most visitors don't come to study history. They come to enjoy the delights of the Cape Cod National Seashore, to swim, lie on the sand, listen to the surf, hunt and fish, dig clams, watch birds, comb the beaches for shells, rocks, driftwood and other treasures. The national seashore stretches for more than thirty-five miles along the ocean and for five along the bay, in several sections, and more lands are being purchased gradually.

The charm of this place lies not in spectacular sights such as one encounters at Yosemite or the

Nauset Beach Lighthouse, one of several lights on Cape Cod, is perched high upon the sand cliffs of the great outer beach near Eastham. Elevated 114 feet above the water, its light is visible to ships more than twenty miles out at sea.

Grand Canyon, but rather in the subtle beauty of the marshes, with their flat islands, winding streams, yellowlegs, blue herons and herring gulls. Diligent bird watchers can spot 250 different species during the year. One of the fascinating sights when the tide is low is a herring gull flying along forty feet up, a clam held tightly in its hooked bill. For countless ages the gull opened the clam by dropping it onto some boulder, but now it concentrates on an easier target, the national seashore's large paved parking areas. Sections near the marshes are sprinkled with clamshell bits.

The national seashore does have two spectacular features. One is the magnificent wall of cliffs, sixty to seventy feet high, where the Cape's tablelands meet the Atlantic. The first panoramic glimpse of the great outer beach from these cliffs —as from Highland Lighthouse—has been called "one of the most memorable experiences in America." People tell tall tales about the winds here blowing back pieces of wood cast over the bank and Thoreau once recorded that boys and men "amuse themselves by running and trying to jump off the bank with their jackets spread, and being blown back."

North of these impressive cliffs are eight square miles of some of the most spectacular dunes on the Atlantic coast. The building material came from the highlands to the south—gnawed out of the cliffs by wind and wave, carried for miles by ocean currents, then picked up, shaped, shifted and reshaped by centuries of winds. People who have braved this wilderness during the winter, when the northwest winds blow, report that you can see dunes change shape in an hour. Some are free-moving, others stabilized with beach grass and low-growing dwarflike trees.

The foundations of Guglielmo Marconi's wireless station, where in 1903 he tapped out the first wireless message from the United States to Europe, may still be visited. But the encroaching ocean is 165 feet closer than in Marconi's day. This hungry sea has gobbled up whole islands. Billingsgate Island, for instance, once lay in Cape Cod Bay, about half a mile off Jeremy Point. There are persons who remember the lighthouse there, and before that a try yard for rendering whale oil. Once the island pastured twenty horses—but now it's gone, appearing as a shoal at low tide.

It was shoals off the Cape that caused the Pilgrims to change their minds and settle in New England rather than down around New Jersey. The *Mayflower* turned back from its southward course after narrowly escaping disaster.

The Park Service has converted an abandoned Coast Guard station into a sea-rescue museum. There are several self-guiding nature trails. One leads through pitch pines, into a bushy valley and on to a spring believed to be the one used by the Pilgrims; another skirts an azalea-blueberry bog and descends into a kettle hole created when masses of ice, hundreds of feet high, remained after the glaciers themselves had gone.

People are flocking to the Cape Cod National Seashore in ever-increasing numbers (in 1964 there were 1.8 million visits; in 1975 the number had jumped to nearly 5 million). For here on this historic peninsula with its shining sands, its rolling dunes, its woodlands and its ever-changing seascape is the answer to what so many city-bred Americans seek—the peace and contentment of the unspoiled outdoors.

In the Pilgrim Heights Area of Cape Cod National Seashore, dune roses proclaim their defiance of salt spray, intolerable for less hardy species. This 1700-acre section of the seashore was a gift from Massachusetts to the national park system.

BEWITCHED BY THE GREAT SWAMP

ROBERT C. FREDERIKSEN

Rhode Island's Great Swamp State Wildlife Reservation is an enchanting place, both for what it has and for what it doesn't have.

It has wildlife, of course. Deer, Canada geese, bass, foxes, rabbits, wood ducks, turtles, pheasants, raccoons, snakes, mink, muskrats, mute swans, a lone pair of ospreys, trout and pike.

It has flora, too, in a wide and astonishing variety from arctic moss to semitropical orchids. Also rhododendron, dogwood, birches, sweet fern, oaks, trillium, bullbriers, alders, maples and jacks-in-the-pulpit. Someone once estimated the swamp contains 4000 species of plant life.

Insects, too. Bloodthirsty mosquitoes, deerflies, common flies, bees, no-see-ums, horseflies, wasps, leeches, hornets—all big, tough, hungry and in numbers beyond belief.

Also tucked away in the swamp's 2748 acres, of which one third actually is dry land, are such random items as three cemeteries, one of which has been lost for years, 30,000 feet of old stone walls, segments of three rivers and a brook, a remarkable plank walk running beneath a power line, a mile-long dike, six miles of dirt roads and acres of wheat, corn and rye for the game to eat.

The swamp, which the state bought in 1950 for $23,400, has these things because it doesn't have people, although one of its functions is to provide sport for hunters and fishermen.

Nor does it have autos (except for work vehicles, transportation is by shanks' mare, canoe or horseback), smog, outboard motors, radios, billboards, television, chain saws or a square inch of concrete or asphalt pavement.

I stumbled on the swamp a few years ago while leading a Boy Scout canoe trip. Like others before me, I fell under its spell of timelessness, solitude and variety. Standing on the dike, finished in 1961 for $45,000 to maintain the water level in the swamp, it's hard to believe you are in one of the most densely populated states in the nation.

The swamp, lapping at the high ground called Great Neck, is the most spectacular part of the huge reservation. From the water, reflecting every change in the big sky, emerge countless islets, tussocks of waving grass, wood-duck nests put out by the state and the whitened trunks of drowned trees. Beyond rise old fields and woods blending from green to blue in the distance.

Oddly, the swamp seems noisy because of the warbling, chirping, chittering, quacking and piping racket of the huge bird population, particularly at dawn feeding time. By contrast, the roar of a train on the New Haven Railroad main line, Navy planes or outboards on Worden Pond seem hushed and far away, never more so than on a soft rainy spring afternoon when the world is veiled in gray.

I've gone back to the swamp many times. I've gone in on foot, by canoe and by car, with special permission. I've flown over the swamp and landed on Worden Pond with Bill Snow, a federal wildlife management agent at the time, who used to keep his plane at the hangar there.

I've seen a great horned owl whistling through the trees on the Chipuxet River, watched fuzzy goslings being convoyed by their vigilant parents, heard loons, pushed big snapping turtles out of the road, surprised a fox, dabbled hot feet in the water, slept in the sun, seen the ospreys guarding their nest, the mist rising and the rain dappling the dark water.

One of the minor miracles of the place is its accessibility. It's only about fifty minutes south of Providence. To reach it, one takes Liberty Lane, either from South County Trail (Route 2) or from the Kingston Road (Route 138). A large wooden sign at the grade crossing over the New Haven Railroad main line marks the entrance road, which is of dirt, like all those in the swamp. It leads to the headquarters buildings, maintenance shops and garages, which are manned during the daytime, and a short distance beyond, to a chain that blocks the road. Autos may be left in the parking lot there.

Anyone is welcome. There's no permit or charge. All you need is a good pair of legs, a canoe or a horse. No horseback riding during the hunting season, however. You might get shot accidentally. Take only pictures and leave only footprints.

The swamp will do the rest.

The ruby-tipped branches of a blossoming red maple stretch over a Great Swamp stream in early spring. Colonists from Massachusetts Bay, Connecticut and Plymouth won a decisive battle with the Narragansett Indian tribe here in 1675.

CONNECTICUT'S PASTORAL PERIMETER

JOEL LIEBER

Each summer, legions of New Yorkers are lured into Connecticut's Litchfield County by the pastoral magnetism of its gentle hillocks and lush farmlands, its winding streams, plentiful lakes and quiet, small-town atmosphere. Connecticut's largest county occupies roughly one eighth of the state's territory, the northwestern section that borders New York State on the west and Massachusetts on the north.

Each succeeding summer finds more and more city people renting acreage in this beautiful and unassuming region. They take over houses, farms, reconverted barns and hunting lodges for either full-time vacation sites or weekend escape purposes. Hideaway prices depend on the size of the house, whether or not it's situated on a lake and its view of the next valley.

Yet nothing about the region's yearly horde of visitors suggests an invasion comparable to that of Bucks County or Fire Island. There are no "in" artist colonies, and the only built-up vacation area is on the main part of Candlewood Lake, which lies south of the county's borderline.

Litchfield County has a special charm, an almost mystical power of enchantment, and its residents are well aware of these facts, but it's difficult to pinpoint just how these elusive qualities are felt. The Litchfield magic surely has something to do with a rare bucolic tranquillity just two to three hours from New York's hurly-burly. It's a calm area—with the exception of bustling Torrington—its rhythms serene, its woodlands bountiful, its spell enduring.

Even the cadence of town names bespeaks Litchfield's durable qualities: Still River, Washington Depot, Kent Furnace, Swift Bridge. The climate, too, gives a clue to the area's magic:

Well over a century old, the West Cornwall Bridge still carries daily traffic over Connecticut's Housatonic River. To cross the 242-foot span, pedestrians once paid two cents, equestrians four cents, and teamsters with wagons a dime.

37

clear, fresh summer days filled with the sweet scent of pasturelands and the tangy, sharp smells of abundant pine forests; evenings fragrantly cooled by the breezes blowing down through the foothills of the Berkshires.

Of all its graces, Litchfield County is perhaps richest in lakes, antique shops and state parks. Nowhere in the county are you ever more than half an hour from a lake for swimming and boating. In the south these waters consist of Lake Waramaug, Bantam Lake and the easterly finger of Candlewood Lake. To the north are Tyler Pond, Silver Lake and Wangum Lake. All the lakes have both public and private beaches, and at most places you can rent boats for two-hour sessions.

Apart from the lakes in this pastoral section, streams and rivers are forever winding and crisscrossing through the farmlands and fruit orchards. The serpentine, tree-canopied Housatonic River, with its swift rapids, accompanies Route 7 at the road's edge.

Other waterways, like the Naugatuck, Shepaug and a profusion of fast-running streams, border secondary roads throughout the state. Look to the side of any road in the county and four times out of five you'll find a stream rushing beside you.

The many stores selling old bits of quaintness are dwarfed by the honest-to-goodness realities of Litchfield County—the thick forests and tracts of rich fertile earth, the state parks. Testimony to these clean, well-kept and carefully supervised woodland preserves are the estimated 500 families that camp out every summer weekend in the county's well-maintained state parks: Black Rock, Lake Waramaug, Haystack Mountain, Mount Bushnell, Mount Riga, Ivy Mountain, Mohawk Mountain, Dennis Hill, Kent Falls, Humaston Brook, Mount Tom and Macedonia Brook. There are certainly enough to choose from, and many adventurous families spend each summertime weekend camping out at a different Litchfield County park.

Every weekend you see caravans of trailers and bridges of tents nestled under the tall pine and spruce trees in these state parks. The tents range from bleached army-surplus items to the latest pastel-colored extravaganzas. Cooking odors drift among the pines, and there's always a child running from a stream with a dog right behind.

One of my favorites, Macedonia Brook State

Park, just north of Kent, resembles a raw forest, with some forty miles of trails winding up and down the heavily wooded mountains. And always, twisting and dancing in and out of the hills, are the rushing streams—in this case, Macedonia Brook and its tributaries.

The broad, flat peak of the mountain at Macedonia Park has an excellent view of the entire countryside, and as you come down the road on the far side toward the remote Kent School you see isolated but prosperous-appearing farms guarding the lonely slopes, farms where the nearest neighbor is a mile away.

In addition to all this natural glory the region has specific sights to see. One of the most splendid

Falls Brook cascades over the lower section of Kent Falls, which drops a total of 200 feet in a quarter-mile stretch. The brook passes through a great hemlock grove before joining the Housatonic River south of the West Cornwall Bridge.

38

is the waterfall that cascades down the rocky ledges at Kent Falls State Park. It drops a total distance of 200 feet—not a straight drop, but in gradual stages, with flat rock platforms every thirty or forty yards. On several such platforms the water has eroded natural swimming craters, and there is nothing more refreshing on a hot summer day than a dip in these brisk, cool pools. A path ascends alongside the falls, and picnickers turn off and set up their barbecue equipment.

Old covered bridges are also among the leading sight-seeing attractions. Best known is the structure at the town of West Cornwall. For fifty years this ancient wooden bridge crossing the Housatonic has been a famous tourist attraction, with its walled-up sides and roofed-in top. It could have been built for the purpose.

A few miles south of Kent a dirt road leading west can take you into a planted pine forest, with rows of tall trees marching right to the edge of the Housatonic. The route follows the west bank of the Housatonic and is entirely undeveloped, the woods dense and overgrown, and only one burned-out house along the way. The wildlife is so bold that you'll see rabbits and woodchucks darting in front of your car. So infrequent is any intrusion here that the resident animals feel the woods are still theirs. It scarcely seems credible that such unspoiled freshness is possible just ninety miles from New York City.

THE ADIRONDACKS

The Adirondack Mountains of northeastern New York got their name from an American Indian insult: The Algonquians who hunted in the forested ranges west of Lake George and Lake Champlain were scornfully called *Adirondacks* ("bark eaters") by the powerful Iroquois, their neighbors to the south. The Adirondack Forest Preserve, created in 1885 and protected since 1894 by the New York State constitution, comprises 2.4 million acres intermingled with private land. There are four main mountain ranges, with forty-two peaks over 4000 feet; the highest is 5344-foot Mount Marcy, a favorite destination of hikers. The landscape, based on billion-year-old rocks, is rugged but softened by time. Innumerable lakes and streams, as well as the mountain slopes, lure vacationers all year round.

The two peaks of 4185-foot Wolf Jaw Mountain rise behind an upland orchard near Keene Valley in the Adirondacks. Behind Wolf Jaw, a few miles to the southwest, is Mount Marcy. In the soft air of an early fall afternoon the apple trees are laden with ripe fruit and the sugar maples are just beginning to turn color. Most of the wild flowers, such as the black-eyed Susans, have lost their rays.

Young maples grow from crevices in the Cathedral Rocks near the Ausable River East Branch south of Keene Valley. The East and West branches meet at Ausable Forks and drain through Ausable Chasm into Lake Champlain beyond.

A hobblebush, a kind of viburnum, blooms along
Cascade Brook Trail near Blue Mountain Lake. In mid-May
every Adirondack mountain valley has its own
fern-bordered brook rushing among mossy rocks.

Violets blooming in tall bunchgrass beside Cascade Brook
Trail in the Adirondacks lend color to the spring
woods. The 4.35-mile trail leads to a shelter on Cascade
Pond, where there is good trout fishing.

THE SPECTACLE
OF NIAGARA

WOLFGANG LANGEWIESCHE

Niagara Falls, that tired old tourist sight, came to life for me not long ago when I looked it over from my little airplane. What an astonishing thing we've got there! It's not tired; only our way of looking at it is tired. For the ground tourist the approach to Niagara is flat, and since an industrial area has grown up around the falls they are surrounded on both the United States and Canadian sides by concrete, asphalt and a strong chemical smell. Only a stretch of lawn and trees reminds you of the wilderness that once was there.

Most visitors go as close to the falls as possible, and watch the waters thundering down. It is fascinating, in a stupefying way. You stand there hypnotized by the sheer force, the untiring action that goes on and on. It fills your mind. But afterward you have a feeling—"So what, really? The water comes to this cliff and, naturally, it falls down."

This is where the air view set me straight. At altitude you see it all at once. You see Lake Ontario on one side, Lake Erie on the other, and linking them the thirty-four-mile Niagara River. Then, coming down lower, you see the falls themselves—where the river, along a front almost a mile wide, plunges over a 182-foot cliff and flows off through a deep, narrow gorge seven miles long. And right away, with a flash of understanding, you see the main fact about Niagara Falls: The falls are moving; the seven-mile-long gorge is merely the track the falls have made as they moved. This instantly reverses all your ideas. On the ground it seemed that the water fell because there was this low place for it to fall into—the gorge. Now you see that it's the other way around: The falls are the cause, the gorge is the result. From one mile up, Niagara Gorge looks remarkably like the track eaten into an apple by a worm.

The Niagara River at the American Falls in western New York plunges 182 feet to Maid of the Mist Pool. A larger amount of water drops over the 176-foot-high Horseshoe Falls, beyond Goat Island and the boundary with Canada.

The falls have moved at least 500 feet upstream, toward Lake Erie, since they were first reported by Father Louis Hennepin and other French missionaries in the seventeenth century. They have been under engineering survey since 1841, and rates up to five feet per year have been measured. Most of the movement has been in the middle of the falls, giving them more and more of a horseshoe shape. The movement is in steps. Now here, now there, a chunk of rock breaks off at the brink, where the water goes over, and that part of the falls thereby moves a few feet upriver. Every few years a big chunk lets go. Then the townspeople feel a trembling of the earth, and there's a flurry of news in the papers. People ask: "Is the beauty of Niagara fading? Is something wrong?"

Nothing is wrong. It's a natural law: All waterfalls tend to migrate upstream. Most of them in moving back also tend to fade out. As the rock at the brink wears off, the fall becomes less steep—century by century it shallows out, becoming a string of rapids, then a mere stretch of fast water. That's why waterfalls are rare: They tend to destroy themselves. But Niagara has a special setup that keeps it going. Underneath the river is a layer of hard rock about eighty feet thick. Below that are layers of softer rock. The water runs over the hard rock without making much of a dent. When it reaches the brink it plunges—straight down, creating a terrific whirlpool at the foot of the cliff. This whirling action excavates the softer rock—backward. So the waterfall undercaves itself, and in time a piece of the top ledge, no longer supported from underneath, breaks off. Then that portion of the falls moves a step upstream. The constant undercaving keeps Niagara always fresh, steep, powerful; the constant breaking-off at the brink keeps it moving back. So, through the centuries, digging as they went, the falls have moved seven miles.

In this mode of operation Niagara differs from the elegant waterfalls you find in mountains, where a thin stream of water comes down a mountainside, half-flying—like Bridalveil Fall in Yosemite National Park. Some of these falls are much higher than Niagara, and perhaps more beautiful. But they lack the mass and cutting power. Niagara belongs among the heavyweights—where a whole solid river plunges bodily over a cliff.

From the air I could also see how Niagara Falls got started in the first place. This, too, you understand the moment you see it. Seven miles downriver from the falls the whole country drops off, forming a bluff that overlooks the lower country

45

and Lake Ontario. Over this bluff the big waterfall first formed. But the real sight at Niagara Falls is the gigantic movement of the falls themselves, digging the gorge. And it is a sight full of meaning; it is mankind's clock!

Here is how it works: The first appearance of the sort of man who inhabits the globe today, *Homo sapiens,* is believed to have occurred during the fading-out of the last Ice Age. The worldwide springtime that melted the ice also brought the first flowering of art. This timing the prehistorians deduce from geologic and archaeologic evidence, and also from the art itself—the wall paintings of the caveman, which show reindeer and other cold-climate beasts in southern Europe. But how long ago was this fading-out of the Ice Age? For answer you turn to Niagara, the great clock.

The logic is a simple one-two-three. First, the Niagara River must have started running at the fading-out of the Ice Age. It couldn't have existed before, because all was solid ice here and for 300 miles farther south, all the way to the Ohio River.

Second, we know where the falls started: at that bluff—and how far they have traveled: those seven miles. And third, we know about how fast the falls have been moving. One century is not quite long enough to establish a reliable average.

But still, it's a calculation that their age must be between 10,000 and 30,000 years.

Till recently the longer estimates of Niagara's age have been generally believed. But a group at Yale tackled the problem with a new time clock, using atomic analysis of bits of wood buried by the glaciers. And they gave the nod to the short estimate that Niagara Falls is probably 10,000 years old. If this stands up, it brings the Ice Age startlingly close to historical times. It makes the rise of *Homo sapiens* even faster and more spectacular than anybody had believed. But whatever the time lapse is, modern man and Niagara Falls are still about the same age.

And so Niagara Gorge, considered a Grade-B sight by many tourists, becomes a fascinating thing to see. This, you might say, is the course of man's career on earth—so far. Look at the sight-seeing point called Niagara Glen today. By the time the falls had got there we had probably learned to tame animals and grow grain. Perhaps when the falls had reached the wide place called the Whirlpool, we had learned to write, and recorded history had begun. When they were at the point where two railroad bridges now cross the gorge, the Greeks discovered liberty, reason and beauty. And at the time that the falls reached

today's International Bridge, Christ was born.

The falls are still moving. In my plane, as I circled, I could observe the streamlines of their flow and action as on some laboratory model. At the center of Horseshoe Falls, at the most upstream point, a new, smaller horseshoe has been forming, a horseshoe-in-a-horseshoe, reaching still farther upstream. I could see how this place attracts the oncoming river. Green, solid masses of water kept hurling themselves into this spot as into a fierce, gigantic sink. Naturally, the more water that flows into this spot the more violent is the undercaving, and the farther this spot grows!

Our own century has tamed the falls a bit. A lot of water that used to take the big jump now goes through the electric power plants, both American and Canadian. These plants simply take water out of the river above the falls, run it through their turbines and spew it back into the river below the falls. However, by international agreement the hydroelectric plants leave at least half the river's flow for the tourists during daylight hours in the tourist season. At other times the flow over the falls is down to about a quarter.

Still circling, I now understood for the first time the real difference between the American and Canadian (or Horseshoe) falls. The American Falls are a spot where the Niagara formula no longer works. They get only about 10 percent of the water, while Horseshoe Falls get 90 percent. Because the volume of water is so much greater, Horseshoe Falls are eroding far more rapidly—which means they are moving more noticeably. And when they get to Buffalo and one day tap Lake Erie direct—what's going to happen? They could drain most of the Great Lakes in one spectacular flood; that sort of thing has happened in geologic history. But it won't happen here, according to present forecasts, because the falls won't get to Buffalo. About two miles above their present location (perhaps 2000 or 3000 years from now) the falls will start biting into a different rock structure: The soft underrock will be missing. This means their special formula will have been played out.

In that case, the gigantic falls should gradually change into mere rapids. For, unlike the mountains and canyons of our West, Niagara is a short-time glory that wasn't here yesterday and will be gone tomorrow.

About 4 million gallons of water a minute thunder from the brink of the 1000-foot-wide American Falls. Bridal Veil Falls, on the right, is separated from the main falls by Luna Island. The deepest water at the brink is about forty inches.

THE HUDSON RIVER VALLEY

From its birthplace in New York's Adirondack Mountains, the Hudson River winds south, gathering tributaries and strength. At Troy the Mohawk River cuts in from the west; pieced out by the Erie Canal, it links the Hudson to the Great Lakes. For the rest of its 150 miles the Hudson is an arm of the sea; oceangoing vessels tied up at Albany rise and fall 4½ feet on the tides. Steeped in history since Henry Hudson sailed the *Half Moon* upstream in 1609, the valley is especially noted for its Revolutionary War sites. The river, in places over three miles wide, is bordered by glacier-rounded hills and, at its southern end, by the cliffs of the Palisades.

From the lawn of Boscobel, a restored nineteenth-century mansion,
visitors may enjoy a sweeping view of the Hudson Valley some fifty miles
north of New York Harbor. The name of the estate is taken from the
Italian words bosco bello, *meaning "beautiful woods." Buildings of the*
West Point Military Academy poke above the foliage to the right.
To prevent the passage of British ships during the Revolutionary War,
a great chain of two-foot iron links, 1700 feet long and weighing
180 tons, spanned the strategic Hudson at this point.

WALKING IN THE ALLEGHENY FOREST

EDWIN L. PETERSON

Early in the afternoon we pitched our tent under the black cherry trees at Twin Lakes in Allegheny National Forest, near the northwestern corner of Pennsylvania. While we worked, the cedar waxwings looked on. If they disapproved of our presence, they gave no sign of their displeasure, nor did the chipmunk who supervised our labor from his station on the stone fireplace.

While I finished making camp, Tom walked over to the pump for a bucket of water. We cooled ourselves with long drinks of the icy pump water, watched the cedar waxwings for a while and then took the path that led through the grove toward the lake. In a few minutes we came to a footbridge crossing the inlet to the lake. There two youngsters fished in desultory fashion for the speckled trout that lie in the shadow of the bridge. Ahead lay the lake, the thin band of beach and the broad lawn where bathers sprawled, enjoying the turf, it seemed, more than the cold water.

We passed among the bathers and took a woodsy path that bordered the lake. For a while a scarlet tanager led us along the path, but shortly he took his black and scarlet way across the lake. We walked on under the tall cherry trees and maples and among the ferns and wood sorrel that crept in upon the trail. After a time we came to the bridge across the spillway, where we stopped to listen to the roar of the overflow, to see an angler bringing in a nine- or ten-inch brookie, and to look at two young ladies who took pleasure in nothing more important than sunlight and the sound of tumbling water. On the bank of the spillway we picked a handful of wild strawberries and then went on through the woods and back to the beach. "It's hard to believe," Tom said. "Waxwings and wild strawberries and trees and deer, and right in the middle of everything a place to go swimming. I wasn't born in the right place."

Late in the afternoon we followed the inlet up the valley, stopping long enough to watch the brook trout rising in small pools overhung by heavy cover and in the abandoned beaver dam a half mile up the stream. The dam was a beautifully desolate place of darkness and ferns and laurel and of trees rising naked and black from the water. Hemlocks on the western shore cut off the sunlight and dropped heavy shadows to the opposite shore. Neither leaf nor bird was in motion, and the only sound was of water trickling through the brush of the dam. We stood there quietly for several minutes, caught up in the spell of timelessness and desolation, of death rising from the black water. Then I heard Tom say, "Look! Quick!"

I looked upward. Against the reflected light of the sky the great creature swept toward us, like a bird from the prehistoric past, its tremendous wings outspread and slowly flapping. Almost directly over us and perhaps a hundred feet high in the air, the bird hesitated and folded its great wings against its sides. Then it plummeted downward like a dead thing stricken in midair. Forty feet away from us it hit the water with a tremendous splash and in almost the same instant was rising from the spray with a fish—no doubt a trout—clutched in its talons. Almost over our heads the bird wheeled.

"An osprey," Tom said. "I never saw one so close." I was still too startled to answer.

We left the beaver dam then, and the black water and dead trees, and walked quietly back to camp. On the dirt road some girls were singing.

After dinner, while Tom wandered off in search of deer, I spread out our map of Allegheny National Forest on the picnic table. It is a huge tract of land, thirty-seven miles long by forty-three miles wide. The simple map on the table showed a half million acres belonging to the people, maintained for their profit and their pleasure. The light had gone from the grove when Tom returned. "Four," he said. "Three small does and a fawn. There must be as many deer up here as there are people."

The morning was perfect for our drive to Hearts Content, the road to which, one would think, should be paved with gold. Instead it is a dirt road that winds through miles of fine young timber as carefully managed as a farmer's crop of corn. Ferns grow along the roadside, and laurel and rhododendron, and sometimes, in a sunny spot, patches of wild strawberry plants are speckled with red.

White pines a hundred feet tall tower above shade-tolerant hemlocks and hardwoods in the Hearts Content Scenic Area of northwestern Pennsylvania's Allegheny National Forest. The pines established themselves after forest fires in 1644.

Presently we came to a roadside marker that told us we were opposite Hearts Content—an area of a little more than a hundred acres of virgin hemlock and white pine. We parked the car and walked down the path into the woods. As we entered the forest the bright light of day began to fade into a woodsy dimness. A hundred and fifty feet overhead, the crowns of the tremendous trees blacked out the sky, and all around us, as we went deeper into the woods, was that strange stillness of the forest, like the stillness of fog at night, so quiet that the chittering of a red squirrel seemed raucous and irreverent.

Some of these trees were tall before the *Mayflower* set sail from England. To stand beneath them in perfect silence, to be willingly dwarfed, to sense rather than to see their grandeur is a chastening experience. Among these ancient inhabitants of the earth, our mortal pretensions are so out of place that we forget them. They dissolve into the silence and the twilight, and we stand alone and honest and humble among those that take their sustenance from earth and sky.

For an hour or two, saying very little, we walked among the great ones. Not until we were back at the car, I think, did we speak naturally. Then Tom said, "It's only eleven miles from here to Ludlow." He looked at his watch. "Let's try it," I said. He did not know that I had a special reason for wanting to see the Tionesta forest.

Not far from where we parked the car an obscure trail led down the hillside into the darkness of the forest. We followed the trail for a few hundred yards until it separated into two trails.

"You try one, and I'll try one," Tom suggested.

"Let's take an hour," I said, "and meet here."

Being alone made a difference, as Tom had guessed. It made the trees taller, the forest larger, the silence deeper. No wind moved among the distant branches, and no birds sang. If deer, turkeys or squirrels were in the woods, they made no sound.

For a mile or more I walked down the dim trail, looking back from time to time to keep my bearings. There was little undergrowth—an occasional small hemlock or a beech sapling courageously trying to find its way to the light. A few ferns showed green against the dark floor. When I stopped walking and sat down on a great log, the silence was more intense than ever, for my clumsy feet had been making a dreadful ruckus among the leaves. It was not an oppressive silence but so expansive, so pervasive, that it seemed to cover the whole earth.

From where I sat, my eyes caught a straight line of seven magnificent hemlocks, twenty or thirty feet apart. They were in a straight line because, about two centuries before, a great tree had come tumbling to the earth, had slowly crumbled into humus and had become a nursery for hemlock seedlings. Now the seedlings, nurtured on the decaying humus, were themselves old trees, markers of the long grave of their patriarch, and the dead and the living were in close communion.

Sitting there, I thought of another time long ago, and I wished that every boy in western Pennsylvania could spend at least one hour of his life in Tionesta forest. He might not be deeply impressed at the time, but he would remember the experience, I think, forever, just as I was remembering, even then, my first sight of these trees.

My father took me to see them when I was a boy. Before we went, he told me many things about the forest. Some of the trees were hundreds of years old. They were virgin trees, he said. I did not know exactly what he meant, but I had a maiden aunt who often came to visit us, and I hoped the trees were not like her. He told me about the elk and deer and bison that used to roam the woods and about the Indians who hunted there. They were all gone now, he said, except for a few deer and the trees.

The next day, when we got to the forest and started along the trail, I was disappointed. The trees were tall, of course, and their trunks were big, but they looked much like the big trees in the hollow behind our house. The trees in our hollow were oak trees, though, and maybe that made the difference.

Although my father was ordinarily a fast walker, we went down the trail slowly. Sometimes he would stop beneath one of the big trees and, with his eyes, follow its trunk up to the branches at the top and the bit of blue sky beyond. I did, too. They *were* big trees. I talked a good deal while we walked, but my father hardly talked at all. Once he put the palm of his hand gently on a tree and kept it there a long time. He was just looking at his hand on the tree trunk.

It was dark and shadowy and quiet in the woods, and the spell of it all began to seep into me. In spots, sunlight found its way through the branches and made bright brown splotches on the fallen needles. From down in the valley a sound came up, a sound like thunder.

"What's that?" I said. My father looked down at me. "It's a grouse," he said, "a grouse drumming." Then he walked on, slowly.

I had never heard a grouse drumming before, and I wanted to ask him about it, but this was not the right time. To me it sounded more like buffalo. I had never heard a buffalo, either, but I had read about them and about how, when the herd was moving, it made a sound like thunder. Maybe my father was wrong. Maybe a few buffalo had escaped the white man's notice and the Indian's and were still living there.

Ahead of me, my father did not look so tall as usual. I saw him stoop down, looking at something on the ground. When I came up to him, he was selecting little hemlock cones and putting them in his white handkerchief.

"What do you want them for?" I said.

"I just want them," he said. "Maybe I'll plant them in the backyard. I just—want them." He put the handkerchief carefully into his coat pocket. "Remind me to take them out of my pocket when we get to the car," he said. "I don't want to crush them."

As we went on, I kept thinking about the buffalo and the elk and about the Indians, too. I asked my father about the Indians.

"It isn't very likely," he said. "They're gone now, along with a lot of other things. I wish I could have seen them then, the trees. You couldn't get your arms around them, no, not two of you. They're gone now," he said, "except for just a few, like these."

I was still thinking about the elk and the buffalo.

"Here," he said, "try to put your arms around this one."

I tried, just to please him, but I knew I couldn't do it. My arms seemed shorter than usual, and the bark hurt my face. He was pleased, though, that I had tried, for when I turned around he was smiling—a strange smile that in some mysterious way seemed to come partly from him and partly from someone else.

"But it's a nice idea," I heard him say, still smiling, "about maybe the Indians still being here."

Where the trail turned uphill, the forest was not so dark. My father talked a lot as we were going uphill, but I was thinking of too many things to hear all that he said. When we got back to the road again, I turned around to look at the trees once more.

Now that I knew them, they looked different. They were the biggest, the greatest trees I had ever seen. I could still feel the bark under my fingers and the hurt of the bark on my face, and I could see the branches, black and high in the sky. I hoped that they would live forever, that my father would live forever, that nothing would ever die, not trees nor Indians nor buffalo. I was exalted and sad at the same time.

My father reached into his coat pocket and said, "Here, boy, have an apple." He had another one in his pocket for himself. Together we rubbed them on our pants to make them shiny, and then we ate them on the way back to the car.

Now, forty years later, I stood in the same forest, remembering an important boyhood experience compounded of tall trees and quietness and the drumming of a grouse. Little had changed except for the absence of the tall man. Even the exaltation and the sadness were the same, though older and a little wearier.

THE WEALTH OF JERSEY'S "BARRENS"

JOHN T. CUNNINGHAM

Thirst quickly overtakes a July visitor to New Jersey's Pine Barrens, and here we were floating down the tea-colored Oswego River without a drop of water in our canoe. Such lack of foresight is not in character for my canoe mate and guide, Frank McLaughlin, executive director of the New Jersey Audubon Society. I asked him how long it might be before I could get a drink of water.

"A second, maybe two," Frank replied. "Lean over and drink your fill of good Oswego water."

I drank suspiciously at first, then deeply, of a cool, dark liquid that had a faintly pungent, cedar taste, as if flavored by the evergreens that line both sides of the meandering river. There are few places in the East where a person dares drink from a stream, but the Oswego flows clean and sweet. No factories have invaded its watershed. No humans pollute its pristine banks or throw beer cans into its unsullied waters.

I drank, and we coasted downstream looking for the rare bog asphodel that Frank promised me would be in full bloom on the riverbank on the first of July. Just north of Martha's Furnace we found a breathtaking stand of this lovely flower—cluster after cluster of the bright yellow spikes; and their golden sheen lingers in my memory.

"This is the largest stand of bog asphodel in the

world," Frank told me matter-of-factly, as if such wonders were everyday occurrences.

Bog asphodel gives me still another reason for hoping that at least part of this great, little-known New Jersey wilderness will be saved for posterity. Even after 300 years of colonization and natural growth, these wildlands still encompass around 1.3 million acres—about one fourth the entire area of the state. Parts of the Barrens are less developed than they were 125 years ago.

Unused land attracts attention in a booming world. It lures romantic souls who seek clues to its historic past. It entices naturalists, botanists, bird watchers and flower collectors who are familiar with its unusual flora and fauna. It affords ample opportunity for thoughtful research, whether in varieties of flora or in the care and feeding of pine trees. The Jersey Pine Barrens are one of America's most challenging natural frontiers.

Great stretches of the Pine Barrens inevitably must succumb to civilization. Philadelphia is less than thirty-five miles to the west, and New York City lies not more than a hundred miles to the northeast. People, following industry, are moving to New Jersey at the rate of 500 a day.

But despite pressures for "development," all is not lost. Sections of the Pine Barrens have been set aside for state forests, parks, natural areas or public hunting and fishing. The 99,000-acre Wharton Tract, the nucleus of which was bought by New Jersey in 1954 because of its potential for underground storage of water, has paid huge recreational, conservation and historic dividends not originally anticipated. Most excitingly, a movement has been started by the New Jersey Audubon Society to set aside a major portion of the forest land as the Pine Barrens National Monument and Reserve. This would embrace the heart of the forest, nearly 550 square miles.

National monument hopes are based primarily on two tiny rarities—the diminutive curly grass fern, found nowhere else in the United States; and the bright-colored little Pine Barrens treefrog, found only here and in two other small, isolated colonies, one in North Carolina, the second in Georgia.

Perhaps for the first time in their long history the Pine Barrens will be understood, studied, utilized and managed. At last people may become aware that the very name Pine Barrens is a serious misnomer.

Pine Barrens indeed! Here is a land of incredible varieties of flora—the place of turkey beard, pyxie moss, cranberries, two score wild orchids, laurel, pitcher plants, golden crest, sundews, bearberry, bog asphodel, blueberries and at least 400 other varieties of flowers. It is a region of more than 150 species of birds, a place for deer, muskrats, raccoons, harmless snakes, frogs, flying squirrels and even an occasional beaver lodge.

The basic tree is pitch pine, which once grew forty to eighty feet tall. Now, because of repeated forest fires, pines more than fifty feet tall are seldom found, and most average only thirty to forty feet. Intermingled with these are scrubby oaks that are so little nourished by the thin soil that they often break off fifteen to twenty feet above the ground.

On first visits the cognomen Pine Barrens might seem justified. I remember well my first exposures about twenty years ago. The roads stretched straight and uninhabited from one small rise to another. Pine trees pressed in from all sides. I had to know the area before I loved it.

Botanists have shared this affection for at least 170 years. One of their favorite early haunts was a ramshackle old inn at Quaker Bridge (now a nearly forgotten crossroad deep in the Wharton Tract and less accessible than it was 150 years ago). The first recorded discovery of the curious little fern *Schizaea pusilla* was made at Quaker Bridge in 1805.

Since then *Schizaea* has called botanists again and again. This is the most unfernlike of ferns. It grows chiefly at the base of white cedars or in the damp hummocks, bogs and moist, sandy flats on the edges of white cedar swamps. It seldom attains a height of more than four inches and is difficult for the uninitiated to spot. A fertile frond grows out of the fern, whose leaves seemed to original discoverers to be "curly grass"—accounting for its common name, curly grass fern.

One charming description of the finding of *Schizaea* appeared in the *Botanical Gazette* in the fall of 1884, when a party of fifty, "including ladies and Britishers," tramped through the Pine Barrens in late-summer temperatures in the 90s. The writer said: ". . . The zeal of the excursionists, which was emulating the temperature, reached its highest point when the cry ran along the line that the *Schizaea* was found. There was a succession of disappearing forms down the railroad embankment into the thicket, where all, great and small,

Pitch pines like these bordering a stream in Lebanon State Forest flourish in New Jersey's Pine Barrens. Conservationists are battling to have a large section set aside as a national reserve to protect the Barrens' rare plants and animals.

went down on hands and knees to gather the precious little ferns of such unfernlike aspect."

Frank McLaughlin pointed out the grass fern to me. While our excitement did not reach the 1884 height (there were only two of us), I shared Frank's enthusiasm and fully agreed when he turned to me and said, "These stands are as important as the fossil beds of Nebraska—and in more danger of extinction. They should be preserved."

I have not seen the other rarity most cited in connection with a Pine Barrens National Monument, the small treefrog called *Hyla andersoni* or Pine Barrens treefrog. As Roger Conant has written, this denizen of the swamps, bogs and brown waters of the area is rarely seen "unless one follows the call of the singing male to its source."

The little treefrog calls *lank-lank-lank* (some say *quonk-quonk-quonk*)—repeated at the rate of about twenty-five times in twenty seconds on warm nights, at a slower rate if the air is cold. The breeding season is in late spring, and only then can the Pine Barrens treefrog be seen.

"There is only one way to catch him," said Frank. "You wait until you hear the *lank-lank-lank*, then run toward it, stopping abruptly on the last *lank*. Keep this up until you locate him. When he *lanks* again, you can even pick him up—but if you move between *lanks*, he will scramble away."

Frank added that it is a "great sight to see dignified naturalists romping through bogs between the *lanks*." Someday I hope to see that scene and even more to see the beautiful little green treefrog with its characteristic lavender stripes bordered by white. Frank promises that I will.

I *have* seen the handsome, if secretive, northern pine snake, another rarity that grows to upward of four feet, and has been found at a record eighty-three inches in length. This black and white snake slithering through the pine needles has a noisy hiss and can be frightening. It is harmless, except to small mammals and birds' nests, and can climb trees to seek out eggs, although it usually burrows in the sand.

Many Pine Barrens flowers are rare, if not unique as in the sense of the *Schizaea*. The southern yellow orchid, for example, is found at Sim Place Bog. This is the northernmost limit of the flower.

Close by, within eyesight of the southern yellow orchid, bearberry spreads away from a sandy road. This is a plant of the Far North, as far as the tundra land—and in that proximity of southern orchid and arctic plant is another story of the Pine Barrens. Here North and South meet botanically. Witmer Stone in 1910 catalogued sixty plants that are usually associated with Canadian provinces but reach their southernmost limits in the Pine Barrens. He also listed 164 "southern" species whose northernmost limits are in the Pine Barrens.

For a century and a half naturalists have wondered about the eerie, fire-scarred Plains southwest of Toms River. The Indians had shunned it, and with good reason. Here grow pine trees whose rings show they are thirty years old—and they stand not more than four or five feet tall. Growth seldom exceeds twelve to fifteen feet on the Plains, even in trees fifty years old. Stunted trees spring largely from shoots on old trunks. Their shrunken, seemingly forsaken appearance has made this a lonely, forlorn region where legend is bound to be rife.

Many a theory has been advanced to account for the aborted growth. Indians felt the soil was bewitched by evil spirits. Later a theory was advanced that the chemical nature of the soil could not support good growth, but comprehensive tests do not show the soil to be worse than the rest of the Pine Barrens. There is widespread—nearly unanimous—belief among scientists and foresters today that fire is the chief culprit.

The Plains are broken into two sections, one astraddle Route 72 about seven miles east of Chatsworth, the other to the south on both sides of Route 539. Between the two lonely reaches of pygmy trees and vegetation is a rich bottomland known as Sim Place. Dr. Silas Little, Jr., of the Northeastern Forest Experiment Station in Lebanon State Forest, and George Moorehead, state forester, took me there one afternoon to prove what the absence of fire can do. I saw one of the most impressive stands of native pines in all of southern New Jersey.

"Why?" I asked Si Little.

"No wildfire," he answered simply. "This is protected—by cranberry bogs along one edge, by the Oswego River on two other sides and by a canal on the fourth side."

The Pine Barrens face a constant threat of being eliminated. Gone then will be the sweet water of the Oswego, the orchids, the *Schizaea* and *Hyla andersoni*, the golden crest, the laurel. Often we brood at our capacity to destroy. Only occasionally are we cheered by our capacity to save—as by a Pine Barrens National Monument.

Words of Frank McLaughlin keep coming back to me: "God put that Pine Barrens there for us today. He gave us time to think and years to plan."

We have the Pine Barrens today. But will we save them for those who will follow tomorrow?

The Pine Barrens of New Jersey are a haven for colorful and unusual plants. White fringed orchids, just starting to open (top left), display deeply cleft flowers in July and August. Cranberries (top right) thrive in moist, acid bogs. The deep red fruits are popular with songbirds. Commercial cranberry growers call redroot (above) a weed. Shoots and stems contain a red juice used in making dyes. The trumpet-like leaves of the pitcher plant (left) collect water, and their "one-way" bristles imprison any insect as it enters. Eventually the insect drowns and is digested by the plant.

Part II

MOUNTAINS, MARSHES AND LOWLAND SHORES

Delaware Maryland District of Columbia
West Virginia Kentucky Virginia
North Carolina Tennessee South Carolina
Georgia Florida Alabama
Mississippi Louisiana Arkansas

DELAWARE'S WILD LANDS

WILLARD T. JOHNS

"First you need people who love the land—people who truly appreciate the land's historic, scenic or wildlife values and want to achieve a balance between these values and the necessity for industrial or economic development. And then you need a crisis."

In those words, Edmund H. (Ted) Harvey, president and founder of Delaware Wild Lands, Inc., described the underlying formula behind one of the nation's most unusual and successful citizen conservation efforts.

Organized in 1961, Delaware Wild Lands is a private, nonprofit corporation dedicated to the preservation of unspoiled natural areas in that state. The corporation is convinced that the most effective way to do that is to raise money, buy up, set aside or restore.

We visited the Diamond State (nicknamed from Thomas Jefferson's reference to Delaware as "a jewel among the states") to see what was behind the success story of Delaware Wild Lands. For two hot, sunny days in mid-August we tramped along ocean and bay beaches, waded through coastal marshes, walked the shores of mysteriously beautiful cypress swamps and hiked across fertile farmlands rich in colonial history. With Ted Harvey and his son Rusty, we learned what this small group has done in our second smallest state to help Delaware maintain its rural charm despite a booming population growth and spectacular industrial development.

They took us first to Trussum Pond, near Laurel, Delaware, and then to the Great Cypress Swamp, which straddles the Delaware-Maryland state line in Sussex County just west of Selbyville. Here, as in very few places north of the Deep South, you can see and experience a miniature wilderness in which the earth's evolution suddenly and dramatically comes alive. Here, the giant bald cypress trees—last of their race to be found so far north—tower above the dark, coffee-colored swamp waters like living giants from the

past. It is a place where you can picture in your mind's eye the Mesozoic era of our planet's geologic history, complete with flying reptiles and dinosaurs. Some 80 million years ago, this unique swamp covered much of Delmarva peninsula.

Today, this tract of 11,000 acres owned by Delaware Wild Lands on the headwaters of the Pocomoke River—"black water" in the Algonquian language—is about all that remains. Generations of shingle-makers and farmers clearing land reduced the cypress swamps to remnants.

Most people had given up all hope for perpetuating the Delaware bald cypress after fire and drainage had all but destroyed its last remaining strongholds. But Trussum Pond and portions of the ravaged Great Cypress Swamp were bypassed in the parade of progress.

Before they were lost forever, Ted Harvey returned to his native state after many years of living in Florida and traveling the world. He never had lost his love for the lands he had known as a boy, lands that his father had shown him and lands that had instilled in him deep respect for trees, history, natural beauty and things wild and free. He was shocked and saddened to find, however, that Delaware had changed in his absence. Places he had visited with his father were no longer recognizable; progress had changed the landscapes with real-estate developments.

In 1961 Harvey heard that 1200 acres of the Great Cypress Swamp were for sale. He didn't have the purchase price of $80,000, but it didn't take long to interest some of the women in the Wilmington Garden Club in this enchanting and unique ecosystem of bald cypress, white cedar, swamp magnolia, sweetleaf and exotic flowers such as the white fringed orchid. Together they formed Delaware Wild Lands, Inc. For the first few years all of the money used by the group to acquire and manage their lands came through private donations.

But then there occurred a crisis, the second element in Ted Harvey's formula for success in any program of this type. An oil company began to purchase some 6000 acres of land as the site for a huge oil refinery along the Delaware coast. Conservationists everywhere were outraged over the threat this industrial development posed not only to the natural beauty and character of

The distinctive trunks of bald cypresses rise out of Trussum Pond on James Branch in southern Delaware. Broad buttresses give them stability in soft soil. Mature trees may approach 120 feet in height and three to five feet in diameter.

the state but also to a great aquatic resource and to the wintering grounds for a great portion of the waterfowl of the Atlantic Flyway.

Today, the company still owns the land, but it has never started construction of the refinery. And, although it wasn't intended that way, it has protected the coastal land and given outstanding impetus to Ted Harvey and his group which, as it were, lost a battle but won a war.

For the last five years a public appeal for funds with which to continue the group's land acquisition program has brought in more than $60,000 per year. Thousands of Delawareans, both rich and poor, have contributed to the cause. Ted fondly recalls a crumpled one-dollar bill that arrived in the mail one day from an old lady who wrote that she didn't have much money but she wanted to do a little something to save the Delaware she remembered as a girl.

From Trussum Pond and the Great Cypress Swamp, Delaware Wild Lands has moved on to greater, and perhaps more significant, land acquisitions. The group presently owns some 20,000 acres, acquired at a cost of about $6 million. In a small state such as Delaware, these acres are highly significant. Unlike some properties acquired by citizens interested only in land near them, however, these lands were not purchased entirely for their individual features. Working with state conservation agencies, Delaware Wild Lands acquires land not just for its natural resource value but also for its future potential of fitting into an overall plan for the entire state.

Some of the land has already been turned over to the state government, particularly its Board of Game and Fish Commissioners, so that it can be managed to maintain Delaware's wildlife resource. Other lands are being managed and improved to restore their native plant types. All are available to the public, although mass recreation development will not be planned because such use is not compatible with keeping these miniature wildernesses as they are.

Later we talked with Fred Hudson, one of Delaware Wild Lands' field men, about the program of replanting bald cypress, southern white cedar and pine on areas where these species once grew before lumbering, drainage and farming destroyed much habitat. We heard Ted Harvey

Waters from Trussum Pond show their true colors as they flow over an old mill dam. The roots of bald cypresses and southern white cedars produce the tannic acid that gives this unique swamp's clear water its deep amber cast.

and his son express their dreams of someday getting water control devices in the drainage ditches so that there could be fishing and proper water levels in the swamplands of Sussex County. We listened in agreement with their hopes of restoring and protecting the Pocomoke River from its source to Pocomoke Sound on Chesapeake Bay.

We explored the Blackbird-Appoquinimink salt marshes of southeastern New Castle County where Delaware Wild Lands has purchased over 2100 acres seriously threatened by heavy industry and drainage. Finally, we tramped over Kingston-upon-Hull, a 2000-acre Kent County farm, rich in

colonial history and in natural resource value. As we were leaving the farm a magnificent buck deer, head held high, bounded across the road in one mighty leap. It seemed to us that, perhaps more than any other single thing, that tremendous stag typified what Delaware Wild Lands means.

A people with a love for their land, coupled with a crisis: Those are the elements Ted Harvey said were necessary to success in any citizen effort to save natural areas from material progress. But there is still another element to it, one that Ted Harvey didn't mention but one that became increasingly obvious to us. Conservation also re-

quires leadership—an intangible, indescribable element of service to humanity that cannot be measured except by results. Ted Harvey, and now his son Rusty, have that mysterious but entirely convincing type of leadership. So do all of the loyal people connected with Delaware Wild Lands and all of the Delawareans who have contributed to the program. It is a leadership with dedication, devotion, loyalty and a sincere desire to serve all of the people of a state, region or nation. In the final analysis real conservation embodies all of the qualities of service to your fellowmen that places their future ahead of your own.

ASSATEAGUE ISLAND NATIONAL SEASHORE

Wild ponies roam the dunes and marshes of Assateague Island National Seashore, a slender strand off the Atlantic coast of Maryland and Virginia. The longer, Maryland portion of thirty-seven-mile-long Assateague had been slated for private development when a 1962 winter nor'easter slammed into it, creating havoc. Subsequent reassessment led to designation of the entire stretch as a national seashore in 1965. Beautiful beaches are backed by sand dunes protecting the marshy lowlands. Most of the seashore's Virginia end is a wildlife refuge. Two miles of the Maryland section are used for camping. The balance is administered by the National Park Service for a variety of recreational activities.

The sun rises over the Assateague sand dunes (above), brightening saltwater ponds and marshes where many shorebirds breed. Good feeding awaits migratory waterfowl in this sanctuary on the Atlantic Flyway route. Smaller than horses but larger than Shetland ponies, Chincoteague ponies (right) have long, shaggy coats. Legend holds that they are descended from Moorish ponies that swam ashore from a shipwrecked Spanish galleon.

TOWPATH ALONG
THE POTOMAC

WILLIAM O. DOUGLAS

The bright days of Indian summer are choice along the Potomac. Maples are crimson; sumac and dogwood, a rich dark red; gum trees and papaw, yellow; willow oak, a dull gold. There are autumn days when the leaves have not yet fallen and no breeze touches the trees. Then it's as if the woods were holding their breath, lest a leaf be lost. On such a day I was headed west along the Chesapeake and Ohio Canal towpath. There was hardly a sound in the woods, none but the cawing of a raven and the scolding of a squirrel as my dog Sandy—the Shetland sheepdog who traveled the woods with me—scouted the thickets where the hawthorn and honeysuckle entwine. Suddenly a gust of wind touched a stand of sycamores. Down came scores of leaves, no longer flat and pliant, but dry and slightly cupped. They scattered far, the wind spinning them in gentle gyrations. Each kept a horizontal plane, landing bottom down in the waters of the canal and dancing in the soft waves like dainty skiffs.

Out of Washington going west there is water in the C&O Canal for the first twenty miles or so. This waterway, built by mules hauling scoops, and men with picks and shovels, was finished in 1850. President John Quincy Adams had turned the first spade of dirt in Georgetown on July 4, 1828. The canal was part of George Washington's dream; it connected Cumberland, Maryland—about 185 miles to the northwest as the Potomac flows—with Washington, D.C., and it brought mostly coal to tidewater on the Potomac. The railroads soon followed, however, and the competition became intense—too severe for the canal. But it remained in operation until 1924, when stubborn economic facts intervened. The barges—ninety feet by fourteen and a half feet—pulled by mules, have now

Only canoes can navigate this section of the Chesapeake and Ohio Canal, near Harpers Ferry. The canal, now mostly dry, followed the north bank of the Potomac for 185 miles above Washington, lifting barges through seventy-five locks.

67

disappeared. The restored locks with gate beams made of oak still stand.

The canal has abandoned stone lockhouses where the lock tenders used to live. There is one on the Washington end over which two great sycamores tower. On the fall day I walked the towpath, the pale color of the house, the mottled bark of the sycamores and their yellow leaves made an exquisite pastel. A flock of blackbirds whirled overhead in unison, swooping and turning en masse before settling in treetops to chatter in a lively community meeting. A dozen turkey vultures caught a current of air as they soared high over a stretch of woods. They would stay with us all winter. So would the white-crowned sparrow, the junco, the redheaded woodpecker and the wrens. But the robin I saw in a walnut tree was headed south. So was the blue jay disappearing in a huge tulip tree.

This was the ebb tide of autumn. The oak and walnut had dropped their nuts. So had the numerous hickories that flourish in the valley: bitternut, pignut and mockernut. The towpath was littered with them. The papery, transparent husks of the box elders were empty. The Siberian crab apple, growing like a miniature shrub, was in fruit. Earlier it had showed white, handsome, long and slender-stalked flowers; now its yellowish fruit, about three quarters of an inch in diameter, was wrinkled and shrunken. The scarlet berries of the dogwood had mostly dropped; its silver gray, squarish terminal buds were conspicuous, conveying the illusion that spring was close at hand.

White and purple asters were among the few remaining wild flowers, and there were occasional bushes of the pale snapweed still showing yellow flowers. The dayflower made a blue carpet over some edges of the towpath, its petals heart-shaped and clasping. Swamp smartweed showed a delicate raceme of whitish flowers. Growing high above the canal was the halberd-leaf rose mallow. Some of the flowers were still in bloom; their delicate flesh-colored petals with purple bases were more in keeping with spring than with fall.

Those clear November days when the temperature dips to the low 30s have their own rewards. Then the leaves are down, rustling underfoot. The shining sumac—the one with resin dots on its branches and fruit—is heavy with bunches of seeds. The mimosa (the old silk tree from Persia introduced here over two centuries ago) stands like a plume, its pods hanging forlornly. The pods of the honey locust are turning black underfoot. The sycamore catches the eye when the forests are barren. Its smooth bark looks as if it is in sunshine even when clouds hang low. On a sunny day in late autumn the sight of a stand of naked sycamores lifts the heart. Quite often one great horizontal limb extends over the canal in a protective gesture. But most of the branches, slightly twisted, reach for the heavens. The bark flakes off in irregular patches; it has a mottled effect in any weather—light gray, pale tan and chalky white. In November the limbs are hung with balls that burst and scatter seeds far and wide. It is from them that the tree gets the name buttonwood. This tree, the largest deciduous hard tree in North America, was a boon to the early pioneers, though the wood was almost impossible to split. Cross sections were once used for oxcart wheels. A section from a hollow tree made a good hogshead when boards were nailed across one end.

On a bright November day one leans into a sharp wind out of the west. Freezing weather has come; little life is abroad. The waters of the Potomac are low and sluggish. The muskrats are holed up for the winter. So are the turtles, the friendly blacksnakes and the less friendly copperheads. One seems to have the woods all to oneself. A gray squirrel scolds from a sweet gum. A kingfisher, perched on a limb that overlooks the waters of the canal, flaps lazily away. A flock of pigeons turns and disappears down a ravine. This is the time to be alone—surrounded by the stark grandeur of naked trees.

There are times in the winter when the temperature drops to the 20s. If that happens for successive days the canal freezes and Washington turns out in great numbers for skating. Fires are built and families bring their lunch and make a day of it. Some winter days have shown the Potomac wilderness in sheer splendor. I remember a bright, breathless day when the temperature was below 20° F., and new-fallen snow three inches deep lay crisp on the land. It powdered trees and shrubs alike and stood stiff like frost on the branches of the hawthorn. The Potomac was white with frosted ice, not showing the channels that keep it open most of the time. The canal was frozen, but the hour was too early for skaters. I was the only one abroad. At least I thought I was, until I saw the fresh tracks of a rabbit. Later there were signs that a squirrel had been foraging. At Widewater a host of starlings swooped down over the glistening ice as if to land, only to turn upward in a wide spiral and disappear over the river. A hawk streaked across Widewater and a bald eagle soared at great heights. A cardinal hopped from limb to limb in a willow oak, which bears nuts bitter to our taste but liked by squirrels and some birds.

All was silent, except the crunching of the snow underfoot. When I stopped, I could almost hear my heart beat. Yet I was less than a dozen miles from the heart of Washington. My wilderness, though small and confined, was real. It was in miniature the immense northland stretching to the Arctic Circle and beyond.

One misty March morning I came to a section of the towpath above Harpers Ferry, West Virginia, that had been washed out by spring rains. The river was running in the canal for a mile with the frenzy of a western mountain stream before returning to its channel. To get through I had to climb a bluff 200 feet above the river. When I reached the top there was so much fog that the Blue Ridge, rising on the opposite shore, was vague and indistinct. The river had an angry roar. Soon a cold wind came blustering out of the north, sweeping the mist before it and making a small stand of red cedars fairly sing in the gale.

The coming of the buds is one reason why March is my favorite month along the Potomac. They fill the air with expectancy. The willow, box elder and the sweet gums show their buds early; one can smell them where the stand is thick. And the Potomac Valley is especially inviting in a spring rain. Some storms bring a hard torrent, but these rains are usually soft, some of them barely more than mists. Then fog comes in thin wisps. The Virginia shore shows dimly on the river. Islands come and go. Familiar shorelines and promontories are distorted, strange. Everything is so out of focus it almost seems that one walks in a dream. Mystery upon mystery unfolds as cliffs acquire new shapes, points of land new character. Even old, familiar sycamores seem strange and new at first glance. These gentle spring rains and fogs transform the valley so completely that one can hike with fresh wonder and excitement.

There is ceaseless delight and amazement when man lets the wilderness grow without hindrance around him, when he keeps the waters inviolate. Then he glimpses the universe that put him in molecular relation with its smallest as well as its greatest parts. Man's task is to do more than share life with other people. His true destiny is in sharing life with all the other living things in the universe. One who knows the wilderness at its full glory appreciates how dreadful and oppressive it would be if we ended up with nothing but people on this earth.

SENTINEL IN THE FOREST

MAURICE BROOKS

A fire tower is a comforting sight, in settled country or in the wilderness. It stands as evidence that someone cares about the forest and has made plans to keep it growing—green and productive. When fires start, and they will, the lookout in his tower sets in motion a chain of action, a planned attack that sooner or later will lead to the control of any blaze. This is a welcome thought.

I invite your attention to Gaudineer Knob in southeastern West Virginia, and to the tower the United States Forest Service has erected on its summit. Don Gaudineer, for whom the peak was named, was a ranger in the Greenbrier district of the Monongahela National Forest. When fire threatened his family he gave his life to save them, and so a fine mountain bears his name.

The tower area is about thirty minutes in latitude south of Washington, a strange place for the red spruce forest that covers slope and crest. Elevation, however, tells the story. Gaudineer Knob is 4445 feet above sea level. In average temperature and length of growing season this mountaintop is climatically a part of northern New England or eastern Canada. Many plants and animals present would be at home in New Brunswick or north of Lake Superior. Here a precious bit of Canada spills southward along Appalachian ridges.

Cheat Mountain range, of which Gaudineer is a part, is well watered, and so for much of the year fire danger is minimal or nonexistent. During spring and fall, however, things are different, and there is the ever-present threat of a blaze.

Today, however, Gaudineer fire tower stands empty, a memorial to the dedication of the heroic forest ranger for whom it was named. Lookouts no longer climb the tower to watch for forest fires even in the dangerous dry season. Detection of fires is now accomplished almost entirely by airplanes. But the deserted fire tower on Gaudineer Knob is still an unsurpassed location from which to view the breathtaking vistas of the Monongahela National Forest.

In the panoramic sweep from Gaudineer there are few cleared areas. Most of the landscape is forested, with second-growth spruce on the heights and northern hardwoods—beech, birch and maple —on the lower slopes.

Two miles south of the tower, a paved highway, U.S. 250, crosses the mountains, but the road is out of sight. Beyond it is a beautiful wilderness, a ridge known locally as Back Allegheny, with an elevation always above 4000 feet. For almost twenty miles no road follows its crest, and none crosses it except a one-time logging railroad. A mile or so north of the tower is West Virginia's one remnant of original spruce forest.

The Forest Service welcomes visitors to Gaudineer Knob. For business uses, and for the public's convenience, their engineers have built a gravel-surfaced road to its summit. Picnic areas are screened by dense spruce hedges. There are tables and outdoor grills, and a well provides cold water. Besides, *mirabile dictu*, there are few biting flies, even on a warm July day.

Visitors may climb to a platform surrounding the glassed-in cubicle on top of the tower, although the structure is no longer manned. It is the ideal setting for picture-taking or for quiet reflection on the grandeur of the forest.

The fire tower atop Gaudineer Knob in West Virginia commands a view of second-growth red spruce forest. Seed for the new forest spread from a small stand of virgin spruce that escaped the axe through a fortuitous surveying error.

There is an interesting layering of living things apparent in the sixty-foot climb. At ground level the characteristic Gaudineer birds in summer are juncos and winter wrens. A dozen feet from the ground, magnolia warblers are abundant. Red-breasted nuthatches search along the higher branches, and golden-crowned kinglets hunt tiny insects in outer twigs. The thirty-foot level is a good place for blackburnian warblers; I found my only nest of these birds by looking squarely into it from halfway up the tower. The tallest of young spruces bear cones, usually near treetop. When red crossbills are abundant, as they are some years, they feast on spruce seeds, using their crossed mandibles as chisellike tools to pry open the cone scales.

Some of West Virginia's finest mountain country surrounds Gaudineer Tower. Just eastward is the long range of Middle Mountain, and along its crest the Forest Service maintains a road, forty miles through high country, most of it wooded and all a delight. Spruce Knob, at 4860 feet West Virginia's highest point, is just visible on clear days.

To the south, Gaudineer Tower overlooks the upper reaches of the Greenbrier River. Down through a valley sheltered by high mountains on either side, the river flows through the great white pine forest.

To the north and west, Gaudineer looks down on the Cheat River country, a land of heavy forest, all of it high and much of it roadless. So abundant is precipitation that vegetation from

ground cover to forest crown grows in layers, each of which shelters its appropriate animal species.

The Gaudineer region is at the center of the highest and most extensive mountain mass between the White Mountains of New Hampshire and the southern Blue Ridge in Virginia, North Carolina and Tennessee. To a remarkable degree it combines their qualities and characteristics and therein lies much of its attraction for naturalists. At times all the bird voices seem to be those of the north woods, but suddenly one also hears a yellow-breasted chat, a hooded warbler or a blue-gray gnatcatcher. The whole effect is delightfully bewildering.

No matter what the season there is always something worth seeing round and about Gaudineer. In autumn the foreground of the lookout's view is a sea of young spruce tops. In nice counterpoint to this dark green is the blaze of color on maple, birch, beech and basswood just downslope. On fair days hundreds of monarch butterflies drift southward, perhaps to winter in the Everglades. Occasional hawks pass over.

Fall warblers, just as confusing as they are supposed to be, feast on aphids that infest spruce twigs. Chipmunks constantly scurry, and red squirrels are busy cutting and piling cones which will be their winter's food supply. Wild turkeys, safe enough from the hunter so long as they stay in rhododendron tangles, gobble at dawn and dusk.

This is a season of bright fruits, much of the color being supplied by deciduous hollies. In this area are three species of holly that shed their leaves but flaunt a harvest of red fruits.

Winter is a silent season on the heights. Few birds can find food under heavy snow and ice, and few care to weather the arctic storms that sweep the crests. Every spruce needle acquires a coating of frost crystals, sparkling decorations that may last for weeks. Varying hares, whose fur turns winter white, search for highbush cranberries, a favorite food at all seasons. A few ravens live on discards that other creatures overlook or reject. Snow is often drifted high.

Spring comes slowly, and with many false starts. Along the south foot of Gaudineer Knob is a narrow swampy area, Blister Swamp. Here northern balsam fir grows, exudations on its trunk causing blisters and accounting for the local name of the area. On warm nights, perhaps in April, spotted salamanders emerge from hibernation, seek forest pools for their mating and deposit their egg masses. As frost leaves the ground, earthworms become active, and woodcocks arrive to probe for them and to build nests, even though there still is danger that snow will cover the eggs.

Farther up the slopes, where snow lingers, it will be May before spring wild flowers open under bare branches of northern hardwoods. Toward the last of that month, painted trilliums and pink lady's-slippers blossom just as leaves are opening on the trees. Among the spruces, flowers are few: oxalis and Canada mayflower are most common, and here and there heartleaf twayblades, tiny

orchids of the north country, show their cleft-lipped blooms in early June.

Birds, too, are slow in reaching the high places. Until insects hatch, there is little for birds to eat in a spruce forest. Juncos need make only a short altitudinal migration; they arrive with the first snowless days. Hermit thrushes also are hardy, and they are often scratching for food in early April, a month before the other nesting brown-backed thrushes—wood, veery and Swainson's—appear. Northern water thrushes begin singing in April, at home here on the heights well away from water. Most other summer residents are on their breeding grounds by mid-May. Frost or even snow may yet come, but the birds are ready to nest.

The summer visitor to Gaudineer must divide his time. He cannot afford to miss the massed beds of mountain laurel and rhododendron, these at their best as June turns to July. He must allow enough hours for wood warblers: From the foot of the mountain to its summit, twenty-two warbler species are summer residents, more kinds than are known to nest on any other Appalachian peak. If he has an interest in the cold-blooded vertebrates, he will want to see the little gold-flecked Cheat Mountain salamander, a creature not known to occur outside this mountain range.

Just at dusk, varying hares, now in summer brown and white, come out to eat grass beneath the fire tower. The platform above affords good views of their feeding and playing. Also out are the flying squirrels, the larger northern species near the southern limits of its range. Sometimes one will pause for a moment on an exposed snag near the tower. Winter wrens are still singing, juncos chirping and magnolia warblers sounding as though they were scolding the children.

But the dusk really belongs to the thrushes. Their full chorus begins earlier; at first most of the birds are well downhill, where wood thrushes will remain. As shadows creep upward, veeries and hermit thrushes seek the light toward the summit. Veeries usually keep to the undergrowth, but hermits like to sing from the highest tip of a spruce. Closest of all in approach to the tower are Swainson's thrushes. They seem reluctant to miss one daylight moment, one ray from the summer sunset. As the tower is on the highest point, so the birds are drawn to it in the dusk. Finally, singing must stop, there are a few sleepy chirps—then silence. The June day has ended.

This is fine country, and I keep returning to it. I am happy that it is protected—the tower is a symbol and a promise.

NATURE'S UNDERGROUND CATHEDRAL

BILL SURFACE

Exquisite, multicolored flower formations decorate the ceiling. Sculptures of Christmas trees, animals and waterfalls embellish the walls. Eerie, moonlike craters pit the floor. Indeed, so intriguing is its catalogue of wonders that 1.9 million visitors a year are drawn to Mammoth Cave, one of the world's largest and most majestic caverns. "Caves are as different as cities," says John Aubuchon, superintendent of Mammoth Cave National Park. "But Mammoth Cave is the capital of them all."

It could uphold this reputation on length alone. Opening under a hillside in southern Kentucky, thirty-two miles northeast of Bowling Green, Mammoth Cave has 225 known avenues winding over five levels, and a circumference of twelve miles. Stretched out, the cave would extend at least 180 miles—or more than the distance from Philadelphia to Washington, D.C. Yet visitors need walk only a few feet past the entrance to begin appreciating this exotic natural phenomenon. Here they are in a rotunda as large as Grand Central Station. One of the two access tunnels, aptly named Broadway, is wide enough to accommodate an interstate highway, with plenty of passing room, for most of three consecutive miles.

Every step in Mammoth's passages offers sights that seem incomparable—until the next turn. In the vast "auditorium" beyond the first bend, for example, is a natural stone pulpit reputedly used by evangelists with remarkable effectiveness. Pointing to five nearby tunnels, they could readily evoke "gateways to purgatory and hell." Farther on, dripping water has spun gravel around and around tiny cracks in the limestone floor until it has carved twenty-three seemingly bottomless pits as circular and smooth as silos. The water also sculpted rust-colored columns thrusting up 104 feet, resembling Egypt's Temple of Karnak. Most major caverns have two or three such pillars, but

Mammoth Cave has forty-seven—including one taller than a twenty-story skyscraper!

Endless rows of sparkling white stalactites—formed by calcite deposits in dripping water adhering to the ceiling—hang like huge icicles, while cone-shaped stalagmites rise to meet them. Where they meet, a column is born. Other formations that began as stalactites now mimic fish hooks and inverted trees—with no scientific explanation for their bizarre shapes. "We call them stalactites gone crazy," says naturalist William Westphal, of the National Park Service.

On a special expedition a visitor may admire needle-size formations so delicate that they "dance" at the slightest touch of heat or air current. Farther on, huge boulders are so precariously perched above the trail that they make some tourists think that slides are imminent. Such fears are unnecessary. Since air filtering into the cave through miles of streams and damp crevices keeps the temperature at 54° F. the entire year, there is no expansion or contraction in the ground to disturb the boulders. There's no record of anyone having seen a single stone fall in Mammoth Cave.

Mammoth's contrasts are endless. After stooping and twisting through a narrow corridor referred to as "Fat Man's Misery" you enter a room large enough for a basketball court. Minutes later you're walking on a narrow ledge, looking into deep gorges. From a section so arid that it is named the Sahara you proceed toward one of the cave's eight waterfalls. Among Mammoth's other aquatic wonders, some of which are not accessible to visitors, are two crystal-clear lakes, a dead sea surrounded by sixty-foot walls and partially covered by a natural bridge, and three rivers that alternate from calm, navigable streams in summer to turbulent rivers that rise or fall up to six feet an hour during winter.

Many of the one hundred species of subterranean creatures inhabiting the cave are unlike any others in the world. Crickets, descendants of insects that lived in the cavern centuries ago, patrol the corridors with two sensitive antennae alert for their enemies or their next meal. These crickets, wingless and pale, have so totally conformed to the dark, damp environment that they die if exposed to daylight for a prolonged time.

An even more astounding adaptation to a murky world has been made by fish. Translucent and eyeless, these small fish navigate Mammoth Cave's waters by means of a keen acoustical system that enables them to find and eat invisible microorganisms in the water.

The world's most stupendous cave is, in essence, part of a similarly impressive cave region. At least forty smaller (but still sizable) "wild" caves are known to be within the 52,000-acre Mammoth Cave National Park, and almost every farmer owning hilly land within a twenty-five-mile radius is apt to have a cave or two on his property. All are a product of the unusual topography: Instead of draining into creeks and ditches, rain empties into the area's approximately 10,000 sinkholes and then flows through underground streams, leading to the Green River, systematically gouging new passages and weakening the earth above. New sinkholes appear so suddenly that many a farmer in that area has had a cow or dog fall into a "sink" that was level ground the previous day.

As water entered similar sinkholes millions of years ago, it seeped through cracks in the gray sandstone until it reached the seemingly impenetrable limestone beds. But when carbonic acid (formed when gases in the air are dissolved in water) came in contact with limestone, the resulting solution slowly dissolved many limestone beds and eventually carved great channels that became lakes, then rivers. While the flowing water collapsed many underground corridors, the strongest and possibly largest cavern remained virtually intact. Then, as the underground water table dropped, a new route was cut toward the valley of the Green, and in time the cavern's four upper levels were drained.

As the waters subsided, the limestone reacted to its unnaturally dry condition by oxidizing to form calcium sulfate. The evaporation of calcium sulfate through porous limestone formed gypsum crystals of varying shapes and colors, which were forced outward into the cave. They eventually encrusted one room with snow-white gypsum bubbles as uniformly spaced as if they were fitted by interior decorators. In rooms where the pores were of uneven size, other bubbles burst into exotic patterns resembling lilies, roses and daisies, and rich designs that would do justice to a highly skilled embroiderer.

Minerals such as calcite and iron oxide color many overlapping stalactites to resemble orange and white draperies. A glimmering, dripping wet stalactite is still growing. But if water drips too fast to evaporate as it drips, the calcite in it may form flowstone in crevices.

One foamy-looking formation so closely resembles a waterfall that it is named Frozen Niagara. At seventy-five by forty-five feet, it is probably

older than the real Niagara Falls, since, some geologists maintain, cave onyx grows only one foot per 1000 years.

Pre-Columbian Indians, carrying cane-reed torches, ventured up to three miles into the cave's top level to scrape from the walls gypsum crystals that were possibly used as paint bases, fertilizers and medicinal salts. Less adventurous Indians apparently used the rotunda near the cave's entrance for tribal councils and for storage of clothing, coffins and other artifacts which, radioactive-carbon dating techniques reveal, were placed there from 400 B.C. to 100 A.D.

Warren County Land Certificate No. 2428 shows that in 1798 one Valentine Simons entered "200 acres of second-rate land . . . including two salt-peter caves." Simons was astonished on July 9, 1812, to receive a seemingly foolish stranger's offer of $116.67 for "those hills with the big cave." After he accepted, he was further astounded to learn that by sundown the cave had changed hands three times. By August a mere half of the cave had been sold for $10,000. The "cave speculators" were after the saltpeter, an ingredient in the gunpowder being produced for the War of 1812.

Later the cave's auditoriums were often illumined by lanterns for musical and dramatic performances—by such as Swedish soprano Jenny Lind and actor Edwin Booth. Then the discovery of new "rooms" in 1923 precipitated feverish searches for new entrances to the cave. Nearby farmers neglected crops to explore remote passageways; one even succeeded in digging another entrance. Such desecration of the area did not subside until 1941, when the state and federal governments acquired the land for a national park.

Mammoth Cave's guides feel that their sons can have no greater ambition than to "guide the Cave." Typical is Lewis Cutliff, a third-generation guide born only 300 feet across the hollow from the cave's entrance. He went away to college and taught junior high school. But he couldn't get "caving" out of his system, and returned to be a guide. "No matter how many times I walk through," Cutliff says, "Mammoth Cave fascinates me just as much as it did the first time."

And that is perhaps as precise a summary as any that could be made of the lure of this fabulous underground cathedral.

Cleveland Avenue is one of several Mammoth Cave galleries decorated by deposits of gypsum crystals formed from evaporating water and forced through porous limestone. Probably thousands of miles of passages remain unexplored.

THE BLUE RIDGE NATIONAL PARKWAY

The Blue Ridge National Parkway is a 469-mile highroad linking Shenandoah National Park in Virginia with the Great Smoky Mountains National Park on the North Carolina–Tennessee border. Its northern tip lies near one of the highest sections of the Blue Ridge Mountains, between the Piedmont and Shenandoah valleys. On its southwesterly trek, the road winds along mountain crests at elevations of 2000 to 6000 feet. Designed for leisurely motoring, the parkway substitutes wooded vistas for the more usual roadside congestion. Numerous highway overlooks give travelers a chance to see the blue haze characteristic of these ancient Appalachian mountains. At many overlooks, signs beckon to motorists to leave their cars and follow well-marked footpaths. Toward its southern end, the parkway curves around 6684-foot Mount Mitchell, the highest point in the eastern United States, then leads through the Cherokee Indian Reservation to the Great Smoky Mountains National Park.

Pink azalea and white dogwood add spring color to a Blue Ridge Parkway vista north toward Buchanan, Virginia (lost to view in the cloud-filled valley). Beyond the valley, the prominent peak is 2995-foot Purgatory Mountain; to the right are The Knob and Short Hills. Floral displays along the parkway vary widely because great ranges in altitude (649 to 6053 feet) create, in effect, different seasons.

OUR
FIRST NATIONAL
SEASHORE

DON WHARTON

On the thin, windswept string of barrier islands that form the Outer Banks of North Carolina is a stretch of seventy miles of unspoiled beach. Here you will encounter only shorebirds, scurrying crabs and an occasional surf caster.

As you walk against the salty wind you need not worry about any slick promoter's ruining this shoreline with hotels, cabanas, cabins and concessions. It is preserved and protected for you and your grandchildren and their grandchildren. For it is Cape Hatteras National Seashore, a unit in our national park system.

From the air the narrow islands occupied by the national seashore resemble a wishbone floating in water. The point of union is at Cape Hatteras, from which one clavicle stretches out forty miles to the north and the other thirty miles to the southwest. At the cape the bone is nearly three miles wide; elsewhere it's generally less than a mile and at some points only a few hundred yards from the ocean to the sound. The whole is one of the nation's major geographic curiosities. Some scholars believe the Outer Banks were once much farther out and that over the ages the ocean has driven them ever closer to the mainland. Others say they were part of the mainland. The rest of us simply marvel that the narrow ribbon of sand is there at all, beaten as it is by water on both sides and blown ceaselessly by winds and gales.

The Gulf Stream is only fifteen miles off the cape. It comes driving up from the south, and here runs head-on into cold currents from the north. The result is treacherous Diamond Shoals, formed offshore for fourteen miles. You can stand at the cape and witness one of the world's most dramatic demonstrations of the majesty of the sea. As the two major currents collide you see spectacular spray dashing twenty, thirty and more feet into the air, not from water striking rocks but from water striking water.

One of the joys of the national seashore is not only to bathe in the surf, swim in the sound—but also to wade in history.

The first English colonizing attempt in America was on sandy Roanoke Island, which lies in the sound just back of the Outer Banks. It was on the Outer Banks in 1903 that the Wrights made the first successful flights in a powered machine

heavier than air. In both world wars German submarines haunted the area—one man tells of climbing the lighthouse at the cape during World War II and seeing four tankers burning simultaneously. This lighthouse is the tallest in the United States, a climb of 268 steps.

But many visitors come to get away from the works of man. On this wilderness shoreline human effort seems puny compared with the power of wind and sea. The inlet through which the English ships brought our first colonists was closed by drifting sands at least 150 years ago. A few miles south, visitors see a long-abandoned highway bridge over dry land—the waters cut an inlet here around 1730, and closed it up 200 years later. The Wrights flew at the base of Kill Devil Hill, a sand dune ninety feet high. But the wind has piled up other dunes here nearly twice that height—and kept them moving, covering live forests in their paths and uncovering dead ones left behind.

The national seashore draws thousands upon thousands of visitors the year round. More than half come during the summer, but the other seasons have their attractions, too. More and more people are beginning to recognize the particular charms of an autumn seashore—the sea, the skies, the vegetation, even the sand, take on strange and marvelous colors in autumn. Fishing is at its best this time of year.

In early winter people come to watch the arrival of the greater snow geese—about 10,000 of the 35,000 known population of the fowl feed for weeks on the roots of salt-marsh grasses. Then in late winter many visitors like to watch commercial fishermen hauling nets in the surf. In spring come bird watchers.

There are now ten national seashores, but that is not enough. We should plan for still more until our great system of national parks, with their scenic wonders, is matched by an equally great system of national seashores, with their opportunities for public recreation in the inspiring surroundings at the edge of the sea.

Century-old Cape Hatteras Lighthouse warns ships to steer clear of the "Graveyard of the Atlantic," grim nickname for the perilous waters off North Carolina's Outer Banks. Sea oats and beach grass help to slow down erosion of the dunes.

North Carolina

THE GREAT SMOKIES

GEORGE LAYCOCK

A grim-faced farmer nailed the plank to an oak tree beside the road and stepped back to appraise his warning. The message, printed on the board, was plain enough. "Let the Cove people alon. Get out. Get gone. 40 mile limit."

Today, if you drive down that same narrow mountain road, as hundreds of thousands of people do every year, you will neither see the sign nor detect the attitude that prompted it. The farm on which the warning was posted, and all the rest of Cades Cove, is a scenic, peaceful section of the Great Smoky Mountains National Park, the most heavily visited of the nation's thirty-eight national parks.

Since 1956 roads have been repaired in this national park, visitor centers built, and new camping grounds, picnic areas and trails completed. There have been even more of those little signs warning visitors not to feed the bears. Back in 1941, only four years after the park was dedicated, it was the first national park to log a million visitors in a year's time.

Why do millions of people converge on these great timbered mountains in the middle South? They come because of the mountain scenery, the bears, the fishing, camping, hiking and the big open spaces. There is room to spread out in the Smokies. The park itself contains 515,200 acres of timberlands straddling the wilderness ridge that separates North Carolina and Tennessee.

Settlers from the British Isles moved into these mountains in the early 1800s and built their simple cabins back in the coves. For decades they were free of outside influence and almost self-sufficient with their farming, hunting, fishing and berry and nut gathering. They became fine craftsmen, adept at making their own cane-bottom

The dark hues of evergreens set off the brilliant dress of hardwoods in the Great Smoky Mountains National Park. Autumn's pageantry reaches its peak during late October in the Great Smokies of North Carolina and Tennessee.

80

chairs, spinning wheels, roof shingles, musical instruments and handwoven fabrics.

Meanwhile, the outside world had bypassed them and pushed onward to the West Coast. The Smoky Mountains people were cut off from progress, and if they realized this at all, it did not worry them. Let the world leave them alone; they would do as much for the world.

But, out beyond their mountains, men were gradually forming opinions certain to disrupt the mountain family's quiet existence. By the 1920s there were people beginning to view the Great Smokies as more than a huge natural barrier between Tennessee and North Carolina. Knoxville citizens traveling through national parks in western states began to realize that they had a good thing right in their own backyard; they began talking about the fine national park they could have just to the south of them. The first successful organization to work for the park was an association of Knoxville businessmen, set up in 1923.

Since the birth of Yellowstone in 1872, Congress had established a total of eighteen national parks. But there was a big difference between these regions and the Smokies. In such parks as Yellowstone, Mount Rainier and Glacier, the government already owned the land. Congress had only to take it from the public land reserve and declare it a national park.

In 1923, however, the proposed Smokies park lay in 6600 privately owned tracts ranging from the holdings of large timber companies to summer home sites. The thought of acquiring title to all these lands and forming the sweeping mountain slopes into a single unit under public ownership would have frightened off weaker men.

When boundaries were eventually established, President Calvin Coolidge signed the bill creating the park. This was May 1926 and there was still a big hurdle ahead of the civic workers struggling to get the park established. The federal government was willing to take over when the states could deed 150,000 acres to the secretary of the interior as a start. The projected cost was $10 million.

Fund-raising campaigns were organized on both sides of the mountains. Workers collected gifts and pledges from private citizens and even pennies from schoolchildren. These campaigns brought in $1 million. Then Tennessee and North Carolina bonded themselves for $2 million each, but this totaled only half the funds needed. On March 6, 1928, however, came the announcement that the Rockefeller family would match locally raised funds. Once again, there was jubilation through the mountains and dancing in the streets of Knoxville.

The federal government, in February 1937, made the final appropriation to buy land and complete the purchases for the Great Smoky Mountains National Park. The first superintendent, J. Ross Eakin, had already been on duty there since 1931. The park was finally dedicated at Newfound Gap on September 2, 1940, by President Franklin D. Roosevelt, who stood with one foot in North Carolina and the other in Tennessee.

Since then millions of Americans have learned what those pioneer planners saw in the Great Smokies.

The Smokies are among the world's oldest mountains. Their history reaches back 500 million years and begins with the forming of sedimentary rocks from masses of sand, mud and gravel, perhaps in the bed of an ancient sea. Other rocks formed on top of these rocks, and the stage was set for a long series of geological upheavals known as the Appalachian revolution. This, we are told, was 200 million years ago, and it built the Smokies.

Then, endless erosion, which is still under way, transformed the landscape into valleys and ridges and great peaks. And through the millenia, the carpet of green matured across these slopes, over the 6000-foot peaks and down the far sides. Today, more than 95 percent of the park is covered with timber. And 40 percent of it is still virgin woodland, protected for all time now from the axe and saw.

Trees have made the Smokies famous. More than a hundred species of trees grow on these mountains, a greater variety than is found in all of Europe. In the lowlands are hemlock, ash, sugar maple, beech and red oak. And along the high ridge running down the center of the park is a Canadian zone. Here, in a spruce-fir forest, are plants and animals like those a thousand miles to the northeast in New Brunswick. Here also is fall color unmatched anywhere.

Scattered through these ancient forests are many trees of record proportions—a cucumber tree measuring eighteen feet around, a sugar maple thirteen feet around, a yellow birch taped at fourteen feet around and a yellow poplar more than twenty-four feet around. Within the park, say the botanists, are 1300 kinds of flowering plants, 350 mosses and 230 kinds of lichens.

Far up on the slopes and ridges are occasional bald spots, the closest the Smokies come to a timberline. No one is quite certain why trees don't

grow on the "balds." In June the azaleas, rhododendrons, dogwood and redbud splash the balds with yellows, reds and oranges. Then visitors in hiking clothes walk the park's 600 miles of foot trails to the high places where automobiles do not take them.

This dense blanket of vegetation across the mountains gives off the moisture that hangs over the slopes in a bluish haze. The Cherokees noticed it and named their mountains for it, and the white man agreed—the Great Smokies come honestly by their name.

There are wild turkeys throughout the mountains. One of the better places to encounter them is around Cades Cove. Ruffed grouse are there, especially where the old farms have not yet grown

Junglebrook, a restored pioneer homestead near Gatlinburg, preserves the history of the hardy English and Scotch–Irish who settled the Smokies. Life here, pioneers said, was "great for men and dogs, but hard on women and steers."

back to mature timber stands. High up on the ridgetops you may encounter Carolina juncos in their summertime nesting grounds. They migrate in winter, but instead of going south they simply go down the mountainside. And, after a six-month sojourn in the milder climate there, travel back up the slopes for the summer again. Beats going all the way to Florida.

There are deer in the Smokies and an occasional bobcat, but the animal that attracts by far the most attention is the black bear. During summer

83

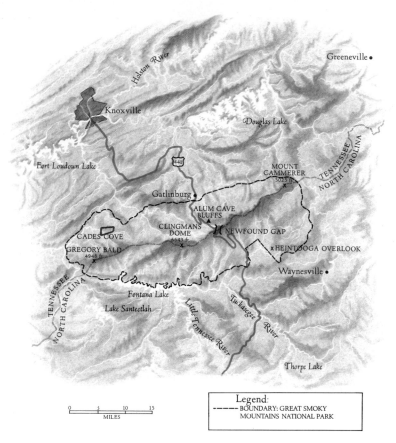

months visitors can hardly drive over the trans-mountain highway (U.S. 441) without seeing one or more bears—the animals are credited with many a traffic jam.

The mutual attraction between people and bears creates endless problems for the park rangers. There are signs all over the park warning against feeding the bears. The bears sometimes tear the signs down, but for the most part they ignore them. So, for that matter, do a lot of the people. And often they are either arrested by rangers for illegally feeding the bears or are carted off to the hospital for stitches and sedatives.

Most of the injuries occur when a visitor teases a bear or promises him food and then withdraws it. One camera-carrying tourist in the park was severely injured by a bear he was trying to push into his automobile. He was trying to get the bear behind the steering wheel so he could take a picture of it as it sat beside his wife.

Fishing is good in the Great Smokies. There are 600 miles of trout streams inside the park. Only artificial baits are permitted. The season runs from May 16 to August 31, but if you are willing to turn back all fish under sixteen inches, you may fish the year round in the West Prong of the Little Pigeon River in Tennessee and in Bradley Fork and its tributaries in North Carolina. The Park Service calls these "Fishing for Fun" streams. Residents need a fishing license from the state in which they are fishing, though visitors may fish anywhere in the park with a nonresident license from either state.

Within the national park are seven major campgrounds and a number of secondary campsites. Others are located near the park. Most of the campsites have accommodations for trailers as well as for tents, but there are no electric or sewer connections for trailers. Elkmont, with 340 campsites, is the largest. Since the sites are not reserved and demand is heavy, experienced travelers claim their space early. Park headquarters, in Gatlinburg, Tennessee, supplies lists of campgrounds as well as lists of trail camps along the footpaths.

There are seventy-one miles of the famed Appalachian Trail within the park, extending down the ridgeline of the Smokies. Hiking time for this section is six to eight days. Along this trail are thirteen primitive shelters where the venturesome and the rugged may pause for a night on their hiking vacation.

It is those who take to the foot trails who see the Smokies best. There are things they could see no other way—the azaleas on Gregory Bald, the cliffs of Alum Cave Bluffs and the sweeping view from Mount Cammerer.

Highest point in the park for the motorist to reach easily is Clingmans Dome (elevation 6643 feet). Today, from Newfound Gap, you can drive

84

an easy six miles of well-engineered blacktopped road to the peak. And, once there, you can climb the observation tower, the top of which is the highest point in the park.

Park naturalists keep busy helping visitors see the wonders of the Great Smokies and understand what they do see. They will offer you a free list of the half dozen self-guiding nature trails scattered throughout the region. And on these little trails, ranging in length from a quarter of a mile to a mile, the do-it-yourself naturalist can wander idly through the woodlands, reading about the creatures and plants he encounters. Meanwhile, the crew of naturalists are presenting slide shows and lectures at the various nature centers and campgrounds. But their service is not by any means limited to such sedentary guidance. They plan and lead a whole series of half-day and full-day trail hikes.

When you go to the Smokies, take along comfortable clothing, including rain gear, hiking shoes and a warm sweater or jacket for the cool evenings. In spring and summer it is good to carry an insect repellent, especially if you are camping.

Sometime during your Smoky Mountains visit you will want to drive down to Cades Cove. Park officials let the farmers stay in these broad meadows between the mountains and raise grass and livestock, by special Park Service permit. A few families descended from original settlers still live there and farm some 2000 acres. You will see their cattle grazing in the Cades Cove meadows. And here you will get one of the best remaining impressions of what life in this isolated region was like before outsiders turned the Smokies into a wilderness playground.

The old gristmill with its overshot waterwheel steadily grinds white cornmeal for sale to visitors. Nearby, the old Cable home still stands where Becky Cable operated her general store for the Cove people. If Becky thought, back in 1900, that fifteen customers made a big day, she should be there now, when visitors are numbered in the hundreds of thousands.

Despite all its use, this most popular of our national parks is still largely wilderness country. There is still space here for citizens who want to sample the fresh air of the high altitudes and see the haze-shrouded mountains and the virgin timberlands. With all its attractions, as well as its being open the year round and having a location not far from the eastern population centers, it is no wonder that the Great Smoky Mountains is our most visited national park.

SOUTH CAROLINA'S SEA ISLANDS

EUGENE B. SLOAN

If you're looking for a place to go camping during the winter months, try the Sea Islands along the coast of South Carolina. In these lush subtropical islands it is possible to pitch a camp— or gaze from a motel window—at settings which nature has preserved in primitiveness, and yet there are enough of the usual amenities of life and facilities nearby to make the area suitable for an individual or a family group to vacation happily.

Not all of the islands are accessible by automobile, and many off the coast near Beaufort, uninhabited but breathtaking in their unspoiled state, must be reached by boat.

Among top spots accessible by bridges, Hunting Island, seventeen miles southeast of Beaufort, and Hilton Head Island, a few miles farther south, close to Savannah, Georgia, are representative of a vast, wide area of islands, channels and beaches.

Camping along the beaches is possible at Hunting Island and Edisto Island State, Parks. Facts about these beach parks can be obtained from the South Carolina Department of Parks, Recreation and Tourism, Box 71, Room 1, Columbia, South Carolina 29202. The camper who selects a state park campground pays a nominal fee for the use of a campsite and available facilities, such as bathhouses, tables, water and electricity. Edisto Island, which is 50 miles southeast of Charleston, also has a nature trail. Campers in all areas should remember to be mindful of the usual hazards of insects, sunburn and sand.

At Hunting Island the fisherman can literally throw his line into the Atlantic from his tent, and yards away he can wade into the surf with a saltwater rod and reel and bring in almost anything, using nothing more than shrimp or fish for bait. The different species that can be caught in an afternoon might include spot-tailed bass, whiting, flounder, sheepshead, ocean cat, trout, stingray or sand shark. Occasionally, a surf caster may have the time of his life battling for forty-five minutes with a giant tarpon, though this is a rarity.

Subtropical breezes stir the sea oats growing on the shores of Hilton Head Island. When William Hilton, a seventeenth-century English explorer, came upon the island he called it "the goodliest, best and frutefullest ile ever was seen."

A lighter sport, one almost tailored for children but sure to produce a meal fit for a king, is crabbing. This game takes mostly time, a stout cord, a light hand net and a small hunk of fish head for bait, which can be used over and over again. Once the cord, with bait tied on the end, is dropped near the water's edge, the first victim comes along. If close to shore, the crabber can see the red and blue claws of the quarry settle down for a meal, and at this point the net is gently eased into the water or to a position where the bait and crab may be pulled up. Crabbing is very profitable in tidal creeks, for here the waters are calmer and it takes only a couple of hours to procure a peck or more. When the crabs are boiled, by dropping in piping hot water, you get some of the finest meat in the world for cocktail tidbits, soup or crab cakes.

There is also an infinite variety of natural attractions, in addition to fishing, with widespread appeal. Nature study is one. Almost every vista and scene is ever changing, a panorama of pure magic, where young and old, amateur and naturalist, can feast in sheer delight. Want to see an alligator? Raccoon? Deer? Pelican? Snowy egret? Palmetto tree? You will see these, and more, in their natural habitat or setting. Thousands of virgin acres in this wilderness offer them protection, and on recently inhabited islands certain areas have been set aside to insure this protection permanently.

Walking up a springtime beach after the tide— or sometimes at night—you may see the almost extinct sea turtle. By flashlight or moonlight the dark outline of the hulking reptile may lumber across the sand in search of a spot to scoop out for her nest. Many weeks later—warmed by the sand— the eggs will hatch into small turtles, which will make their own way into the sea, alone and forgotten by their mother.

The beaches never appear the same from one day to the next. A stroll always provides new interest, especially for children, who like to pick up sand dollars, sea horses, sea biscuits and conchs. And then there is the often beautiful driftwood piled on the shore.

Besides sports and nature study, the Sea Islands offer to the visiting camper an opportunity to see relics of history dating back almost to the discovery of the New World, uncommercialized and, in some cases, unpublicized. Often the camper discovers them by accident as he follows a trail through the woods, overgrown by vines or hidden by a clump of myrtle.

On a number of the islands old, perfectly preserved forts or remains of forts, Indian mounds and elaborate houses languish from a long-ago era. Much of the construction within the Sea Islands is of tabby, a now-lost art that was created by the African slaves. An impervious material of concretelike qualities, tabby was made by firing oyster shells in kilns or pyres. The shells are

still clearly visible in the texture of the exposed surfaces.

If the camper brings his boat along he'll find excellent facilities available at such towns as Port Royal, Charleston and Beaufort. The Inland Waterway runs through the group of Sea Islands and at Hilton Head it is possible to stop off at splendid marinas.

Sight-seeing of the entire area is a lot of fun, with many towns, communities and cities to choose from: Bluffton, Beaufort, Pritchardville, Burton, Charleston, Sullivan's Island or Hilton Head. Excellent golf courses are located at Hilton Head.

At no point in the Sea Islands is the camper far from habitation, and procuring food is no trouble. Truck farms provide fresh vegetables in season and there is always a quantity of seafood on the market. The climate is ideal, with sunshine the majority of the time. Winters here are so mild that usually only light wraps are needed.

South Carolina's beautiful Sea Islands will captivate those bent on wintertime camping.

LAND OF THE TREMBLING EARTH

BEN LUCIEN BURMAN

The guide thrust his long pole into the water and sent the boat toward the shore. "I'm going to show you something you've never seen anywhere," he said. He left me sitting in the boat and stepped onto the bank. To my amazement the grass and small trees that formed it began to sway drunkenly as though from an earthquake. The guide walked forward. Some skinny pines a short distance away rocked crazily, and the grassy earth tossed like a stormy sea.

When the guide had made his way back to the boat I stepped gingerly onto the bank myself. The weird spectacle was repeated. I saw the reason in the mucky tangle of vegetation at my feet: I was walking over an immense floating sponge. I looked into the distance. As far as the eye could reach there were similar spongy islands, some floating, some anchored, set in streams and pools crowded with water lilies. They were part of that strange phenomenon known as Okefenokee Swamp.

I had come that morning to this mysterious natural wonder near Waycross, Georgia, not far from the Florida border and only five miles from U.S. Highway No. 1. Though thousands of tourists pass this way every year, the swamp has remained one of the most primitive and untouched parts of the United States. It is a national wildlife refuge, comprising more than 360,000 acres of prairie and cypress jungle. From its dark waters is born the storied Suwannee River, which flows across part of Florida and empties into the Gulf of Mexico.

I climbed back into the boat, and the guide, Will Cox, a towering, brawny figure with a weather-beaten face, put down the pole. In the stern a swamper named Lynt, wearing a brown plastic helmet that gave him the appearance of Stanley exploring Africa, started the outboard motor. We headed into an old alligator trail. Through a strange, dreamy world we wound our way past queer-shaped pitcher plants four feet high that ate insects, and iris of all the colors of the rainbow.

"This swamp's so wild there's plenty of it ain't ever been surveyed," said the third swamper in the boat, a short, jaunty youth named Oral. "Ain't too many years ago a fellow killed a man out here. Everybody knew he done the murder, but they never could try him because nobody knew in what county the killing was done."

We drifted through an endless stretch of brown cattails. A flock of egrets and a heron soared up before us. Will reached over the side of the boat, pulled up a plant and rubbed the thick leaves between his hands. Foamy suds quickly appeared. "Poor man's soap," he said. "Plenty of swamp people use it for washing clothes." A moment later he broke the pad of a pond lily and exposed a worm an inch long. "Poor man's bait," he said. "The fish here like it best. Lord kind of looks after poor people in the swamp, seems like. Got everything they need in it—just have to reach out and take it off the shelf."

In the distance was a tall tree with a vague shadow in the topmost branches. "An eagle nest," said Will. "We call it a swamp lighthouse. You use it as a marker to tell your way around."

"Eagles got the swamp all divided up," remarked Oral. "Each eagle's got him a territory three miles long and three miles wide. When the young eagles grow up, the old man eagle carries 'em off a little ways, puts 'em down and tells 'em to stay three miles away. If they come back, the old eagle whips 'em till they cry."

The swamp changed now. The reeds and lilies gave way to a tangled forest of cypress. We skirted the edge, our heads at times brushed by Spanish moss drooping from the branches. Once there was a grinding noise beneath our hull, and I thought we had scraped bottom. An instant later a huge alligator crawled out from under and scrambled up the muddy bank. We drew up alongside a cypress hammock known as a "house"—a dense thicket tangled with vines and Spanish moss—and went ashore to sit in the shade and smoke. My companions began to talk of life in the swamp before it became a park, when the few isolated inhabitants, like pioneers everywhere, found food for their families with their rifles.

"There was a wonderful shot around here named Luke Johnson," Oral said. "Had cataracts

A male anhinga perches watchfully on a cypress knee. Some call it snakebird, for it swims with only head and slender neck showing. Bald cypresses cloaked in Spanish moss add a primeval splendor to Georgia's timeless Okefenokee Swamp.

on both his eyes, but he could still beat anybody with a gun. I was with him one night when we was looking for a wildcat that was killing his young pigs. It was pitch-black, and I couldn't see nothing. All of a sudden Luke raised his gun and fired and a wildcat fell out of a tree. Luke had killed him just by the sound of him crawling in the branches."

We set off again and coasted along a shore dark with cypresses. A tunnellike entrance showed through the trees. "It's the bear crossing," said Will. "Like the elephant walks they have in Africa. Bears been using this for hundreds of years." Okefenokee is a bear paradise. Some years ago about 1500 were counted in the park, and their number is constantly rising.

As we started back toward park headquarters I saw the strange phenomenon of the mirrors of Okefenokee, the most perfect reflections I have ever seen. Some ingredient of the swamp plants or the soil, or perhaps the brown stain of the cypress roots, transforms the water into an immense and flawless mirror. The trees towering above us now showed below us as well, so that for an instant I had an odd sensation of riding upside down.

Next morning, with Will and Oral, I began exploring the enormous area of swamp that lies outside the park. Over narrow, deep-rutted roads we traveled, sticking often in mud or sand, and digging our way free. This was turpentine country. The pine trees had wide slashes in their trunks, and little metal cups caught the dripping gum that would later be turned into paint or medicine. We arrived at an isolated frame house set under some live-oak trees. It was a picture of early America, still miraculously surviving today. Hollow gourds, housing families of martins, stood on high poles in the yard, put there by this swamp farmer so the birds would give him their pleasant company and warn him of prowling snakes. A water bucket hung on a windlass over a moss-covered well, and nearby were the great round stones used for grinding the sugarcane that made syrup.

"Ain't nothing in the world like living in the swamp," said our host, a silvery-haired old man. "There's swampers around here that are rich, but they go on living the same old way. They ain't going to be happy unless they got their feet in swamp water."

We drove all day through the swampy wilderness and at sunset swung back to the park. Lynt was waiting with a boat at the dock to take us on a night excursion. Will brought aboard several flashlights and an acetylene lantern. He and I sat in the bow, and Lynt and Oral sat in the stern as we glided off. It grew dark quickly. The swamp, mysterious in the daytime, became ghostly. We reached a wooden platform in a remote section, got out and, after a quick search for snakes, sat down on the damp boards.

Everywhere frogs were croaking madly. There were leopard frogs, tree frogs, rain frogs, peepers —all the forty-odd varieties naturalists have found that make up the thundering frog chorus of Okefenokee. A nearby frog began an odd noise like a man pounding with a hammer. "It's a carpenter frog," Will declared. "He's straightening his nails." The sound grew sharper, more staccato. "Now he's hammering the nails in," said Will.

Strange cries drifted through the trees: the bark of a pursuing fox, the scream of a wildcat, the agonized wail of some animal as it met its end in the grim pattern of life and death in the swamp.

We sat talking and listening until midnight and then climbed into the boat again and started home. Oral, who had relieved Lynt at the rudder, was slow in making a turn that Will ordered, through a towering wall of cane. There was a heavy thud at the stern and the boat stopped. "Hit a stump," Oral said. "I think she's broke the propeller." He pulled the shaft out of the water. One blade had been broken off, and the other was badly bent. "Looks like we ain't going to get home for a long time," he said. I began thinking of all the people who had been lost in the swamp, the lucky ones who emerged in a week or two, almost dead from insect bites and exhaustion, the others who never did return but whose skeletons were found years later.

Oral and Lynt started working on the damaged propeller with a wrench and hammer. When at last the bent blade was straightened, Lynt started the motor. The boat moved sluggishly forward. I looked at my watch. It was 4 a.m. Soon the sun was rising like a disk cut from molten iron. Ospreys dived near us, searching the water for a fishy breakfast. Herons scratched the lily pads to find worms. When we reached the stretch of spongy prairie where I had walked two days before, Will stopped the boat to let me step out once more and make the grass and trees sway giddily. Then we moved on toward the park entrance.

The red men who once hunted the swamps and plains of America have given rich, poetic names to many parts of our country. But never have they chosen a better name than the one they gave to this place of wonder and mystery. Okefenokee means Land of the Trembling Earth.

INTO THE
RIVER OF GRASS

ROGER TORY PETERSON
AND
JAMES FISHER

The Everglades really begin at Lake Okeechobee, a hundred miles from the tip of Florida. The
whole south end of the great peninsula that constitutes the Sunshine State is a vast complex of
swamps, saw grass and water. The water, swelled
by rains, flows—or rather, oozes—until it merges
imperceptibly with the tidewater of the Gulf of
Mexico. It is wider than the broadest river on
earth—fifty, sixty, even seventy miles across. The
Indians called it *Pah-hay-okee,* "grassy water."

This sea of saw grass, sodden and waterlogged
in summer, drying in winter, is a fantastic plain of
slough and swamp. Between sixty and sixty-five
inches of rainfall in the course of a year, mostly
in spring and summer, are caught by this sponge
of low vegetation, the Everglades, and flow slowly
southward through it—flow visibly only when the
water runs high after the rains. Over a third of the
Everglades is neither water nor land but something between the two. Here and there are higher
spots, dry all year round, which are dominated by
cabbage palms or even the rare wild royal palm,
growing in the rich black soil of plant decay that
the Calusa Indians used to cultivate and the Semi-
noles still do.

Below the saw grass is the muck, the sticky
basis of the great slow bog-river; below the muck
is a sedimentary oolitic limestone. Like all such
limestones that water comes in contact with, it is
dissolved partly away. Here and there are islands
where the limestone comes to the surface; most of
them run north and south as the dissolving stream
flows gently past them. Upon these hammocks
West Indian trees grow in jungly tangles: Caribbean pine, gumbo-limbo, blolly, paradise tree,
mastic, royal palm, cabbage palm. Underneath
there is often a tangle of saw palmetto, and the
sinister strangler fig grows on, grows over, envelops and finally suffocates its host trees.

To the east, along the coast, the busy towns—
Palm Beach, Fort Lauderdale, Miami, Coral Gables, Homestead—all stand on a limestone ridge

that is comparatively high, as much as twenty-
five feet above sea level. But the average height
of the Everglades above sea level is not much
more than eight feet. Within the last century
there has been considerable lowering because
of rash experiments in clearing and burning,
which have resulted in the oxidation and denuda-
tion of the muck, the sticky black Everglades soil.
To man, the Everglades have been a continuous
challenge. He has involved himself in drainage
schemes far more costly than he ever dreamed,
many of which have been disastrous failures.
Land won from the sloughs and swamps, and
densely peopled with fruit growers and catch-crop
market gardeners, has been drowned more than
once, with heavy loss of life, when violent hurricanes pushed the rising water over it.

To drive roads through the Everglades, men
have had to blast right through the muck down to
the limestone bedrock and build on that, which is
why the great road out of Miami across the Everglades, the Tamiami Trail, was fifty years building, and why there is a block about twice the size
of Rhode Island in which there are no main roads
at all. Nothing but Okloacoochee Slough, Big
Cypress Swamp, the largest of the Seminole Indian
reservations, the ruins of Sam Jones town and

seventy miles of rather abortive canal from Miami to Lake Okeechobee.

Everglades National Park embraces nearly 1.5 million acres—more than half of that part of Florida lying south of the Tamiami Trail. The mangroves occupy the entire southwest half of the park, growing wherever the water is salt—all over the islets or keys in Florida Bay, around the entire coast and around the multitudinous creek and river mouths. Mangrove forest pokes up all the rivers until with the last of the tidal salt water the growth is only of hedge thickness.

One of the most gratifying results of the creation of national parks and nature reserves in the United States is the tameness of the indigenous wild animals, a phenomenon that dates back into the last century and the early years of Yellowstone. It is true that, in many other parts of the world, protected wildlife has become ridiculously tame. But only in North America, so far, has it been possible to combine the national park (where man is encouraged) with the nature reserve (from which, at least in the old days, man was supposed to be kept away). Here, on Anhinga Trail, under our feet clattering over the boardwalk, floated sleepy alligators. Quietly on its huge yellow feet a purple gallinule bobbed and jerked about the water-lily leaves, and stepped, like a proud chicken, a few feet below us.

On a bush overhanging the slough sat a water turkey, the trail's own anhinga, turning its head from side to side to watch the visitors. There were a few egrets—both snowy and American egrets. And like a ghost among the sedges at the slough edge stood a really rare bird, the great white heron of America. The history of the Florida herons, of the desperate straits to which they were reduced by plume hunters at the turn of the century, has often been related. The great white heron suffered along with the others. But it does not seem ever to have been brought near extinction by humans; indeed, nature has probably been harder on it than man. Its breeding has always been confined to the mangrove zone of Florida— to Florida Bay and the chain of Florida keys, in which the special Great White Heron National Wildlife Refuge was established in 1938. At that time the species had been decimated by the hurricane of 1935, which also took such a toll of human

Egrets, herons and white ibis winging across a winter sky suggest the astonishing diversity of birdlife in the Everglades. The park's vast sea of saw grass is dotted with hammocks (slightly elevated islands supporting shrubs and trees).

life in the keys. Just after this catastrophe, an aerial surveyor from the National Audubon Society could find only 146 birds in nine tenths of their range. But so remarkable are their powers of recovery that seven years later between 1500 and 1800 birds were discovered.

We must have stayed a couple of hours with our tame great white heron of Anhinga Trail. All was quiet, except for a continual stream of human visitors chattering away on the boardwalk; the anhinga never left its post. The alligators floated, and a huge one, which we had not seen before, swam up very, very slowly; we heard another growl in the distance. Under the sunning, lazy body of the smallish alligator, many slender garfish nosed about with rippling fins.

After consuming about half a gallon of root beer and cola—with a salt pill to balance up—we pushed on southwest, farther into the wilderness. After some sixteen miles of good, unsurfaced road, with a verge on one side alive with dragonflies, through a landscape of saw grass and low cypress islands, we found ourselves among the mangroves. In the narrow belt where the mangroves began we saw a few extremely slender palms of a new, rather rare species, *paurotis*, towering over the other vegetation.

We ate our sandwiches and drove on toward Cape Sable, a broad peninsula joined to the mainland by a narrow isthmus. On the north side of this isthmus, at its narrowest point, stands the Coot Bay ranger's station, fitted out with a gasoline depot and a fleet of motor and outboard craft. It was in the finest of these boats that our friend and guide, Joseph Moore, the park biologist, took us deep into the glades where mangroves grow to fifty feet on some of the wooded keys. Moore navigated unerringly across the bight of Coot Bay and through narrow, dark passages arched over with mangroves. Herons flew overhead, and a pack of white ibis scattered on our approach.

These Everglades rivers in their salt mangrove sections are the last real refuge in the United States of the manatee, one of the few surviving representatives of the Sirenia, spatula-tailed, cleft-faced, vegetable-eating aquatic mammals. The usual evidence of a manatee, or sea cow, is a disturbance or "boil" of water. We didn't see even this, but we got to the East River rookery, where

An American egret flies over Fisheating Creek, west of Lake Okeechobee, against a backdrop of bald cypresses festooned with Spanish moss. Once nearly hunted to extinction for its feathers, the bird is now a common sight in the Everglades.

countless wood ibis, white ibis, snowy egrets, little blue herons, American egrets and Louisiana herons nested. The main island looked like an overloaded Christmas tree, as if someone had tried to make snow out of candle wax. All over the mangroves was a frosting of white birds, parents standing on guard or bending over flat, dirty nests. On top of the trees were gatherings of unemployed-looking wood ibis. As we got nearer, they took off with a great balancing and tilting of wings, bowing and bill-clattering all the time.

We had to start back quickly—while there was still daylight enough to light our way. Threading through the tall mangroves of East River, we were soon on the open choppy water of Whitewater Bay, and then entered the tea-colored channel that would lead back to our mooring at Coot Bay. This channel had been dredged recently by the Park Service, but Moore showed us the site of an ancient canal dug by the Tekesta Indians in pre-Columbian times, perhaps about the year 1200. Centuries of silt had filled it in, but its straight course could still be traced through the vegetation. He also pointed out, growing on the higher ground beside it, a modest tree whose name—

Colorful roseate spoonbills (and one snowy egret) perch among red mangrove roots at the edge of a brackish pond in the southern Everglades. When feeding, spoonbills wade through shallows, wagging their bills from side to side.

manchineel—is enough to send a shiver through those who have had any experience with it. Rain dripping from its leaves raises huge blisters; eating its fruit brings agonizing death.

No mangrove forest in the world can compare with the one we had been passing through. Usually low-growing elsewhere, the trees attain a height of fifty feet around Whitewater Bay and over eighty feet near the mouth of Shark River, a few miles to the northwest. These glossy-leaved trees, with their elevated root systems and pneumatophores, catch the silt, hold it, consolidate it and slowly, steadily, build the land.

On the long road back (it was twenty-seven miles to park headquarters) we caught sight of four or five raccoons hunting for crayfish along the ditches. Caught in the glare of our headlights they shambled into the shadows like high-rumped miniature bears. We stopped briefly at Anhinga Trail; an alligator bellowed in the distance, but all was silent again when we walked out on the wooden pier. We swept the pool with our flashlight and could spot the alligators motionless on the still water. Lining up the beam, we caught their bright red, rather sinister eyeshine. A silent show of fireflies, flashing intermittently in the blackness, accompanied us back to the car while a chuck-will's-widow chanted softly in the distance. It was late when we got back to neon-lighted Miami.

SCENIC PARADISE IN ALABAMA

JOHN GOODRUM

The Alabama mountain country is not really on the superhighway to anywhere. Interstate 65 slices through the area from north to south, and Interstate 59 chops off the southwestern corner. Travelers in a hurry avoid the region, preferring the faster highways connecting the South's major metropolises. And this may well be the area's greatest blessing.

This is a region of great natural beauty, with a quiet and compelling charm that annually attracts millions to its pristine retreats and its crystal-clear blue waters. Yet thus far it is largely free of commercialized tourist attractions. The region's appeal lies in its natural beauty and the wide variety of quiet and relaxing activities it offers. The nature lover, the history hound, the water-sports enthusiast, the hunter and the fisherman are equally at home here.

The Tennessee River enters and leaves Alabama at its northern corners. It winds gently in a wide-mouthed "U" over 200 miles as it crosses the state. Tennessee Valley Authority dams on the river's main stream create a chain of four huge lakes, whose fingers probe the valleys of the Appalachian foothills.

The climate is as gentle as the geography, mild and temperate almost year round. Only for a few weeks in midwinter is the weather poor; and spring, summer and fall bring warm, sunny days and cool nights.

The best way to enjoy this scenic paradise and its many attractions is to establish a headquarters at one of the numerous lakeside campsites or, if you want all the comforts of home, at one of the modern motels along the route. Within a few days, leisurely visits can be made to most of the outstanding places of interest, with ample time left over for full enjoyment of the lakes themselves. This region does not lend itself to hurried travel.

U.S. Highways 72 and 43 converge at the western end of the region, where a cluster of scenic and historic attractions await. Here you may get your first look at the TVA system at Wilson Dam, one of the giant concrete monoliths creating the mountain lakes. This is the world's largest single-lift navigation lock, where commercial tows are raised a whopping hundred feet in a single lock filling.

Only a few miles south of the Tennessee River down U.S. 43 are two of the region's most beautiful natural sights.

In Rock Bridge Canyon giant rock towers reach 285 feet above a shimmering spring-fed pool on the canyon floor. A natural bridge provides passage across the deep canyon, where many species of fern, wild magnolia and mountain laurel combine to present a year-round spectacular.

A few minutes drive to the east is one of the most beautiful and astonishingly different scenic attractions to be found anywhere. But be prepared for a shock. Stepping into the Dismals Wonder Gardens is like taking a giant step backward in time. Scarcely inside the entrance, you are swallowed up in an undisturbed forest where giant hemlocks, sweet gum and tulip trees crowd together to close out the modern world. Mysterious fissures wind through towering rocks and exotic rock formations loom ahead unexpectedly. Phantom waterfalls and rippling brooks provide a natural accompaniment to the unreal scenery. As darkness swiftly descends, you are suddenly conscious of the glow of millions of tiny lights from a natural wonder, the Dismalites, tiny phosphorescent worms that twinkle in the dark.

Traveling east on U.S. 278 brings you into Bankhead National Forest. Getting the most from this visit requires parking the car and hiking along the well-prepared forest trails, past rocky bluffs, through limestone canyons and hardwood forests.

At both Brushy Lake and Corinth in the forest there are excellent facilities for picnicking, camping, swimming and boating. Both are on clear blue lakes, and both provide good facilities for trailer parking and family cottages at modest rates. They are quiet, restful places to spend the night, where the only sound to disturb your rest is the rush of the cool night breeze through the treetops or an occasional splash as a big fish leaps clear of the glass-smooth lake water.

A leisurely hour's drive south of Huntsville is Guntersville. Guntersville State Park is just a few miles northeast of Guntersville. Almost surrounded by fingers from Guntersville Lake, it provides quiet and scenic relaxation. There are two developed camping areas and one undeveloped area.

This northeastern corner of the state is one of the most beautiful regions to be found anywhere, with rugged, thickly wooded mountains and clear blue streams coursing through the valleys. Largely untouched by commercial interests, it is a place where you soon lose touch with the outside world.

Many developed caverns and numerous unexplored caves are in this rugged corner of the state. DeSoto Caverns, named for Spanish explorer Hernando DeSoto who visited the caves in 1540, are famous for their onyx and crystal formations, and also feature a display of recently unearthed Indian burial relics. They were the first officially recorded caves in the United States. Indian Agent Benjamin Hawkins reported the existence of DeSoto Caverns to President Washington in 1796.

Sequoyah Caverns, located near Alabama's border with Georgia and Tennessee, are noted for their crystal-clear underground lakes. Like California's giant sequoia trees, Sequoyah Caverns are named for Sequoyah, the Cherokee Indian who developed an alphabet for the Cherokee language.

Russell Cave National Monument in the extreme northeast corner of the state is one of the most important archaeological finds of recent years. Archaeologists have unearthed many layers of magnificently preserved artifacts, dating back from 6200 B.C. to 1650 A.D. Since the cave is now open as a national monument, there is no admission charge.

Even in summertime, cave temperatures are low (about 60° F.). A sweater or a jacket is a must. And a flashlight is a great help for fuller enjoyment of the caverns.

The avid fisherman (and what fisherman is less?) finds plenty of action here. There are 180,000 acres of fish-laden waters. Here the smallmouth bass is found, including a one-time world's-record-breaking ten-pound, eight-ounce papa. Largemouth, white, striped and spotted bass, crappie and other native gamefish are abundant.

Guntersville Lake is a fisherman's paradise. In early spring seasoned fishermen concentrate on white bass in the tributary streams. April, May and June are the best months for white crappie and black bass. Bluegill fishing becomes popular about mid-June, after the first hatch of mayflies, and continues until August. Then white-bass fishing picks up again when these fish gather in the open lake to feed on thick schools of small shad. In the fall and winter there is good sauger fishing at the head of the lake, along road and railroad fills and in the tail water below the dam. Crappie and bass are also taken in the fall in deep water.

These lakes, with their broad, open expanses of clear water, are ideal for sailing, boating and water skiing. The gentle shorelines make all water sports, including swimming, easier, and camping in the thick forests that line the lakeshores is virtually a year-round activity.

ISLAND OF ADVENTURE

ROSS E. HUTCHINS

Enclosed within and among the branching mouths of Mississippi's Pascagoula River, just before it flows into the Gulf of Mexico, are numerous bits of higher land that are, in truth, islands. One of these, perhaps a hundred acres in extent, I claim as mine. I do not know who actually owns it, and I care not whose name is on record in official land titles. Perhaps this piece of high ground belongs to no one. As far as I am concerned it belongs to me and to the creatures that dwell there and, for lack of a better name, I call it The Island.

The Pascagoula, known to the Indians as the Singing River, divides into numerous passages as it meanders southward through the marshy savanna; there are more than a thousand miles of channels and bayous, all interconnected in a confusing network. My island is remote, lonely and isolated, and in this lies its fascination. Every man, in fact or fancy, has an island, a refuge. This island is mine.

My first trip to The Island began on a warm day in late autumn when the bald cypresses along the bayous were tinged with rust-colored foliage. Unlike most other conifers, these cypresses are deciduous and would, I knew, eventually shed their foliage, leaving gaunt limbs etched against the winter sky. My conveyance was a houseboat or, more properly, a river yacht, named *Likilikit*. My companions and I had gone aboard the boat at an isolated fishing camp hidden deep in the vast Pascagoula Swamp. We had taken on stores of

Autumn foliage surrounds the dual arches of Natural Bridge, spanning a 148-foot-wide ravine near Haleyville, Alabama. Soft shale under the arches was long ago eroded by a stream, leaving harder layers of sandstone high and dry.

gasoline and food sufficient to last a week, since, once we left the dock, there would be no further contact with civilization until our return.

The *Likilikit* was thirty-five feet long and of shallow draft, ideally suited to bayou and river cruising. Like a seagoing vessel, it was self-contained, having all the conveniences and luxuries needed for a pleasant life beyond the borders of civilization. My companions were fishermen and, like all devotees of that sport, had only one thing in mind—the catching of fish. As is usual on most such expeditions of which I am a part, I was the offbeat character, tolerated but not exactly understood, because my interests are unusual. While others are fishing or engaging in "normal" pursuits, I am turning over logs to see what is hidden underneath, or collecting and photographing plant and animal specimens. But I have become accustomed to being considered a little peculiar and am happy that some people do try to understand my interests and even attempt to help me.

My usual gear for such an expedition consists of about a hundred pounds of photographic equipment, plus jars of preservative and collecting nets. On this trip I was advised to purchase a fishing license, since it was unlikely that a local game warden could ever be convinced that I had merely come along for the ride. This would be just too unbelievable, since no one ever goes into the Pascagoula Swamp except to fish. So, in order to forestall possible embarrassment, I acquired a license allowing me to catch fish even though I had not the slightest intention of wetting a hook.

I climbed to the top deck of the houseboat. There, fifteen feet above the water, I watched in fascination while we followed the tortuous channel that meandered across the marsh-grass plain. Here and there, colorful blooms added gay touches to the otherwise pastel landscape stretching to the horizon. The channel of the bayou was often barely wide enough to permit the boat to pass, and from my vantage point I could see, far away, other channels that wound through the grassy plain, their courses marked in places by rows of cypresses both living and dead. Lonely crows often sat quietly upon dead snags while birds of many other kinds fluttered over the waving grass. Once, as we rounded a bend, a small alligator lay half-asleep in the water, but, as we approached, it slowly sank from sight and was seen no more.

The cypresses along the bayou were all draped with long streamers of gray Spanish moss swaying gently in the breeze. It was like a scene out of some childhood fantasy, strange, exotic, unreal,

languid. I felt as if I were living in some fanciful dreamworld as the changing scene slowly unfolded, bend after bend. Now and again the channel widened and mudbanks appeared where snowy egrets waded sedately in the shallows, their white forms reflected in the still waters. Sometimes muskrats sat half-hidden among the stems of the tall marsh grasses beyond the water's edge. Elevated as I was, above the waving grass, I had a bird's-eye view of my surroundings.

It was all intriguing and mysterious and I longed to explore this grassy world at closer range. The tide was out, with the result that the water was draining from the marsh, leaving the soft black muck exposed. Out of this muck grew the dense stand of marsh grasses and other vegetation, the bases of their stems discolored and crowded close together. Between these stems ran dark passages that appeared to be inhabited by some sort of animals, but we passed along too rapidly for me to determine what they were; this was a matter that would have to wait.

As the houseboat cruised down the twisting bayou I continued my vigil from the upper deck, sweeping the marshy world beyond the channel with a powerful telescope to obtain a closer look at the passing scene. At last the bayou widened and then emptied into a broad expanse of water that was the main channel of the sluggish Pascagoula River. The waters were coffee brown and flowed gently along between high banks.

The houseboat swung out into the current of the river and headed north, following closely along the western bank. Water birds, alarmed by our passing, took wing and flew up the river; otherwise there were no further evidences of life except turtles sunning themselves on infrequent sandbars and half-submerged logs. Sometimes the banks were heavily forested; at other times we passed growths of tall marsh grass which waved rhythmically in the undulations created by the boat. Once, as we rounded a bend, a number of large yellow butterflies were seen crossing the river toward the east. They fluttered along, low over the water, and then away through the forest as if following a compass course. Now and again large dragonflies alighted upon the houseboat, their cellophanelike wings momentarily at rest.

Eventually, after several miles, we rounded an abrupt bend and came to a straight section of river where a meandering bayou opened into it, creating an island that was higher than the surrounding land. The island was dominated by tall, spreading live oaks, some of which leaned far out over the river. Beneath the trees, along the sandy shore, rose a dense growth of palmettos, their fanlike fronds imparting a tropical atmosphere. Unknown to me, this was to become my island, a parcel of high ground surrounded by brown waters. In time I would come to know its intimate details like the palm of my hand. I had found my Shangri-la, though it would require time to realize it.

After snubbing the boat securely to a stout, overhanging cypress, my companions prepared to try their luck at fishing. I had other ideas. Rigging a gangplank, I stepped ashore, feeling much as Christopher Columbus must have felt when he landed at last on an island of the New World.

On this first reconnaissance I found the island to be about a hundred acres in extent. Near its center was a cypress-ringed lake of considerable size. Along its muddy margins grew an almost impenetrable barrier of bamboo or cane and buttonbushes. The rest of the island was covered by dense, junglelike vegetation.

After a general survey of the island I sat down on a rotting log and quietly took stock of my surroundings. Above me towered a great live oak, its trunk nearly a yard in diameter. Ten feet from the ground the first large branch emerged and extended out over a marshy area for nearly twenty feet. It was gnarled and twisted, its bark was deeply fissured and along its top grew masses of epiphytic ferns and mosses.

Beyond the oak lay the open water of the lake, and, as I watched, a bright red male cardinal dropped down in a shaft of sunlight and alighted on a bush. He sat quietly for a time, then hopped down to the ground, looking in all directions. Soon I became aware of his more somber-colored mate, who was perched some distance away. After a minute or so she joined him and they continued to search their surroundings for any sign of danger— at least such was my interpretation of their actions.

As I sat quietly observing them it gradually dawned on me that they had something in mind, that all this searching had some purpose. After a time, the male, satisfied at last that it was safe, flew down to a small pool and began fluttering his wings, tossing up a spray of droplets that sparkled in the sun. Now I knew why they had been so concerned about possible enemies. In bathing, a bird's feathers become wet, making flight difficult. This is the way of all wild creatures; eternal vigilance is a necessity to survival. One moment of laxity and some enemy is apt to exact its toll.

After a few seconds of bathing, the male cardinal flew up to a low bush and fluttered his wings

to shake out the water. Then, while he preened his feathers, the female flew down for her turn.

After the cardinals had finished their toilets and departed, I continued to sit on the log, enjoying the island's remoteness and solitude. Upon a nearby limb I detected a movement and then, as my eyes became adjusted, I found that I was looking at a green chameleon. As I watched, it turned from green to brown and then to green again. When it slowly lifted its head, its throat pouch pushed downward, exposing an area of red skin. Several times it followed this procedure, bobbing its head up and down. This, I knew, was a male engaged in its mating ritual, but I saw no female, and he soon became interested in a fly that had alighted on a nearby leaf. Rapidly his tongue flashed out and the luckless fly was gone. On another tree I saw two blue-tailed skinks, or lizards, chasing each other. Around and around the tree they ran, then disappeared into a tree hole.

For a long while I sat on the log watching the play of woodland life going on around me in this undisturbed and isolated habitat. Slowly the light faded from the sky and dusk descended over the island and the marshland. From far away I heard the bellow of a bull alligator and the evening cries of marsh birds. From willows near the shore I heard the muted chirps and flutterings of redwing blackbirds as they chose roosting places for the night, and from across the river came the call of a great horned owl, eerie and primitive.

My afternoon's cruise down the twisting bayous and my short excursion on the island had been fascinating in the extreme. After supper I climbed to the top deck of the houseboat to enjoy the solitude and the night sounds of river and forest, thrilled at the sense of remoteness. This marshland has two separate and distinct personalities. By day, under the blazing sun, its waters sparkle as if set with a thousand gems and the trees along the bayous are mirrored in the surface. As night closes down and the full moon rises, both marshland and the forest are transformed into a strange dark world against a backdrop of starry skies. Soft breezes, blowing from across the river, caress the face and carry the heavy scent of woodland blooms. Moss-draped trees that seemed very ordinary in daylight take on weird, grotesque shapes.

On this night the full moon was slowly rising above the forest across the river, making a moon-path over the water that undulated and shifted as currents slowly moved beneath the dark surface. As I sat watching the river I heard, now and then, the plop of striking fish and other sounds whose

origins I could only guess at. From far overhead came the voices of migrating geese and I lifted my eyes to watch their broad "V" as it moved slowly southward. Following some built-in compass, the geese passed overhead, to merge, at last, with the rosy glow that still suffused the sky, leaving me with a sense of wonder as to their precise means of navigation. From the now-empty expanse above, my eyes dropped down to the river where a broad wedge-shaped wave moved slowly across the moon-swept water toward the opposite shore. Looking closely, I could see that it was created by some swimming animal with its head just above the surface. No doubt it was an otter, since they are fairly common in this marshland.

As darkness increased, from everywhere around me came mysterious night sounds, rustlings and buzzes. What caused the rustling noises I do not know, but the hums and buzzes were the voices of katydids and crickets sawing out their nocturnal tunes. Bats circled over the river, at times touching the surface, at other times flitting through the trees as they fed upon night-flying insects. They moved on silent wings and I heard no sound, but I knew that the bats were locating their prey by uttering high-pitched squeaks which were echoed off the insects' bodies and picked up by the bats' sensitive ears in a sonarlike technique called echo location. The bats darted among the trees, never touching a twig.

These were the sights and the sounds of the marshland night, and as I climbed down the ladder to my bunk I reflected that here was a place where time stood still, where 1000 years or 10,000 years made little difference. Changes come to most places: Forests are cleared and the land brought under cultivation to feed the expanding population; highways are built through wilderness areas, making them so easily accessible that they are soon littered with discarded cans and bottles, the debris of civilization; cities and towns expand their boundaries, gradually overrunning the surrounding countrysides. By contrast, this vast savanna remains unaltered by the heavy hand of man, a place where the only visible changes are those brought about by the seasons. Here I could walk through an island forest or paddle down some nameless bayou, seeing little to remind me that men had passed that way before.

Spreading over St. John's Bayou in the West Pascagoula River, a venerable live oak supports numerous streamers of Spanish moss. The live oak, one of the most impressive of southern trees, bears shiny green leaves all year round.

103

LOUISIANA'S DELTA COUNTRY

Louisiana's 15,000 square miles of Mississippi River delta is a fascinating latticework of bayous that glow at night with phosphorescent life, verdant swamps, and picturesque towns with sidewalks and houses perched on stilts. Blue geese crowd onto sandspits, otters and "M'sieu Mus'rat" forage for crawdads and shrimp around marsh roots, and sleepy alligators bask on islands of "trembling land," newly built by vegetation and river silt. A fifty-mile chain of wildlife reserves and recreational areas, almost a half million acres, are added enticements of the region. Tourists can explore much of this unique land by car, then continue with a guide by floatplane, balloon-tired marsh buggy or canoe.

(Above) *Tiny leaves of duckweed, one of the world's smallest flowering plants, float on quiet water in the 113,000-acre Salvador Wildlife Refuge in southern Louisiana. The plentiful duckweed forms a substantial part of the diet of ducks and geese.*

(Far Left) *Water tupelos, adorned with beards of Spanish moss, shade a bayou in the Salvador Wildlife Refuge near New Orleans. The name bayou derives from a Choctaw Indian word meaning "sluggish stream." The labyrinthine bayous teem with life in near-tropical profusion. Decaying plant matter attracts worms and shellfish, which lure fish and, consequently, the furred animals and long-legged water birds that feed on the abundant fish.*

(Left) *The water hyacinth has been called the world's most exotic nuisance. The colorful weeds float on air bladders under their leaves, clogging delta waterways, halting boats and killing aquatic life by shutting out light and air. In a single growing season ten small hyacinths can cover an acre.*

FLOATING THE BUFFALO RIVER

BERN KEATING

Fishing and scenery—these are almost the only natural resources left in the Buffalo River watershed in northern Arkansas. But who wants more? Certainly not the fishermen, botanists, nature lovers and vacationers who float down the stream year in, year out and all year round.

They ease their own canoes or twenty-foot flat-bottomed johnboats into the Buffalo, or hire boats and guides from professional outfitters. They shove off into the clear, swift-running water and let the current carry them downstream between forested banks, with only an occasional flip of the paddle to steer around a rock. Their goal is fishing or scenery watching—or stillness. One blind man, a veteran of many floats, describes the Buffalo trip as being "an escape into blessed silence."

Paradoxically, all this is possible because, in the dreary annals of man's despoiling, the Buffalo River has come full cycle. Early settlers abused the land, cut the forests and wiped out the game. They rendered the mountains too poor to support man, so after World War II man began to move out.

Now, decades later, the hills have again clothed themselves with forests, the game has returned and the streams run clear between banks uncluttered by industry. The few domestic animals visible from the river add a pastoral grace note.

To exploit this most intangible of raw materials—natural beauty—a curious industry has sprung up: float trips.

Floaters divide into two groups—canoeists and johnboat floaters. Canoeists rarely fish, often carry binoculars and usually cover twenty miles in a day unless a special interest in botany, bird watching or geology compels them to make stops along the way for inspection trips ashore. Johnboat floaters usually fish by plug-casting for large-mouth black bass, spotted black bass, goggle-eye —or, above all, the prized smallmouth bass, a scrapper that can weigh six pounds or more. Because the smallmouth bass thrives in the cool swift waters running over limestone shelves, anglers rarely float more than twelve miles a day.

Many johnboats are propelled by five- to ten-horsepower outboard motors on specially built raised mounts to provide only a five-inch draft. Canoeists have snobbish disdain for johnboaters for disturbing the silence with even so faint a mechanical sound as the purr of a midget outboard.

Both classes of floaters regard anybody discharging firearms as a barbarian unfit for exposure to the charms of the Buffalo. (Far from shooting snakes on sight, the true float fisherman welcomes a swimming water snake as sure sign that fish are about to bite.)

The Buffalo is floatable the year round downstream from U.S. Highway 65. Above that point, during the month of August the river goes underground for a stretch of several miles downstream from Woolum. The stretch from Pruitt to U.S. Highway 65 is floatable for a longer period into the summer than the twenty-mile stretch from Ponca to Pruitt, where some of the most magnificent scenery lies. Along this reach of the river, the water level drops in May and isn't high enough for floating till October.

Even botany students can enjoy the fall or winter trip, for a thousand flowering species begin blossoming with the witch hazel in January and continue through the Indian pipe in late fall. And, of course, the early spring floaters who put in at Ponca see the woods at the peak of their blossoming. The two biggest upriver group floats take place Thanksgiving Day and New Year's Day.

Floaters put in at many different locations. Convenient launch points for a trip down the Buffalo River include Pruitt, Ponca Point, the bridge over U.S. Highway 65, the Arkansas Highway 14 crossing and Buffalo Point, only one and a half miles beyond the Arkansas Highway 14 bridge. The three-day float from Buffalo Point to the juncture with the White River runs through the wildest section of the stream.

Congress made the stream a national river in 1972 and authorized the purchase of roughly 100,000 acres to protect the riverbanks and adjacent woods from "progress and development." In the words of the National Park Service: "The Buffalo River remains one of the few rivers still possessing exceptional wilderness value."

Hidden natural wonders await adventurers along the Buffalo River in the heart of the Ozarks of northern Arkansas. From a towering cliff, a waterfall plummets 200 feet to the floor of Hemmed-in Hollow, a short hike from the river.

Part III

LAND
OF THE LONG
HORIZONS

Ohio Indiana Illinois Wisconsin
Michigan Minnesota Iowa Missouri Oklahoma
Kansas Nebraska South Dakota North Dakota

OUR GLORIOUS GREAT LAKES

NOEL MOSTERT

The Great Lakes are the immemorial surprise of middle America, its finest color; they are the greatest natural wonder of the whole continent, and yet, I am convinced, the most undervalued and unsung. My own introduction to them came in the early 1950s from the spectacular stretch of Canadian Pacific track that runs along the north shore of Superior. The train comes drumming down from the bushland plateau, doubling and turning in the cuttings, and suddenly the emerald water heaves below, spreading from the white, empty sands to a horizon as vast and open as the sea. That far horizon has always struck me as being the truest measure of North America's breadth: It is hard to grasp that a land should contain several freshwater seas so big that a ship can steam out of sight of the shore for a day or more, or even founder in giant waves, as happens from time to time.

Yet there they are, these changing, changeless lakes, flung upon the map, almost dead center, spilling eastward and southward across the Middle West. Ontario, the only Canadian province that fringes them, sprawls along their northern coasts, and eight states—New York, Pennsylvania, Ohio, Michigan, Indiana, Illinois, Wisconsin, Minnesota—crowd their lower shores. More than 40 percent of America's total dollar income from farming, mining and manufacturing is earned around their basins; 80 percent of Canada's industry is settled in this area—so that in a most literal sense it is the pulsing heart of North America.

This is the largest group of lakes in the world and the biggest body of fresh water, covering 95,170 square miles in surface, draining an area of 295,200 square miles and flowing to the sea at a rate of 240,000 cubic feet per second—more than

A summer squall lashes southern Lake Michigan off Indiana Dunes State Park near Gary. The Great Lakes can spawn raging storms, with gale winds that whip up violent seas: During a 1958 blow a 640-foot steel freighter broke in two.

the Seine, Thames and Danube combined. The lakes were the single greatest asset this land endowed to its pioneer man. Their spacious waters were a natural highway for the exploring French and, two centuries later, for the main westward rush of settlement. And when iron ore was discovered on Superior's shores, in the mid to late nineteenth century, the cheap transportation provided by the lakes became the lever of continental prosperity and boom. It established the American iron and steel industries, and made America the industrial giant of the world.

Let us approach the lakes the best way: along the course of history, up from Montreal along the St. Lawrence and its seaway. We book on a big Swedish freighter that has crossed the Atlantic with Scandinavian luxuries for North America and will go into the lakes to pick up grain and general cargo for Australia. Under way, we slide out of Montreal harbor and nose through the deepening twilight into the first lock of the seaway, at St. Lambert. Suddenly a siren wails, bells ring, booms descend and the lock gates start swinging shut. At the same time lights flash red, and a drawbridge behind us descends while another in front rises, the heavy road and rail traffic shifting imperturbably and without pause from one to the other. There is a roar of water, the ship rises and in minutes we have been lifted high enough to continue onward.

Through our first night and the following day, other locks lift us steadily higher, into Lake Ontario. This is the smallest of the Great Lakes—193 miles long, east to west—but it is deep, with a maximum sounding of 802 feet. While the other lakes have distinct personalities, Ontario's is more elusive. The Niagara Falls escarpment with its sheer thunderous drop has been an effective barrier between this and the other lakes, and the St. Lawrence sluicing out its eastern end draws Ontario's attention seaward. Its commerce has always been in that direction—or south, to New York. Its mood is sedate. Here are no vulgar echoes of the westward push, the immigrant scramble; that essential pioneer familiarity of the upper lakes is missing.

On the bridge the pilot tells us that the lake sailor speaks a different nautical language. The lakeman came originally from the farm, and he brought with him a homey terminology. He goes steamboating, as he describes his calling; he calls the rail his fence, the bow the front end. When a propeller loses a blade he says the boat has "thrown her bucket." After the seaway brought in oceangoing ships, pilotage was introduced and

enforced, and the lakeman has grudgingly come to recognize that the Great Lakes are no longer his private preserve.

In the morning we enter the Welland Canal, whose twenty-seven miles and eight locks will lift us over the Niagara Falls Escarpment to Lake Erie. We drift through the canal, past orchards and towns. We sail between backyards, then past the back porch of a small farmhouse. Next morning we break out through the last lock into Lake Erie. The ship suddenly begins to sway. Doors bang and the air pours cold and strong through the porthole. We are at sea.

Though Superior is the worst storm lake, with waves reported as high as thirty-five feet, Erie is the one that is talked about: a killer of small craft. It has a reputation for treacherous flash storms. The shallowest of the lakes, it can be pale as glass, and as smooth—then a few hours later be insensately churning under a fugitive sky. Its shores are low-lying, its beaches often narrow, and except for the gritty imprints pawed by industry in that dense line of cities between Buffalo and Toledo on the south shore, it is succulently pastoral.

All day we push southwest. By evening the air is much colder, and a rainstorm washes away Cleveland's profile as we pass in through the breakwater and tie up there. We never really see the city; in the morning it remains hidden in dark mist, and the foghorn on the breakwater sounds steadily. The cargo winches are busy, and the ship lists to starboard as the cranes work the port side, probing and nodding over the hatches like weird skeletal giraffes at feed; crates of beer and canned fish swing upward.

At dusk we pass the Detroit River lighthouse, situated at the junction of river and lake. Detroit lies beside us now, an immense suffusion of light on the mist, with glowing red patches from the torches of the plants at River Rouge. The night rattles and growls with the sleepless discontent of industry on the nearby shore. A strange melody as one lies in one's bunk, listening.

In the next day and night we run the 206-mile north-south length of Lake Huron, the second largest of the lakes. Its deepest sounding is 725 feet, and its shores are sparsely populated. Except for Bay City, Michigan, Owen Sound, Ontario, and the twin cities of Port Huron, Michigan, and Sarnia, Ontario, it is still wild country. You can smell the North here; the wind has the resinous taste of pine, and stings from having blown a long way across cold water.

We enter St. Mary's River at the upper end of

Huron at twilight. The river is wide and still. On either side of it the forest comes down to the water, a stony shore; the country behind rises to low, hunched mountains. The overwhelming impression is of absolute silence. Not even Huron itself seemed so wide, so empty, so soundless as these woods pressing thickly to the very edge of the water. A gull, solitary as fear, the only movement in this primeval desolation, rises beside the rail and then wheels and soars high and catches that final light on its wing, floats for a moment, then vanishes.

Our destination now is Fort William, Ontario, at the top of Lake Superior. Superior is 350 miles long, the largest freshwater lake in the world. It is also the deepest of the Great Lakes—with the maximum sounding at 1333 feet, its bottom lies several hundred feet below sea level—and it holds more than half the water of the entire Great Lakes system. There is an antique stillness on Superior, a feeling of immense, brooding age. Round-humped mountains along the shores look like burial mounds of the gods, their surfaces having been rubbed to a hard, glacial polish through eons of cold sleep. It is even in the very look of the water, a serene surface overlaid upon inscrutable depths.

Out through these ancestral mists move the long lake barges bearing prairie grain and Minnesota ore. If there is a distinctive sound that man has brought to this region, then surely it is the harsh clanging of shunting freight cars that re-echoes night and day in the ports—Marquette, Duluth, Superior, Fort William, Port Arthur—where the trains crawl in with their mile-long loads of golden seed or tinted nuggets.

We slowly steam up to Fort William. The town wears the look of any city: sidewalks, paved streets and urban architecture. Yet the gleaming tracks and lines of cars, fringing the wilderness, strike me as being among the most remarkable things we have experienced so far; one feels that one has indeed come to some junction of the continent, between past and present, between frontier and factory. Forty-eight hours later we pass through the Straits of Mackinac and enter Lake Michigan. Michigan, the only one of the lakes entirely within the United States, is the lake that built Chicago. It is the main route of the oceangoing ships. Its shores are green and tangled in the north, and white with dunes to the east.

Now the whole lake has gone glassy, and the sky is black. There are distant rumbles, and suddenly the wind comes. In no time the ship begins to lift and roll. The bulkheads creak; the curtains swing; lightning illuminates the whole ship. From that windless dusk to this black rage. A steward comes in to secure the porthole. "Tomorrow Chicago," he says, as if to convince himself as well as me. It still doesn't seem true. He should have said Cherbourg or Southampton. Chicago? I lie and listen to the water.

FANTASY IN SANDSTONE

FREEMAN TILDEN

In the oil and gas fields to the east of Ohio's Hocking Hills State Park, the drillers talk of a certain "Big Injun sand," which they strike some hundreds of feet below their rig. They are probably referring to a cliff on the Licking River east of Newark, where the Indians once painted a big black hand pointing toward a ridge on which excellent flint for arrowheads and spearpoints could be found. The geologists have chosen, since this cliff exposes an interesting type of rock, to call the formation the Black Hand sandstone.

The casual visitor may ask what difference it makes what geologists call any particular kind of rock. After all, he has come simply to look, to admire, to rest, to picnic or merely to find a cool valley on a blistering day. Yet for all of that, the ordinary tourist cannot visit an extraordinary park like Hocking Hills without wondering how its scenic marvels came to be. What happened to create all this? Why here, rather than somewhere else in Ohio? And under what circumstances?

There is one brief—and reasonably accurate—answer to such questions: Black Hand sandstone. It is the type of the sandstone formation that results in the strange and beautiful effects seen in the six units of the park. And the amazing thing about these areas is that each one has a perfectly clear character and quality of its own.

If this Black Hand rock, more than 200 feet thick in some parts of the park, had all been of the same character, or composition, the picture would have been entirely different. But this rock is divided into three distinct zones. The top zone is firmly cemented and stoutly resists weathering. The bottom zone is similar, but you will

probably see it only at the lower falls at Old Man's Cave. The middle zone, however, is more susceptible to weathering and erosion. Throughout the park big and little instances of the results of this zonal difference in the sandstone can be observed.

This difference accounts for what are called the "caves." They are not true caves, though none the less spectacular for that. They are really rock shelters similar to the many that housed the prehistoric people of our Southwest. There can be little doubt that these "caves" of Hocking Hills were used by generations of historic Indians. Otherwise, why would such quantities of ashes, the result of years of campfires, have been found in Ash Cave? As late as 1890 the pile of ashes was three feet deep, a hundred feet long and thirty feet wide. A good many forest trees went into the making of such an accumulation.

The approach to Ash Cave leads to a surprise. You have been coming through a narrow gorge densely covered with many kinds of hardwoods and hemlocks and pines, and suddenly you emerge from the forest in full face of the great overhang, the largest overhanging ledge in the park's units. It is a big horseshoe with an arc of 700 feet and nearly 100 feet high. As usual in Hocking Hills, a little cataract comes pouring down into a pool at the foot. This stream is a small one, save at times of heavy rainfall, but even so, the spray from the plunge of the water eats constantly at the softer zone of the sandstone.

Old Man's Cave has been voted by many as the outstanding beauty spot of the state. Certainly it is the most popular of the six associated areas. But other eyes might choose elsewhere. For my own part, I found that Cedar Falls pleased me best. It gave me that little tug at the heart that cannot be explained or justified; it just is. Let us take cheerful thought that there is some special attraction for everyone.

It is probably true that Old Man's Cave is the most extensive example in the park of what the forces of erosion can do when a softer layer underlies a more resistant rock. If you start at the lower end and go up the easy trail to the head of the gorge, you will see Old Man's Creek cascading over the harder rock at the high Upper Falls. Here the undercut ledges are the result of older streams

A waterfall plunges ninety feet into Ash Cave in Ohio's Hocking Hills State Park. The rock overhang was named for a huge pile of ashes found by the first settlers in the area—apparently the remnants of countless Indian campfires.

115

of water that deepened the bed to its present level.

Numerous potholes tell the story of swirling rock material that gradually bored down into the sandstone. In the north wall of the gorge, high above the stream, is the great overhang where, the story goes, a fugitive from West Virginia lived as a hermit for many years after the Civil War. It was an ideal place for a hermit then. In these days he would be somewhat annoyed by the thousands of visitors who come every year to clamber among the boulders and cool themselves in the dense shade, where remnants of Ice Age plants are still growing out of reach of the sunlight.

Rock House, unlike the cavelike shelters of the overhangs, is a true cavern, though still not like the caves that are found in limestone formations. At the head of a valley, a sheer cliff of the Black Hand rises from the stream bed. Here is a natural wonder that the casual visitor finds difficult to understand. What produced it? Certainly not the same forces that acted to create Old Man's Cave. Rock House is a tunnellike passageway through the cliff, open at both ends and 200 feet long, with windows topped by Gothic-type arches and supporting columns between. Geologists tell us that the cavern resulted from the "jointing" of the rock; but what force actually excavated this great room? The explanation that weathering was responsible, breaking down the rock into grains of sand that were removed by wind in the course of a million years, sounds fantastic, but the experts assure us that it is true.

Rock House has been a tourist attraction for more than a century. As early as 1835 "a sixteen-room hotel, complete with ballroom and livery stable," standing where the park shelter is today, housed many an important person.

Less welcome guests have made use of Rock House over the ensuing years. It was an ideal hideout for highway robbers, horse thieves and other fugitives, and also for the elusive bootleggers who flourished in the days of Prohibition.

Cantwell Cliffs is the most northerly of the Hocking Hills State Park units. Here the erosion of Buck Run has produced another kind of scenic phenomenon. It is a showy example of the manner in which the undermining in this kind of rock creates one escarpment after another, as the resistant cap rock collapses when the middle zone is eaten away. The trail here winds its way through narrow passages among huge blocks of fallen, "slumped" rock. One of these narrow spots is called Fat Woman's Squeeze. It isn't clear why the sex distinction was made. According to life

insurance actuaries, gross overweight is impartially distributed. Maybe some plump lady actually got stuck, although the passage is not quite as narrow as it looks.

Between Rock House and Old Man's Cave is Conkle's Hollow. This is real, almost untouched wilderness. The trail up the gorge, one of the deepest in Ohio, is one of the easier gorge trails in the area. Hemlocks, birches and other hardwoods screen out the sunlight. Near the upper end of the hollow the cliffs are almost vertical, while at the back end of the gorge a series of waterfalls cascades into a small plunge pool.

Downstream from the Lower Falls of the area of the Old Man's Cave is another gorge, wider and deeper than the first, called the Lower Gorge. If you were to follow the trail through this, it would lead you to Queer Creek and so on to Cedar Falls, and you would then be halfway between the two caves of Ash and the Old Man.

In order to preserve the unspoiled beauty of Cedar Falls, the Ohio Department of Natural Resources has provided only the bare necessities for visitors. I hope it may always be so here, for this is as charming and peaceful a spot as can be found anywhere. The falls themselves weave lacy ribbons along two grooves in the rock face as they drop to the pool below; and the forest growth, with great sleek beeches—and what is lovelier than the delicate bark of these trees?—raising their shapely crowns high above the fern-covered glen, gives the impression of a remote, happy island saved from the modern march of enterprise.

Here at Cedar Falls there is quiet; there is restoration for a tired mind or body. It is not exciting, like the tumbling chasm that brings the major number of visitors to the cave of the hermit. A series of steps lead one to the falls.

Ohio has done well to preserve these choice areas, and also the considerable surrounding state forests. Beginning with the acquisition of a block of land that included the Old Man's Cave region, the state has widened its holdings since 1924 to include many thousands of acres of forest and the cluster of park units described here. The alluring qualities of these parks are demonstrated by the fact that, though most of the usual facilities for physical recreation are missing, they draw an increased number of visitors year after year.

A hemlock grows from the top of a boulder along the trail in Conkle's Hollow. Walled by towering cliffs of Black Hand sandstone almost 250 feet high, this rocky gorge in Hocking Hills State Park is one of Ohio's deepest.

THE INDIANA DUNES

Two battles have been raging in and
around Indiana Dunes State Park on
Lake Michigan's south shore: Within the
park an endless struggle goes on between
sand-carrying winds and sand-stabilizing
vegetation, and in the surrounding
land conservationists combat urban
inroads on the dunes area. The state park
is an oasis of pearly beaches and includes
an unusual blend of bog and forest.
More than 1000 plant species grow here,
from cactus to arctic bearberry. The
winds build the dunes from sand lifted
off the beach. Stabilization starts when
grasses bind the sand, so that more
complex plant communities can follow:
shrubs and then pine forests. These in
turn condition the soil for the last stage,
lush forests of hardwoods such as
black oak. These stages may span 1000
years, and each of them can be seen
in the Indiana dunes. This park is the
core of the new Indiana Dunes National
Lakeshore, into which land from
the nearby areas is being incorporated
as it becomes available.

The Big Blowout (bottom) *punctuates the Lake
Michigan shore twelve miles east of Gary in Indiana
Dunes State Park. Looking like an explosion crater,
the blowout was shaped by wind-borne sand. One
area of loose sand on a dune may tip the balance,
spelling erosive doom for the binding plants; winds
cut across the dune; a blowout forms. The sands
move inland, smothering growing trees and perhaps
uncovering gaunt remnants of a previously buried
forest. Such a "dunes graveyard" at the Big Blowout
contains the stark remains of white pines* (top left).
*Elsewhere on the blowout, beach grass gains a
foothold, restarting dune stabilization* (top right).

ILLINOIS: HEARTLAND OF AMERICA

DONALD CULROSS PEATTIE

I'll call Illinois the best.

I don't expect anyone to agree with me except several million natives of the Prairie State, my friend former senator Paul Douglas and the spirit of Adlai E. Stevenson.

Why do I say Illinois is best? It has no gorgeous scenery, no stately antebellum mansions, no hallowed customs and no true cosmopolitanism like New York City's. In fact, just the opposite. For me Illinois is the best state precisely because it is so American.

More, it is heartland. As Castile is of Spain, as the plain of Beauce is the granary of France, or Tuscany of Italy, so Illinois is core America. Yes, even in the large number of the foreign-born in Chicago. It is American in its unappreciated beauty of plainness, something that Thoreau would have understood perhaps, something that the three poets of the state who really sound to me like Illinois have given voice to—Sandburg all the time, Vachel Lindsay sometimes and Edgar Lee Masters in the one truly great book of poetry that he produced, *Spoon River Anthology*.

Illinois is beautiful, it seems to me, as only a great fertile plain can be beautiful. If I cannot have a range of snowy mountains, then give me a great teeming plain, and not mere hilliness which shuts off rather than provides a view. In Illinois you can see right down to the horizon. You have 180° of an arc of sky, be it the aching blue of spring, when meadowlarks and bobolinks throw the twinkling gold of their songs into your ear, or a sky with vast moving clouds, castle-in-Spain clouds, in the days of summer thunderheads.

A tree, too, on the prairies has meaning for me as mere woodsiness never has. When in Illinois you need a tree, for shade or the vertical breaking

Bromegrass waves in the August sun near Galena, in northwest Illinois. Contour plowing of fields checks erosion. These fertile farmlands were a gift of the Ice Age glaciers, which made their greatest southerly penetration in Illinois.

121

of the horizontal lines, there is a tree. In one of the first accounts of the Prairie State, "Waubun, or the Early Day," by the wife of a captain at old Fort Dearborn, the single beauty of a far-off poplar is described, now near and clear, now mistily distant on the prairies. So with me, a cottonwood is a short-lived queen whose last golden raiment falls from her smooth body in the hour before the little death that is winter.

"Yes," I hear some saying, "I have been to Illinois several times. I motored across it as fast as I could." Or, "I took a train, pulled down the curtains against the sheer monotony of the state, and went sound asleep until I was well away."

Good-bye, stranger; next time take a faster train or a plane; step on that accelerator; my state is not for you.

I am sorry for you if you had no time to go to Starved Rock with its wild primroses, the true subarctic mistassini primrose with pale lavender petals and yellow throat. Francis Parkman found it worth his while to go there in the days when travel was difficult, to see the spot where, on a high natural castle of rock, soldier-explorer La Salle established a French fort in 1682 and, according to legend, a band of besieged Illinois Indians later starved. They would not be dislodged and stayed, in their pride, till death overtook them.

Yes, and I'm sorry that you could not see the lofty and murmurous virgin white pine groves. You didn't know we had such places? No, how could you? These spots don't advertise on billboards, they don't charge admission. Illinois is the least touristical of states. Nobody comes to Illinois for the climate, heaven knows; nobody comes to see the sights unless in Chicago. Illinois is just itself, soliciting nobody. Yet La Salle and the Jesuit priest Marquette said of it, over and over: Beautiful, beautiful!

I never heard a place where birdsong and the spring song of the frogs sounded so sweet. If you camp out on some hillock where swamp and orchard and prairie grass meet, you will hear full more than half of the species of land birds of eastern North America—the wild telegraphy of crows, the *flick-up wick-up* of flickers (called highholers in Illinois), the golden rolling call of orioles, the jingling doorbell cry of redwings. And there is always the raucous call of herons (farm boys

An autumn sunset gilds the bluffs of Garden of the Gods Recreation Area in Shawnee National Forest. Oak and hickory trees hug the erosion-cut 400-foot cliffs. Part of the Illinois Ozarks, these rocks are about 200 million years old.

call them cranes) and the warning cries of king rails to their tiny coal-black chicks.

And the frogs! What I still hear in my dreams is the rising, bubbling sound of the swamp tree frogs, a thin *pee-yee-yeep*. And the trilling tree toads that prophesy rain.

The state flower is the modest violet, and it is a good choice, for there are scores of species—the butterfly, the sister, the hooded, the larkspur, the longspur. What some call dogtooth violet is a member of the lily family. And that flower called shooting star, with its upward-and-backwardly-flaring petals, like some pointed comet head rushing to earth, is really a close relative of cyclamen.

In early spring, when the plum thickets fume with snowy blossoms on the dark, gnarled old finger-twigs, comes the moment when millions of spring beauties spread a carpet under the thicket. In autumn the prairies change with the rough purple of ironweed, the royal purple of liatris, the purple and mauve of joe-pye weed, the smoky drift of asters through the woods.

For there are woods, of course—the prairie groves and, in every county, a strip called "the river woods." But there are three completely characteristic trees besides the cottonwoods: the bur oaks and the red haws (we called them thorn apples) that lean old elbows on the ground, making a perfect playhouse for every Illinois country child, and, towering above, the shagbark hickories that, like Homer's soldiers who fought naked in their leathern armor, stand soldier-straight in their long strips of bark that is forever being sloughed off and replaced.

I love, too, the old-timiness of Illinois towns, with their streets deep-shaded in vaulted elms and their yards never fenced against neighbors, so that the children run in and out of each other's frame houses or play favorite dusk games all over the block, while june bugs bang against the screens.

You can follow up the towns that lie on the path of the Lincoln-Douglas debates. They fought in Ottawa, in Quincy on the Mississippi, at Alton, at Galesburg and in Freeport, where 15,000 came from all about to hear these two, and stood in a light drizzle or sheltered in their wagons.

These towns are still there, not totally changed from the days of the great debates. Only in Chicago have Lincoln's quiet traces been obliterated. Elsewhere his greatness marches invisibly across the wide, plain land. For there are mighty footsteps in the prairie grasses, as they bow before the wind—footsteps of a brave and simple past, leading to a confident tomorrow.

WISCONSIN'S TWENTY-THREE APOSTLES

HOWARD MEAD

As far north as you can go in Wisconsin, clustered in the clear, cold waters of Lake Superior off the blunt tip of the Bayfield Peninsula, is the Apostle Islands archipelago. These twenty-three incredibly beautiful islands—some 50,000 acres of rock, sand and forest—vary in size from a tiny sand spit hardly large enough to hold a range light to 12½-mile-long Madeline Island (which boasts a year-round community, a golf course designed by Robert Trent Jones and a rich history). On the islands' sheltered sides there are bright sand beaches washed by small gentle waves, but on the lake-facing shores it is quite different. Here, where the brownstone rocks absorb the full crack of the great storms that sweep across the lake, their faces are hollowed and chewed.

Like most of Wisconsin's landscape, the Apostle Islands were formed by glaciers. It is some 18,000 years since the last huge ice sheet began its final ponderous, halting retreat, releasing, as it went, torrents of meltwater that gouged out the valleys separating the Apostles from the peninsula and from each other. What the glacier began, the endless washing and pounding waves finished. But even before the first glacier came, a million years ago, this land was ancient. It is probable that the Lake Superior region was almost the first to emerge from a global ocean 2 billion years ago.

But the Chippewa Indians, who settled on Madeline Island about the same time Columbus landed on this continent, knew nothing of glaciers or emerging land masses. According to them, their great hero Nanabushu made the Apostles. One day, the tale goes, Nanabushu cornered his enemy, the Great Beaver, in Chequamegon Bay. To make a trap, Nanabushu built a dam across the bay. (The Chippewa name for Chequamegon Point

Frozen surf adds a fanciful frosting to the caves and rock outcroppings of Stockton Island's northeast shore. Second largest of Wisconsin's twenty-three Apostle Islands in Lake Superior, it also goes by its French name, Presque Isle.

124

was *Shagewomekong*, or "Soft Beaver Dam.") And so powerful was his digging and scooping that huge clods of earth fell behind him into the lake and these became the Apostle Islands.

The Chippewa built a great city on Madeline that may have had a population of 12,000 or more. And for 120 years they lived in comparative safety, tending their nets and harvesting corn and squash and beans from their vast gardens. But they are gone. Famine led to cannibalism and, the legends say, the spirits of the dead walked at night and globes of fire danced above the marshes. To them the island was cursed, and for 200 years no Chippewa would stay overnight there.

As early as 1622 the explorers came, and then the missionaries, and finally the traders, who were searching not for the Northwest Passage nor for souls to save, but for furs. In 1659 two Frenchmen, Médard Chouart, Sieur des Groseilliers, and his young brother-in-law, Pierre Esprit Radisson, built a tiny log fort near Ashland—the first fur-trading post in Wisconsin. In his journal Radisson wrote what amounted to the first advertising copy about the area. "In that bay," he wrote, "there is a chanell where we take stores of fishes, sturgeons of vast biggness, and Pycks seaven feet long."

What these men saw and felt is not forgotten. They wrote copiously, and some of their artifacts are preserved in the snug little museum on Madeline Island. But their physical marks have disappeared. Part of the charm of the Apostles is that in all the time since man first came here he has hardly been able to change them. Nature tends to obliterate man's scratchings.

Even the signs of those men who toiled here in the recent past scarcely show today. The lumberjacks cut off all the big timber that could be floated easily to the sawmills on the mainland. But today the scars they left are covered over with a lush second growth of mixed hardwoods and pines. And the quarries that provided the brownstone fronts for many of New York City's buildings are overgrown and forgotten. Gone, too, are the halcyon days of commercial fishing.

With the coming of the lamprey and the passing of commercial fishing, some of the mystique of the area was lost. It was disturbing to know that the deep crystalline waters of Lake Superior were all but empty of the great fish. There are signs, however, that the lamprey has been routed and the trout are coming back. In fact, we bought a couple of handsome ten-pounders in Bayfield a few springs ago, when everyone in the area whom you asked about the fishing said, "Terrific!" They

were catching the native fish and the big coho salmon as well. The fast-growing coho, stocked in Lake Michigan several years ago, is spreading throughout the Great Lakes much faster than anyone believed possible.

Among the Apostles there is an island to appeal to every man. Out of the bewildering variety of choices, your favorite might be Stockton, with its particularly handsome beaches, one of which, on Presque Isle Point, "sings" as you walk across it. Or it may be Devil's Island, the northernmost bit of land in Wisconsin, with its fantastic deep, water-hollowed caves. Each island has a distinct personality and none will disappoint you.

To know the tranquillity these islands offer, you must walk their beaches on a golden midsummer's day and feel the lake's cool breath as it swishes, bubbling and flowing in a rhythm that you feel as much as hear. To understand the awesome power and fickleness of the great lake you must sit on the ancient scarred rocks and watch the wind-driven waves shatter into thunderous fountains of spray. Each island is its own world. And every man who has learned to love these islands accepts them, and the surrounding blue expanse of lake, on their terms, not his.

HIAWATHA COUNTRY

GENE CAESAR

On the front side of most road maps, Michigan is merely a mitten; and when inhabitants of its industrialized palm say, "Up north," they usually mean the forest and lake country where the fingers would be. Yet within this state's boundaries, literally above "up" and north of "north," lies a land of taller pines and more-primitive lakes, of wild orchids that bloom unseen and rare rocks that gleam undisturbed in the depths of more-immense forests. In light of its color and spectacle, Michigan's Upper Peninsula has long been a place

Morning sunlight pierces the darkness of the forest in Tahquamenon Falls State Park on Michigan's Upper Peninsula. A tree with a vinelike, twisted trunk is silhouetted against a dense forest of red and sugar maples, beech and birch.

known to surprisingly few. It has been relegated, in more ways than one, to the back of the map.

Part of the reason probably lies in sheer superlative. In the nearer north, there is enough space and silence to atone for the crowded sidewalks and production-line thunder of Detroit. Where coyotes prowl the woodlands close to home, no need may be seen for wolf country. Certainly the Upper Peninsula is no longer inaccessible. A $100 million bridge was completed across the Straits of Mackinac in 1957, opening the peninsula to even the most impatient visitors, and rendering the once-remote province so accessible, in fact, that conservationists began worrying about the despoliation of its wilderness. Yet the U.P., as the land beyond the bridge is generally called, has become, if anything, a little wilder since then.

This claim may sound capricious. No one has yet devised a computer for gauging wildness in wilderness; and, like desirability in women, this delicate essence may rest somewhat upon difficulty of attainment, upon remoteness itself. From this standpoint, some of the U.P.'s old magic should have fallen under a shadow the moment the Mackinac Bridge replaced the slow ferryboats. But the slight psychological loss has been more than balanced by a heightening of contrasts. Northward across the peninsula from the bridge —which has become more of an attraction than the peninsula itself—there waits an older man-made wonder, the famous locks at Sault Ste. Marie, which handle more traffic than the Panama Canal. Connecting the two is a third—the multi-lane marvel known as Interstate No. 75, which stretches unbroken to Detroit. But the widest superhighway becomes a pitifully thin line through the north-woods vastness, accenting the forest as an obsolete two-lane highway never could. And whatever the forest gave up in acreage, it more than got back in dignity, because billboards are no longer allowed.

The Upper Peninsula has 4000 inland lakes, 12,000 miles of streams and 1700 miles of Great Lakes shoreline. Its area is greater in size than the four states of Massachusetts, Connecticut, Delaware and Rhode Island combined. Moreover, Michigan's Upper Peninsula is larger than either Belgium or Switzerland.

Interstate 75 is a thread of false first impressions across only the peninsula's easternmost tip, a distance of fifty miles. In every part of the U.P.'s 384-mile-length there are places wild enough to tingle the spine. An hour's drive west of Sault Ste. Marie, for example, north of Hulbert on Highway

M-28, lies the dark green country of the Tahquamenon River. Here no work of man has affected the two giant waterfalls that look for all the world like fizzing cascades of root beer. This is the little-changed land that inspired "Hiawatha": "In the solitary forest, by the rushing Taquamenaw." Both the lore and setting of Longfellow's epic Indian poem were taken from the researches of a scholarly squaw man named Henry Schoolcraft; and in Schoolcraft County today there is a 145-square-mile labyrinth of swampland and pattern-less wooded rises that a dozen bridges couldn't disturb. This is the Seney National Wildlife Refuge, where more Canada geese can be seen than anywhere in Canada, and big pike can be fished from their nesting ponds.

Where M-28 veers northward to Munising, automobile traffic finally moves on Lake Superior's shore, and then not for long. To the right, seen best by excursion boat in a thirty-seven-mile round trip, that shore consists of high sandstone cliffs interlaced with mineral oxides of wildly varied colors and sculptured by storm and wind-driven ice into shapes suggesting everything from cathedrals to battleships. At Marquette, the lake-shore turns into a series of huge docks where ore boats are loaded by automation. And where Highway M-28 slants on down past Negaunee and Ishpeming, the world's largest iron mine lies beneath it, a shaft in each town. But sitting brooding and powerful to the northwest, best seen by a side trip up the shore to the road's-end town of Big Bay, are the craggy, pine-backed hills that the maps call the Huron Mountains. And in those hills, timber wolves still prowl.

They bother no one and are rarely seen. Bears can be watched in summertime at practically any township dump, but men have lived a lifetime on the edge of wolf country and glimpsed nothing more of these wariest of animals than their big pad marks in the snow. And those pad marks, incidentally, won't be found in Maine or California or Oregon, or even in the most remote high-country basin of the Rockies. If, as poetic outdoor writers so often insist, the howl of the timber wolf is the essence of true wilderness, then Michigan's Upper Peninsula and the neighboring Wisconsin and Minnesota forests happen to be the only true wilderness this country has left outside of Alaska.

Waves, rain and frost have carved the 150-to-200-foot sandstone cliffs of Pictured Rocks National Lakeshore. Hiawatha is said to have spent his childhood in this fifteen-mile stretch of Michigan's Upper Peninsula fronting on Lake Superior.

THE SOURCE OF
THE MISSISSIPPI

WILLARD PRICE

He stood his ground, snarling, trying to make up his mind what to do. I blocked his path. The river behind him cut off his retreat. I took another step forward. Like a flash the bobcat wheeled, fled to the river's edge, spanned the river in one great leap and disappeared in the forest.

The river was the Mississippi, at this point only ten feet wide. It was just a babbling brook, with very little to babble about, for it was not old enough to know much. Two minutes ago it was born. A hundred yards back it had issued from Lake Itasca past a wooden marker designating the spot as the river's source.

Forest-girdled Lake Itasca lies in northern Minnesota about 150 miles south of the Canadian border. Its discoverer, Henry Schoolcraft, fixed upon it as the true source of the Mississippi. Searching for some name that would suggest True Head, he came upon the Latin words *veritas caput*. That would be too long a name—so, with skillful surgery, he chopped off the first and last syllables and came out with Itasca.

"You can get awfully messed up in there." That was one comment when we mentioned our plan to canoe down the first reach of the Mississippi.

We did get awfully messed up In spite of the fact that I had the able assistance of our two sons, Bob and Jonathan, it was rough going. We started out in high spirits. My wife, Mary, had departed with the car to a point where the road crossed the river. There she would wait for us. Considering the wiggle of the little stream on the map, we estimated that the trip would take an hour.

It took five. We had scarcely left the lip of Lake Itasca when a disjointed old stone bridge, perhaps dating back to lumbering days, blocked our way. We had to pull the canoe out, beat a passage

From Y-shaped Lake Itasca in northern Minnesota, the Mississippi sets out the wrong way, flowing north in the foreground, but soon makes a U-turn. Elk Lake, visible in the upper right, is one of several lakes draining into Itasca.

131

Every few dozen yards a fallen tree blocked our way and we would carry the canoe around it through almost impenetrable underbrush.

When we had begun to think of spending the night on a bed of leaves under a blanket of mosquitoes, the trees suddenly parted and there was the road bridge. The yellow car waited patiently and Mary a little less so. We flung the canoe on top of the car and drove to Lake Bemidji State Park where our twenty-one-foot trailer stood within a few yards of the north shore of Lake Bemidji. The river flows out of Lake Bemidji in a noble stream 200 feet wide, contrasting strongly with the ten-foot rivulet in the first reaches. It is now navigable for small craft. We need no longer carry the canoe —it will carry us. So begins a 400-mile canoe trip down one of the most delightful of rivers.

The Mississippi is secretive. It is almost unknown to many people who live within a few miles of it. Over some stretches the road hugs the shore, and magnificent views may be had of the river and its maze of islands. But for the most part the highway does not attempt to follow the river's meanderings. You may drive from the Canadian border to the Gulf, following the general route of the Mississippi, and scarcely be aware of its existence. If you are determined, you can reach it by small side roads, often unpaved. And, of course, it can be seen from the bridges.

But by far the best way to see the Mississippi is over the bow of your own boat. It is easy to imagine oneself a Joliet or a Marquette paddling down this undiscovered river. It flows today as it flowed then between unbroken walls of dark green conifers and snow-white birch. It slows in lilied swamps or speeds down narrow chutes between threatening boulders. It embraces charming islands and swirls rudely around rocky capes.

It is clear and pure for hundreds of miles before its confluence with the turbid Missouri, and when it pauses long enough to smooth the wrinkles from its forehead, its clean surface reflects the flight of kingfishers and herons and black terns. You may paddle for half a day without sight of a bridge or a house or a human. It is your river, for your boat alone. If after hours of solitude you see another boat, you are surprised and a little indignant.

There's a long carry at Grand Rapids. A dam has taken the place of the rapids that gave the town its name, and above the dam the river is surfaced with several acres of logs waiting to be ground into pulp and turned into paper in a local mill. This is one of the longest of the fourteen carries around dams on the way to Minneapolis.

through the prickly brush and carry the canoe around to the stream below the bridge.

We repeated this performance at four more bridges, all of them slumped too low to permit the canoe's passage. We were seldom in the canoe even when it was in the water. We were wading alongside, hauling or lifting the boat over pebbly shoals or rocky ledges. The shallows periodically gave way to deep holes, and we were soon soaked to the hips. Then the forest fell back on both sides, and the stream meandered through a marshy meadow a mile wide. We could stay in the boat now. The water was twelve inches deep, but there was no discernible current to help our paddling.

The river had no interest in the shortest distance between two points. It looped back and forth upon itself, tripling and quadrupling the distance to our objective. We longed for a straight course and a fast one. But when we got just that, we were far from satisfied. The river finally left the swamp, became straight and swift, and plunged down a chute several miles long between high banks supporting tall trees that met above to form a kind of tunnel.

Though the river was fast now, we could not be because the rapids were too shallow for navigation. We waded through the rocks, hoisting the canoe over the worst of them, stumbling into holes, feeling our way through the half-dark. Dusk had brought out the mosquitoes in millions. They eagerly lapped up the repellent we had spread on.

There navigation for large craft begins, and every dam is supplemented by a lock. From Minneapolis to the Gulf, one need never beach one's craft.

As we neared Brainerd, white rapids tumbled over unseen rocks, and we slid along with toboggan speed. The current was full of whirlpools that would sometimes twist the boat out of control for a moment but were never powerful enough to upend it and suck it down as the whirls in the lower river sometimes swallow logs.

Great blue herons and kingfishers sailed from one forest wall across to the other, and deer came down to the shore to drink. If deerflies are any indication of the presence of deer, there must be great herds in these woods. The deerflies sailed around and around our heads, and we were continually dropping our paddles to swat them. Our conversation was punctuated with impolite exclamations, the whang of dropped paddles and resounding slaps on tortured skin. It is hard to understand the regional distribution of insects. We had had no deerflies on other stretches of the river, only mosquitoes. Here there was not a single mosquito, but clouds of deerflies.

Then, suddenly, we rounded a bend into the wind—and there was not a single fly. But we had no sooner congratulated each other before we encountered the hardest job in all our canoe experience. It looked so easy. The current was strong and we expected it to carry us along with little or no effort on our part, but a violent headwind developed. Many travelers down the Mississippi have complained of the south wind. Generally it is only a breeze; this time it grew into a gale.

It was like trying to paddle through a stone wall. The opposition was so strong that if we stopped paddling for an instant the wind promptly blew us upstream against the current. The blasts all but whipped the paddles out of our hands. Many times we ran into sea-size waves, the result of upstream wind against downstream current. The river was a half mile wide in places—much too wide for comfort in that wind. An Army helicopter from nearby Camp Ripley returned time and again to see if we were still above water.

Whenever the wind battering our eyeballs would let us, we realized that the river was beautiful. Hundreds of islands lay between the low shore on the right and the high rugged bank on the left. But it was often difficult to pick the most direct channel through the islands. At one place there were five broad passages to confuse us. We ran into rapids repeatedly, and the rapids were full of ugly rocks.

The wind and waves were so noisy that, sitting only ten feet apart, we could not hear each other speak. The waves curled and broke over us, the surface was churned into whitecaps, and we seemed to be afloat on a sea of whipped cream. Finally we were ready to give up the struggle. But then what? A night on an island, the wind chilling us through our wet clothes? If we could just find a house, we could telephone. There was no house. Even the helicopter had deserted us.

It got worse when the river began to broaden into a lake at Little Falls. The lake was one roaring rush of water, the wind dead against us. But at last we spied a small pier. We pulled in behind it, walked half a mile back through the woods until we came upon a farmhouse. It was the first time we had fallen short of our objective, but we acknowledged defeat with the greatest pleasure.

The canoeist paddles through much of Minneapolis scarcely aware that the city exists. In the heart of Minnesota's greatest metropolitan area the river still struggles to maintain its privacy. It passes through a sylvan canyon closed in on both sides by wooded banks some hundred feet high. Soon an unimportant-looking little stream comes in from the right. This trivial trickle is one of the most loved waters in America. It is Minnehaha Creek, immortalized by Longfellow. We disembarked to see the bronze of Hiawatha about to bear his sweetheart across the stream just above the Falls of Minnehaha.

A little after the advent of the famous creek, we passed under old Fort Snelling, for more than thirty years the northernmost post of the U.S. Army. Here the Minnesota River quietly joins the Mississippi. As if this reinforcement gave the river the courage to face the world, the Mississippi now flows through the busiest part of St. Paul, fully exposed to view and affording docking facilities for large river craft. So far as commercial traffic is concerned, the Mississippi begins at the Twin Cities. There the Falls of St. Anthony block off the upper reaches.

We had now come to the river of big boats. The Mississippi from the Twins to the Gulf was once famous for its floating palaces, with great side wheels or stern wheels, with tall chimneys crowned with iron plumes, with murals and chandeliers and sumptuous cabins and good food and a deep whistle and gay music on the calliope.

There are a few of the old steamboats left. We boarded one, the *Avalon*, at a St. Paul dock for an excursion downriver. Aloft a steam calliope was playing "Cruising Down the River."

THE GLACIERS' GIFT TO IOWA

R. V. CASSILL

Across the northern counties of Iowa the roads lie straight as the boundary tapes on a green tennis court. The flat horizons are calibrated monotonously by farmyard elms and the little groves of trees that shade our evenly spaced small towns.

This is a genial, workaday countryside—not in any ordinary sense seductive to the tourist. A stranger might drive 200 miles across the state without spotting terrain that invites him to more than a casual roadside picnic. Yet if he chose the right roads, the same 200 miles would provide him a choice of natural pleasures and resorts worth a longer stop, for the glaciers that rubbed out Iowa's hills and valleys here left a scattering of lakes.

It is true that these lakes of ours, dwindling in size from 5700-acre Spirit Lake to nameless ponds and kettle holes, are merely the fringe of the lake region that spreads across Wisconsin and Minnesota. Our lakes show where the glaciers ran into Iowa conservatism and stopped. Maybe they are ours only by the grace of a political boundary, but when the weather settles warm in May, something in Iowans looks as far as Clear Lake or the Okoboji region without caring what goes on beyond them. We respond to a distinctly native mixture of the memory and desire that turn other people in *their* states toward *their* north and *their* blue water.

One of the chief pleasures of visiting the Iowa lakes is to find these waters reflecting images of the past and, if you can, to sense the qualities that have made them inordinately precious to Iowans. From the time the railroads closed in on them in the 1870s and 1880s, Clear Lake, Spirit Lake and West Okoboji have been Iowa's summer resorts. Before Iowa became a state, discriminating Indians used to pitch their wigwams on the lakeshores in hot weather.

For an insight into our possessive pride in these lakes, leave your car and walk a hundred yards into Cayler Prairie. The prairie is now a state monument a few miles from Okoboji water. It was not set aside as a natural rarity but rather to save a bit of the commonplace of another age from the plows that have changed the rest of the state. Within this preserve there is nothing but native grasses, some tall, some short. The tallest whiten at their tips, tracing lacy patterns, like frost on a windowpane. The shorter grasses suggest the underbrush of a miniature jungle. Even now, with farms at your back (toward which you can turn if you need reassurance), to stare up those wave-slanted prairie slopes is to have a direct, sensuous experience of vastness and an intimation of terror. On the prairie you need the lake over the hills as a soldier on a tedious sea journey needs an island.

In the days when Okoboji, Spirit and Clear lakes were becoming resorts, a lot of Iowa still looked like Cayler Prairie. Now it's all farms and towns. Good towns, but inland towns; inland towns par excellence. I think there may be some inarticulate frustration in everyone who lives this far inland, an unappeased racial memory of the water voyage that brought us to this continent. You can hear that memory grumbling if you park your car on the main street of a town like Humboldt on a shadowless afternoon in July.

It's hot there, first of all, and the obvious relief from such heat is a dip in cool water. But as my Iowa relatives would say, "If that's all you need, you can get in the tub and turn on the electric fan." The Iowan needs more than that. However busy the afternoon traffic may be in Humboldt, the wide, straight street, open to the sky, seems to sleep. In this midcontinental doze, there's a kid coming down the sidewalk with the heat striking through the soles of his sneakers. He stops at the window of a hardware store, blinks and stares at some gold, scarlet and steel-colored fishing lures on a display card. He reads the advertising as though it were an enchantment. Behind the window display, toward the back of the store, there are green and blue shadows like those the boy has seen when he opened his eyes underwater. He fingers the money in his pocket. His lips gape and close, gape and close, like the mouth of a resting bass. He wants one of those lures as no wide-awake fish will ever want it. He knows that Humboldt and the street behind him are all a dream. He will wake up when he gets to Clear Lake among his peers and puts that lure down where it belongs.

Rippling under summer skies, a sea of prairie grass slopes toward Bear Lake, near Iowa's northern boundary. Bordered by cattails and willow trees, the lakelet is to the west of 5700-acre Spirit Lake, in the Kettleson Hogsback Area.

AUTUMN ALONG THE MISSOURI

The bluffs along the Missouri River overlook some of the most picturesque landscapes in the middle United States. The wide vistas result from the river's ceaseless gnawing at its easily undercut sandy banks. In some places erosion has created a level valley bed fifteen miles across and 100 to 300 feet below the surrounding land. In other places, where the river runs beside sheer limestone bluffs, the valley is relatively narrow. The flat river bottoms between the bluffs include some of the finest farmland in Missouri; the soil is enriched by fertile silt carried by the river from as far away as the foothills of the Rockies. In the fall the flow of the river is reduced and sandbars emerge from its muddy, brown surface. In March, when melting snows and spring rains are cascading down the bluffs, the Missouri River may increase its volume by fifty times and inundate its broad valley floor.

A Missouri bluff thirty miles west of St. Louis overlooks a section of railroad and a bend in the Missouri River. A combination of soil and climatic conditions along the bluffs gives these oaks, maples and hickories some of the brightest autumn foliage in the state. Each fall hikers enjoy the colors by taking to trails first blazed by Daniel Boone, who came to Missouri from Kentucky in 1799.

UNPREDICTABLE OKLAHOMA

ANGIE DEBO

When it was proposed that several pieces of unconnected territory be put together to form the state of Oklahoma, someone noticed that the projected commonwealth was shaped like a butcher's cleaver. The story is that members of the Constitutional Convention were determined to adopt that handy utensil as the state seal, and it required shrewd maneuvering to circumvent them. The figure is graphic if not poetical; the long, narrow strip on the northwest now known as the Panhandle is the helve of the implement, and the Red River boundary forms its hacked and dented edge.

Outsiders seem to think every one of the state's 69,919 square miles is exactly like all the others: as Kyle Crichton wrote, "a large flat piece of ground covered with oil wells, wheat fields and a crop of long, rangy individuals." But it probably has more kinds of country, more kinds of weather and more kinds of flora and fauna than any other area of similar size in the United States.

Geologists have traced these differences to a time remote in the earth's history. Hundreds of millions of years ago the sea advanced over much of the region, and mile-deep layers of rocks were deposited. During the ensuing period most of Oklahoma stood near sea level, thus forming great swamps in which plants flourished; but the sea flooded it from time to time, putting down layers of mud and sand and covering the vegetation, which was eventually converted into coal. Great earthquakes folded all these rocks into corrugations—if one can imagine an elongated layer cake crumpled into washboard folds—or even broke them and shoved them over each other. The tops of these folds have long been worn off, but remnants of the more resistant rocks form Oklahoma's four mountain uplifts: the Ozarks of the northeast, the

An early spring landscape near Jones in central Oklahoma is brightened by the magenta blossoms of a redbud, the state tree. To the left, an American elm spreads its shade over a country road lined with dried stalks of Johnson grass.

Ouachitas of the southeast, the Arbuckles of the south central and the Wichitas of the southwest.

Later the sea covered only the western part of Oklahoma, depositing red sands and shales. These Red Beds give the characteristic color to the western half of the state. This about finished the job except for a much later invasion of the sea from the south and the deposit of rocks along the southern margin, the work of wind and streams, and a lava flow that came over the western border of the Panhandle to form the Black Mesa. The rest of the Panhandle is deeply covered with rock debris washed down from the Rocky Mountains.

The whole surface of Oklahoma slopes from northwest to southeast. Many long rivers flow in parallel lines southeast across the state. Perhaps one should not say "flow" of these twisting, shallow sheets of water moving lazily over wide beds of sand. In the western half each of these streams is bordered along the northeast by a strip of sand two to eighteen miles wide, blown up out of the river by the south wind. Sand can still be seen rising from the dry bed on any windy day.

Sometimes these rivers are filled with water, which sweeps down in a swirling torrent bearing soil and uprooted trees, breaking over the low banks, destroying farms and tearing out bridges. In earlier days pioneers trying to cross the treacherous fords were drowned in these sudden rises or engulfed in quicksand.

But it would not be like Oklahoma to have only one kind of river. From the Ozarks and the Ouachitas come clear streams rippling over rocky beds. There are no more agreeable combinations

of shade and waterfall and mossy bank than one finds along the Illinois, the Sallisaw, the Poteau, the Kiamichi or the Mountain Fork.

The rainfall also varies, from a near-arid average annual precipitation of less than seventeen inches in the western Panhandle to fifty-one inches, which is above the national average, in the southeast.

The Oklahoma climate is of spangled sunshine —with variations. Spring comes early with a flash of mockingbirds' wings, moving powerfully across the land like an army with banners. Summer is dry and scorching with cool breezes at night (about six weeks of that). Autumn is golden and perfect; it begins the middle of August or the first of September and lasts till after Christmas. Properly speaking, there is no winter; the period is filled with weather left over from the other seasons— spring days alternating with autumn days, an occasional summer day, and once in a great while a howling blizzard. But all the seasons are likely to be jumbled: snow in May, hot winds in March, spring showers in November, with hailstorms or even tornadoes thrown in for good measure. Only sultry days are practically unknown; the wind takes care of that.

Of course there is a reason for this unpredictable weather. In United States weather maps showing the generalized path of storms, Oklahoma is a little white island surrounded by sweeping black lines—a fortunate isle set in a tempestuous sea. But when a storm sweeps across the border, it strikes hard.

At such times the thermometer may drop in

140

twelve hours from 80° F. to below freezing; and most of the drop comes in the first hour or two after the wind swings to the north. I remember very well a change of that kind that occurred, I believe, about the middle of April in 1938. It was the noon hour of a perfect spring day, and I was sitting under a tree enjoying it all. I happened to be facing the north when I felt—I could almost swear I saw—the wind veer sharply, and an icy blast swept across the bright landscape. By the middle of the afternoon the snow was whirling, and by night the railroads and the highways were blocked with drifts. Hundreds of schoolchildren from three states were at Enid to march in the spring band festival. The wires were down, so frantic parents could not contact their thinly clad offspring. Enid took them into its homes until the roads were opened. Of course the drifts soon melted, but the trees had to put out a second crop of leaves and spring had to begin again.

With all kinds of soil and all kinds of weather, Oklahoma should, and does, grow many kinds of plants. Botanists say that only about 5 percent of our species are found in all parts of the state; in other words, nineteen out of twenty reach the limit of their range here. And in unspoiled portions of this still-new land the abundance as well as the variety of wild flowers is astonishing. Sheets of color blot out the green of the prairie; banks of color glow through the timber. Flowers bloom every month of the year.

The mountainous eastern end of the state is heavily forested. In the northeast are hardwood—oak, elm, hickory, maple—and some pine (southern yellow pine); south of the Arkansas River are hardwood and much pine; and in the extreme southeast along the sparkling streams grow the tulip tree and the cypress. The largest tree in Oklahoma is an ancient cypress near Eagletown; it measures fifty-six feet in circumference and is ninety feet high. Here in the spring is the breathtaking beauty of the flowering dogwood; in the winter, the waxy green leaves and bright red berries of the holly.

Crossing the state from north to south through the rugged sandstone hills and extending into the eroded margin of the Red Beds lies the belt of tangled blackjacks and post oaks known, and dreaded, by early travelers as the Cross Timbers. Fingers of the same blackjack–post oak jungle extend northwest on the hills that flank the rivers.

As one follows the streams west and the other timber falls away, the cottonwood becomes increasingly conspicuous. It is poor for fuel and worse for lumber, but how could dwellers in a prairie land live without the beauty of its craggy white branches and its polished, twinkling leaves? Also extending far west are the wild plum—in the spring a white drift of bloom, in the summer good for marmalade—and the redbud, the official state tree, most popular of all Oklahoma plants.

As the plains grade west into a drier climate and a ragged land of gypsum hills, the grass becomes bunchy and the blackjack thickets on the strips of river-blown sand give place to shinnery oak and sagebrush. Increasingly common are the yucca, which is also known as soapweed or bear grass, with its sharp, spearlike leaves and its tall stems of fragrant, waxy flowers, and the cactus—especially the prickly-pear, or hog-ear, cactus—with a fleshy, thorny body and fragile blooms.

In the Panhandle, sagebrush and clumps of grass still grow on the sand hills bordering the streams, but the flat top of the plains is indeed the "short-grass country." Flowers bloom here, too, mostly yellow flowers. On the rugged, lava-capped Black Mesa grow piñon trees strayed from New Mexico and a few western yellow pine. Thus Oklahoma flora runs the gamut from the great cypress of warm, low southeastern valley to the brave piñon of windswept height.

Zoologists say that the range in species of native Oklahoma animals is probably greater than that of any equal area in the United States. Denizens of the timbered East were at home in the Ozarks and the Ouachitas; Rocky Mountain species strayed to the western sections; Great Plains animals found the prairies their natural habitat.

For birds Oklahoma is a meeting place of North and South, East and West, plain and timber. There are more than 250 varieties, 200 of which stay the year round. Geese and ducks fly over, flocks of gulls from the Gulf of Mexico visit the state, and dense clouds of blackbirds wheel and twist and settle on feed lot and pasture. Meadowlarks and cardinals stay all winter, filling the air with their clear notes on every sunny day. Robins also remain the year round.

Of the migratory birds, orioles, hummingbirds, mockingbirds, catbirds, kingbirds and the scissor-tailed flycatcher are among the most common. The mockingbird is the universal favorite. All day and all night he pours out his joy (one wonders when he eats), his slender body atilt on treetop or house roof or floating up into the air borne by the surge of his song. Once in a while a belated one stays all winter, when he may be heard singing rather sadly on some crisp night.

HIGHROAD UNDER THE BIG SKY

THAYNE SMITH
AND
CLELLAND COLE

It was April 1965. A group of prominent Kansans were joined by national figures in traveling a scenic and historic route that wound and twisted across the width of Kansas. Near El Dorado they stopped on a high plateau overlooking miles of lush, tall prairie grass, in the heart of the famous Flint Hills. One in the group remarked, as his eyes scanned scenic beauty for many miles to the north, that it was "a superb experience with America's last great belt of true prairie."

Today, through the action of the state and the painstaking work of a few promotion-minded individuals, the route is marked for all to see. It is called the Prairie Parkway.

The Parkway actually is composed of 250-plus miles of federal, state and county all-weather roads, extending from the historic cattle city of Elgin, on the Oklahoma border, to the famous Pony Express Station at Hanover, near the Nebraska border. In 1967 the Kansas legislature passed a bill adopting the route and directing the State Highway Commission to mark it.

The purpose of the Parkway is simple. The proposal for its establishment, as first submitted to the state by former governor John Anderson, sought it as "an integral part of the national park system, as a fitting and nationally significant presentation of the last major vestiges of the True or Tall Prairie that once existed in a wide region of the Midwestern United States."

To date the Parkway is only a state project, but federal and national park system approval is pending in Congress.

Prime mover of the Parkway since its inception has been Bill Colvin, editor of the Manhattan *Mercury* at Manhattan, Kansas. He started in

1964 to promote the Prairie Parkway, and not only enlisted the help of many Kansas officials and boosters but called on cities along the proposed route. Response was immediate and gratifying. In a matter of weeks the National Park Service had experts study the proposed routing and made recommendations for slight changes. The aid of other states was also sought in a plan to make the Prairie Parkway a four-state route, extending eventually from northern Oklahoma through Kansas, Nebraska and a part of South Dakota.

If federal designation eventually comes, Colvin has said, the Park Service would participate in the establishment and construction of a number of turnout and overlook areas along the Parkway route.

In the meantime no one really need wait to see just what the ultimate Parkway will include. The Kansas portion of the route—although it might

A windmill pumps water for livestock near El Dorado, Kansas. Although they have been largely replaced by electric pumps, the steel windmills still symbolize the American Great Plains much as Dutch windmills typify Holland.

later be changed a little here and there—is clearly marked for everyone to follow.

In many areas the route skirts through virgin tall prairie-grass areas, where miles upon miles of Flint Hills are lush green in summer and harvest brown through winter months. Cattle graze in contentment on many areas adjoining the Parkway route, but otherwise no signs of civilization mar the visitor's view.

The Parkway boasts other attractions, too. Almost every city along the route is a history book in itself. The Pony Express Station at Hanover, the last of the stations on the pioneer mail route, is now an excellent Kansas museum. Near Blue Rapids and Marysville is Alcove Springs, a landmark and rest spot on the Oregon Trail, one of the first wagon-train routes to the Pacific coast.

At Randolph, on K-16 Highway, the Parkway crosses the state's longest bridge, spanning the upper end of Tuttle Creek Reservoir, which offers excellent outdoor recreation of every description.

Manhattan is the home of Kansas State University, the first land-grant school in the nation. A little farther south, Council Grove—already a

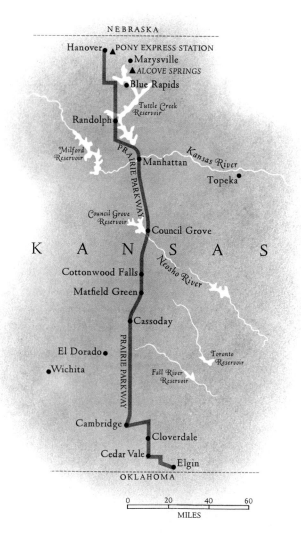

national historic landmark—is one of the state's most prominent historical cities. It was the birthplace of the Santa Fe Trail, boasts the famous Post Office Oak, Kaw Methodist Mission, the Last Chance Store and the Custer Elm. Another fine lake, Council Grove Reservoir on the Neosho River, offers excellent camping, fishing, hunting, swimming and other outdoor recreational opportunities. Farther along the route, the oldest Kansas courthouse still in use is located at Cottonwood Falls. Matfield Green, in the heart of the best-known grazing lands in the world, is the center of the largest segment of remaining bluestem prairie.

Much of American history is laid in this prairie country, and every American should see for himself the infinite sky and the nearly infinite horizons of Kansas.

NEBRASKA'S GREEN SEA OF DUNES

EDWIN WAY TEALE

I have learned that whatever has life has individuality. No two ants, no two sparrows, no two cows, no two children are ever identical. It is only our lack of perception that leads us to conclude that all bees in a swarm, all fish in a school, all sheep in a flock are just alike. And so it is with the years and the days and the seasons. No two are ever the same. The summer season my wife and I traveled in Nebraska had been characterized by more than average rainfall. Everywhere we went we saw the innumerable consequences written in green.

From my boyhood in the dune country of northern Indiana, I expected to find the sandhill region of Nebraska an area of bare-topped mounds and drifting sand. Instead, as we wandered east to Valentine and south to Thedford and west to Scottsbluff, we traversed a sea of green hills that rolled away to the horizon. All the high knolls of sand had been clothed and stabilized by a surface layer of grass. The dunes were green dunes. And in the hollows between spread the luxuriant "hay meadows" that had attracted the first settlers.

For 20,000 square miles, for more than 15 million acres, for an area sufficient to absorb the states of Massachusetts, Connecticut, Delaware and New Jersey, the largest area of dunes on the North American continent extended around us. Mainly in the north-central part of the state, it occupies over one fourth of the area of Nebraska. It is a land of hay and cattle. In pioneer times hay was used to pave temporary roads across stretches of open sand. It was also twisted into tight rolls and burned in the stoves of homesteaders. Grass was then, as it is today, the wealth of the region. Here the sign we had seen so often along the way, "Help Prevent Forest Fires," became transformed into "Help Prevent Grass Fires." The green dunes represent the richest beef-producing region of Nebraska. They support pure-breds, Angus and Herefords, black cattle grazing across one range, red-and-white cattle across another.

But always just below the wealth of the grass lies the sand. During years of drought, every break in the sod is probed by the wind, expanded by the gales, often turned into blowouts of extensive proportions. To dwellers in the area, dunes scarred by such blowouts are "whitecaps"; the storm winds that produce them are "howlers." Even in that year of exceptional moisture, when an unusual fifteen inches of rain had already fallen in the region, we saw numerous evidences of the loose, fine-grained material, the substance of the hills.

Where boundary fences climbed steeply up a slope, they were bordered by lines of raw, pale yellow sand. There the hooves of the cattle, walking in single file, had broken through the grass. Around the wooden windmills where the rangeland animals came to drink, the ground was trampled and the sand lay bare. These windmills were never high and towering, although their blades were from 6 to 12 feet in diameter. Once we passed a row of curious two-toned telephone poles running across an open field. Each pole was weathered almost black except for a striking band of satiny yellow that encircled it a few feet above the ground—the product of constant rubbing by the cattle. Around the base of each pole there ran a ring, a circular path of open sand.

All through these green dunes, houses stood remote and far apart. Side roads were few. We were in a wild, lonely, windy land with a special beauty of its own. After the fire of the sun had burned low at the end of the first day, we wandered for nearly a hundred miles through the "lake country" south of Valentine. Much of this area, embracing the greatest concentration of small bodies of water found among the dunes, lies within the boundaries of the Valentine National Wildlife Refuge.

Already, pintail and blue-winged teal, the earliest migrants, floated in rafts on the larger ponds. Wilson's phalaropes swam in clusters, spinning like water beetles. We counted more than 500 of these robin-size shorebirds on two small ponds. Turning about in almost exactly the same spot, a phalarope was once seen making 247 revolutions without stopping. The feeding activity of these birds is of considerable benefit to man. Their diet at this time of year consists largely of mosquito larvae.

The solitary charm of the dune country is best appreciated in the evening and in the early morning. It was being accentuated, when we started out one morning, by the subtle shadings of the dawn light. At the time we awoke, I remember, neither of us had the slightest idea what day of the week it was. And what did it matter? For that glorious season we were living by sun time, by moon time. We had no other appointments than those with nature.

Blooms of the night, yellow primrose and white evening star, were still open in the dawn. All across one wide stretch where Queen Anne's lace bloomed, red-and-white Herefords fed as though in low-lying mist. In the rich meadows between the dunes, haying was over and new stacks rose close together like the tents of an encamping army. The sun rose; through rents in the broken eastern sky slanting rays descended.

It was in such a spotlight that we saw crossing the road before us a home-going rattlesnake. We slowed down. It coiled on the highway. I pulled up beside it. It gave no ground. We looked almost directly down on it from a distance of hardly more than a yard. Its head was lifted, weaving from side to side. Its rattles blurred and shrilled, its coils were in constant motion, its shifting body seemed at once fluid and as taut as a tempered steel spring. Never before had I seen so lively a rattlesnake.

North of the Dismal River, at Thedford, we turned west to follow the road of the "potash towns" through the heart of the sandhills. In the days of the First World War, potash for gunpowder was obtained from the dry lake beds of the surrounding dunes. Factories hastily took shape. Communities along the way became boomtowns in a period of short-lived prosperity.

Along most of the roads we traveled, small birds, particularly sparrows, would dash wildly across before us. At the last moment, as though on a suicidal impulse, they would plunge directly down into the path of the onrushing machine.

Why did they descend into a zone of greater peril when they could have zoomed upward and let the speeding car shoot harmlessly past below?

To do that, we decided, would have been a reversal of the age-old instincts of the bird—as much a reversal as for us to open our eyes wide instead of automatically blinking them shut when a dust cloud sweeps around us.

When it is hard pressed, a bird instinctively dives to increase its speed, letting gravity add to its momentum. In darting across the road with a car bearing down on it, it feels the need to cover the distance as soon as possible. It does what instinct demands to shorten the time. It pitches downward. Again and again I saw small birds disappear in front of the car and looked for their bodies in the rearview mirror, but their burst of speed had really carried them safely across. To fly upward and let the cars go by below would be safer still. But in the life of the bird, instincts are old and automobiles are new.

As I think back over our memories of the heart of the sand hills, two—one concerning birds, one concerning plants—return with special vividness. We had come to a little saddle at the top of a rise on a particularly lonely stretch of the road when we discovered six sharp-tailed grouse ahead of us. A seventh, apparently a young bird, had been killed by a passing car. Its six companions seemed bewildered by the tragedy. They wandered about the crushed body or stood irresolute in the low vegetation of the roadside. None flew away when we came to a stop beside them. Even under normal conditions these birds are surprisingly tame during the summertime. To keep more of the little family group from being hit by speeding cars, I tossed the body of the dead bird up the embankment off the highway. Even then the grouse retreated only slightly. They remained nearby as though bewitched, chained to the spot, unable to leave. The huddled flock stood still in full view when we drove away.

The second recollection is associated with a wide valley among the sand hills east of Hyannis. The green wall of a ridge rose on our right as we crossed the flatland. For nearly a mile along its lower flank ran a broad, irregular band of brilliant yellow. We stopped and studied the distant stripe through our field glasses. Here, as we had never

Northern Nebraska's grassy sand hills stretch for miles in this early morning view from 1000 feet up, near Crescent Lake National Wildlife Refuge. Small lakes and dunes up to 300 feet high cover a 24,000-square-mile area.

→

had it before, extending acre after acre, was that strange leafless plant, the naked dodder.

Love vine, pull-down, strangleweed, devil's-hair, hairweed, clover silk, this parasite of many names is a relative of the morning glory. According to a late monograph, there are about 170 species of dodder. Nearly forty that are injurious to agriculture grow in the United States. In many places along the way we saw the tangled masses of the threadlike stems splotching fields of clover with their color or overrunning weeds beside the road. Here among the green Nebraska dunes the luxuriant growth of the dodder reflected the greater-than-usual rainfall of the season. This annual plant thrives best during wet years.

Wherever it grows, its story is the same. From the sprouting seed, a slender thread pushes above the ground, drawing itself out to a length of from two to four inches. And as it elongates, it circles, groping blindly for a suitable host. If it fails to find one it shrivels and dies. If it succeeds it coils itself around the stem. Small wartlike suckers appear on the surface of the thread, penetrate the stem of the host and become fused with it just as a grafted twig becomes part of a tree. Through these the dodder absorbs food material from its host. Because it does not have to manufacture its own food, it can dispense with roots as well as leaves. As soon as the parasite is well attached, the vine below the first coil dies. The plant has now lost all contact with the ground. Henceforth, by draining away fluid from its victims, it will thrive and grow, spread its tendrils from plant to plant, often end by forming tangled mats of threadlike yellow or orange-yellow stems many feet across.

During those midsummer days the flowers of the dodder—minute and massed together, white or cream or pink, sometimes yellow—were preparing the way for the little pods that would hold from two to four seeds apiece. As many as 3000 seeds come from a single dodder vine. Their exteriors are dull and slightly roughened. Commercial dealers separate dodder from red-clover seeds by a treatment of iron powder, which adheres to the rough surface of the dodder seeds and enables magnets to pull them out.

These minute seeds, often overlooked, are distributed by irrigation water, in baled hay, among flax and alfalfa seed. They can pass uninjured through the digestive systems of animals. And they retain their ability to sprout for years. Even a severed fragment of a dodder vine retains for several days its power to coil and grow and develop new suckers.

An old-time superstition in the South had its origin in this ability of the parasite. Also the local name, love vine, apparently was similarly based. By swinging a fragment of love vine three times around the head and throwing it to the rear, the superstitious person sought to discover if a sweetheart was faithful. If, three days later, the dodder was found attached to some plant and growing—as was almost invariably the case—all was well.

Throughout the dunes of Nebraska, on our last day there, we encountered that phenomenon of summer on the western plains, the passing showers of the one-cloud rains. Miles away we would see a cloud drifting toward us, trailing below it a smoke gray veil of falling rain. It would pass overhead. Large drops would drum on the roof of the car. For half a mile or more we would ride on spattered or steaming pavements. Then sunshine would be all around us again and the narrow swath of the rain would sweep away across the countryside. At times we would see as many as half a dozen widely spaced clouds come riding over the hills from the skyline, each with a pendent rain veil beneath it.

Once, far to the south, where a heavy downpour descended in a gray column beneath a cloud, we glimpsed a thin line of lightning run for a split second, without a sound, down the center of the falling rain. Always the showers were of short duration. Always blue and sunny skies lay between the clouds, just ahead.

Clouds for a hundred miles around—angry, violent clouds, wind-torn and flushed in the last light of the sunset—marked the sky on the evening we came to the summit of Scotts Bluff. This sandstone eminence, beyond the dunes near the western edge of Nebraska—famed in the annals of the Oregon Trail—rises a sheer 750 feet above the valley of the Platte. In the early hours of that evening, lightning glared all around the horizon. One-cloud storms were rushing through the sky, across the wide reaches of the plains. Beyond the Wyoming line, twenty miles away, a dark tower, the black column of a falling deluge, reared against the hearth-glow of the west. Storm on storm advanced toward us. Yet before we left almost all had spent themselves, and the serpentine of the Platte River, winding away off to the east, glistened faintly with the light of reflected stars.

White-faced Hereford cattle graze below Chimney Rock near the North Platte River in western Nebraska. The 500-foot-high landmark signaled the end of monotonous plains travel for nineteenth-century pioneers on the Oregon Trail.

THE BLACK HILLS

BADGER CLARK

To us, the inhabitants, the Black Hills of South Dakota are a priceless and everlasting possession. Whether one owns a house and lot, a little valley ranch, a crazy quilt of mining claims sprawling over a mountain or not an inch of their pine-shaded surface, the Hills belong to us and we belong to them.

An elliptical island of mountains rising out of the rolling sea of the northern Great Plains, the range occupies southwestern South Dakota and projects into eastern Wyoming. Near at hand the Hills are a changeless dark green; at a distance of thirty miles they are black; and at fifty they turn blue. Whatever their color phase, however, the Hills are always proud, looking down on the plains with a calm superciliousness which has its basis in the fact that they are among the world's older mountain ranges. They are not lost in some great system, like the ranges of the Appalachians or the Rockies, but are an exclusive group, standing so close to one another that their pines can whisper across the gulches, and drawing their green skirts primly about their toes at the outer edge of the crowd.

Down in the southern Hills, at the former Fossil Cycad National Monument, is a different rock, rock that was once alive. The now-fossilized cycads, rare enough to be placed under the protection of the government, were an ancestral tree of palmy or ferny appearance which may have been the many-times-great-grandfather of the ponderosa pine. They wagged their green-plumed heads in the wind when this region was tropical, quite some time ago, and they are now turned to stone.

The Hills are so rich in charms that they have hidden part of them underground, deep down below daylight. There are about a dozen known natural caves and probably twenty more unknown. Patient Mother Nature through the ages has used her spare time in lining them all with calcite crystals, generally in the forms known as dogtooth and boxwork, and in many dainty colors.

It is characteristic of Nature's extravagance that she should place such works of art in form and color where they would blush unseen for hundreds of centuries, but they have come to light now—or, rather, light has come to them—and they are annually admired by thousands.

The Black Hills, as I said, are very old mountains. More youthful ranges, such as the Alps and the Himalayas, show wide expanses of nudity, in the fashion of young people on the beach; but the Hills, in their green and vigorous old age, have become conservative and are clothed from neck to ankle—in ponderosa pine. Ponderosas, perhaps catching the habit from some of the scalawags of the early days, have had several aliases—rock pine, bull pine, western yellow pine—but ponderosa is their right name, according to the scientific folk who should know. And they make a beautiful garment. Whether they form the straight red pillars of a forest with centuries of maturity behind it or thickets of thirty-year-old saplings, whether they are climbing up a mountainside or marching down one, the ponderosas never lack charm. Individualists all, they vary much in form, and the eccentrics among them seem to pick out the most impossibly rocky spots for their homes and to grow there triumphantly, while the human onlooker wonders what they have for nourishment, save air. They go clear up to the high, broken horizons and hobnob with the blue sky, and in the night they seem companions of the stars.

The Black Hills pines are no match for the California giants in size and age, but they do not lack dignity. The Hills were one of the first forest reserves, set aside under President McKinley. The U.S. Forest Service has served them well, and by the control of fires and the scientific "harvesting" of mature timber it has preserved the 5000 square miles of the Black Hills National Forest so that it is almost as fresh as when the first pre-Columbian Indian followed a fleeing deer into the woods.

The streams of the Hills are all creeks. In the grandiloquent early days, one or two were named rivers, but you can disregard that. Charming creeks they are, of the mountain variety, gleaming over rocky shallows, glooming in trout holes, strolling around the edges of green meadows or dancing along through the shade of spruce and birch and quaking aspen, and singing all the way. With

Great stone spires, aptly named the Needles, thrust skyward above the forested slopes of South Dakota's Black Hills. Each spire is a bundle of upright granite columns divided by joints of softer rock that is slowly crumbling.

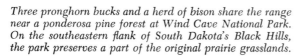

Three pronghorn bucks and a herd of bison share the range near a ponderosa pine forest at Wind Cave National Park. On the southeastern flank of South Dakota's Black Hills, the park preserves a part of the original prairie grasslands.

the creeks we have a galaxy of little lakes: blue mirrors reflecting the piny mountains that surround them, and only seldom ruffled into lilliputian breakers. Black Hillers are mostly ardent fishermen, but I suspect they take out a license as much to have an excuse for sauntering along the creeks as to catch trout, for the sportsman never raises his eyes from his fly without finding some pleasant bit of landscape to contemplate. If he goes alone and in silence, as a good trout fisherman should, he is likely anywhere to start a buck, which will go scampering away through the woods, holding its tender summer antlers back over its withers to avoid striking them on overhanging branches.

In Custer State Park and Wind Cave National Park one may see elk and buffalo by the hundreds, as the old-timers saw them long ago. The state park, one of the largest of its kind, aims to preserve its territory as nearly in its primitive beauty as is possible. No hunting is allowed there. The little

mountain meadows ("parks" in the western vernacular) are untouched by the mowing machine, and their waving bluegrass, jeweled with flowers, is not disturbed except as the buffalo trail up from their foothill pastures in the fall to graze on it as a sort of Thanksgiving feast and a change from their usual prairie grasses. The roads, hotels and tourist camps occupy only a tiny fraction of the park. The rest of the 120,000 acres literally belongs to the animals, the trees and the grass. They own it, even as the people own the towns.

But why bother about details? The Hills are—well, they're the Hills, that's all. A thousand efforts have been made to describe and name them. Pioneer writers spoke of their "gloomy fastnesses," but that was in a day when a hostile Indian or a road agent might be encountered in any clump of brush. Then they were called "the richest hundred miles square on earth," which is still used. Then people who loved them and thought their name was not cheerful enough proposed to call

them the Purple Mountains. And of late the local newspapers have bestowed upon them the nickname of the Magic Mountains. Yet there is something artificial about all these, and perhaps the old "natural" names you find among them have a truer ring—names like Poor Man Gulch and Lame Johnny Creek and Shirttail Canyon.

One evening fifty years ago three clergymen started out afoot to attend a religious gathering in a nearby mining camp, but in the dusk they took the wrong fork of the trail. Next day the local paper, with a commendable effort to keep a straight face, announced that the reverend gentlemen had failed to reach their meeting because they got lost in Go to Hell Gulch.

The Hills are still at least two thirds wild and, as in any mountain country, are likely to remain so. In spite of the towns and the tourist camps and the sawmills and the mines and the ranches, there are many rugged, forested square miles that don't see a human being from one year's end to another.

Which, in this trampled, tamed, tired old earth, is as it should be. But the Hills have not the stern, austere, almost threatening aspect of the greater ranges. They are friendly little mountains, and to the traveler across the plains, weary of topping one level, unbroken skyline after another, they rise up and say, "Come on in out of the wind and rest yourself."

There are things here to please people of many tastes, from the artist to the scientist. The only one who is at a loss is the person with a passion for the many-windowed canyon walls of a great city. After my more than fifty years among the Hills, half of that time living intimately with them in a situation where I see more hilltops in a week than I do people, I am beginning to know them a little. They have given me many of the ingredients that go to make life engaging and satisfying, but I am most grateful to them for the gift of three things that today's world seems to seek without finding— freedom and quiet and peace.

153

THE BADLANDS OF NORTH DAKOTA

North Dakota's Badlands occupy a loosely defined area of several hundred square miles near the Montana border. They were whittled out of grassy plains by the Little Missouri River and its tributaries. Hills and buttes striped by multicolored rock strata fill the area, threaded with a maze of gullies and gorges. The name comes from Canadian fur trappers who spoke of "bad lands to travel across." Such curiosities as burning coal mines and petrified forests are interspersed with cattle ranches. Some of the area's most spectacular scenery has been incorporated into the north and south units of Theodore Roosevelt National Memorial Park. As a young man Roosevelt ranched for several years in North Dakota and gained a keen awareness of the need for conservation.

In Theodore Roosevelt National Memorial Park's North Unit, the Little Missouri River, slicing eastward to join the Missouri, has exposed gray and buff clays alternating with bands of black coal.

Part IV

ROCKY MOUNTAIN WILDERNESS

Colorado   Wyoming
Montana   Idaho

THE ROCKIES AND THE GREAT DIVIDE

DAVID LAVENDER

Many people assume that the Rocky Mountains and the Continental Divide are synonymous terms for a single long chain of hills. The misconception arises, I suppose, from the precise line of dots with which the divide is indicated on most maps and which makes it seem as dominant and as singular as the ridge of a house.

It is singular, to be sure—a great splitter of waters and the only natural pathway in the United States by which a person can walk, in theory at least, from Canada to Mexico without wetting his feet in some stream or another. It is not isolated, however, and it is not always dominant. Though its ultimate course is, roughly, from north to south, it wanders along as erratically as a ribbon dropped by a careless girl. In southern Wyoming it sinks so limply into a gray sage desert that it is perceptible only to sophisticated instruments. In New Mexico it abdicates its sway entirely; its streams become meager, its forests scraggly, its ridges devoid of majesty.

The shifting course of the divide and the variety of its satellites have created a chaotic geography and pockets of climate at variance with the normal rules of thumb.

From Montana south into New Mexico there is a series of broad flats that are variously called parks, basins and holes. In their own way they are as dramatic as the mountain peaks. Novelist D. H. Lawrence flatly declared that the Taos Valley in New Mexico is backed by the most beautiful skyline he had seen anywhere in the world—not nation, world.

Part of the charm that led Lawrence to such hyperbole arises from the feeling of release that

Leafless western willows bordering a southern Colorado pasture catch the glow of a winter sunset. In the background Blanca Peak, the tallest mountain in the Sangre de Cristos, rises 14,317 feet at the center of a towering trio.

the openings bring to the viewer. Much of the mountain scenery is austere, violent, constricting. Then suddenly the land spreads out. There are not even many trees. Streams coil quietly through meadows rather than dash headlong among boulders. Cattle and sheep graze as pastorally as they do in Iowa. There is no feeling of Iowa, however. Always on the horizon loom the snow-streaked peaks of another range.

Because of the mountains that border them on the west, the larger parks and valleys are not as moist as one might expect from their elevation. They lie in rain shadows. When warm air drifting east across the desert strikes the western ranges of the Rockies, it lifts and cools. Water vapor condenses into clouds—on summer afternoons one can literally watch the billowing cumuli take shape out of nothing—and moisture falls. Then, the crossing completed, the air settles into the basins and valleys, warms again, and seldom will yield more water until meeting another uplift.

Thus the between-range valleys and parks of the Rockies are arid, but most are either so high that evaporation is slow or so narrowed by rain-breeding ranges on their eastern sides that true desert conditions do not appear. In low, wide openings real parching develops—in Wyoming's Bighorn Basin, where Buffalo Bill Cody spent his fortune trying to develop irrigation; along the eastern skirts of Colorado's San Luis Valley, where Sahara-like dunes of fine white sand have been apotheosized as a national monument.

In a similar manner temperatures also escape the dominance of elevation. Generally speaking, the plains east of the mountains are colder than the high country. When the first of the major Rocky Mountain ski resorts, Sun Valley, Idaho, was advertising its carefully coined name, it attracted a good deal of surprised attention in the East by flooding publicity channels with pictures of tanned male skiers stripped to the waist amid the snowbanks. Miners, of course, had learned long before that it is possible to be more comfortable in sheltered basins at timberline or above than in valleys that lie three quarters of a mile lower and look kinder but are not.

A wry joke in the upper Green River Valley of Wyoming says that the snow there never melts; it just blows around until it wears out. And yet no

Douglas fir and aspen dot the slopes of 14,150-foot Mount Sneffels in the San Juan Mountains near the Great Divide. Some 5000 feet below the peak, cattle graze placidly on the pastures of a ranch in the San Miguel River canyon.

cold snap lasts unendurably. Warm, dry winds—chinooks—roll over the mountaintops, lift temperatures and suck up the snow.

A myth has grown up that the high country influences the basic nature of the people who dwell in it—men to match the mountains, so to speak. The notion has certain superficial points to recommend it. Altitude, dryness and long successions of sunny days do produce an invigorating climate. Tremendous vistas, ever changing under each day's varying slant of light, do fascinate even those who are used to the scene. A stroll beside a Montana lake or a vigorous climb to the top of Grand Teton can be cleansing to the spirit.

And yet, for those who would write about the Rockies in terms of the human spirit, their sense of remoteness from petty human problems is their ultimate deception—as if the height of a peak or the depth of a canyon somehow bears relevance either to human grace or to human cussedness. No. Mountain conditions may change patterns of living but not the natures of the men who produce the patterns.

161

GREAT SAND DUNES
NATIONAL MONUMENT

Wind and sand have combined to create huge mounds hundreds of feet high at the
Great Sand Dunes National Monument in Colorado. Tons of sand, blown from the arid
San Luis Valley by southwesterly winds, are stopped in their eastward flight by the Sangre
de Cristo Mountains. The winds drop their burden on the growing dunes, which
are constantly changing their shape and position.

The Great Sand Dunes are the tallest in the United States; some may top 700 feet. The twenty-five-square-mile dune area is mostly devoid of plant life, but the dunes may bury a growing forest only to reveal its lifeless trunks when the sand moves on. Usually the dunes creep about three feet a week, but strong winds may whip them seven feet a day. The tall cottonwoods standing here between rabbit brush and junipers, at the left, and willow brush may become victims of the smothering sands.

ROOFTOP OF AMERICA

DONALD AND LOUISE PEATTIE

Going west over the old buffalo plains, you see at last on the wide horizon what looks like a low, gleaming cloud. So it appeared to the first American who wrote about the mountains of Colorado, young Lt. Zebulon Pike. But when he raised his spyglass to it, that day in 1806, he saw that the cloud was "a great peak"—Pikes Peak, we call it now in his honor. And as he and his little band toiled eagerly toward it, peak beyond peak the Front Range of the Rockies reared higher, coming nearer, swathed at the base in dark evergreen forests and topped with the glitter of snows. Now the Americans unfurled their flag, to snap proudly in the wind from those cold heights, while all shouted their cheers.

And that is just what you will want to do, when first you see that great storm of frozen earth-waves rising in a long wall. For what lies beyond it is your holiday, your green vacation in a region literally tops in America.

Colorado holds more high summits than any other state. Here is air so dry and never-breathed-before that it enters the lungs like rapture. Here is a wilderness welcoming with campsites; here are ghost towns and live towns, and highways crisscrossing the Continental Divide by alpine passes. Here you can spend days knee-deep in wild flowers, hip-deep in singing trout streams. It's cool enough here in July for forests of Christmas trees to grow, and warm enough to picnic coatless among them. And the skies are mostly as clear as a great blue bell, unless there breaks one of those hair-raising mountain thunderstorms—a tantrum soon over.

The capital of this Rocky Mountain empire is

A grove of quaking aspen stands out in stark relief against somber peaks bordering Snowmass Canyon near Aspen, Colorado. Aspens provide the Rockies with their brightest autumnal colors—from dazzling yellows to fiery oranges.

the high-hearted city of Denver. However, most of us go to Colorado (and maybe over its borders into sagebrush Wyoming and sunburnt New Mexico) not for urban pleasures but to enjoy the spectacular western nature that is the prime adventure in America. So go from Denver to Boulder and then into Rocky Mountain National Park; if you never saw more of Colorado than this you would still have tasted of its best. There are over 400 square miles of it, gemmed with lakes reflecting boughs and boulders, and laced with streams born but minutes ago from glacial ice and summer sun. In one glance you behold white peaks against clear azure—and a long valley brimming with lupine and gentian, larkspur, harebell and Indian paintbrush; and the pride of the state, its columbine, grows so big here it seems like a garden runaway, eloquent—in its spurred and airy grace —of summer freedom.

If you are a mountaineer, you'll find sixty-one summits over 10,000 feet above sea level in the park, with Longs Peak (14,255 feet) the outstanding challenge. To less ambitious eyes dozens of other mountains look just as noble, and a car will take you right over them on the Trail Ridge Road. There, above timberline, where the alpine flowers crouch before the planetary gales, you may gaze out over the Rockies—wild, grand, unspoiled, a sea of tossing whitecaps stretching away and away, world without end.

Some of the towns down there are right out of our favorite westerns. Gold was discovered around Denver in 1858, and the next year the prairies were streaked white with "schooners" bearing the legend *Pikes Peak or Bust!* For sixteen years men were fevered by gold, as they prospected every gully and slope, undaunted by snow and avalanche, starvation and Indians. Though the easy pickings of gold gave out, dramatically, luck held, for silver was suddenly found. Towns like Leadville, Telluride, Cripple Creek and Fairplay sprang up overnight, growing crazily along the windings of canyons or climbing beside the lode above timberline. In them all, boom and bust (or, in miners' Spanish, *bonanza* and *borrasca*) followed the same pattern, as the price of gold and silver rose or fell, as veins pinched out or new strikes were made.

Heading north from Denver you may climb up over Rabbit Ears Pass to Steamboat Springs. You may pull up by a stream to rent a pan and sift the gravel for gold. After samples of such fun, you can then head south—over Loveland Pass or Wolf Creek Pass, over the Medicine Bow Mountains and

the dreamy Sangre de Cristos. You may stop to peer fearfully into the depths of the Black Canyon of the Gunnison; or you may cross the Royal Gorge on the world's highest suspension bridge, from which you can watch the Denver and Rio Grande trains forging along at the bottom like toys. A week of such adventuring, and your head will be in a happy whirl of snowy summits, echoing gorges, roaring streams and marching, marching forests.

Those great trees, seemingly dusted with moonlight, are blue spruce, Colorado's state tree. The ones with the pencil-slim outlines and somber foliage are Engelmann's spruce. Those long-tailed, black, white and green birds flying up from the road are magpies, and that's a crested jay scolding from the branches. If you draw up to photograph the doe and her fawn at the wood's edge, you can know by their big ears that they are mule deer. If you hold a peanut or potato chip high in the air a Clark's nutcracker may fly in to take it from you; if you hold it close to the ground, a ground squirrel will probably be your guest. And you may even see an unkempt doglike creature slinking off into the timber, a coyote, blood brother of loneliness.

Later or sooner you will discover Aspen, a town of 2000 persons that has become world famous. When the silver boom closed with the last century, Aspen, isolated in its cup of mountains, was forgotten. But its steep, snowy slopes brought it to life again in the 1930s. Now it is a sports resort known to skiers the world over. In summer Aspen's cultural festival draws flocks of visitors to lectures, concerts and forums, conducted by renowned artists and intellectuals.

While winter and summer are Aspen's big seasons, we'd choose to be there in autumn. For it is in late September and early October that the trembling aspen sends all the mountainsides to glory. Turning from pale summer green to gold molten with sunlight, these white-stemmed trees stand like angels against the naked blue of the fall sky. They pour down the slopes in sheets of fire colors, and troop, brilliant and whispering, through the somber masses of silent spruce and fir.

When you go to Mesa Verde National Park, way down in the southwest corner of Colorado, over the giddy twists and grades of the Million Dollar Highway, you'll be journeying not only miles into lonely splendor but centuries back in time. Mesa Verde is Spanish for "green table," and that precisely describes this lofty plateau which rises out of the burning desert, covered with an aromatic

166

forest of juniper and piñon pine and carved with deep canyons. In the niches of these walls you'll behold the silent, ancient habitations of the Indian cliff dwellers. Now they are gone, those people who loved the things you are loving—this desert sun and air, the scent of juniper, the far croak of the ravens sailing over the chasm—gone 200 years before Columbus came upon America.

The man who discovered Pikes Peak predicted that its awesome height could never be conquered, but now a paved road and a cog railway run right to the summit. Next favorite excursion is to the Garden of the Gods, that fantastic wilderness of massive, strangely shaped red rocks set amid gnarled junipers older than Methuselah. Go early when the young day is fresh, and nobody is there but the gods and you. You, and high in bright morning the wheeling swifts and the white-crested giant Pike.

This is a high spot in travel adventure. Nowhere in Europe is there grandeur of this primeval kind. True, the Alps are picturesque, but better than a picture is a window open on the West. And such are the passes of the Rockies; through them, just yesterday, journeyed the pioneering heroes of our Homeric age—Lewis and Clark, Marcus and Narcissa Whitman, Kit Carson and Jim Bridger. In all our struggle to conquer a continent, it was the Rockies, above all, that tried and proved the American will. And even in our day, when those perils are past, this range, the very backbone of our country, makes any man who comes to it stand tall and breathe deep with native pride.

Cliff Palace at Mesa Verde National Park, Colorado, is the nation's largest cliff dwelling. It was built by Indians about 1200 A.D. and occupied for a hundred years. The well-like structures, called kivas, were underground ceremonial rooms.

THE YELLOWSTONE NOBODY KNOWS

ERWIN A. BAUER

One July evening a few years ago, in a seldom-seen corner of Yellowstone Park called Trout Creek, I watched a wildlife spectacle that few if any Americans will ever see again. As dusk settled on the sagebrush hills and changed them from pale green to gold, grizzly bears began to gather from all around. They seemed to materialize from nowhere. Some walked slowly, cautiously; others came running.

They came to this spot alone, in pairs and in families of three and four until there were thirty-two of the brutes in our vision at once. In the group were giant grizzlies as well as tiny cubs, boars as well as sows—altogether about one fifth of all the grizzlies left in the United States outside of Alaska.

"I drive out here many evenings during the summer," Frank Craighead told me, "but this spectacle never grows old. I'm always thrilled by it."

Along with his brother John, Craighead has been working on a wonderfully interesting and exciting project. With grants from the National Science Foundation and the National Geographic Society, plus aid from the Park Service and the Environmental Research Institute, the biologists are doing a life history and ecology of grizzlies within the park. At this same spot on Trout Creek they've trapped, tranquilized, weighed, measured, blood-tested and tagged bears (some weighing more than 800 pounds) at considerable personal risk. They've attached transistor radios to some of the bears to track their movements. And their findings may well save grizzlies for future generations to see.

"Aside from the conservation aspect of this study," Craighead told me, "this is just another part of Yellowstone Park that nobody really knows."

That comment rang a bell. Each year millions of people visit the park. Some simply drive through, others tarry a few days, while still others spend an entire vacation. But the unfortunate truth is that only a handful ever desert the main roads to see what lies beyond. Most visit Old Faithful Geyser, Mammoth Hot Springs, the Fishing Bridge and the black bears—the Yellowstone of the summer tourist. But far too few follow the trails into the Yellowstone nobody knows.

A man can spend his lifetime vagabonding the Yellowstone backcountry and still not see all there is to see. After our visit with the Craigheads, Jim Graff, my two sons, Park and Bobby, and I decided to go off and do some exploring of the park on our own. What we found was a paradise for anyone or for any family that genuinely loves the outdoors.

We started at Yellowstone Lake, which is the highest body of water of its size in North America. It would have been easy to launch a boat at West Thumb or Lake and catch a limit of three cutthroat trout apiece by trolling within sight of the docks and steaming hot springs. Hundreds of tourists do it every day. But that wasn't enough. We wanted to see what was on the other side of the lake where no roads reach and where no powerboats are permitted.

"If you can get to Peale Island in the South Arm," a ranger had advised us, "there's fishing you have to see to believe."

To reach Peale we chartered a runabout at West Thumb to cross to Plover Point and the remote Plover Campground. It was strange to see this developed campground completely empty while those at Old Faithful, Canyon and the other tourist centers were crowded beyond capacity. At Plover we transferred our gear from the runabout to light aluminum skiffs powered by oars and elbow grease to cover the last few miles. A cloud of mosquitoes speeded up the job.

Rowing into a fresh wind wasn't an easy chore, and the truth is that we never did reach Peale Island. But it didn't make much difference. About halfway we sought the shelter of a sandy point to wait out the wind, and stayed there.

If any human being had visited this place recently, it wasn't evident among the bear and moose tracks that engraved the soft earth all around. And the trout cruising in easy fly-casting range were about as unsophisticated as trout can be.

Sixty thousand gallons of water a minute plunge over the Lower Falls of the Yellowstone when runoff from mountain snowfields reaches its peak. From an overlook at the brink, visitors can watch the river begin its awesome 308-foot drop.

168

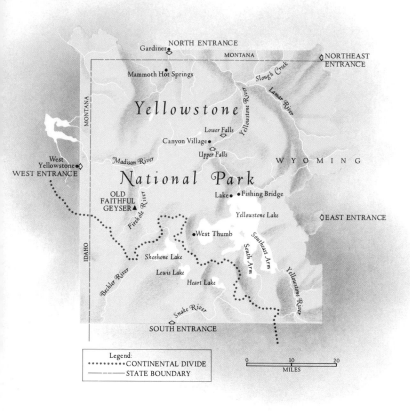

Many of the best spots along the lower Yellowstone are those where smaller rivers such as Deep Creek, Crevice, Cottonwood and Hellroaring join the main stream. I remember Hellroaring especially, because it's the place where Bobby, then aged twelve, caught his first big trout. It cavorted crazily all over two pools before Bobby subdued it and sat on it (for safety purposes) while he extracted the hook.

"From now on," he said, "this will always be my favorite river." But the next day Slough Creek became his favorite. After that it was Buffalo Fork. Then the Madison River.

Before we eventually left Yellowstone, my oldest and fly-fishingest son noticed that all of the great fishing in Yellowstone is less than a day's hike from the highway. "There are stretches of the Firehole," he said, "that are very handy—but the fishermen never go there."

Park proved his point one evening. While I repaired a flat tire, washed a barracks bag of clothes at the laundromat and bought some groceries at Old Faithful, the lad hied himself to a steamy pool on the Firehole less than a mile away —just a mile from those throngs of tourists. When he returned soon afterward he was carrying a matched pair of brown trout that measured seventeen inches long.

When writing about Yellowstone, it is hard—maybe impossible—not to be carried away with the fishing. But that isn't the only part of the park nobody knows.

Not all of the hot springs and geysers are located where tour buses travel. And not all of the wildlife, in fact not even a fraction of it, is posed where car-borne cameramen can film it. I saw more moose while casting in Slough Creek one evening than I would have in driving around for a week. And all of them watched my efforts with complete disinterest.

There are many other reasons besides the strange geysers and extraordinary fishing to retreat from Yellowstone Park's beaten tracks, and bird watching (or bird photography) is one of them. Of course you can see birds, maybe as many as 200 different species, without unbuckling your seat belt. But the odds are much better in your favor if you will leave your car behind and walk quietly along the trails.

Park cast a wet fly, allowed it to sink, and instantly his rod was dancing. Bobby cast a spoon and he had a strike. I delivered a Blonde Wulff into the wind and a cutthroat inhaled it a split second later. Three casts, three fish.

Then we watched the passing show of birds. White pelicans and gulls nest in the Southeast Arm to the east. One gull made passes at Bobby's spoon as he tried to retrieve it. A fine bald eagle cruised by at close range. And all day long, not ten miles from crowded Fishing Bridge, we never saw another fisherman. In many respects this is a fisherman's park and promised land.

Let's select the Yellowstone River itself to prove the point. From the lake's outlet downstream to the Upper Falls it offers good fishing, even though a road is seldom farther than 200 yards away. But from the Grand Canyon northward to the park's northern boundary it's virtually undisturbed by anglers or anyone else. Viewing the river and the canyon from lookout points far above, few tourists suspect that it's even possible to get down into the canyon. But we discovered that it can be done. We found, in fact, that almost anyone would be able to ride (or hike) in and out of the canyon at Seven Mile Hole in one day's time—with a couple of hours to spare for fishing at the bottom!

Old Faithful Geyser can hurl 10,000 gallons of water into the air during a four-minute eruption. Its spout, usually around 125 feet high, may reach 180 feet. The performance occurs about every hour and has not failed in a century.

170

Besides the Canada geese, mallards and pintails, my notebook reveals that I also saw ravens, whisky jacks, ospreys, California gulls and such uncommon birds as a violet-green swallow, a western tanager and a number of mountain bluebirds. Add also a pair of trumpeter swans, an elegant species that teetered on the brink of extinction for too many years and still isn't seen every day.

Bird watching has many rewards, and I would advise carrying a camera. Pictures of the birds you "shoot" on summer trails will bring you pleasure later on and far away.

There is even something for the adventure-boating fan in Yellowstone's backcountry. Although most park waters are closed to watercraft, a few are open. One of these is Lewis Lake, which lies on the west side of the South Entrance road. Another is Shoshone Lake, which is farther west and not accessible by any road. The two lakes are connected by a thin channel, usually navigable.

Beginning at the Lewis Lake campground, it's possible to launch a shallow-draft skiff or cartop boat (outboards are not allowed now) and make the trip to Shoshone. During low-water periods in midsummer, it may be necessary to wade and drag the boat behind through some shallow sections of the connecting channel, but it's worth it. Besides the elegant scenery, there's a remote geyser basin to explore, and this particular portion of the park has more than its share of wildlife to see. Moose will stand and watch like sidewalk superintendents as you cruise past them.

On any summer day Old Faithful Inn (or Mammoth or Canyon Village) is a swarm of humans, but walk a quarter mile in any direction and you are free. You will see no sign that anyone has ever been there before. Suddenly you will feel like a discoverer, an explorer. Now you can know how John Colter and Jim Bridger felt. You feel good, exhilarated. You may see only chipmunks scurrying for cover, but then again you may see or hear the flutelike bugle of a bull elk or the eerie howl of a coyote. Sounds, as well as sights, can be high adventure.

All at once you realize how much you don't really know about this first and largest national park.

Almost nobody knows very much.

Scalding water carrying dissolved lime built the terraces of Mammoth Hot Springs. Lime is deposited continuously so that the formations slowly grow in much the same way as cave stalactites; the colors come from algae and minerals.

GRAND TETON NATIONAL PARK

The Teton Range rises with startling abruptness in western Wyoming's Grand Teton National Park. The name derives from Grand Teton, the tallest peak at 13,766 feet. The eastern side of the range is one of the world's most spectacular mountain landscapes because the foothills that usually surround high mountains are absent. About 60 million years ago a series of upheavals began, which raised the Tetons almost like a huge stone block— originally about 20,000 feet high, forty miles long and thirteen miles wide. The upheaval was less abrupt on the western side, where foothills do exist. Glaciers, remnants of which are still among the peaks, scooped gorges from the mountains and deposited a layer of rocky debris in the valley of Jackson Hole. The valley and slopes, once covered by ice, are now a sanctuary for the rare trumpeter swan, elk and bear.

The clear waters of the twisting Snake River rush southward nearly 7000 feet below the snowy peak of Grand Teton (in the center here). At the water's edge, aspens, willows and cottonwoods put on a flashy display of fall color against somber evergreens. Swift despite its meanderings, the Snake shows open water even when the valley floor is blanketed with snow.

MONTANA'S MISSION MOUNTAINS

HELEN GERE CRUICKSHANK

My husband Allan suddenly stepped hard on the gas, and as our car shot out of the thicket bordering Montana's Mission Creek, I almost froze in my seat. We were virtually face to face with a bull bison that we had surprised standing in a circle of bare sand just off the narrow road. His heavy head was hanging low as if weighted with dreams, but in a fraction of a second, with amazing lightness on his slender legs, he swerved to a charging position and actually seemed to be plunging toward us. As we sped past him, the bull pivoted and took off in the opposite direction like an express train.

From High Point on the 19,000-acre National Bison Range we had spotted a bison herd on the far side of Mission Creek. Hoping to approach the herd close enough for good pictures, we had dropped cautiously down the steep slope by a series of oblique switchbacks, rumbled across the bridge spanning the creek and unexpectedly encountered the lone bull.

As we caught our breath, Allan drove on slowly, one eye on the dusty road, the other on the herd of bison.

The herd was widely scattered as the big mammals grazed over the rolling, golden prairie. Behind them the Mission Mountains rose like a vast blue wall. We were on the Pacific side of the Continental Divide in northwest Montana, where the Mission Range rises in the Flathead Lake region and terminates north of Missoula. Though short as mountain ranges go, it has some rugged 10,000-foot peaks where snow lies all year.

Rising abruptly toward the sky, the western slope overlooks one of the most beautiful valleys in all America and one extremely rich in wildlife. Now, as I watched the bison herd, I noted they

The National Bison Range in northwestern Montana protects nearly 500 bison, one of the few remaining herds of the New World's largest land animal. The range includes nearly 18,500 acres of rolling grasslands and scattered forests.

177

were grazing in a spot where no sign of man was visible. The scene must look precisely as it had looked when the Plains Indians hunted these animals, which supplied them with food, clothing and shelter.

Allan braked the car. As he stepped out with his camera, a western meadowlark exploded from the ground. It held a great mouthful of worms and, alighting on a stone, began to scold us. Allan looked about carefully. Under the shriveled leaves of a balsamroot he found the nest, woven of fine grass, tucked into a tiny hollow.

This was a lucky bonus, for he had been too busy to search for a meadowlark's nest, though the birds' flutelike whistles, ringing from one side of the Bison Range to the other, had been a constant joy. Their rollicking, musical songs are truly called the spirit of the prairie.

Since the four young were fairly large, there could be no delay in photographing the meadowlarks. Ground birds, if disturbed, are likely to coax their youngsters to leave the nest. As soon as Allan finished photographing the bison, we put a blind beside the nest and spent several days working there. Both adult birds fed the young, coming to the nest with their bills stuffed with insect larvae.

One of the most abundant mammals on the range is the pronghorn. This fleetest of American mammals is the only member of its family found exclusively in North America. The male is called a buck, the female a doe, but their offspring is a kid, not a fawn. When only four days old a kid can outrun a man.

Early in summer the does and kids were usually in small groups, while the bucks were solitary. Sometimes we failed to notice the bucks at a distance, for their color closely matched that of the prairie. When we approached they threw up their heads alertly, and as the distance between us narrowed, they were off—sometimes bouncing as if they had springs in all four legs.

Allan was particularly anxious to make close-ups of a buck, for some bucks had beautiful heads. Not far from our meadowlark nest, one such handsome male apparently had a favorite daily grazing territory. He appeared curious about the blind but offended by its presence. Each time we arrived he trotted back and forth, pausing every hundred feet or so to stare, head held high. He stamped with one foot at each stop and gave an explosive, snorting cough. When he turned his back we could see the rosette of long hairs erected, like two white cushions fastened to his rump.

On the day we removed the blind from the meadowlarks' nest, the pronghorn was in his usual place on the hillside. I announced that I was going to try for a picture of the buck, and Allan gave me a "How silly can you get?" look. I knew pronghorns can travel up to sixty miles an hour and make leaps as long as twenty feet. They can maintain a steady rate of twenty-five miles an hour for a considerable distance. I had no illusion that I could outrun a pronghorn, but occasionally it is possible to approach an individual of some wary species, and I had hopes for this buck. Off I went under the hot sun.

Nearer and nearer I approached the quietly grazing pronghorn. At last he filled the viewfinder frame, and I worked the shutter of the camera furiously. Then the buck lay down and began to chew his cud as calmly as a pet cow. When he started off again I followed and took more shots. Each time he passed a thistle he took a swipe at it with his horns. After my last exposure, I returned to the meadowlarks' nest and Allan took up the stalking where I had stopped. Gradually the pronghorn climbed higher until at last it stood on the very top of the hill, and there Allan left it.

One day we were having a fine time photographing blue grouse until we heard an ominous buzz and faced a stocky four-foot Pacific rattler. We promptly forgot about the grouse, and as the rattler coiled with its arrow-shaped head pointed at us and its rattles hoisted high from the coil, we shifted immediately to reptile photography. Allan approached the rattler closer than it liked, and it shook its tail furiously. When Allan withdrew to change films, the rattler relaxed. It still held its tail aloft but stopped shaking it and stuck out its dusky, forked tongue inquiringly.

Ninepipe National Wildlife Refuge was a much better place than the range for water birds. Allan was particularly anxious to find the nests of black terns, birds that skim over all the potholes in the area as they search for food. Finally he discovered a group nesting at a small, muddy pothole in a pasture just outside the refuge.

We drove through the dust to a pink farmhouse to ask permission to photograph the terns. Approval was given cordially, and we returned to the refuge, left the car high on a dike, carried the equipment through a dense tangle of thistles, rolled under a barbed-wire fence, crossed an irrigation ditch by means of a narrow, very limber board, and were promptly attacked by the terns.

My sun hat was a protection, but Allan insists

a hat interferes with quick work in setting up the blind and camera. As a result he took the brunt of the attack, for the slim little terns were courageous in attempting to repel what they thought was danger to their eggs.

As we prepared the blind, an audience began to gather. Cows and calves formed a semicircle, lowered their heads, began to chew meditatively, and stared. A beautiful Arabian horse joined them, and as a hundred eyes gazed at the blind, I left Allan to photograph his terns.

Later I spent a few hours in the blind and rejoiced at the delicate frosting of silver on the black terns.

The parent birds exchanged duties from time to time, with much discussion about the three dusky, speckled eggs before one left and the other settled down to incubate. Allan was fortunate enough to see the three mottled bits of down emerge. Soon after drying, the baby terns were able to swim about and hide among the cattails, then find their way back to the nest when the parents brought food for them.

As the summer heat intensified we often abandoned the Bison Range and Ninepipe for the cooler, wooded Mission slopes. Birding was good there, and we frequently chose the country road that led to McDonald Reservoir, passing through a farm gate into a pasture choked with second growth and low shrubs such as mock orange and wild roses.

We found bunting nests in shrubby tangles, but early in the season most were robbed by chipmunks, garter snakes or other hungry creatures. Many were parasitized by cowbirds. But the buntings persisted, and as July progressed many nestfuls of young buntings were raised.

At the end of the car trail, which can scarcely be called a road, lies McDonald Reservoir in McDonald Canyon. Perpendicular McDonald Peak is reflected in the green water. Prairie falcons nest on the sheer cliffs, and so do ravens. Both species are always ready to challenge loudly anything that displeases them. From time to time we located, through our binoculars, a family of mountain goats grazing high on one of the little alpine meadows near the summit.

Throughout the summer there was constant change. One day when it rained in the valley there was snow on top of the Missions, and black swifts nesting behind the waterfalls found that their flying-insect food had temporarily vanished from the heights. Then they swooped down to feed over Mission Creek, where the insects remained lively.

One sweltering afternoon in July Allan put me in a blind beside a rock wren's nest on the hot, dry southern slope of the Bison Range and then went off to stalk three bighorn sheep he had spotted high on Red Man's Ridge. As I drooped in the heat I was startled by a pounding roar and looked out to see the three handsome rams with great curling horns thunder by within ten feet of the blind. In the Mission Valley there never was a dull moment.

In this valley, through which U.S. Route 93 passes, there is elbowroom to spare and a delightful place to stay. From the west windows of our motel we looked at Ninepipe across the highway and watched the sun sink behind the purple Salish Mountains, while skeins of geese, honking loudly, set off to graze in the fields and western grebes went through their noisy courtship antics.

Best of all was the large pothole outside our east windows. Its waters reflected in endless variation the highest Mission peaks towering skyward two miles beyond. There was always activity around, above and on the pothole. An American bittern sometimes stalked along the shore hunting for a frog or small fish to take to its young in a nest a mile away. Ducks, gulls and terns fed only a dozen feet beyond our window. Pied-billed grebes built their floating nests among the rushes. The bushes bordering the pond were alive with blackbirds, and Allan found many of their nests.

In the grass close to the pothole Allan discovered a sora's nest with eleven eggs in it. He put up a blind, but when he returned for his camera he feared he was too late. An egg had hatched while he was working, and the incubating sora had taken the young away. The shot was worth a try, however, and to Allan's delight, back came the bird to continue her interrupted incubation. Ten more times that day the sora left the nest to escort another and yet another young bird, as soon as it dried off, to her mate, which then took charge of it.

We left the Mission Valley on the last day of July, with a certain contentment because agriculture and wildlife share with equanimity the beautiful land beneath the Mission Range. We had found a sense of leisure there.

In this age of haphazard "progress," of speed, restlessness and diminishing natural resources, the valley offered us conditions conducive to reflection and thought as well as the opportunity to observe wildlife that has vanished from most of America.

GLACIER NATIONAL PARK

Montana's Glacier National Park is the handiwork of Ice Age glaciers, which chiseled the park's valleys and dug more than 200 lakes within its 1583 square miles. Ten thousand years ago northern Montana lay beneath a vast ocean. Its rocks are among the oldest sedimentary formations on earth, and some strata still retain impressions of waves and salt crystals from that long-departed sea.

*Blossoms of bear grass, the most conspicuous flower in Glacier
National Park, carpet an approach to Pollock Mountain. In this oblique
view the flowers, which are two to three feet high, appear nearly as
tall as the 6664-foot mountain. Bears are said to eat the plant,
but it is more definitely known to be food for the park's elk, Rocky
Mountain goats and small rodents such as the spruce mouse.*

IDAHO:
"SUN IN THE
MOUNTAINS"

Idaho is one of the strangest states in the union. No other has a topographical structure so varied and sometimes so appalling. Idaho lies among a group of states each of which has a more definite geological integrity. It is homologous in the north with Washington or western Montana, in the far south with Nevada, in the southeast with Utah, and upon its eastern boundary with Wyoming.

It is, in consequence, a state that seems to have been parceled from many, and it offers not only unusual and dramatic changes in scenery but also remarkable shifts in altitude. Idaho drops in a long, broad incline from almost 6000 feet in the east to a little more than 2000; then, in the west, it lifts over mountain ranges and sinks into Lewiston, the lowest point in the state. And lying between Canada and Utah, and between the frozen Teton peaks and warm Pacific winds, it perhaps offers more extremes in temperature and weather than any of its neighbors.

In some of Idaho very little snow falls and that little rarely remains long; in other parts, even in valleys where farms are many, the snow in February may lie eight feet deep. The streets of Boise may be bare while a town thirty miles north is buried to the gables. Parts of the state harvest full crops without irrigation, and others lie brown and barren through the summer months. In some sections deer, exhausted by lack of forage, may freeze to death; in Lewiston and the Treasure Valley areas, at the very same time, large orchards may be getting ready to burst into blossom. Within southern caves in January wild animals may lie indolently fat in warm chambers; and mountain goats on the great watersheds look across deserts of snow that have completely buried evergreens.

Idaho has huge semiarid reaches, but it also

A blossoming field delights a holiday visitor to Salmon National Forest in central Idaho. Idaho has 20,689,977 acres of national forest—more than a third of its total area—including 6.4 million acres set aside as wilderness reserves.

probably has more running water than any other state. There are flat, formidable tablelands that defeat everything but sagebrush and coyote, but there are also more lakes than have ever been counted, and nobody quite knows how many remain undiscovered and unexplored. The state has broad benches slabbed out of basalt that reach like vast gray pavements from county to county; but it also has, one on the border and two within, the deepest canyons in the United States. There are alpine pinnacles where the ice never melts, and so many hot springs that in some cities the water is piped into homes for heat.

South of the Lemhi and Lost River ranges and running east from the Big Wood River is a magnificently desolate steppe of 3400 square miles. Much of this is porous volcanic terrain with countless vents and cones, caves filled with ice, and superchilled springs. A small portion of it has been set aside as the Craters of the Moon National Monument.

These corrugated lava flows of a former time have left phenomena called sinks, and into these rivers disappear, to emerge, at last, far away into hundreds of thousands of springs, many of them gushing from walls of stone and others rising high to tumble in waterfalls. Lying for 1000 miles within Idaho or on its boundaries, the Snake River (Mad River, the French-Canadians called it) has cut a gorge across the width of the state, and across the southern flank of the lava steppe it has eroded a stupendous path. In some places the river lies hundreds of feet under walls of stone and pours over cascades or flows in shadow under the outpourings of buried streams; farther in its journey, on the Oregon-Idaho line, it flows through Hell's Canyon more than 7900 feet below He Devil Mountain.

From automobile or train or plane window Idaho seems a rolling mass of loneliness and waste. A more impervious area would be difficult to find, or one more inviolable within its empire of aridity and rock. Much of it can never be used, save for grazing, and must lie here forever as it is now under the journeyings of people. But for those who know the area and have stood within its strength, it is a splendid and timeless region upon which 1000 centuries will leave little mark. This part of Idaho looks as if the sky had poured boulders upon it or as if it harbored a vegetation of stone. Such a land is not for everyone.

It is chiefly just this land that people see as they travel across the state to the Pacific Northwest. They come in from the humid Middle West

A wooden hoist for hay bales awaits the next harvest beside an old log cabin used as a barn in mile-high Swan Valley. Now among the richest agricultural regions in Idaho, the valley was at one time a haven for the rare whistling swan.

or the industrial East, where landscape seldom breaks into rugged and terrifying extremes, and they find this region awful in its aloofness and inexplicable in its calm. There is no shadow in its bald glare and no witchery in its horizons; it is candid in sunlight and alien and ageless in its mood. Those passing through the state doubtless think of Idaho as an appalling desert with an oasis at either end. But this region is only a very minor part of the state.

Eastward from it lie the farmlands of the upper Snake River Valley, famous for potatoes; and here, under irrigation, what was once a desert of sagebrush is now one of the most fertile and productive areas in the West, running from the entrance of Yellowstone Park to the city of Pocatello. From the sky it is a network of canals, and the farms covering it look in June like a great green blanket. In October hundreds of thousands of bags of potatoes stand in long rows; trainloads of sugar beets reach almost across the cities; alfalfa hay is stacked against the winter.

A great chain of mountains on the Idaho-Wyoming boundary fences this valley in the east. Upon the north it is rimmed by the Continental Divide. And in the west are the magnificent Sawtooth, White Cloud and Pioneer ranges. Here are peaks reaching altitudes of more than 12,000 feet, with many tiny valleys, some holding lakes, some fertile, tilled basins, and all of them walled in by the forested slopes of other ranges. A larger basin (about 14,000 square miles), holding smaller ones within its area, is that in which the Salmon River and its tributaries lie. At no point does the elevation fall below 4000 feet, and most of the basin is considerably higher than a mile.

The Salmon River, nicknamed the River of No Return, is a phenomenon in itself. It is the headlong and furious stream that the explorer William Clark entered in 1805, only to turn back after he had followed it fifty miles; and it is a river that, until the advent of the jet boat, few others ventured to navigate. It rises in the eastern slope of the Sawtooth Mountains and flows northwest for thirty miles. Then it abruptly turns eastward through a canyon, finds a small valley, picks up the South Fork and swings into the north. For about a hundred miles it flows northward, gathering two more rivers and several creeks; meets the

North Fork, which has come down out of the Bitterroot Range; and turns suddenly westward. Thirty miles later it gathers the Middle Fork. In 200 miles it has come no closer to the Snake River, its point of delivery, than it was at its source. But now, as though having learned by trial and error, the Salmon plunges into a deep gorge, picks up two more rivers and takes its cold subterranean way down a canyon for another 200 miles to its outlet.

The surrounding country is no less awesome than the river. Here are hundreds of peaks—many of them unnamed—more lovely lakes than have been explored and thousands of acres of timber in which there has never been the sound of an axe. Much of this is an undiscovered wilderness and it presents some quite overwhelming contrasts. It has broad sweeps of ragged peaks and high, almost inaccessible ridges where mountain sheep live—but adjacent to any of these more formidable reaches, and in almost any direction, are lakes of utmost loveliness and serenity, or impassable forests of fir and pine, or meadows where wild flowers grow dense and knee-deep, or river gorges

dropping sharp and sudden to the white-capped waters below. Shadow and jungle growth hide innumerable small streams where the fish have never seen an angler.

From the tallest peaks there is a drop of more than 10,000 feet to Boise, less than eighty miles southwest of the headwaters of the Salmon River. Here in western Idaho are the gently rolling watersheds of several rivers, of which the largest is the Snake. These valleys, from the Sawtooth foothills to the Oregon line, have an unusually mild climate. The winters are temperate, with occasional zero weather and with snowfall varying from a sleety mist of rain to snow measured by the foot. The summers are long and cloudless, and irrigation is necessary, as it is in all of Idaho except the north. In these valleys more than a half million acres are under irrigation. When, in late spring, the westerly winds come from Oregon, the fragrance from the orchards and fields rises in the air and the sky is swept clean to its deepest blue, with the cool northern background hazy in white or purple mist. In every way the western valleys are unlike the rest of Idaho.

During autumn roundup ranchers move beef cattle from higher pastures to cold-weather ranges in Swan Valley, Idaho. The state's level farmland, once primarily pasture, is now extensively cultivated; hilly land is used for grazing.

Coeur d'Alene Lake in the upper Panhandle has the nebulous reputation of being the fifth loveliest lake in the world. Superbly scenic highways run along its shores, and the timber in its down-sweeping backdrops is so dense that it is almost blue-black. More rain falls here than over most of Idaho, and even at the lower altitudes where cities lie, winter snow sometimes reaches a depth of eight or ten feet. Nevertheless, the region, lying as it does within western winds, has a surprisingly mild climate for its latitude, and often is not as cold as parts of the state 600 miles farther south.

This small scenic wonderland belongs topographically to eastern Washington and is in much closer kinship with Spokane than with Boise. It is, indeed, so remote in both interests and distance from most of Idaho that a resident of the Snake River Valley feels less at home upon coming here than he would feel in Montana, Wyoming or Utah.

Far south, against the Nevada line, another remarkable contrast is to be found. In Owyhee County is a region larger than Rhode Island and Delaware, and most of it so barren and bleak that even sagebrush and greasewood grow precariously, and what is thought to have been in part an ancient lake bed is an overwhelming waste. The Snake River cuts across its northern extremity, but even here, in bizarre desolation, with black basalt towering in vivid bluffs against pale sediments, very little grass and only a few stunted trees grow. Much of the county is sprinkled with ghost towns, largest of which is Silver City, 6000 feet up.

But this northern stretch of Nevada, lying unexpectedly within the boundaries of Idaho, is not a level tableland of desert. It is anything but that. Channeled and gouged and eroded, scabrous and cragged, it is a huge supply of steppe materials that have never been ordered and flattened out. The whole region, laid down under the dramatic sculpturing of turmoil for a long period, is today one of the most picturesque terrains in the West; it is because of the enormous shifting of valleys and mountains ages ago that the whole area now presents such terrifying aspects.

Just east of Owyhee County lies a section of the Snake River Valley, one of Idaho's principal valleys, and this, too, not long ago, was a prairie of sagebrush and buffalo grass, coyotes and rattlesnakes and horned toads. Here is the state's most dramatic chapter in reclamation, and a valley now no less fertile and productive than others famous for potatoes and fruit.

Perhaps more than any other state Idaho has retained much of its wild character, with a minimum of destructive intrusions by man. The purity and beauty of its forests, lakes, mountains, rivers and canyons have become a resource far more valuable to the nation today than mere minerals and logs. Perhaps it should be called "the last wilderness," for its wild lands and rivers and lakes are unmatched by those of any other state except Alaska.

Idaho is the eternal American dream of new and untamed frontiers, the challenge against which our character as a people was formed. But now there is a fundamental difference: When its last forest is cut, its last river dammed, its last mineral dug up, our nation will be poorer, not richer. It is possible that Idaho might best serve itself and the rest of the country by remaining relatively undeveloped and unchanged.

This could prove to be the greatest glory of the state whose name in Indian means "Behold the sun in the mountains."

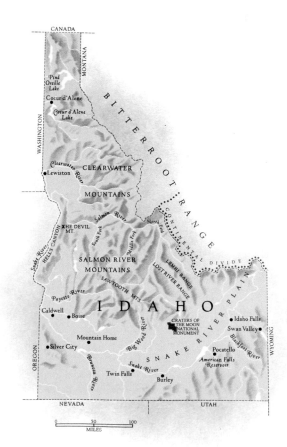

Part V

RED EARTH AND SUNBAKED SAND

Texas   New Mexico

Arizona   Utah   Nevada

TEXAS'
TREASURE ISLAND

WILLIAM M. HALL

Padre Island is a long gleaming strip of sand and surf that extends from Corpus Christi to Port Isabel and separates the blue waters of the Gulf of Mexico from the mainland of Texas. It is a land of many moods, exciting challenges and rare opportunities. It is everything to everybody, depending on the whims, the desires and the nature of the individual.

To many it is simply a wilderness where one can escape the anxieties and complexities of our time. Where solitude is desired, it would be difficult to find a more perfect place than this subtropical island. To some it is a land steeped in legend, where gold and silver lie embedded in the offshore reefs, dumped into Davy Jones's locker as ships of the Spanish Main foundered and sank beneath the storm-tossed seas; a land where adventure beckons, where primitive conditions pit a man against the elements of nature and where it is possible to lose oneself in the vast stretch of shifting sand and rolling waves. To such Padre offers the perfect rendezvous.

To others it is a beachcombers' heaven, a rich field for the exotic bits of flotsam and jetsam that so delight the eye and fill the mind with visions of their mysterious origin and significance. The island abounds in trinkets swept in by the tides or buried in the sand—ancient Spanish silver reals, historical odds and ends, old buttons, curious coins, pistol balls, driftwood and strange creatures of the sea. Beachcombing on Padre is an adventure in living.

Some like the plush motels, the spacious parks and the crowds that throng each end of the island. Still others come to fish, to hunt, to watch the

A young great blue heron stands in the brilliant noonday sun on a Padre Island dune amid sea oats and railroad vine. More than 350 species of birds inhabit or regularly visit Padre Island, the largest national seashore in the U.S.

myriads of birds or to photograph and paint the ever-changing face of sky and land. For those so inclined there is a happy anticipation and fulfilled delight in the pursuit of their specialty on Padre.

Padre Island does, in fact, have many faces, each appealing in its way, each beckoning with a provocative, come-hither look, promising much, giving more. The choice is up to the individual. Along this snow-white strip of dunes, history has carved an intriguing legend of adventure. Long before a white man set foot on its shores, it was the home of a savage band of Indians. The cannibalistic Karankawas roamed the sands, fished in the tropical waters and lay in wait for the victims who were soon to tread their native haunt. Then came that seafaring Spaniard Alonzo de Pineda, who discovered the island on the feast of Corpus Christi, in 1519. The island—actually a strand of narrow, contiguous islets—was called Las Islas Blancas, "The White Islands."

For close to 300 years after Pineda's arrival the island remained remote, a place visited only by an occasional pirate, a few shipwrecked victims of some of the storms that periodically rake the region, and perhaps an adventurous Mexican renegade or explorer. About 1800 Father Nicolás Balli braved the stormy reaches of the island, seeking to tame the savage Karankawas. This Spanish priest remained on the island some thirty years. With his nephew, Juan José Balli, he established the Santa Cruz Ranch, about thirty miles from the southern tip of the island. From Father Balli, Padre Island received its present name.

Around 1847 Capt. John Singer, a brother of Isaac Singer, developer of the sewing machine, landed on Padre with his wife and son Alexander. Their schooner had been shipwrecked near the glistening sands. Singer envisioned a prosperous shipping business on the island, but gave up the idea and established a ranch instead. The Singers took over the Santa Cruz area of Padre, later buying it along with much of the rest of the island. For about fifteen years they held undisputed possession of the island, demonstrated the practical value of cattle raising on the sparse rangeland and paved the way for the development to come.

Another pioneer who arrived on the scene before modern oil exploration and real estate development began was Patrick Dunn. Dunn was a bold and daring swashbuckler who built a home and ruled the island with an iron hand. This self-styled "Duke of Padre" was known as Don Patricio by his Spanish-speaking ranch hands. He established title to a great area of the island, and from the late 1870s until the land boom following

Near the ranger station one of the last two stands of live oak remaining on Padre Island struggles for survival. Only about fifteen feet tall, these fifty-year-old trees are less than half the height of live oaks the same age growing in good soil.

World War I was lord and master of Padre. His ranch was the largest ever established there. His home, made from the salvaged timbers of ships lost along the shore, was unique, impressive and sturdy. But the great storm of 1915 destroyed it completely. Undaunted, Dunn rebuilt the house and continued to dominate the island for a number of years. He allowed no one to intrude on his paradise, driving away fishermen, treasure seekers and naturalists alike. He sold his interests sometime during the 1920s to Col. Sam Robertson. With this transaction, the slow march of progress on the island had its real beginning—development that would not have been possible if Padre could not boast of a host of visitor attractions.

Padre Island is one of the greatest migratory bird flyways in the world, a place where many species come for protection, winter residence and abundant feeding and nesting facilities. There are also scores of interesting native birds. White and brown pelicans abound. The American and snowy egret, the tiny blue heron, the great blue heron, Wilson's plover, the laughing gull, black skimmer and redwing blackbird are plentiful. And it is always a delight to the serious bird watcher to spot the famed whooping cranes at the nearby Aransas National Wildlife Refuge.

For the fisherman there are close to 300 varieties of fish in the waters of the Gulf of Mexico and Laguna Madre. And the lure of lost fortunes continues to haunt treasure seekers wherever stories of sunken vessels loaded with gold and silver are told. The mouth of Brazos Santiago Pass, at the south tip of Padre, is the resting place of a number of ships that sank less than a hundred years ago. There is the *S. J. Lee,* which sank in 1873 with a fortune of $100,000. The *Texas Ranger,* carrying $200,000, went to the bottom in 1875. The *Ida Lewis,* with $20,000 aboard, also sank in 1875, as did the *Reine des Mers,* with $100,000 in her hold.

Legend persists that Captain Singer managed to save his money when he lost his ship somewhere along south Padre. But when he hastily fled from Confederate troops at the beginning of the Civil War, he is believed to have buried about $80,000 in the sand dunes near his ranch homeland. So far as is known, the money is still there, waiting for a venturesome treasure hunter to find and lay claim to it. The chances of discovering any of this legendary loot are remote. But many valuable finds have been made by dredging up schooners that were felled by Padre Island's more treacherous storms.

For half a century sporadic efforts were made by various individuals to convert Padre Island into a wildlife sanctuary or national park. Little came of these efforts until finally the state of Texas deeded an eighty-mile strip of the island, along with its submerged lands, to the federal government. In 1963 President Kennedy signed a bill designating the area a national seashore, setting aside 134,000 acres, 100,000 acres of which are on the island itself, with the remainder extending into the Gulf and Laguna Madre.

Continued development will inevitably make Padre Island grow in importance as a national year-round playground. But there is no doubt now that the area within the national seashore will remain an unspoiled vista of shifting sands, blue waters and solitude.

BIG BEND NATIONAL PARK

Bounded on two sides by a colossal curve
in the Rio Grande, Big Bend National Park
lies in the southwestern tip of Texas.
Its 700,000-acre area is an unspoiled
mixture of canyons, mountains and desert
expanses, which have been called the
"lonesomest, hottest, chilliest, driest,
wettest, orneriest and prettiest" parts
of Texas. Though much of the park is
desert, it is by no means devoid of life.
More than a thousand species of plants
are found within its boundaries.
Cottonwoods and willows grow in the
lowland river valleys; creosote bushes and
many cactuses flower on the desert floor;
piñons, junipers, firs and ponderosa
pines dot the rugged mountain
slopes. Deer, coyotes, foxes, hoglike
peccaries, mountain lions and more than
200 species of birds also live in the park.
"Big Bend," Ludwig Bemelmans wrote, "is
what Beethoven reached for in music; it
is panorama without beginning or end."

*Brooding beneath a leaden sky, two peaks in the
Chisos Mountains suggest why the range may have
taken its name from an Indian or Spanish word
meaning "ghosts" or "enchantments." The stilettolike
leaves of the Spanish dagger, which often
reaches a height of ten feet, add to the scene's
forbidding aspect. This species of yucca, whose
pointed leaves can inflict painful injuries,
is rarely found outside the confines of the park.*

MY SOUTHWEST

JACK SCHAEFER

Many people have come to my Southwest in search of many things, of gold and health and farmland and rangeland and business opportunity and simple vacation playground.

Some have found what they sought. More have not. Its deficiencies have defeated them. But all have found an incomparable place in which to search. And many of those who have failed have yet succeeded, have found riches other than those sought and have stayed in the land of failure to become rich in living.

But first, a defining. What piece of land is covered by that name Southwest? There are definitions by the dozen. Some expand it eastward to take in Texas; others northward to include part of Colorado and Utah; still others westward to the Coast. But my Southwest consists of just New Mexico and Arizona.

Two states and yet one area. It has always been so. In the American territorial days these two, roughly what they are today, were a single piece, New Mexico Territory; before that, a single province of Mexico. Before that, the major part of a single province of the Spanish colonial empire. And before that, the range of the Amerindians whose descendants still hold much of it: the nomadic Navaho and Apaches, who roamed and raided through it, and the Pueblos and Hopis and Zunis and Papagos and Pimas and Yumas, who dotted almost every part of it through the prehistoric years with their stone and adobe dwellings, now seen as weathering ruins.

That is my Southwest, west of the South and south of the West, Indian range and Spanish-Mexican province and American territory and states and still all three together and at once. Time passes over it and the pattern of the past remains. History makes markings upon it, and these are small, scattered, lonely, lost scratchings on the surface of the huge, indifferent land. What it was it is and will be.

It is a land where man and his works do not dominate, a land of vast stretching distances, a land of infinite variety and natural wonders, a land of sky and sunlight and color. And the sky is not a sorry flattened overcast that hangs pressing on the earth, but a limitless depth of the very space in which the earth itself is poised. Deep blue over New Mexico, lighter blue over Arizona, it sweeps so vast over the distances that entire storms can be seen scudding across it.

Sunlight is a living presence, more and purer and more golden than that of boasting Florida and California. There is a wide strip across the southern portion of both states that has sunshine 80 percent of all daylight hours of the year. And this is sunlight in all its phases: a magic mantle over the land during the day, a miracle of luminance on the ridges and far mountains in late afternoon, a superb always-different panorama of color in the evening setting. . . . Color! Color is everywhere, the full range of the earth's palette, ever changing, always renewed. My Southwest is a place where nature continues to play the artist through every moment of every day.

It is a land, too, that holds history in the palm of a huge protecting hand. Its high, dry climate preserves relics of the long past and adds through each successive epoch to its mighty outdoor museum of antiquities. The southwest, in addition, is rich in the resources needed by modern industry: copper, uranium, coal and natural gas.

Time takes on new dimensions here, is not pinned to the immediate pressing present. This is both the oldest and youngest part of the continental country. Here have been found remains of some of the oldest civilizations in the New World. Here the aboriginal inhabitants, when the countries of Europe were just coming into being, had already developed a culture that endures, not much changed, to this day. Here the Spanish were administering the region before a single colony fretted the Atlantic coast except in one insignificant piece of Florida—which was theirs, too. And yet this is almost the youngest section of the nation as such. New Mexico was the forty-seventh, Arizona the forty-eighth of the states, both admitted as late as 1912. And it is only in recent decades that Americans—Anglos—have in any real sense been making markings upon it.

What I have been trying to state in these wide generalizations derives directly from deficiencies, primarily the lack of water. Just a simple increase in the average annual rainfall and my Southwest would cease to be. Its strange, rugged mesas and ridges and mountains would soften and diminish into the rounded hills and elevations of other regions. Its *vegas*, plains, deserts would become prairies inviting the plow. The splendor of its sky would shrink to the overcast of moister areas. Its sunlight would lose much of its golden glory. Its wilderness would give way to fast-spreading settlement. The living presence of history would dwindle, the exhibits of the outdoor museum crumble away, the land be overrun by us Anglos, disregarding, pushing aside, erasing the other cultures.

Out of its poverty, its deficiencies, my Southwest creates its riches.

> I wander with the pollen of dawn
>   upon my trail.
> Beauty surrounding me, with it I
>   wander.

So sings the Navaho, the man unafraid, unsuccumbing to the cynicism of a commercialized age, unafraid of song straight from the heart. And his land is the poorest, the most deficient of all.

It is the very essence of my Southwest, the Navaho Reservation, vast in extent, barren, compounded partly of grassland and more of painted desert and dust-devil plain and canyons with great red cliffs strong and startling against limitless blue of sky. Beauty abides there always, the stripped-clean beauty of the even-breathing days of the summer of the high levels and the harsh, brutal beauty of the sandstorms and bitter searching winds and bitterer cold of winter.

Not far up Canyon del Muerto, the canyon of death, are petroglyphs on the cliff wall, painted long ago, showing Spanish soldiers riding across the rock. High on a nearby ledge lie bones of Navaho women and children who were slaughtered in hiding when Spanish raiders discovered them. All through here, when this had become American territory, tramped Anglo soldiers under Kit Carson when he was forcing the final surrender. Nowadays Navaho roam with their flocks through the canyons. The land is theirs again, because that same Kit Carson insisted that they be given the reservation promised them. The wise among these Navaho know what is really here. Beauty surrounds them, the living beauty of the land and the time-softened beauty of remembrance of recurrent tides of human history, and with it they wander.

That is what people come to my Southwest to find, those who come with open eyes and open mind. They come—all kinds and from everywhere —and my Southwest welcomes them. For the more sensible, the network of modern civilization is a series of stopping points from which they can go forth to see the true Southwest.

Most people come here, the first time anyway, determined to *do* the region, at least an aspect of it. They have itineraries plotted, schedules laid out. My Southwest offers each more than the most frantic scurrying could possibly cover.

Natural wonders? The entire region is one great natural wonder, a mosaic of individual wonders. Take any highway, any road, any old wheel track, and you run headlong into them. Hike anywhere in any direction and soon you will be lost in them. Simply scoot across on a federal highway and still you will see aplenty.

Ancient ruins? There is hardly a square mile of the region, save the highest mountain slopes, that has not been a homesite for some prehistoric people. (Prehistoric here means pre-Spanish, before the keeping of written records, our style.) Local archaeological clubs, with the aid of professional archaeologists, turn up new traces everywhere. Highway construction is often interrupted by the uncovering of previously unknown ruins.

Wilderness areas? Not just sparsely inhabited land but real wild wilderness? The national forests, more than 22 million acres of them, offer plenty of that. The vast Pecos Wilderness at the headwaters of the Pecos River, much of it wildlife sanctuary, is still country to satisfy a Daniel Boone. The Gila Wilderness, larger than Delaware and Rhode Island combined, rugged beyond belief, is still largely inaccessible except to those hardy enough to pack in.

My Southwest has more than enough of everything they come to see to keep visitors busy every moment!

And that, of course, is arrant nonsense!

To come here and dash about, determined to *do* the region, is to defeat yourself at the start—to bring into it something foreign. My Southwest is not a collection of sights to be seen, a museum to study, a zoo to visit. It is an experience to be shared, a romance to be lived, a beauty with which to wander.

Slow down. Perhaps simply stop and stay awhile. There is no need to dash about trying to cover it all. There is always tomorrow, or the next visit, or the one after that. Mary Austin said it a half century ago. *This is the sense of the desert hills, that there is room enough and time enough.* The slowing down comes first. Imperceptibly it claims you, an easing of tensions. You begin to look about with new vision.

197

CARLSBAD CAVERNS NATIONAL PARK

Carlsbad Caverns National Park in southeast New Mexico is the site of the largest, most beautiful subterranean caverns known to man. Visitors may take a three-mile tour that dips 829 feet below ground, and view a seemingly endless variety of fantastic rock formations. Each evening during the summer the cavern's bat colony, which numbers in the thousands, can be seen spiraling out of the natural entrance.

Carlsbad Caverns contain the largest known underground chamber, a fourteen-acre gallery called simply
the Big Room. This airy grotto is a showplace of cave
formations. Delicate stalactites hanging in the Doll
Theater (left) give it the look of an ornate stage.
In contrast to the stalactites, which form like icicles
from deposits on the ceiling, the thirty-six-foot
stalagmite, the Totem Pole (above), grew as water
dripped onto the floor from overhead.

NATURE'S GAUDIEST PAINTPOT

FRANCIS AND KATHARINE DRAKE

Some people think of Arizona as a sunbaked wilderness. It is not. It is a land of magnificent, infinitely varied scenery—mountains, lakes, forests, vivid deserts. It is a land of immense distances, where the wind really "blows free," where the vault of the sky seems vaster and the stars look more brilliant than anywhere else, and where the people have time for friendliness.

The climate is a balm for all seasons. The state is cut diagonally by the mighty Mogollon Rim, a towering rock rampart over 5000 feet high. North of it is a high plateau, cool and clear through the long summer. Skies sparkle over bright red cliffs and mountains, a strange place of dry highlands once the beds of ancient oceans and swamps, still holding deposits of seashells, sharks' teeth and dinosaur tracks. South of the rim, stretching down to Mexico, is the low country, a desert actually covered with cactus, cottonwood, sage, live oak and, in spring, wild flowers. Blazing hot in summer but warm and welcoming thereafter, this is a winter playground, set apart from others by the crystal air that tastes like dry champagne.

The highway north from Phoenix skirts little towns with such improbable labels as Horse Thief Basin, Bumble Bee and Broken Arrow, then swings into what seem to be the veritable gates of Valhalla. Instinctively the foot comes off the accelerator. On either side of the road, great red buttes and pinnacles rear up 1000, 2000 feet high, each named for its peculiar shape—Cathedral Rock, Coffee Pot, Thumb, Submarine, Mushroom. Here nature has dipped into her gaudiest paintpots, staining the sandstone cliffs with every hue from geranium red through amber to white.

Rabbit brush dots the eastern edge of the 3000-square-mile San Francisco Peaks Volcanic Field, north of Flagstaff, Arizona. These cones were vents for gases escaping from volcanoes which began erupting some 2 million years ago.

201

You approach a rock-rimmed gem called Sedona, a town suffused with sun, shade and glow, so neat that it regularly figures in Uncle Sam's "Ten Cleanest Cities." Side trails lead into the mountains and canyons, best seen from Sedona's fleet of tasseled pink jeeps, which zip up pathless crags at 45-degree angles, skirt dizzy precipices with the aplomb of mountain goats.

The Oak Creek Canyon road leads north through some of the most gorgeous scenery in the West, winding beside a quicksilver trout stream set in virgin timberland. Soon, almost-tropical blooms give way to the first alpine flowers, the maples and aspens to piñon and fir. You climb the Mogollon Rim in a series of hairpin turns, and come out on a highway running straight as an Indian arrow between rank upon rank of tall ponderosa pine. Up ahead are the snowcapped San Francisco Peaks, home of the Navaho gods.

Soon the way changes abruptly from wilderness to busy town—Flagstaff, nearly 7000 feet high, gateway to the high country.

Some eighty miles north of Flagstaff, with little warning, the road ends at a heavy guardrail. Beyond, the earth falls away into radiant space and absolute silence. In front of you, barring your way, is one of the greatest wonders of the world, the Grand Canyon—4 to 18 miles across, 217 miles long, a mile deep. The remote depths are colored with every flaming hue. Birds fly far below, but there is no other living thing visible, and not a whisper until the ear catches the distant sound of water. The eye strains, and sees a little brook, its surface slightly rippled, flowing between the walls of the Inner Gorge. The ripples may be fifteen feet high, and the "brook" is the swift Colorado River, sweeping from its source in the Rockies 1000 miles away and carrying some half million tons of sharp dirt and gravel a day. This is the force that has carved one of the deepest chasms in the world.

What makes the canyon so staggering, however, is not just its appearance and size—you could pile four Empire State Buildings one atop the other and still not reach the rim—but the fact that it shows the whole story of our world, displayed in brilliant horizontal bands, each millions of years thick. The bottom is 2 billion years old; then come strata after strata, age after age, spread before

Daisies and California poppies carpet the desert floor when spring comes to Tonto National Monument, east of Phoenix. To the northeast the Sierra Ancha forms a backdrop for giant saguaro cactuses, native only to the Arizona-Sonoran desert.

you like some titanic book. Sometimes the pages are rumpled; where the earth buckled and heaved, seas were formed and dried up, and mountains higher than Everest were raised, only to be worn flat again by wind and rain.

In museums windowed with plate glass, park rangers explain the formations and point to the Painted Desert, a hundred miles away. Sometime, they say, all this will be gone, the great rims will have been worn down, and the brawling Colorado will be a broad stream flowing to the sea. But now it is here.

Arizona is also a place of vast, man-made lakes—Mead, Havasu, Mohave, Roosevelt, San Carlos. The newest is Lake Powell, a turquoise body of water stretching nearly 200 miles, set in a treeless matrix of tomato-colored rock, indented with so many bays and side canyons that the shoreline is 1900 miles long. It was brought into being by the new Glen Canyon Dam. At first sight the dam looks small; only close up does it become immense. It is almost as tall as Hoover Dam, and the bridge beside it is the highest steel arch in the world. You cross the dam to Wahweap, a super motel-marina complex. There you find every water sport from skiing to skin diving, and even, unexpectedly, excellent fishing—thanks to the stocking zeal of the Arizona–Utah Departments of Fish and Game.

Lake Powell provides a safe waterway into nature's remotest stronghold, hitherto seen by few but explorers and Indians. The main channel lies between vermilion cliffs etched by "desert varnish" (a black exudate) into every imaginable picture—lions, castles, clipper ships, Mickey Mouse. Everything is gigantic; even the white "bathtub ring" left by the fluctuating water levels is higher than a house.

There are nineteen arches, the largest and most famous being Rainbow Bridge, just over the Utah border. Boats take visitors up Forbidden Canyon to within a mile of the bridge. Then a trail winds through exotic vegetation to the mighty stone arch—28 feet thick, 278 feet long between the canyon walls and 309 feet above the river that cuts beneath. It is so big that the Capitol dome in Washington would fit snugly beneath it, and sculptured in so many colors that the Navaho named it Rainbow Across the Sky.

Now we followed the old Navaho Trail, which linked the Middle West with California. It runs clear through the Navaho Reservation, a shimmering expanse of colored buttes and mesas—20 million acres in which live about 110,000 American Indians. The man cantering alongside the road is a Navaho and he waves cheerily in response to our greeting. (He cannot be photographed without his permission. Navaho are very proud, and this is his Nation, regained by treaty from the United States.)

His house, or hogan, is solitary—a Navaho doesn't like crowding. Made of juniper logs and red adobe, it is shaped like an inverted cup. Outside is the corral for his horses, sheep, goats. Inside, piles of skins and native blankets serve as beds. There is a loom on which his wife is making a vivid Navaho rug freehand, without a pattern, and a little anvil on which he hammers out bracelets, rings and bow guards to be set with turquoise.

The Nation is filled with U.S. national monuments: Canyon de Chelly, famous even in Spanish days for its cliff-dweller ruins; Petrified Forest, where the trees have turned to stone; Meteor Crater, where the largest object ever to hit the earth lies buried. There are also the three mesas of the Hopi, people who make beautiful jewelry and stage their annual Snake Dance holding live rattlers in their mouths. And Monument Valley, a famous and beautiful place rimmed by tall buttes and monoliths scoured into shapes like cathedral spires, elephant feet, running buffalo.

The whole scene is a living canvas in violent contrast to our own crowded existence. The Indian is locked in a struggle between the old folks—the long hairs, who live "under the blanket," worship the old gods and sing the Night Chant for sickness—and the new generation, which has learned about clean clothes, varied food and having babies in hospitals. Change is treading closer. Yet, however far the Navaho goes—to Yale or Harvard or to the cities—the spell of this ancient land pulls him back, to the blanket, and to the wild heritage that is still ours to see.

South of the Mogollon Rim lies a winter paradise of smoke-colored mountains and Wild West scenery—now also a place of guest ranches and luxury motels with swimming pools, palm trees, golf courses and rodeos.

From Phoenix excellent highways fan out to showplaces like the Apache Trail, a breathtaking drive that snakes along tall cliffs and tops out at Roosevelt Dam, which backs up a lake twenty-five miles long. From Roosevelt the road loops north through the Tonto Basin, a great parkland, and through the Tonto Forest of giant pines. Salt River Canyon, one of the great sights of the Southwest, lies east via Globe. A superb engineering feat built a forty-mile road through cholla, saguaro, yucca and prickly pear to this miniature Grand Canyon cut by the Salt River.

Tucson, 115 miles southeast of Phoenix, was once the center of the old Southwest in its shootingest days. Now it is a winter resort. Not far away is Tombstone—"the town too tough to die" —which has preserved its old stores and long bars, its "opera house" where miners in frock coats sat swilling champagne, its O.K. Corral and its Boot Hill cemetery with the quaint tombstones ("Hanged," "Shot by Mistake," "Died with His Boots On").

So much space, so many notable places to see. Nothing in the magnificent variety of our wonderful land surpasses the color of Arizona, its drama and beauty. These have been the religion of the Indians whose land it was long before the white man came. The first words a Navaho child hears are the prayer: "May he walk in beauty." And when his journey over the gleaming plains is ended, the last words will be those of the Night Chant: "In beauty it is finished." This beauty lives on for us to see, to remember, to think about.

Named for the white plaster on one of its walls, the White House nestles beneath a 500-foot sandstone cliff in Arizona's Canyon de Chelly National Monument. The three-story dwelling was built about 1100 A.D. by prehistoric Indians.

GRAND CANYON OF THE COLORADO

DONALD CULROSS PEATTIE

There is a giant that once claimed dominion over one twelfth of the area of this country—the Colorado River, which has a score of other young giants, only comparatively smaller, working for it in six great states. Their united strength is 5 million prime horsepower. Rearing, bucking, locoed horsepower it was, before puny man threw a halter over it.

Until Hoover Dam was built in 1935, the Colorado was the wickedest stream in the world. For 1000 miles it flows far below the level of the surrounding country, gouging away the land, so that though your life might depend on getting one handful of its muddy waters to drink you could wander till you dropped before you found a way down its sheer sides. Yet it has repeatedly gone berserk in flood. After running low along its bed of gigantic rocks it has in a single night risen to a tide that destroyed everything in its path. Emerging from its prison walls, this torrent devastated vast areas in Arizona and California, every year building higher the barren, queasy delta at its mouth, and lashing restlessly over this wasteland till it spent its rage in the Gulf of California.

Seventeen hundred miles from that muddy mouth rises the pure source of the Colorado. This headstream, called the Green, is the highborn child of the Wind River Mountains in Wyoming. At their breasts of snow the little Green is nursed, and it runs laughing away, down through forests of lodgepole pines, till it reaches the sagebrush plains. There it slips stealthily until it must break through Utah's mountains. Then for the next 1000 miles the river's course is a commingling of horror and beauty. And along that course, through the ages, the Colorado has created the greatest of all natural masterpieces—the Grand Canyon. Here the Colorado, glinting distantly at the bottom of the canyon like a silver thread, seems the least of the spectacle. Yet the river carved that gulf, up to 18 miles across, a mile deep and 217 miles long. The scale of the canyon is so vast that it dawns on one only slowly, and even today the visitor can hardly believe that huge skyscrapers could be tucked out of sight beneath the canyon's many cliffs.

And here the Colorado has laid open the book of life, so that modern man may read the story from a great stone page. Down, down through the great Redwall of Mississippian limestone (300 million years old) the river has rasped. Today it is filing away furiously at the hard black schists and pink granites of the Archean era—rocks so old they antedate the appearance of life on earth.

The canyon's depths long remained unscaled, its river uncharted, though famous scouts and trappers of the West one after another tried to conquer the forbidding current. Time flowed by. Gold was discovered in California, the Civil War was fought, the continent was linked by rails, and still the Colorado, throughout much of its course, remained unknown, unmapped, the most mysterious and terrifying river in the world. Then on May 24, 1869, at the town of Green River, Wyoming, while coolies and cowboys and railroad men and Indians watched, a band of nine men put four boats into the Green's flood. Their leader, Maj. John Wesley Powell, was determined to lick the Colorado with one hand. (He had lost his right arm at Shiloh.) Schoolteacher, botanist, geologist, surveyor, this thirty-five-year-old Illinois veteran, more scholar than explorer, had wrung from Congress and the Smithsonian Institution a small fund for expenses to explore the canyon's 2 billion years of geology.

His men were young and toughened to western life. His twenty-one-foot boats were of stout oak, with air chambers to right them in case of capsizing. Food for ten months, clothing, firearms and scientific instruments loaded the boats deeply as they sped down Flaming Gorge. In Lodore Canyon, at Disaster Falls, one of the boats was smashed to bits. Into Whirlpool Canyon spun the three remaining craft, on through Desolation Canyon and the endless Labyrinth, through Cataract Canyon, past Dirty Devil Creek.

Day after day, driving himself relentlessly, the one-armed Major toiled with his instruments up perilous walls to take observations and map his course. Strong though they were, his companions were exhausted from lowering waterlogged boats on ropes, portaging them for miles over rocks, often making but three miles a day. They were now in the depths of the Grand Canyon's granites.

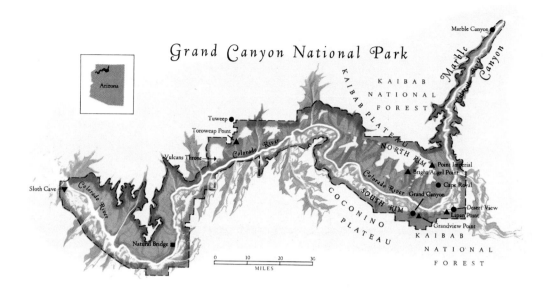

Grand Canyon National Park

With nerves frayed, they broke into quarrels; rocks and rapids no worse than those they had surmounted looked appalling. Indeed, every canyon explorer who ever lived to tell the tale has spoken of a strange river-fear that overpowers even the bravest man, sometimes quite unexpectedly and after weeks of conquering obstacles.

In such a mood, perhaps, three of the Powell party, toward the end of August, took their share of the rations and a duplicate set of the Major's records, in case he should perish, and climbed up out of the canyon. Finally, on August 29, Powell's party emerged from the Grand Canyon, to find men scanning the water—at the anxious request of the government—for their corpses or any fragment of their wreckage. The three who had quit were never seen again. Two years later Powell ran the course a second time, and emerged with complete scientific records. Thereafter he was made chief of the new U.S. Geological Survey and became its greatest organizer.

Today visitors come by the thousands—the great and simple of earth, all in a spirit of marvel. Travelers come from every state in the union, from every country in Europe and Asia, pilgrims to a shrine that is greater than creed.

The Grand Canyon of the Colorado River is one of the wonders of the world, unsurpassed in vastness, antiquity and splendor. Of all the world's spectacles no other has its power to still the restless pulse and uplift the human soul. Here is immensity, almost another dimension. In this abyss the chasms drop away into further depths that disappear into a night of deeps like the ocean's. Here are colors raised to a soundless shout—smoldering reds, purples of shadow recessed into a fathomless past, yellow dunes and shores of seas that vanished ages ago. Far down, where a glint of the river shows, lies the sullen black of Archean rock.

Up from these nethermost realms comes welling silence. Seldom can you hear the roar of the river. You cannot catch the patter, like applause, from the leaves of the cottonwoods on the shelf-like plateau below you. For all sounds are swallowed in this gulf of space. "It makes you want to whisper," I once heard a woman murmur to her companion as we stood on the canyon rim. This is a silence not of death; rather it is a presence. It flows into you like great music. But music made of man works up to a climax and ceases; the Grand Canyon is all climax, a chord echoing into eternity. For that fourth dimension you feel in the canyon is, of course, time—time in unstinted measure. Although it took the Colorado several million years to cut the Grand Canyon, the river is a newcomer. It didn't even begin to flow until seas of past ages, here in these Arizona wastes, had come and gone several times, laying down beds of sediment.

The grinding might of the river, which carries a

A mile deep, 217 miles long, up to 18 miles wide, the Grand Canyon of the Colorado River in Arizona is for most Americans the ultimate scenic wonder. In this view from the South Rim, Bright Angel Creek gleams far below to the right.

➡

million tons of sediment a day, the cold chisel of frost and the little blades of rain together have cut this great cross section of the past. Testimony written in rock is here laid bare for science to read. Indeed, at one glance you perceive that there is a magnificent order running through these fantasies in stone, these reckless outpourings of brilliance. The same bands of rock, distinct in thickness and color and angle, can often be traced along the canyon's length. Like a great stairway the alternating cliffs and plateaus lead the eye up, as one geologic step succeeds another, from the age of chaos, before there was any life, right into the sunshine of the present, where the ponderosa pines stand tall in the dry Arizona air, where the browsing deer gaze mildly, where wild flowers dance to the very rim, and the mind of man ventures forth to understand the beauty it beholds.

Perhaps the most spectacular feature of the Grand Canyon, its Redwall limestone cliff, stands about halfway up the chasm and is practically vertical for the canyon's entire length. The cliff's average height is 550 feet—almost exactly that of the Washington Monument. Though it is actually gray-blue limestone, the surface of the cliff has been stained to a sunset hue by iron salts washing out of the rocks. The purity of the limestone indicates that it was formed in a wide and quiet sea full of beautiful seashells and fish of a type no longer known.

Above the great Redwall come alternating layers of red sandstone and shale 1000 feet thick, which show the fossils of insect wings and fern fronds and the quaint, stubby-toed tracks of extinct animals related to our frogs. Then there must have followed a long period of desert conditions, for the next layer, pale-hued, seems to have been formed by windblown sands. The topmost layers are a yellowish limestone, laid down in warm seas, we can be sure, because so many fossilized sharks' teeth and corals have been found in them.

For ages untold after the river came, the canyon grew, glowing with summer's fires, glistening with winter's snows, time passing over it like the shadows of the clouds that give it its ever-changing expressions. In the fullness of that time came men to live in its shelter, prehistoric red men whose dwelling places, more than 500 of them, have been found in the side canyons. A thousand years,

Just downstream from Upset Rapids, the Colorado River flows beneath 4000-foot cliffs. The river, which has been at work for 10 million years, is still carving its awesome canyon by the abrasive action of its debris-laden waters.

perhaps, these tribes lived here. And after they were gone there passed nearly a thousand more years before a little band of weary Spaniards, soldiers of Coronado, stumbled to the rim and saw the canyon. But they were seeking gold, not scenery, and felt disappointed, not elated.

Then came Spanish missionaries, American trappers and explorers. Always the canyon awed and baffled them; they could not find a way down its sides, and because of its great length it forced them hundreds of toiling miles out of their way into the deserts. Then in 1858 bold young Lt. Joseph C. Ives, having forced his way in a steamboat upriver to the site of the present Hoover Dam, led his little party of army engineers, guided by Mohave Indians, afoot into the depths of the Grand Canyon. Here he visited the friendly Havasupai tribe, which lived then and still lives in one of the side canyons, down where the climate is subtropical the year round. "Ours has been the first party," reported Ives, "to visit this profitless locality." Then he added the rash prediction that it would doubtless be the last. Eleven years later came Major Powell from the other end of the canyon.

Now, a hundred years after that historic trip, visitors to the South Rim alone may number 18,000 in a single day. Some of that number will travel by mule train down Bright Angel Trail to the canyon's floor, cross the raging river by a suspension bridge and mount to the North Rim.

Though the two rims face each other across only twelve unbridgeable miles, it is a journey of 214 miles by car from one to the other. Nor can you visit the North Rim except in summer; some 1200 feet higher than the South Rim, it has a delightful climate in July and August under the shade of aspen, spruce and fir, but is winterbound with ten to fifteen feet of snow much of the year.

But there is no day that you may not visit the South Rim and find the sun warm upon the cheek and the air perfumed with the incense of piñon smoke from a Hopi Indian hearth. Here in a few paces you may step forth from the confines of your everyday life and face the fact of the canyon—the grandest and most boldly stated fact on earth. As down and down through rock of ages the river has cut, it has revealed to us how life comes up and up. And through the beholder surges a sense of the power of the divine will. The Grand Canyon is a sight with the impact of revelation. Said the Dutch-American author and journalist Hendrik van Loon, "I came here an atheist, and departed a devout believer."

211

THE MYSTERIES OF MONUMENT VALLEY

ROBERT DE ROOS

Stand with me on the red sand floor and look around. Everywhere mesas and buttes, some of them 1000 feet high, rise sharply and separately from the rose-gold dunes. Distances are deceptive. The monuments seem close at hand one moment, far away another. Also, they appear to change in shape from minute to minute. This is Monument Valley, in northern Arizona.

The valley is impersonal in its immensities, yet curiously intimate. As you study the formations, they take on "personality." Some are vaguely architectural—ruined temples, fortresses, banks, skyscrapers, rugged castles. Others recall roosters, rabbits, witches, mules, babies, profiles of great men. In the constantly shifting light, they seem to pulse and glow.

Monument Valley straddles the Arizona-Utah border north of Kayenta, Arizona, on the Navaho reservation. The valley is enormous—forty by fifty miles. But most of the monuments rise in a relatively small area about sixty miles west of the Four Corners, where Arizona, Utah, Colorado and New Mexico meet briefly. Although the monuments seem to change, actual transformation is imperceptible over the years. The age of the sandstone is immense: Geologists believe that the red de Chelly (pronounced de Shay) sandstone was laid down as silt from Colorado mountains some 230 million years ago. Later, the whole area was inundated by an ancient sea that covered almost half of North America. During the flood, Monument Valley was completely overlaid by silt eroded from the first Rocky Mountains. After the sea receded, an earth convulsion formed the present Rockies, and the whole Colorado plateau was tilted and broken. Within the last 50 million years, the top silts eroded away. What remains is the core of the old de Chelly rocks capped by later formations. Long-dead volcanoes have left a legacy of lava plugs, dikes and fumaroles.

I went into the valley one morning with Harry Goulding, the tall, shy trading-post owner for whom the valley was his life. In the morning light the monuments seemed subdued, but as the sun rose in the sky it began to play tricks with their colors. "Watch the monuments grow," Goulding said. That was the illusion. As we wound down to the valley floor, the monuments slowly "grew" until we were utterly dwarfed by their bulk.

We stopped our jeep at the foot of Merrick Butte. Harry plucked a bit of mint sage, aromatic and bearing a purple flower. "This is the purple sage Zane Grey wrote about," he said. He pointed out other vegetation: Mormon tea, squaw tea—and baby bush. "We call it cliff rose," Goulding said. "The Navaho named it baby bush because they used the middle bark, a talclike fiber, to keep their babies from chafing." He laughed. "The Navaho knew about disposable diapers before we ever heard of them."

We churned through drifted sand around the base of the North Mitten and the South Mitten, monuments the Indians called the Big Hands. It was almost uncanny the way the perspective changed as we moved: It was as though the monuments wheeled gently around us, changing their positions and relation to their fellows.

We drove through Sourdough Pass, where the rocks look like stacks of flapjacks six feet in diameter, to a lofty dune where we looked across a wash at the Totem Pole, a slender needle spire as high as a forty-five-story building. The spire seems to defy all rules of gravity. It has a notable list, is cracked almost in two. Nevertheless it stands—part of what the Navaho call the Yea-Bechai group. "To the Navaho this group recalls their winter sings—the Yea-Bechai," Goulding said. "To them the formation depicts robed and plumed dancers coming out to sing in single file."

A trip across the valley is full of surprises. One day we came upon a great half-dome which had been weathered out of a solid-looking cliff. High in the dome was a hole, eroded through the rock. "You can see why the Indians call this the Big Hogan," Goulding said. The huge cavity looked like a greatly exaggerated hogan (the domed mud and timber house of the Navaho), complete to the chimney hole. Nearby was another tremendous hole, cut through a bluff in the shape of an

A Navaho sheepherder brings his flock to drink at Sand Springs, a small stream that runs the year round in Monument Valley Tribal Park. Most of the park's 30,000 acres lie in Arizona, but its northern tip crosses the Utah border.

Late afternoon shadows stretch across the desert floor in the Utah section of Monument Valley. At this time of day it is easy to see why "The People," as the Navaho call themselves, gave the valley the name Among the Red Rocks.

ear. In the winter, Goulding said, the wind whistles an eerie song through the window. "The Navaho call it the Ear of the Wind."

Dozens of ruins left by prehistoric Indians prove that this land was once verdant enough to support a fairly large population. There are undeciphered picture writings on the cliffs—paintings and petroglyphs depicting antelope and deer. At the House of Many Hands, an adobe ruin of what was once a large pueblo at the foot of a 700-foot cliff, are the imprints of hundreds of hands, each one different, many quite small. They were printed on the cliff face in white paint that has lasted hundreds of years. Goulding believes that this was perhaps the site of a maturity ceremony for girls, who left their hand prints on the rock as a sign that they had completed the rites.

Monument Valley differs from our national parks. It is Navaho land, owned, administered and

inhabited by the tribe. The Navaho herd their sheep, rear their children, seek out water holes, live and die in this skeletal land. A noble-spirited and stoic people, they are surrounded by grandeur, but there is little grandeur in their poverty-filled lives.

On my last evening I sat on the porch of Goulding's lodge, perched on a shelf of Big Rock Door Mesa. We looked eight miles across his "front yard" to the row of gigantic monuments someone has called Harry's Picket Fence. They stretched in a seemingly straight line across the desert.

The evening show was on! In the slanting rays of the sun, the buttes glowed. I have seen molten copper the same color. It was possible to believe that the monuments held raging fires which heated and colored their sides. The worn, majestic, flat-top buttes flamed with incandescence, scarlet and vermilion against the blue of the sky.

The sunset hour in Monument Valley is a call to Armageddon. And yet it is not at all fearful. There is in the sight something of hope against the night —and an emblem of tomorrow's promise. It is one of the great spectacles of the world.

ARCHES NATIONAL PARK

Arches National Park, located in sparsely-populated southeastern Utah, is an amazing geological showplace. The park's 129 square miles contain more stone arches, windows, spires and pinnacles than any other place in the country. Here visitors can see dozens of natural stone arches in various stages of formation and decay. Their story began about 150 million years ago when the stone was formed by wind-borne sand and sediment from an inland sea. As the sandstone hardened, vertical cracks formed about twenty feet apart. Weathering widened the cracks, and the stone between them became thin fins. As the elements continued to erode the fins, holes finally appeared in their centers. The same forces enlarged the holes, leaving only the arches. Since this weathering is still going on, someday these soaring arches must collapse.

Landscape Arch, in the Devil's Garden section of Arches National Park, is believed to be the longest natural span of stone in the world. Made of Entrada sandstone, the arch runs north and south and measures 291 feet. Prehistoric Indians camped near the arch while gathering quartz for arrowheads; today visitors may pitch their tents in the same area.

STANDING-UP
COUNTRY

PAUL AND MYRIAM FRIGGENS

Halting our pack outfit on a canyon rim, we gazed in awe at Canyonlands, one of America's newest national parks. Before us towered battlements resembling a medieval fortress or a fairytale castle; sandstone skyscrapers that might have been the Manhattan skyline; spires and needles higher than the Washington Monument. Here the Colorado and Green rivers, while slicing through stair-stepped plateaus and down-plunging canyons, have laid bare some 200 million years of geologic history.

It's "standing-up country" ("There's more of it standing up than lying down!" an old-time cowpuncher said) and probably the greatest red-rock fantasy on earth. With Superintendent Bates Wilson we were pioneering the first pack trip since this fifteen-by-thirty-mile, 257,640-acre scenic area in southeastern Utah was set aside by Congress. Located in the wild, remote Colorado Plateau, haunt successively of cliff-dwelling Indians, Spanish conquistadores, cowboys, train robbers, cattle rustlers and uranium hunters, Canyonlands is nevertheless an all-season park, relatively convenient to airlines and traveled U.S. highways. Said Wilson, "I call it a combination of Bryce, Zion and Mesa Verde, plus Grand Canyon spread out so you can see a lot more of it."

A pair of intrepid Spanish padres, Friars Francisco Domínguez and Silvestre Escalante, first reported on the Canyonlands area at precisely the same time that America was declaring its independence—in July 1776. It remained largely inaccessible and almost unknown to the public, however, until fortune hunters opened up some of the region during the uranium boom of the 1950s. President Johnson signed the Canyonlands National Park bill in September 1964.

Flying commercial airlines direct to Moab, the onetime uranium boomtown near the north entrance to Canyonlands, we began our tour with a "windshield adventure." Veteran driver Joe Lemon jeeped us in his trusty "Green Lizard" up

Shafer Trail, a sheer 1500-foot climb to the park, past chilling drop-offs all the way. "It used to be a cattle trail," Joe explained. "Then the uranium prospectors decided to widen it for jeeps. The government people threw up their hands and said it would cost a fortune, so the miners just built it themselves. Bulldozed and blasted from the top down."

Suddenly we came on one of the most striking features of the park—Island in the Sky, an isolated mesa reached by a precipitous, forty-foot-wide neck with drop-offs on both sides. On to Grandview Point, where "standing-up country" rolled out before us to the distant snowcapped La Sal Mountains. Below lay the incomparable White Rim, a border of tough, resistant sandstone

edging the canyons as far as the eye could see. Beneath the rim were clustered delicate minarets, imposing monuments and great waferlike fins—an incredibly rugged landscape carved out by wind and water.

We spent a leisurely day jet-boating down the Colorado. For really adventurous souls there was a specially arranged, six-day rubber-raft journey down Cataract Canyon, one of the roughest stretches of white water in the country. Secretly relieved that we didn't have the National Park Service permit necessary for this hair-raising cruise, we settled for a flight over the colorful Canyonlands—"flying the rocks," pilot George Hubler called it. We shot color film with abandon, and were reluctant to come down.

Weirdly eroded cliffs and spires surround Chesler Park in the Needles area of Utah's Canyonlands National Park. Like many other attractions in the park's rugged southern half, this valley is along a road too rough for ordinary cars.

Another day, with Joe Lemon and his Green Lizard, we lurched the 38-percent grade up Elephant Hill, then descended to a desert paradise gloriously abloom with lilies, Indian paintbrush, phlox, penstemon and cacti. We camped in the Devil's Kitchen, a bowllike meadow guarded by jaunty red-sandstone sentinels with white caps. With the pleasant aroma of our juniper log fire still lingering on the morning air, we went hunting before breakfast for Indian picture writings, some of which, we were told, the ingenious artists

219

sprayed on the canyon walls by blowing pigment through a straw. We photographed several vivid examples, then breakfasted with gusto, silently agreeing with Mark Twain's dictum: "Nothing helps scenery like ham and eggs."

By now we were deep in the fabulous Needles area of the park—55,000 acres of pinnacles, towers, spires, balanced rocks and grabens. The latter are parallel slippages in the earth, which leave valleys or "rifts" up to six miles long and 300 yards wide. Perhaps Canyonlands' most beautiful creations are the Windows in the Sky, arch formations of exquisite artistry. Most spectacular is Druid Arch, a sandstone colossus more than 200 feet high, so called because it resembles England's famed Stonehenge, popularly associated with the Druids. You have to hike a rugged six miles round trip, up canyons and down, to see it, but it's worth the effort.

Finally the day arrived for us to pack in with Superintendent Wilson as he plotted a wilderness trail in the remote south end of the park. "You'll be sampling a ride we hope thousands will enjoy someday," he explained. "But don't expect deluxe service!"

Our freshly shod horses took us across the rocky mesas, forcing their way through the thick undergrowth of piñon and juniper. By midafternoon we reached the rim of Salt Creek Canyon, gasped at the breathtaking panorama, then began our 1000-foot descent by an old cowboy trail. Before long we had to dismount and lead our reluctant horses as they gingerly picked their way among the loose, sliding rocks. Suddenly our trail ended altogether, and our horses slid on their haunches down deep gullies and jump-offs while we followed, lest 2000 pounds of horseflesh crash down upon us. It was almost dark when we at last reached the canyon floor and the sanctuary of Salt Creek. "Of course, we'll fix up the trail for future riders," Wilson promised. Then he added, "But we don't want it to be a picnic either."

After breakfasting in the crisp, dewy dawn, we broke camp to explore new wilderness wonders: meadows soft with desert flowers; delicate Wedding Ring and Angel arches, the latter over 200 feet high, 163 feet wide; and the silent, abandoned ruins of the Anasazi or "ancient ones" who probably inhabited these canyons 800 years ago.

It's one thing to view dioramas of these early cliff-dwelling people in a museum, quite another to come suddenly upon the prehistoric remains of an entire pueblo in a remote, untrammeled canyon. There, sequestered in the rock of a mammoth cliff, stood a series of two- and three-story stone and adobe structures, perfectly preserved and impregnable as the day they were built. "We call it the Big Ruins," Wilson explained. "We think thirty or forty families lived in this single pueblo, and they must have gained access to the cliff by some sort of ladder. On our park inspection we got down from the top by descending a series of wooden pegs drilled in the face of the vertical cliff."

At the end of our stay in the Canyonlands wonderland, Superintendent Wilson gave us parting words of advice to pass on to future visitors: "Come to our wilderness, but be ready to rough it. We want to keep Canyonlands America's most rugged national park."

UTAH'S POCKET SAHARA

JOSEPH WOOD KRUTCH

Every year thousands of tourists pass through the little Utah town of Kanab, on their way northward toward Zion and Bryce canyons or eastward toward the Glen Canyon National Recreation Area. Most of them do not even notice a modest wooden arrow a few miles east of the town which points down a dirt road and is marked "Coral Dunes." Still fewer accept its invitation, and that is perhaps just as well, for the undisturbed beauty of the dunes (some dozen miles from the main road) is one of their charms. On an early June morning my companions and I had them to ourselves in the cool of 5000 feet.

Much of northern Arizona and southern Utah is a land of towering sandstone mesas and buttes, some white, some pink and some coral red. They have been sculptured into fantastic shapes and are gradually being eroded away by water, frost and especially by windblown sand. Some are half buried in debris of particles worn off from their own rock, but still rise sheer above the

The struggle for life on Utah's Coral Dunes is dramatized by a setting sun. Sunflowers thrust their stalks above the constantly enveloping sand; one pine grows in a hollow, but beyond stands the skeleton of another, defeated by the sand.

plains. At the Coral Dunes, on the other hand, the prevailing wind has heaped and shaped sand into dunes as high as twenty-five feet.

Nothing quite prepares one for the climactic view. The approach is across a semidesert, increasingly sandy but with the sand held in place by fairly abundant sage and juniper, together with a few pines. All of them grow less and less abundant, and then one comes upon a true Sahara of drifting coral-colored dunes sloping gently upward on one side, dropping off abruptly on the other; sometimes rippled as though by waves of a seashore; sometimes almost unbelievably smooth and sleek.

At first one is unaware of any living thing except, perhaps, for ravens calling derisively overhead. No animals are visible. But the most casual inspection reveals the fact that they are only unseen, not absent. There are tracks that can only be those of a bobcat and there are other curious little bipedal marks that proclaim the kangaroo rat. Most beautiful, and at first most puzzling, are long lines of the most delicate tracery, sketched across the smooth surface uphill and down. Each one is perfect despite its obvious fragility and all suggest some secret, mysterious workman. What could have made them? Not a small lizard, because there is no trailing tail mark. Certainly not a sidewinder rattlesnake, whose strange tracks are much broader and in other ways quite different.

It doesn't take much looking to find the answer. The tiny workmen are busy everywhere, often no more than a few yards from one another. They are little, shiny, quarter-inch, scarablike beetles. From the order to which they belong, it seems a pretty safe guess that their unresting progress uphill and down is motivated by nothing more spiritual than a search for the droppings of a jackrabbit. But it would not be difficult to imagine that they are artists, endlessly engaged in beautifying the dunes with the perfect but changeless pattern of lace that nature has ordained their six legs to make during many millenia. They will continue to make it for untold millenia hence, unless, as seems not improbable, man destroys their environment even as he is destroying that of many more conspicuous creatures.

Most of the dunes are shifting, and they often march forward in the direction of the prevailing wind. Any sizable plant that manages to get established tends to anchor the sand around it, but more often than not it is overwhelmed by the slowly advancing waves that may ultimately pass over it. Then a shallower bed of sand is created in which a new generation of plants may be able to grow.

Evidence of that process is plainly visible in the Coral Dunes. One may see, for example, the skeleton of a pine killed sometime in the past by an advancing wave; beside it are younger pines or junipers that have grown since the crest of the wave passed by. On the leeward side of one of the highest dunes a single clump of sagebrush is visible; but it is doomed and half buried already.

A mule-ears blossom adds a dash of yellow to the sands of Coral Pink Sand Dunes State Park, near Kanab, Utah. This hardy sunflower, known to botanists as Wyethia scabra, *is found only in the cooler regions of the southwestern states.*

Many wild flowers, able to establish themselves and mature in much less time than the juniper or even the sagebrush, flourish in patches that here and there provide an arresting flash of color, standing vividly against the red of the dunes. Two are especially conspicuous: the large yellow member of the sunflower tribe sometimes called mule-ears, and the lovely blue *Sophora stemophylla*, which, from a short distance, might be mistaken for a lupine and which has no common name. Most surprising in the desert is a little mushroom, the desert puffball.

All the larger plants must send down deep roots, and some of them may survive even an advancing wave of sand by raising their stems higher and higher as the roots go deeper and deeper. This is the method of a handsome yucca of limited distribution named *Yucca kanabensis* after the nearby town. A different solution to the problem is to spread out over a large area and send down two shallow roots every foot or two to snatch from the surface the water of the rare and usually limited showers. This is the method of another characteristic plant, the scurf pea, a single prostrate branch of which may be more than seventy feet long.

Dunes like these are both esthetically pleasing and ecologically instructive. But they are equally interesting in another way. They occur less frequently than mountains or plains or valleys or canyons, but like all of these they are quite distinct and recognizable geomorphic features and, again like the others, they raise in any inquiring mind the question of how and why they came into being.

In terms of earth and atmospheric mechanics, the answer is always the same whether the material be the sands of a seashore, the gypsum grains of the great White Sands of New Mexico, the eroded sandstone of these Coral Dunes or even the ice crystals of the snowdrift. And the forms assumed are so similar that a photograph of the White Sands might easily be mistaken for that of a New England snowbank.

Given a flat, open surface and hard grains of material too heavy to be blown away by the prevailing wind but not too heavy to be moved by it, the dunes are nearly inevitable. If the grains are too light, they blow away as dust; if they are too heavy (small pebbles, for example), they cannot be piled up by the winds. But if they are just right, you get the similar outlines of the same geomorphic feature. Dryness helps, too, because damp sand doesn't blow easily. And there are minor variations in shapes, depending partly upon the character of the winds. But a dune is a dune is a dune.

Geographers tell us that the wind seldom lifts sand particles more than a foot or two, that the grains are usually simply rolled along, and that they come to rest when the wind's velocity decreases. Once started, a dune itself becomes an obstruction around which the winds swirl and deposit more sand.

Because of the variations in wind velocity and sand supply, there are different characteristic shapes in different regions, and those most characteristic of the Coral Dunes are what are called barchans—that is, hillocks with a sloping side up which the prevailing winds blow the sand and a steeper leeward side where the grains have come to their angle of repose.

Though the Coral Dunes of Utah are in many respects typical, there is one fact about them of additional interest: The material of which they are composed has been twice reduced to sand in the course of many millions of years.

The mesas and buttes that surround them are composed of Navaho sandstone formed during the Jurassic period (say, 100 or 150 million years ago). But that sandstone was composed of the detritus or debris from much more ancient mountains long before worn down. Now this Navaho sandstone has itself been eroded away to make the sand which may (given more millions of years) again solidify into stone—either under water or, like the sandstones of nearby Zion, right on the desert itself. In that case they will still exhibit by their cross-bedding the outlines of successive dunes, like those so clearly seen in Zion.

There are few more striking examples of the restlessness of our earth—always building up, tearing down and then building up again as the result of the processes that will probably continue until a completely cooled earth can no longer raise mountains and its whole surface is reduced to a featureless plain.

Just before I arrived at the Coral Dunes, a local newspaper announced the coming invasion of a fleet of sand buggies which proposed to race up and down over the dunes. Fortunately, wind will, in this case, probably erase their vandalism in a comparatively short time. But here is another example of the fallacy of "multiple use." You cannot use the Coral Dunes (now an undeveloped state park) for both sand-buggy racing and the quiet enjoyment of their esthetic, ecological and geographical interest.

WHEELER PEAK SCENIC AREA

Some of eastern Nevada's most exceptional scenic, botanical and geological attractions are in Wheeler Peak Scenic Area, a 28,000-acre tract within Humboldt National Forest. Wheeler Peak, at 13,063 feet, dominates the area, but there are six other summits above 11,000 feet. Lehman Caves National Monument, with large and exceptionally beautiful caverns, is on the eastern slope of Wheeler Peak. Many of the caves and rock shelters bear prehistoric paintings. Close to the scenic area stands Lexington Arch, a limestone span six stories high.

The twisted trunk of a dead bristlecone pine stands in glacial debris on Wheeler Peak's northeast face. Bristlecone pines are the oldest known living things in the world—one tree, now dead, lived for 4900 years.

Wheeler Peak and a curtain of dark evergreens provide a dramatic setting for the flashy foliage of quaking aspens in Lehman Creek Canyon. Wheeler Peak is the loftiest of the Snake Range.

Part VI

LAND OF EVERGREENS AND SHINING PEAKS

California

Oregon   Washington

AMERICA'S HOT SPOT

BEN LUCIEN BURMAN

"It's sure a hot day," said the grizzled old prospector as he slowed his battered pickup truck to glance at a lizard beside the road. "I was looking to see if it was a stick lizard," he drawled. "That's a special kind ain't found nowhere but here. He picks up a little piece of mesquite twig and uses it kind of like a pogo stick when he has to go walking in warm weather, so his feet don't get too hot. Lizards out here got to be extra smart. Like the people."

I could almost believe that tall tale. We were in Death Valley, California, the hottest place in the United States. Thermometers thrust into the ground here in midsummer have recorded an incredible 190° F., only twenty-two degrees below boiling point. The pickup rattled along the highway. Before us lay a fantastic panorama—dazzling white salt beds surrounded by gloomy, towering mountains. Mirages showed here and there, queer-shaped lakes, sometimes with what appeared to be a boat or a wharf, as a huge rock caught the reflection of the sun.

Now we began to climb, and the air grew cooler. We reached Dante's View, where the valley lay spread out before us in all its somber beauty. At our right were the grim Funeral Mountains and opposite them, to the west, the lofty Panamints. Directly under us were the white salt flats of Badwater, 282 feet below sea level, the lowest point in the western hemisphere. At the same time, we could see in the far distance the highest point in conterminous United States, snow-covered Mount Whitney, rising 14,495 feet above sea level. I saw how the surrounding mountain ranges trapped any moisture-laden clouds that might have watered this valley, making it a huge stone bake-oven in which countless prospectors

have lost their lives. Nevertheless, Death Valley is still a mecca for prospectors out of the pages of Bret Harte and Mark Twain. I was traveling with one of them, a weather-beaten gold seeker nicknamed Copperstain.

Leaving Dante's View, we dropped down again to the valley floor. Copperstain pulled up beside a little stream trickling over the hot sand, where some minnow-size fish could be seen darting about. "These here's what we call desert sardines," he said. "But they ain't like any sardine ever come out of a can. When winter comes the fish'll just disappear. And then when the hot weather comes back, there's the fish swimming around again, pretty as can be. Where they stay ain't nobody been able to figure out."

The 3000-foot Death Valley Buttes, here backed by snow-crowned Hunter Mountain, rise from the valley floor northeast of Stovepipe Wells. Mostly in California, Death Valley National Monument covers nearly 3000 square miles.

As we turned up a mountain trail, a cabin showed ahead, near the entrance to an old mine shaft. Once a rich producer of gold ore, the mine was being worked again by some hopeful valley characters, one of whom was known as the Duke of Muddy Water. The Duke, a youngish, well-spoken man with a friendly face somewhat obscured by a heavy beard, courteously invited us to stop for lunch. Afterward he led us to the shaft to see the ore they were getting. Crushing a sample, he showed me how to wash it in the heavy iron pan. As I sluiced the water about, the crushed rock separated, and at last I saw some shining grains on the bottom of the pan. The Duke gave me a magnifying glass, and as I looked again each grain became a gleaming nugget. Suddenly I felt the lure that made these men undergo hardship and danger.

Later Copperstain and I drove down to the flats once more. The heat had increased, and a fiery wind was now sweeping across the salt-flecked plain, drying my face until I thought the skin would split. Off in the distance, sand whirls danced weirdly, forerunners of those huge sand pillars 200 feet thick and 1000 feet high that frequently come rushing across the desert. I remarked about the heat. "You ain't seen nothing yet, brother," Copperstain said. "Compared to what's coming this summer, this here's like a day at the North Pole."

We arrived at the desert center where I was staying, a place quite aptly called Furnace Creek.

Darkness fell, but there was little lessening of the temperature. To touch the wall of my cottage was like touching a hot stove. I knew why the Panamint Indians who once roamed the valley had named this desert Tomesha—"Ground on Fire."

Next morning, early, Copperstain was waiting for me. We swung north awhile, along the base of the Funeral Mountains. Then, climbing a ridge, we came to Hell's Gate, where in midsummer the heat rising from the valley sweeps through like a blast from Inferno.

One day Copperstain and I rode the rocky trails where once the enormous borax wagons with their twenty-mule teams had thundered. We traversed Golden Canyon with its bizarre rock formations like the monuments of ancient Egypt; past Wild Rose Canyon, where the wild burros graze, descendants of the lost burros of many a prospector; past Artist's Palette with its unbelievable colors, as though some madman had hurled barrels of oil paint in every direction, trying to rival a rainbow.

We turned back toward Stovepipe Wells. A small animal hopped across the road. I recognized it as a kangaroo rat, another extraordinary dweller of the valley. One of the few animals that can go their entire lives without drinking a drop of water, it is equipped with a sort of chemical distillation plant that can turn anything it eats into all the moisture it needs.

There was a fascination about the valley that made it different from any other place I had ever visited. When darkness fell at Stovepipe Wells, the strange pure-white bats of the valley would circle overhead, with a beauty of flight that made them a contradiction to the ugliness and horror generally associated with bats. Often I would drive sixty miles at night without seeing the lights of a single car or the shadow of a single animal, just the stars shining with incredible brilliance above the mountains. Only the dullest soul could fail to experience some feeling of the infinite.

I did not want to leave the valley until I had seen the mysterious "dry lake" called the Race Track. "You better go there with one of the rangers," Copperstain said. "This truck ain't in too good shape, and the trail there ain't patrolled. If we broke down and nobody knew, we'd be in plenty of trouble."

On Mesquite Flat, near Stovepipe Wells in Death Valley, wind-patterned sand dunes 100 to 200 feet high cast deep shadows. Some twenty miles away, on the hazy northwest horizon, summits of the Panamint Range shimmer in the heat.

Death Valley is now a national monument, with rangers on constant patrol to protect travelers. Early on my last day I drove to the headquarters at Furnace Creek, where a tall, weather-beaten ranger was waiting for me in a pickup. After an hour we came to a dirt trail. A sign stated that from here on the route was patrolled only at irregular intervals. The ranger began to talk into his shortwave radio: "Leaving for the Race Track. We should be back in three and a half hours." I heard the answering "OK" from the ranger station at Emigrant Junction.

The trail, climbing gradually, wound like a yellow snake across a barren waste encircled by low volcanic ridges. Now and then great frozen waves of black lava surrounded us. It was as though we had drifted back to those convulsive days when the earth was emerging from chaos. Suddenly, in the distance, a great circle appeared, flat and shiny as though cut by some giant hand from a piece of yellow paper. As we came closer, the Race Track looked like a huge saucer, the surface as even as though it had been smoothed by great rollers. We sped two miles across to the other side of the Track, where the ranger brought the pickup to a halt. "These are the Skating Rocks," he said.

Behind an enormous boulder weighing at least 600 pounds was a wide track several inches deep, where the rock had moved across the earth in a ruler-straight path. Beyond were other boulders that had left similar trails. What had made these huge rocks slide in this fashion? "Some scientists believe it's earthquakes," the ranger said. "Others say it's the wind, but it would take a terrific gust to blow a six-hundred-pound rock around. I guess nobody will really know until some scientist camps out here and actually sees one of them move."

Back at the headquarters I picked up my car and set out for Stovepipe Wells. I saw an ominous black cloud in the distant sky. Long streamers of rain streaked down against the horizon. I drove faster, having no desire to be trapped by a flash flood. But soon I saw that trying to outrun the storm was hopeless. The cloud came directly overhead and I braced myself for the deluge. To my astonishment, not a single drop of water fell. The air was so dry and hot that the rain, dropping from the cloud perhaps 2500 feet above me, evaporated long before it reached the ground. Then I remembered that this was a phenomenon that occurred often in the area. It was merely another spectacle in nature's colossal, ever-changing show that is Death Valley.

THE MANY WORLDS OF YOSEMITE

DONALD CULROSS PEATTIE

I am awakened deep in the night by a portentous sound, the thunder of Yosemite Falls—one of the most impressive sounds in the world. Its water strikes the valley floor with a tireless soft cannonading. Above my cabin roof I hear the whisper of the lodgepole pines and the deeper voice of the great yellow pines. Falls and trees give a combined command: "Sleep again, mortal. Peace be unto you. You are in the Great Good Place."

Yosemite National Park, in the heart of California's Sierra Nevada, is to my mind the most beautiful spot in America. Every one of its nearly 1200 square miles is glorious. There are probably more waterfalls leaping into its valley than in any comparable area in the world. The mightiest tree on earth grows there—the giant sequoia, cousin of the coast redwood—as well as other conifers, red fir and white, yellow pine and Jeffrey pine, cedar and Sierra juniper. In among them, waiting for autumn's touch to set them afire, are aspen and dogwood and oak. The dense high forest country (closed in winter) can be penetrated via many miles of road and trail. The valley itself, seven square miles at an altitude above 4000 feet, is open throughout the year—open, too, to the heavens—walled in sheer granite, floored with lush green and jeweled with waterfalls. If spring is the time of wild flowers, if summer makes possible high-hearted, carefree camping and if autumn is the time for woodland color, winter offers crystalline joys of its own. White wonder glistens on evergreen bough and granite slope.

Four roads can bring you into this heartland of the Sierra. The most dramatic leads from the south, where you climb from the foothills into bracing, pungent air until you are suddenly swallowed by the Wawona Tunnel. Coming out of it,

Light from a January sunset touches the mist-shrouded face of El Capitan, a sheer granite monolith rising 3604 feet above Yosemite Valley. In the foreground the Merced River's open water is framed by snow-clad cedars, firs and pines.

you stop, glory-smitten. There lies the long-sought valley, the steep perpendicular of El Capitan soaring on your left; on your right, from mountain heights its equal, gleams the long white leap of Bridalveil Fall, and as far as you can see beckons the wilderness of Clouds Rest. So vast and powerful was the vanished mountain glacier that sculptured out sheer-sided Yosemite Valley that it left above it many "hanging valleys." Flinging themselves precipitously from these are tributaries of the stream that now runs where once the great glacier carved its inexorable way. There is view upon spirited view of stacked or polished rock and peak, of mighty mountain flank streaked by those plunging white torrents.

Upper Yosemite Fall pulses forth in a drop of 1430 feet, tumbles in a cascade and falls again for a total drop of 2425 feet, to smite the earth with a seismic shock that sets it trembling. Bridalveil Fall is more slender and sheer, forever blowing and lifting, sometimes wholly clear of earth; at the right hour its spray catches the sun in a breathtaking rainbow. Ribbon Fall, 1612 feet, is the highest in the park; but when in summer the snowmelt that feeds it is gone, it, too, vanishes, spritelike. Vernal and Nevada falls seem in their season like foaming passions let loose from earth. The full flood of all the falls is in May and June, at the height of the snowmelt.

Enchanting as are these evanescent spectacles,

for strength you must go to the "big trees," of which there are three groves in Yosemite. The giant sequoia is the craggy king of trees, greater in girth than the coast redwood, though not so tall; so broad indeed that roads pass through a tunnel in the standing trunks of two. It may reach the awesome age of thirty centuries. Through the years its ruddy trunk becomes buttressed; its crown may be smitten off by lightning, but its sinewy short boughs remain forever green. Jovelike, it chooses to grow in the high country, at altitudes of 6000 to 8000 feet, where the winter snows may pile up amid these titans in drifts five times the height of a man.

Yosemite is not a place of giants only. The dogwood starring the evergreen dusk, the fragrant masses of azalea, the mariposa lilies, the lupine and columbine, the snow plant that thrusts up from some diminishing snow patch like a crimson fist defiant of departing winter—they, too, belong to the people of the United States. For Yosemite is sanctuary. No stem may be broken, no hunter's gun discharged; only fishing is permitted.

It was the hand of Abraham Lincoln that, in 1864, signed the bill delivering Yosemite Valley and the Mariposa Grove of big trees into the keeping of the state of California. Although the area had been seen by traders and trappers as early as 1833, they had left it unspoiled. For many years Yosemite—it takes its name from the now-vanished tribe of Indians who summered in the valley —was to be reached only on horseback. Then rough roads were built, and the stagecoach came, bringing eager loads. From the railroad's ending it took two or three days of jolting travel over the low country up to a friendly little inn in the mountains on the way to the valley.

There was one man who lived, winter and summer, in Yosemite. John Muir, the great naturalist, went there on foot when he was a young man and dwelt there for much of the rest of his life, sleeping in hollow trees, living on tea and bread. He became Yosemite's most famous guide and interpreter. Through him and his ardent writings there stirred a great wave of public interest in the glories of the Sierra—and in 1890 Yosemite became a national park.

The National Park Service's Nature Guide Service began here. The valley's little museum and nature center, the guided walks and hikes, the nightly campfire programs at which park personnel talk of Yosemite's geologic making, of its plants and animals—all help to increase the enjoyment of some 2 million visitors who come to Yosemite each year.

The pleasures of Yosemite now include mountain trails, a rock-climbing school, bridle paths and a High Sierra ski center called Badger Pass. Saddle horses and pack animals are available, but you must have a guide with you when you leave the valley floor.

The most famous long trail, for hiker and rider alike, is the High Sierra Loop, a fifty-three-mile round trip, provisioned with camps along the way. But even if you are a motorist you can reach the high-slung Tuolumne Meadows, a lovely wide swale abloom with subalpine flowers. Called out of your car by the wild, still waters, icy-cold even in high summer, you will pause on the way at Tenaya Lake, where the tilting sea gulls seem strangely far from home. Or you can drive or hike the few miles up to Glacier Point, from which, in one wide cast of the eyes, you can see the terrible splendor of the ancient glacier's work, the enormous tumbled prospect of forest-clad mountains quickened by two great glittering distant falls. Here, if anywhere, Yosemite's grandeur will overwhelm you.

Yet if, happy on the valley floor, you want only a gentle stroll, there are many enticing trails. And when, deeply fulfilled, you return at day's end, the campfires will be lit in the dusk among the trees, and the scent of their smoke, the sense of fellowship, will draw you in again.

CALIFORNIA'S MAJESTIC SEQUOIAS

STEWART L. UDALL

The tree is king here in Sequoia and Kings Canyon national parks, peering down over a majestic domain of gray granite mountains, deep forests and valleys that make a harsh but welcoming slash in the landscape. It stands, holding silent court over a seemingly untouched panorama, beginning beyond one horizon and going past the other.

This tree, the sequoia, is the largest living thing in the world, gently elbowing aside white firs and sugar pines. It rivals the age of almost any other tree or plant known, its cinnamon red bark and pointed needles quite unchanged from the time when frightening creatures rumbled the earth with their ponderous tread. One can count nearly 4000 years since some of the trees were born, and science believes none has died simply because of old age. They usually find their life-giving roots exposed by slow erosion, perhaps nature's way of returning organic material to the soil. Then they topple and die with a crash, to lie fallen beside other warriors fighting the long battle against time.

There are more than 1300 square miles in the parks, starting at the foothills of the San Joaquin Valley and reaching toward the crest of the High Sierra. It is some 6000 feet above sea level here, and the altitude makes the giant sequoias seem all the more regal. Perhaps at first the height leaves one breathless; then suddenly the vista generates a catch in the lungs, for nowhere else does such a view exist. Save for the efforts of a few, these mighty trees could have disappeared to the logger. The first of the two parks gained federal protection in 1890 so that the trees could be preserved. The culmination of this protection came in 1940 with the establishment of Kings Canyon National Park.

Hale Tharp, a brawny, tanned cattleman seeking grazing land, was the first recorded visitor. He went up the Kaweah Valley near what is now Moro Rock, and listened to an Indian friend tell of lush mountain meadows lying beyond. Heartened, for cattle were his livelihood, Tharp followed

235

the patrol of Indians to the high meadows carpeted with deep, nutritious grass. There, in 1858, he beheld the Giant Forest's sequoias, and set up a temporary home in a fallen tree hollowed by fire.

In 1862 Joseph Thomas discovered the General Grant Grove (now located in Kings Canyon Park), where several outstanding trees reign. It took little time for their descriptions to create a national stir to preserve this virgin land.

Today, it all has changed. The parks are not what they were a century ago, nor are the trees the same. Although most of the changes are too small to measure, the valleys are a bit deeper because of erosion, the mountains a shade lower because of the torture of the elements, and some trees taller. If anything, Sequoia and Kings Canyon have grown more graceful, bearing their years with dignity.

The nucleus of a visit here is the General Sherman Tree, largest of all living things on earth, towering more than 272 feet above the ground and measuring more than 35 feet across the base. Because it is hard to imagine such a tree, perhaps this helps: The trunk alone weighs approximately 1450 tons and has 50,010 cubic feet of wood, enough to build about forty homes. The General Grant is only five feet shorter and contains only a bit less wood.

These giants of the forest live in harmony with their smaller and shorter-lived brethren. The gigantic sugar pines and firs wrest life from the soil, and even without the sequoias their existence would be a pleasing sight. They are youngsters, however, for the General Sherman is believed to be more than 3500 years old, a fertile tree when Christ was born and existing when the great temples of ancient Egypt were being built. It is a living link with history; no, more than with history, with the evolution of our planet. Only one existing thing has been proved older, the bristlecone pine. And the young sequoias may be living after our civilization has become history.

Smaller than the sequoias, but with much value of their own, are the flora and fauna of the two parks. The floor of the forest is covered with dogwood, colorful lupine and the red-flowered snow plant. Meadows are filled with wild flowers— Sierra shooting stars in June, Queen Anne's lace and senecio later. Bears and mule deer roam at

Flanked by fir trees, giant sequoias tower above three tourists near Congress Trail in Sequoia National Park, California. Sequoias have changed little since dinosaur times, and some living trees were growing when the Pharaohs ruled Egypt.

will. This is a rugged land, existing almost as a separate entity from the rest of the West. Beyond the Giant Forest, named by that great Scots-born naturalist John Muir, is the Sierra Nevada's high country, a vast, tilted block on the earth where snowcapped peaks rise to more than 14,000 feet to cast giant shadows on glacial valleys and ice-formed lake basins. This landscape is relatively untouched, remaining as it is by federal decree.

Here the bighorn sheep forages and the wolverine hunts in the alpine solitude, nuzzling through the luxuriant growth of a short summer, growing fat before the chill winds blow away the fragrance of delicate flowers and turn their vivid shades to dull brown.

Great canyons are incised upon the landscape. Gorges along the middle and south forks of the Kings River are more than a mile deep, their steep sides forming a canyon between the great peaks and the roaring waters tumbling over time-polished stones below.

Here there are valleys, miles long and a half mile wide, created when small streams grew larger and carried infinitesimal bits of stone with their downhill fury, then finally hewn to shape by vast fields of ice jamming their depths. The valleys bear silent testament to their past: glacial moraines telling of a time when nature's strength rubbed, scoured and gouged its way through granite, forming the canyon walls we see today.

Some of these valleys are covered with forests of ponderosa pine, incense cedar and white fir, towering above lupine waving in the summer breeze. Deer, bears and bobcats graze or hunt among the trees. Birds flutter against wind gusts, then swoop earthward to grasp an insect in their beaks and retreat to the forest a few wing flaps beyond to enjoy their meal and perhaps sing of triumph. High over all—nearly two miles above the level of the sea—is a mountain wilderness dotted with glacial lakes that mirror the sun and the spectacular surroundings. There is no word that does justice to the area, which is magnificent even in winter when snow festoons the giant sequoias and fills the dips and small valleys.

The region so moved John Muir that he wrote, "No doubt these trees would make good lumber after passing through a sawmill, as George Washington after passing through the hands of a French chef would have made good food."

The sequoias, thankfully, are living, for their peculiar makeup gives them an odds-on chance against every natural enemy—except possibly man.

POINT LOBOS STATE RESERVE

Point Lobos State Reserve on the California coast near Carmel is celebrated as much
for its outstanding rock and surf scenery as it is for the rare plants and animals
that it shelters. A convoluted six-mile shoreline separates the park's two sections: 500 acres
of dry land and 750 acres beneath the Pacific Ocean. Two of the rarest trees in the
country are found here: the Monterey cypress and the Gowen cypress. Sea otters (once
hunted to the brink of extinction), harbor seals, killer and gray whales, and sea lions
live in the coves and offshore.

Monterey pines (above) *are silhouetted against the*
autumn fog in Bluefish Cove at Point Lobos State
Reserve in California. Sea otters can frequently be
observed swimming in Headland Cove (left).
The first Spanish settlers called the area Punta de
Lobos Marinos (Point of the Sea Wolves),
for the sea lions that bark and roar on offshore rocks.

Monterey pines, Monterey cypresses and bluff lettuce cling to the cliffs at Bluefish Cove (left) in Point Lobos State Reserve. The Monterey cypress is one of the rarest cone-bearing trees in the world; the only other native grove exists at nearby Carmel Bay. The trees may live 200 to 300 years. Dead ones (right) often are hung with lichens and reddish algae. Low tides expose limpets clamped to the sandstone (above) at Pebble Beach. Some of the depressions in the easily eroded sandstone are caused by small pebbles, endlessly rolled by the sea.

OUR IMMORTAL REDWOODS

DONALD CULROSS PEATTIE

To step out of the brilliant California sunlight into the astounding dimness and silence of one of the mighty redwood groves of the Pacific Coast is like entering a room—surpassingly lofty—and closing a door behind you. The sheer overwhelming vertical strength of trees that tower up 300 feet and the sense of sanctity they shed are fingers laid upon our restless pulses, bidding them be quiet. To any observer the redwoods must bespeak the strength of our natural resources. They are the last and greatest reminder of the aboriginal abundance of this country of ours.

For the redwood is incredibly resilient. Not only does it reproduce by seeds dropped from its cones, but if it is cut down or burned to the ground, its roots, unless they too are destroyed, are able to reproduce the whole tree again. No other conifer regularly has this marvelous regenerative power. A redwood, where one tree grew before, can send up a hundred shoots from buds dormant in the stump. Of these perhaps half a dozen will eliminate all the others by competition. Each of these will in turn become a tree, standing in a circle of close-ranked columns, and in time they may all become as great as the original trunk. These are not to be considered children of a parent, as would be the case if they had sprouted from seed. They are the actual renewal of life in the same generation. Presumably, if all these new trees were felled, each might again revive. Thus it is hard to see why the life stream in a redwood is not, for all our human mayfly purposes, eternal!

A given individual trunk of redwood may have a life-span of anywhere from 400 to 2500 years. But the present grove of redwoods are the offspring of trees that were standing 30 to 40 million years ago. When you walk between the great ruddy columns where the sun sends down shafts of holy light in long smoky beams, and you tread the soundless carpet of needles that has been piling up through the centuries, you are stepping back into the scenery of the remote past. More humbling still is the thought that these trees will be standing when you and your children and their children are dust. Then strangers will come after you to walk where you walk, and gaze up in awe at the towering boles, and stop to listen as you do to the sigh of the great canopy as the sea wind moves rememberingly among the boughs.

When the gold rush set the first Yankee loggers to swinging their puny axes at boles ten and twelve feet in diameter, our particular redwood was probably over 300 feet high. This was the absolute limit once set by certain English skeptics, who asserted that we Yankees were up to our old tricks of exaggeration. No tree, they insisted, could top 300 feet without falling; the laws of physics were supposed to make it impossible. Unconscious of this, our tree still soared toward the stars—until one day a gasoline dragsaw was brought up to its base; in an hour the growth of

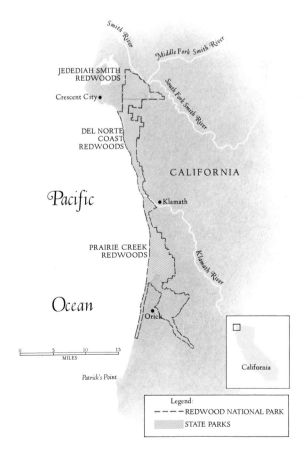

The massive trunks of coast redwoods reach into the fog above rhododendrons in Redwood National Park. Slimmer and loftier than their cousins the sequoias, redwoods are the tallest living things on earth, sometimes exceeding 300 feet.

243

nineteen centuries toppled, with a crash like an earthquake, setting cups and saucers to dancing in the logging camp four miles away.

The redwoods are the densest stand of merchantable timber in the world. No other tree produces boards of such clean length; no other tree is more easily worked by the plane, or takes a higher polish. Very light, it is strong in proportion to its weight. Preserved from decay by the tannin in it, the wood is almost eternal in contact with soil and water; so it makes the best fence posts and wharf piles of the Pacific Coast. It is nearly immune from attack by termites.

The first railroads in California were laid on redwood ties. Pioneer babies were rocked in redwood cradles. Today the famous wines of the Golden State are kept in redwood vats because the wood imparts no flavor of its own to spoil the vintage. Redwood has built many of the towns of California, and the room where I write these words is paneled and beamed with redwood left in its beautiful natural color.

With all these uses for this marvelous lumber it is no wonder that sawmills whine for it, eating ever deeper into the last virgin stands. Yet only a fraction of the Redwood Empire belongs now to the United States. All the rest is in private hands. Under the Homestead Act, Uncle Sam practically gave away this imperial domain; many homesteaders sold out to lumber companies.

Not till early in this century did the public begin to rouse itself. Led by the Save-the-Redwoods League, people all over the country united to buy back, acre by acre, groves that would require a thousand years to be replaced in all their majesty. It is heartening to reflect that these incomparable titans still stand only because individuals in far-off places—Massachusetts, Georgia, Illinois—did their bit to preserve them. Yet most of these people had never seen the forest kings and, presumably, would never see them. It was enough for them that the dollar or the hundred dollars they gave should insure that, far on the other side of the continent, these trees might continue their godlike existence for ages to come.

Some of the groves were saved from the sawmill by garden clubs, some by the American Legion, the Elks and other fraternal, patriotic and women's organizations. More than 250 groves have been named by individuals and groups all across the United States.

In October 1968 President Johnson signed into law a bill that set aside some 58,000 acres of prime California timberland as Redwood National Park.

Actually, half that acreage comprised three state parks created previously to protect valuable redwood forests. But Jedediah Smith and Del Norte state parks, which lie near the Oregon border, are now linked to Prairie Creek State Park by a thin strip of federal parkland along the Pacific coast. The state hopes to discourage further federal "encroachments," but the Sierra Club, the Save-the-Redwoods League and other conservationist organizations have been pressing the government to add more acreage—of watershed as well as redwood stands—to the preserve.

Though creation of Redwood National Park intensified the antagonism that existed between conservationists and commercial interests in California, there could be no denying the park's significance. President Johnson summed it up in words that appear on a plaque unveiled when the park was dedicated: "The redwoods will give instruction to God's work as well as nature's miracles."

OREGON— UNSPOILED SPLENDOR

ARTHUR GORDON

To anyone tired of mechanized living or man-made drabness, a place of dreamlike peace and beauty beckons: the majestic, tension-free state of Oregon. Tenth in size but only thirtieth in population among the states, Oregon stands solidly on the shoulders of California and Nevada, a vast rectangle of almost 100,000 square miles, much of it magnificent wilderness. This is the land the pioneers sought so fiercely in covered-wagon days, the prize at the end of the Oregon Trail. Much of the untamed freedom that they found remains to this day.

Along Oregon's northern border, the mighty Columbia River cuts like a silver sword through the snowcapped Cascades. To the west the Pacific surges against a spectacular mist-shrouded coast. Beyond the Wallowa Mountains in the northeast,

Douglas firs in Mount Hood National Forest frame snowy Mount Hood, sparkling in April sunshine ten miles away. The 11,235-foot dormant volcano is Oregon's highest peak and is visible from almost any point within eighty miles.

Heceta Head is a rocky
promontory on Oregon's coast
about 165 miles south of Portland.
The point was named for Bruno
Heceta, a Spanish explorer and
the first European to see the
mouth of the Columbia River
(in 1775). The fifty-six-foot
lighthouse stands on a cliff 249
feet above sea level; its light can
be seen at sea for twenty-six miles.

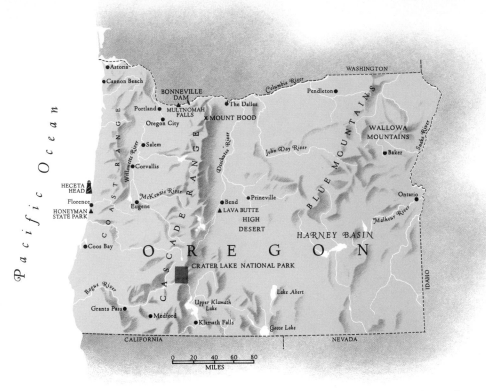

the Snake River has carved a truly stupendous gorge, deeper than the Grand Canyon. The southeastern quadrant is a desert the size of West Virginia, a land of infinite distances and eerie silences, of fossils, rattlesnakes and ghost towns. Yet Oregon also has more sawtimber than any other state, as well as parklike valleys with jade-and-crystal rivers, and shy, lost lakes reflecting sky-piercing peaks.

In many ways the people of Oregon match the land: open, friendly, outdoors-oriented, unplagued by many of the problems that harass the rest of the country. If Oregonians look askance in any direction, it is across the border at their lusty, burgeoning neighbor, California. They fear an overflow of refugees, with pockets full of California gold, who will exploit or ruin the spacious, un-touched atmosphere that is Oregon's pride. When an Oregon newspaper suggested not long ago that perhaps the state ought to build a gigantic bypass from California to Canada, it was not altogether joking.

If progress brings smog, slums, water pollution, trash-strewn beaches and overcrowded highways, the 2 million inhabitants of Oregon would just as soon do without it. They'd rather ski, surf, shoot the white-fanged rapids of such rivers as the Rogue and the McKenzie, hunt elk, deer, bear and fowl, fish for rainbow trout, steelhead or the flashing salmon, send an occasional maverick like the late senator Wayne Morse to Congress, and grow roses the size of cabbages.

The variety that Oregon presents the visitor is bewildering; no single visit can do it justice. But it's exciting to try. Recently, with our two youngest children, my wife and I spent a memorable fortnight there. Here are some highlights as we'll always remember them.

Thanks to the vision of Oswald West, governor in the early 1900s, all but twenty-three miles of Oregon's 400-mile coastline belongs to the people. The result is an endless chain of state-maintained waysides and parks along Highway 101, with excellent camping and recreational facilities. In this vast playground of silver beaches and frowning headlands, summer vacationers dig for clams, lie in the sun or join the happy scav-engers who look for driftwood and the highly prized Japanese fishing floats—beautifully colored glass globes—that often wash ashore. The ocean is cold but swimmable—if you're wise enough to respect the sometimes treacherous surf.

Twice a day, when weather permits, fleets of charter boats set out from towns along the entire coast, often to come back with limit catches of silver salmon—three per angler. In several places you can take your fish to a local cannery and exchange it for neat one-pound tins of somebody else's catch—a great solution to the fish-cleaning-and-transporting problem. At Honeyman State Park, just south of Florence, are the tremendous Oregon sand dunes, some of them hundreds of feet high, where you can take a roller-coaster ride in a dune buggy. Or you can climb them on foot (a heart-pounding workout), and then come leaping down their tawny faces with great skidding strides.

To the north, at Cannon Beach, you can drive

248

your car for miles along hard-packed sand, or look for pale green sea anemones and purple starfish in the shallows at the foot of Haystack Rock, a gigantic monolith that rears like a shark's fin out of surf. Not far away is Ecola State Park, where the view of the coast may well be the most spectacular seascape in the world. In winter people come hundreds of miles just to see the savage, howling fury of gales lashing the rocks with mountainous waves. When you compliment Oregonians on their mild summer climate, they say, "Yes, but you should see our winter storms!"

Beyond the low coastal range lie the lush valleys that lured the pioneers. After the wild coast, these valleys seem pastoral and peaceful, with neat farms and orchards and meadows full of wild flowers. There's something of New England about the country churches and occasional covered bridges.

Portland stands where the Willamette approaches the Columbia, its name determined more than a century ago by the flip of a coin won by a native of Portland, Maine. It is a city of bridges, good restaurants, an excellent zoo and a splendid Museum of Science and Industry.

We drove south from Portland for a look at the handsome state capitol at Salem, its dome crowned by a twenty-four-foot figure of a bearded pioneer holding an axe. We traveled back through Oregon City, capital of the old Oregon Territory, then eastward through the Columbia Gorge, with towering cliffs 2000 feet high laced with waterfalls (Multnomah Falls, dropping 620 feet in two stages, is the highest). Forty miles east of Portland, we stopped at Bonneville Dam to watch the salmon fight their way up the fish ladders on their journey to upstream spawning grounds.

Leaving the Columbia, we turned south into the Hood River Valley (in spring a foaming sea of fruit blossoms), then followed Route 35 as it climbed steeply through immense stands of timber. These forests soar up to the ice and granite backbone of the Cascades, a chain of sleeping volcanoes dominated by mighty 11,235-foot Mount Hood.

Skiers come by the thousands to try the Mount Hood area's variety of ski runs—one is among the world's longest. When we were there in July, we walked to the edge of the glaciers and had lively snowball fights in the ringing silence and pellucid air.

Next day, sweeping down the "dry" side of the Cascades, we were fascinated by the change in vegetation. The great forests thinned out until there was virtually desert country. In marked contrast to the rain-haunted coast, here there are some places that claim 345 days of sunshine per year.

In the long summer twilight we came to Bend, gateway to the high plateau stretching away into the rangeland and desert that occupy the southeastern third of Oregon. The sparkling Deschutes River runs through the center of town, creating a tranquil green oasis. In pioneer days when the dusty covered wagons came creaking out of the desert, this verdant river-curve seemed like paradise to the weary occupants. When they had to push on, they looked back sadly and cried, "Farewell, Bend!" And this, indeed, was its name until an unromantic postal system shortened it to Bend.

This charming town makes a splendid base for side trips. U.S. Olympic ski teams train at Bachelor Butte, twenty-two miles away. To the northeast, the town of Prineville is a mecca for rockhounds on the hunt for agate, jasper, obsidian and quartz. Eleven miles south of Bend is Lava Butte, a 500-foot cinder cone with an observation tower where you can look down into blackened craters dating from the not-so-distant period when this part of Oregon was literally a land of fire. Not far away, beneath lava fields as tortured and barren as the surface of the moon, you can explore the inside of a mile-long tunnel formed by a river of lava that kept flowing after the crust above had hardened.

Two hours' driving from Bend will bring you southward to Oregon's most acclaimed scenic wonder and only national park: Crater Lake, a gigantic rock basin circled by towering cliffs and filled with water that looks like melted sapphires. Five miles across, twenty miles around the rim, Crater Lake was formed thousands of years ago when molten lava draining away through subterranean cracks inside 12,000-foot Mount Mazama caused the whole top of the mountain to collapse in a fiery cataclysm. As centuries passed, rain and snow filled the circular cavity with water so clear and deep—almost 2000 feet—that it reflects the blue rays of the solar spectrum while absorbing the rays of other colors.

The memories that the visitor to many-faceted Oregon takes away with him do not fade: the sun-dazzled lakes and rivers, the shadowed forests, the gilded peaks, the Pacific rollers creaming in, stately and slow. A region as boldly sculptured as this resists change by man. The result is a strong and constant sense of continuity with the past . . . and with the splendor of an unspoiled America.

CRATER LAKE NATIONAL PARK

Crater Lake National Park in Oregon was once a battleground of the gods,
according to legends handed down for generations by the Klamath Indians. A huge
crater—half-filled with clear blue water and surrounded by rampartlike cliffs—grotesque
pinnacles and steep slopes of volcanic debris do help to conjure up such a cataclysmic
scene. Scientists speculate that the entire mountaintop was blown to bits; fiery mushroom
clouds filled the sky, trees were charred black by the intense heat, and incandescent avalanches
rumbled from the summit for as far as thirty miles.

Crater Lake is the deepest inland body of water in
the United States, the seventh deepest in the world.
At a depth of 1932 feet, it only half fills the crater
of Mount Mazama, an extinct volcano that collapsed
after violent explosions some 7000 years ago. The
steep rim of the crater rises nearly 2000 feet above
the lake. Wizard Island (left) juts 600 feet above the
water, and Phantom Ship (above) bears masts of
rock that reach almost fifteen stories high.

SCENIC STOREROOM OF THE EVERGREEN STATE

BYRON FISH

Looking at our country from a geological point of view, it would seem that when the other forty-seven states were put together—long before Alaska and Hawaii had joined the family—the leftovers were stacked in the northwest corner of the landscape. The result was Washington, smallest among western states and a breathtaking, eye-widening collection of amazements.

It took some planning to fit them all in. There were glaciers and sand dunes, cactus and bits of damp jungle growth. There was unused rockbound coast from New England, a leftover length of Grand Canyon. Also to be given consideration were some southern swamps, southwest buttes, midwest prairies and arctic botany—not to mention scores of islands and five snowcapped volcanic peaks. By the time the job was finished Washington wound up with samples of just about everything.

The coast, folded into accordion pleats, stretches about 1700 miles, counting what was placed around Puget Sound. This inland sea is where most of the islands went, including 172 in the San Juan group. And Washington's Olympic Peninsula, which has as many changes in climate and terrain as a whole continent, is but a modest spur jutting into the Pacific.

The peninsula is a low platform with a jagged mountain range in its middle. Damp winds move inland from the Pacific and collide with the mountains; at the highest altitude their moisture turns to snow. This falls on the glaciers and keeps them alive. Below the ice come alpine meadows and the stunted trees of timberline. Next on the slopes is a belt of medium-size trees, then forests of tall, heavy timber. Farther down in the lowlands, where the weather stays relatively warm

and as much as 150 inches of rain falls per year, everything grows to giant size and is festooned with a southern moss.

Thus a whole cycle of nature occurs—ocean moisture to ice fields that feed rivers that flow back to the ocean. Their courses run through many zones—from subarctic to almost tropical growth. In few, if any, other places on earth does this continental process happen in such a small space.

Image Lake mirrors evergreens and storm clouds passing over Glacier Peak Wilderness in northern Washington. On the horizon are the snowy summits of the Ten Peaks Range, part of the Cascades, which stretch from Canada into California.

Some summers ago we met a pair of tourists who had entered Washington by way of Spokane, on the eastern border. As they drove west, they expected the low mountains to grow into snow-topped peaks, the open pinewoods to change to thick forests. Instead of that, the trees disappeared and the earth flattened, first to rolling wheat fields, then to an irrigated plain. After driving 150 miles they came to brown hills, sagebrush and lava-walled coulees where they perspired in desert

heat and dreamed about trees and running water.

"What's all this talk about the Evergreen State?" they inquired.

"Patience," we reassured them. "Go on another fifty miles."

Within an hour they were beginning their climb over the Cascade Mountains, a cloud-stopping barrier that splits Washington north to south and creates vast differences in climate, natural growth and fauna, both wild and human. U.S. 12, desig-

nated a scenic highway, crosses this hundred-mile-wide barrier at its northern end.

On each side of the big range sits a clutter of miscellaneous scenery. The recipe for the east-side mixture calls for about 50 million years of preparation. Boil uncountable tons of rock to liquid. Pour in successive layers until it is a mile or two deep. Fold the north part into a mass of mountains (the Kettle River Range and the Huckleberry Mountains, among others) and leave the rest flat (the Columbia Basin). Cool with five or six ice ages, melting the last one at the edge of the mountains. This will run off in the most gigantic river of all time. It will erode canyons, 1000 to 1600 feet deep, right through the basin lava beds. When this flood is reduced to a trickle, it will be the Columbia—still one of the mightiest rivers on the continent—and it will continue relentlessly to cut its own gorge.

If you wait long enough, the volcanic ash and lava on top of the basin will turn into rich soil—but a lot of good that does under the hot sun, without water! Turn-of-the-century pioneers left a scattering of beaten ranches as monuments to drought.

Where to get water? Block the Columbia with the Grand Coulee Dam. Man's largest concrete structure, it was designed to provide enough water eventually to irrigate 1 million arid acres in the basin. It produces the second biggest dam electric jolt in the nation (almost 2 million kilowatts). And it also provides a never-ending tourist attraction. Among the ancient by-products of the great basin cookout are many animal and tree fossils in the coulee walls, and the world's largest petrified forest, in a state park at Vantage.

In Washington when they talk about *the* mountain they mean 14,410-foot Mount Rainier; it rates the way Fujiyama does in Japan. Other peaks also receive due homage: in the north, Mount Baker; in the south, Mount Adams and Mount St. Helens. These are training ground for mountaineers who intend to conquer peaks in northern Canada, Alaska or the Himalayas. Up on the glaciers, skiers ski right into summer, wearing shorts and sunglasses. They hold a ski meet at Mount Baker in July!

As is true everywhere, Washington's urban areas are rapidly expanding. But along with metropolis there is still space in all forms—ocean and inland seas, glaciers and desert, mountain and plain, forest wilderness and uninhabited islands. Perhaps nowhere else in the world can one have such wide choice of natural treasures, so quickly.

SNOWCAPPED RULER OF THE REALM

ROBERT WALKINSHAW

In one of his poems Victor Hugo tells of his search among the Pyrenees for the Pic du Midi. Standing upon the high mountains, he was unable to distinguish one summit from another for loftiness and grandeur. It was only after he had given up his quest and was far on his journey homeward that he looked back and saw the Pic du Midi against the sky. In the Puget Sound country, whether one gazes from some snow crest or from the blue waters of the sound itself, one can never doubt the supremacy of the mountain that official legend has described as "Rainier, known also by the Indian name Tacoma or Tahoma." So established above the world is this white, broken pyramid that all the southern portion of Puget Sound seems to lie under its shadow.

Compelling as this mountain always is, by reason of its overwhelming mass, it is scarcely for a single hour the same. Before sunrise one may see it in grand relief; only its larger features are discernible. At no other time is one so conscious of the mighty sculpture of its lines. Its dark buttresses reach far along the horizon and sink deeply into the blue hills and forest. When morning arrives above the Cascades, the air of the valleys rises before it in a faint silver mist, like some exhalation of the dawn. It becomes invisible sometimes for hours and, when slowly it reappears, it seems to have been transformed into another mountain. Its foreground of forest is turned to greener blue. Its lines are etched rather than chiseled. One sees the blue of its crags and rockfalls, its mottlings of shadowed snow and the glisten of its upper ice fields. Some days it looks like a vast, dim snowdrift swept up out of the hinterland; on other days it is an indistinguishable surge of mountain and cloud.

Mount Rainier is Washington's highest peak. A dormant volcano, it has been closely watched since a new steam jet opened in the summit cone during October 1969; this could forecast an eruption or produce enough heat to melt glaciers.

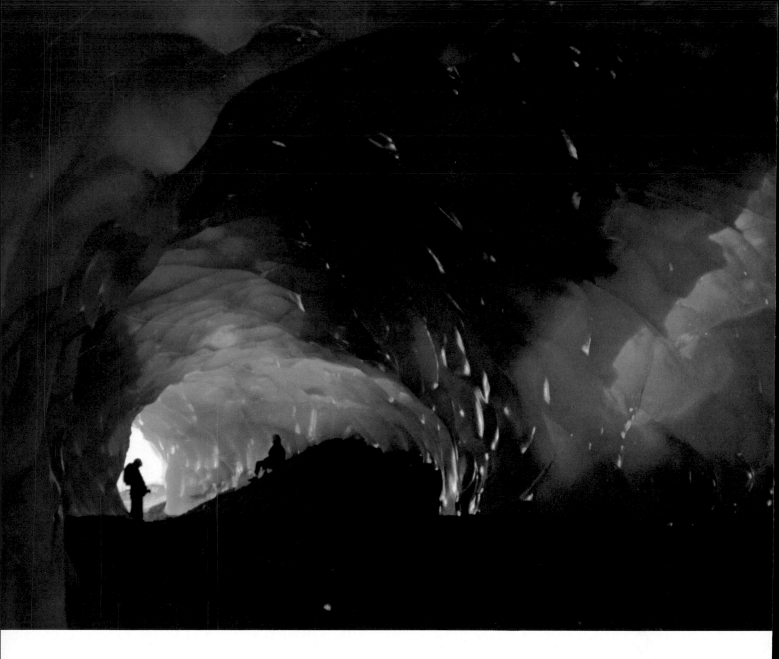

Visitors to Paradise Ice Caves on Mount Rainier see a glacier from inside out. Sunlight filtering through the thick ice glows blue. Started by summer melting and carved by air flow, the caves constantly change their size and shape.

To say that 14,410 feet is the summit of Rainier is to express very little of its wonder. John Muir and Major Ingraham once stood upon that high snowdrift on the western crater and exclaimed to each other, "Surely, this is Columbia's Crest!" It is worthy to be, indeed. One should admit that years afterward Mount Whitney was found to be almost a hundred feet higher. But no mountain which, like Whitney, is merely the highest crest of a lofty range, can ever be worshiped above this single mountain which one can travel all the way around, which rises almost three miles out of the plains and

the sea, and whose flaring base would cover more than all of Rhode Island.

People on Puget Sound can never agree as to where one may see the mountain in its most sublime aspect. For the traveler coming south, there is no more wonderful point than the high road at the north end of Lake Washington. And who in Seattle has not approached the end of Mount Baker Boulevard and seen Rainier like a thing of hammered silver under a Japanese sky? On many a summer evening picnickers at Point Defiance Park in Tacoma have watched it lighten with the alpenglow and die down into a lavender sea.

As one makes the circuit of Rainier, one is aware that every face of it is different and yet, in a large way, the same. Seen from the west, across the Nisqually plains, it is triple-peaked, breaking down into a ruined amphitheater; near Longmire Springs it is a towering pyramid; from Paradise Valley and the south, it is a stupendous snow-crushed mound; from the Cowlitz or Indian Bar to the east, it is a conical mass of rock and ice; above Yakima Park it is a resplendent dome; and from the north one looks upon the awful face of Willis Wall crowned with ice cliffs.

Between the edge of all-year snow and the timberline are the parklands with their tents of alpine fir and brilliant bloom. There are mats of purple heather, squaw grass waving aloft white plumes, tall hellebore standing like giants in Lilliput, and elephant's trunk, valerian, pentstemon, arnica, fireweed, ever ascending in color until they reach a flaming climax. Then autumn comes and the flowers die. But a brighter flame burns after them. All the color of the flowers is not so intense as the fire of the leaves. In September the blueberry and mountain ash cover the hillside with scarlet and rose, as far as the eye can see.

The usual approach to Mount Rainier is from Tacoma. The road carries one across the Nisqually plains and into the broken foothills. Then, crossing Ohop, a little picture valley, one climbs into the higher valley of the Nisqually, past its breathless gorge and, in sight every now and then of its roily waters, all the way to Longmire Springs. An innocent trail that starts here will take the traveler into Indian Henry's Hunting Ground, one of the loveliest of parks, with a mirror lake and flowers blooming as in an English garden.

On up the road past Longmire lies Paradise Valley, a park with meadows so green and alpine firs so beautifully disposed that it seems fresh from some gardener's hand. I first came into the valley on an autumn evening several years ago. Close under the shadow of a mountain greater than any I had ever seen, a waterfall tumbled out of the snowfields into the head of a vast stadium and formed a stream that glistened down its floor; all the slopes were a green and yellow sward set with blueberry and mountain ash in shades of old rose and russet and gold; and when the sun spread in from the west the colors everywhere seemed to flame into living scarlet.

We were a half dozen men who had planned all that summer to climb Rainier, but had not been able to make the attempt until mid-September, after the first snow had fallen. We left at two in the morning so as to make the chutes under the Gibraltar Rock before the ice began to melt. In the semidarkness it was slow work getting up out of the valley to the first snowfields. The névé had

become glinting ice so that our alpenstocks resounded as they fell. The mountain loomed above us, monstrous and dim. After three miles or more we reached Camp Muir in that bitter wind that blows before the dawn. It was impossible to climb the Cowlitz Cleavers before daylight, so there was nothing left but to wring what hospitality we could out of the place. With teeth chattering, we placed two men on the ground. Across them two others were placed, and then two across these. When the undermost two had been sufficiently warmed and smothered, the heap was unscrambled and these placed on top. So the mill continued for several rounds. Life sweetened for us when the sun struck Gibraltar. We picked up, one by one, the peaks along the Columbia River. We were then at 10,000 feet. Looking along the blue and snow-tipped crests, we could see the mountains march evenly in from the horizon like the roll of a heavy sea.

After refreshing ourselves with toast and cold tea, we climbed the Cleavers and made our way to the base of Gibraltar. Then, sneaking along its shelf, high above the glacier of the Nisqually, we reached the chutes. Here we pulled ourselves up, one by one, with the aid of a rope, and came out at last on the snowfields. The crevasses were at their worst. The recent snow made it necessary to test every bridge and to work cautiously around the heads of the chasms, some of which were abysmally deep. Above, we could see the polished rocks of the crater, but whether we switchbacked or climbed directly toward them, it seemed of no avail. We tramped so many steps and rested, and tramped and rested again, until by sheer grinding we came up over the curve of the ice dome.

It was nearly noon before the last man dropped inside the crater, which was filled with snow. A half mile beyond, we saw Columbia's Crest, the snowbank that is the true summit. So, when we had regaled ourselves with more toast and cold tea, we crossed the crater and stood upon this eminence which, but for low-lying clouds, would have allowed us to see eastward nearly across the state of Washington and northward into the mountains of British Columbia. The view to the south was an endless, almost formless chaos of mountains and mist-filled valleys.

The largest steam caves are on this side of the crater. A couple of years before, a party of mountaineers had descended into one of them. The story is told that each man scraped a cup of snow from the roof, dropped a bouillon cube into it and put it over a steam jet. In a few minutes the cups were boiling lustily!

257

When, from this supreme summit, one looks below upon somber-forested valleys lightening upward into pale meadows, and upon these in turn whitening into ice and snow, and considers their climatic changes and distribution of life, one realizes how, in climbing these three miles up the sky, one really travels a distance of more than 2000 miles, through Canada and beyond Alaska. For here is an arctic continent on the lower reaches of which, instead of the musk ox, one finds the mountain goat and ptarmigan; where the Lyall's lupine grows among the rocks; and where, in the upper snows, the mountaineer looks upon no face save that of some lonely adventurer like himself.

THE AWESOME OLYMPIC RAIN FOREST

RUTH KIRK

Walk into Washington's Olympic rain forest and sense time. Trees that are centuries old soar 300 feet high, their trunks like pillars in a nave, and the light beneath them like that filtered through cathedral glass. Colonnades of enormous living trees straddle enormous moldering logs, their combined ages enough to bridge history to before the American Revolution, to before Columbus sailed West, even to before the Norman Conquest.

On some days sunshine spots the forest floor and backlights the crème de menthe green of maple and huckleberry, but these days are counterpoints. Rain sets the theme: Sometimes it is a mere glistening on forest leaves, a wetness against the cheek; sometimes it drums a wild tattoo of pure percussion on roof and windowpane. The rain forest is trees of overwhelming size; it also is "nurse logs" shaggy with moss and seedlings, elk grazing in meadows, salmon spawning in rivers.

This forest clothes the wet west side of the Olympic Peninsula, a thumb of icy mountains, towering trees and wilderness beaches marking

A colonnade of Sitka spruce outlines a fallen tree trunk, or nurse log, in the Hoh Valley rain forest of Washington's Olympic National Park. Because seedlings are well nourished on decayed trunks, such queues are commonly formed.

the northwest tip of conterminous United States. To reach it, you ride the ferries and cross the bridges of Puget Sound westward from Seattle. Then you drive past the screaming saws of lumber mills and pulp mills, past the roar of logging trucks grinding uphill in low gear, and you turn off into a cushioned world of green.

The Hoh, the Queets, the Quinault: Three valleys cradle the best of the Olympic rain forest, a superb forest type found nowhere in the world except the Pacific Northwest, and reaching its full potential only in these valleys on the ocean side of the Olympic Peninsula. Many of the same plant species and patterns of growth flourish throughout the Olympic lowlands and in parts of the Cascade Mountains east of Seattle and along the coastal fog belt from British Columbia to California. They flourish, but they fall short of the mile after mile of prime rain forest that characterizes these three valleys.

Rain forest is more than the mere presence of certain species of plants and animals. Their interaction with each other and with the environment is even more significant. For example, big-leaf maple grows to rounded perfection in a pasture or along a lakeshore—trunk straight, branches angled upward, leaves the only source of green. But in the rain forest its branches droop down as often as they shoot out or up, and its green comes partly from leaves and partly from moss and ferns draping its branches.

Or consider the Sitka spruce. As a species, it ranges from Kodiak, Alaska, to Mendocino County, California; but only on the Olympic Peninsula does it consistently reach great size, monarch after monarch scratching bristly needles against the sky and cascading paper-winged seeds over a wide radius. For years the world's largest Sitka spruce was thought to be one in the Hoh Valley that measures more than thirteen feet in diameter, so huge that eight men must stand with outstretched arms to encircle its base. Recently, however, a spruce more than fifteen feet in diameter was found near Seaside, Oregon, and two spruces larger than the Hoh tree have been found in the Queets Valley. Others are probably awaiting discovery.

The contest is of little significance, however. The real importance of size in the Olympic rain forest is that more gigantic trees of more different species grow together there than anywhere else in the world. Trees in tropical rain forests are generally more varied than those in the Olympic forest, but they do not grow as large.

Spruce is only one of the mammoth trees in the Olympic rain-forest valleys. The largest known western hemlock in the world stands in the Quinault Valley. The largest Douglas fir is in the Queets. The largest red alder is in the Hoh. The largest red cedar grows in the fringe of rain forest near Kalaloch, close by the ocean, and one nearly as large is on a hillside above Lake Quinault.

You can walk inside the trunk of the Quinault cedar, a rotted-out giant like a wooden Carlsbad. Aprons of xylem drape its hollow, and the roots of nursling huckleberries and hemlocks on its flanks hang within like stalactites. You can stride across the inside of this tree for nine long steps, and around its perimeter for thirty-seven steps, walking so close that your shoulder rubs the stringy bark.

The enormity of its trees and the lushness of their vegetative upholstery characterize the rain forest more than other isolated features. However, you can scarcely omit from consideration the arches and tangles of vine maple. ("Cut them out for mules to pass and you find the axe goes through easy, so you think it is as simple as cutting cheese," wrote Louis Henderson, pioneer botanist on the Olympic Peninsula in 1891. "But start to pull a hunk out of the way, and you find how elastic vine maple is when it rises up and thwacks you!")

Nor can you forget the glassy glades maintained by the browsing and grazing of the elk. Or the ground cover of oxalis, vanilla leaf, foamflower, youth-on-age, bedstraw, trailing rubus, liverworts, mosses and ferns. Or the prostrate nurse logs, serving as seedbeds for oncoming hemlock and spruce, green promise of the forest's perpetuation. Or the diversity—a half mile of spruce and hemlock as you walk up the trail, then an alder flat to cross, or a grove of maples by a side stream, then Douglas fir or cedar.

Botanical purists occasionally argue that the Olympic rain forest is not properly "rain forest." They say that more than a hundred inches of rainfall per year is not reason enough to apply the term, because through long usage it has belonged to the jungle belt of the tropics.

Certainly the two forests differ. One is entirely broadleaf, the other dominantly coniferous. One is hot and oppressive, the other cool and mild. Woody vines string everywhere in the tropics; they are nonexistent in the Olympic forest. The trunks are slender and the bark thin in the tropical rain forest; the opposite is true in the Olympic. And whereas up to fifty different kinds of trees typify tropical forests, this northern forest has only four major species—Sitka spruce, western hemlock, western red cedar and Douglas fir.

Nobody could mistake one forest for the other; their species are too dissimilar. Yet in total aspect their resemblance is striking. Each awes you with the height of its trees: Stand close to one, and to see to the top you must tip back your head until your neck hurts. Trees *average* 200 feet in height and range to more than 300 feet! In the world as a whole, trees are "tall" at a hundred feet. (Redwoods hold the record with a tree 367.8 feet tall; the Australian eucalyptus is a close second with a 350-foot tree.)

Each forest has various levels of growth: a topmost canopy of evergreens, a midlayer of deciduous trees, a lower level of brush and a ground cover that is a soft rug in the Olympic rain forest but is sparse in tropical forests because of the poor soil. The evergreens are conifers in the Olympics, broadleaves in the tropics. The deciduous trees in the northern rain forest are predominantly black cottonwood, big-leaf maple and red alder. In the tropical rain forest there are entirely different species, many of which have leaves with grooves that channel surface drainage and tips that end in dripping points. The brush in the Olympic forest is mostly vine maple, huckleberry and sapling conifers; in the tropical forest it is tree ferns and bamboo.

Superabundant moisture characterizes both forests. In the tropics rain falls so evenly throughout the year and temperatures hold so steady that some trees completely lack growth rings (which result from seasonal growth fluctuations). In the Olympic rain forest summer rainfall sometimes totals only an inch or two, but the humidity stays high most of the time, and ocean fog often blankets the valleys, providing moisture.

Both forests impress the beholder with their profuse epiphytes—the ferns and lichens and mosses upholstering the trees. (The term "epiphyte" is derived from the Greek meaning "upon a plant.") Both surprise the uninitiated with their quality of openness—not the openness of a pine forest with little covering the ground except fallen needles, but also not the denseness of a dime-novel jungle requiring a machete to penetrate it.

With each forest the overall quality of growth is what says, "This is rain forest and that is not"— and "quality" remains ever beyond definition. Species and mechanisms are easy to describe—but how do you pinpoint the essence of rain forest, the Oriental *suchness?* How do you define beauty?

WASHINGTON'S WILD AND ROCKY SHORE

WILLIAM O. DOUGLAS

The wildest, the most remote and, I think, the most picturesque beach area of our whole coastline lies under a pounding surf along the Pacific Ocean in the state of Washington. It is marked by Cape Alava on the north and the Quillayute River on the south. It is a place of haunting beauty, of deep solitude. Whenever I hike it, I go in from Lake Ozette, a large freshwater lake, and take the trail west to Cape Alava. It's a good trail, about 3½ miles long, and it passes through a thick forest. Giant Sitka spruce with their powerful upward sweep dominate the trail. This is the tree the lumbermen like for its strength, lightness and uniform texture. It is choice for sounding boards in pianos.

Western hemlocks, a hundred feet or more high, with thick, flat branches, help shut out the sun. Their needles lie in a flat spray; their branches bend down at the tips, giving them a weeping effect. Their shade is dense and, being dense, serves a high purpose. Young hemlocks thrive there; other seedlings are shaded out.

Now and then a western red cedar with its stringy, grayish brown bark, drooping limbs and lacy branches also reaches high to claim a piece of the sky. This is the canoe cedar, which was used extensively by the Indians, not only for canoes but for twine, hats, ropes, nets, baskets and shawls.

Closer to the ocean is the Oregon alder, the tree whose leaves on the underside flash silver in the wind and whose grayish white bark is adorned with blackish splotches. Like the birch and aspen, this tree brightens the woods, as every fisherman knows, since it loves creeks and bays and bogs.

These are the trees that unite to put a green canopy over this beach forest, a roof through which only occasional shafts of sunshine penetrate. Underneath is down timber so tangled and high that a horse can travel only with great difficulty. Logs ten feet or more in diameter are being reclaimed and turned to humus. This is an area of heavy precipitation—nearly twelve inches a

*In the southern Pacific Coast Area of Olympic National
Park, rocky islets stand in the waves that carved them. Unlike the coast between Cape Alava and the Quillayute River,
this part of the park's shoreline can be reached by car.*

month. Down logs are soon covered with thick
moss and lichens.

The trail drops off a dune of loose sand strewn
with logs to a coarse-gravel beach, the site of an
ancient Indian village. This is Cape Alava, which
was, until Alaska was added, the westernmost
point in the United States. One night August Sla-
thar—woodsman and smoker of salmon par excellence—and I camped on the edge of this beach
under an ancient spruce. A raging storm had
driven a fleet of several dozen fishing boats to the
lee of an offshore island. The dim lights of their
cabins bobbed like fireflies over the water. Beyond
them a booming foghorn reminded us, all through
the bitter night, of death and danger.

This beach is one to walk at low tide. The coastline is a series of beaches, usually a quarter or a
half mile long and guarded at each end by a
headland. The points of these cannot be passed at
high tide; then one must climb over them. They
are only a few hundred feet high at most, but their
pitch is steep. Some are thick with the salal bush,
whose berries are dark purple and choice, the
Indians making a drink out of them or drying the
fruit for winter's use. But salal presents a thicket
that is almost impassable.

On one of the first headlands south of Cape
Alava is Wedding Rock, a dark basalt cliff with
broken rocks at its base. These rocks served as a
canvas for ancient artists, who carved lively petroglyphs on them of the killer whale, of Indian masks
and of men.

Each beach is distinctive. On some the sand is
made from dark volcanic rock and packed so hard
that a deer leaves few tracks on it. Some beaches
are filled with a whitish loose sand that flows freely
between the toes. Others have sand too coarse for
packing, streaked with pebbles. Some of this sand
is so loose and heavy that half of every step is lost
in a backward movement. A few beaches are a
millennium from hard-packed sand, being lined
with boulders and ledges of rock that tides without
number have yet to pulverize. Most beaches have
logs strewn along them or piled high on their
upper reaches. Some of them have fallen from the
adjoining forest. Some have broken loose from
booms pulled by tugs far out beyond the dangerous shoals; logs that reach the beach in the winter
have been rolled smooth by summer. There are

giants that have been piled so high by ferocious
waves as to be dozens of feet beyond the reach of
any high tide that comes in summer.

Pieces of ships wrecked on hidden reefs are
often added to the pile. Once Augie and I came
across a fishing vessel quite intact and sitting upright in the sand, as if in a dry dock for repairs.
Here one can find the prized Japanese glass balls
that have broken away from the fishing nets they
helped float, and have drifted thousands of miles
across the Pacific. I once found so many that I had
no room to carry them.

The force of winds and tides is often so great as

to change completely the character of some beaches from one year to the next. On my first hike Augie and I stopped for lunch on a beach of hard sand where a clear, cold stream came tumbling out of the forest onto the white beach. An Oregon alder with mottled bark leaned out over the beach. Dry chips of driftwood made a quick fire, and we propped a stick against a rock to hold our teapot over the flames. The beach was almost as hard as concrete, and extended even beyond the limits of low tide. A spotted sandpiper, feeding near the shore, suddenly jumped into the air after an insect sailing by. The leaning alder, hard sand, the crackling fire and gentle tide made a scene that I carried for years in my memory. My dream was to return to that spot, find an old spruce behind the beach for a campsite and spend several days in the shade of the alder soaking up as much of the solitude as possible. Some years later I hurriedly rounded the point marking the upper limits of my beach. But my leaning alder had disappeared and so had the hard-packed sand. Both tree and sand had gone out in some wild storm. Thousands upon thousands of tons of gravel had been deposited in their place. All that was left of the idyllic scene was my bright memory of it.

Part VII

OUR NEW FRONTIERS

Alaska

Hawaii

ALASKA

HAWAIIAN ISLANDS

THE LANDSCAPES OF ALASKA

THOMAS M. GRIFFITHS

When the summit of Mount St. Elias was sighted from the Gulf of Alaska on July 16, 1741, by the lookout on board Vitus Bering's tiny vessel, the *Saint Peter*, a historic discovery was made for western man. Bering could not appreciate his find; he was ill. He saw only the great difficulties of the return trip. Perhaps some foreboding of his impending death was already coloring Bering's outlook; subsequent visitors have usually taken a more cheerful view. Actually, he saw only the barest margin of his discovery.

Could Bering have looked beyond the 18,000-foot mountain, he would have seen a vast, sprawling territory without a counterpart anywhere in the world, truly a land of superlatives. To sum them up: The highest summit in North America—20,320-foot Mount McKinley—vaults into the brittle sky above the central Alaskan lowland; some of the rainiest slopes on this continent rise from the fjorded coast of southeastern Alaska; stations in Alaska's interior consistently report the continent's lowest winter temperatures. The world's largest carnivore, the Alaskan brown bear, inhabits Kodiak Island and the nearby Alaskan mainland. Cabbages as big as washtubs and strawberries as big as teacups are regularly recorded. Because of the far northern latitude, summer offers eighteen to twenty-four hours of sunlight.

What sort of land is Alaska? Above all it has variety. From the "banana belt" of the southeast panhandle to the frigid coastal plain in the north, it runs a gamut from a temperate West Coast marine climate to that of the arctic tundra. In surface features it shows a similar wide variety.

The Pacific Mountain system is complex. It con-

Glacier Bay National Monument, in southeast Alaska, encompasses 4381 square miles of land and coastal waters. In the foreground, hair seals ride icebergs broken from the glaciers along Muir Inlet; melting glaciers inland form lakes.

tains the highest mountains in Alaska, including McKinley, and an active volcanic belt. These two parts have different natures. The Aleutian chain, which serves as a sort of fine-meshed barrier between the Bering Sea and the North Pacific, contains some eighty recognizable volcanoes, of which at least forty-seven are active. Like a fragmented tongue, the Aleutians flick out westward in a 1600-mile arc toward the Asian mainland. This is a very much alive sector of the ring of fire that girdles the great Pacific basin.

Only reluctantly is the great barrier of the Pacific Mountain system broken by routes to Alaska's vast interior. But once beyond the barrier the visitor reaches the province of interior hills and river valleys. There is a subdued dignity about the region that comes in large part from its sheer expanse. Here, two great arctic rivers—the Yukon and Kuskokwim—gather together hundreds of tributaries, not only from the north flanks of the Pacific Mountain system but also from the south flanks of the Brooks Range, and sluggishly deliver their accumulated burden to the Bering Sea. Along the way they meander over spruce-, birch- and alder-choked floodplains.

Elevations seldom reach 2500 feet. Even at that height the summits are above timberline and are clothed in a green and brown carpet of tundra and frost-riven rock. Stunted black spruce is the tree best adapted to the severe winters, shallow soil and short growing season; it is not uncommon to find a four-inch spruce trunk that shows well over a hundred annual rings.

The river ice melts slowly in spring, but eventually "goes out" in a great flood of jostling cakes that sometimes override the banks—plowing out timber and anything else in their way. For several months canoes, motorboats and airplanes carry next winter's supplies.

In some sections a flight of half an hour will show no evidence of man. This is the region where winter's grip is felt most severely. On clear, cold winter days, when the thermometer hovers near —60° F., the moisture in a breath rustles down one's parka front in a fall of ice crystals. Smoke rises from a chimney for the first thirty feet without a quiver—a perfect cast from the chimney's mold. Men do not exert themselves, lest they breathe hard and frost their lungs. On moonlit

Purple fireweed blooms on the tundra near the foothills of the Alaska Range. Summer here is too cold and too brief for large trees to grow; shallow-rooted plants dominate because only a thin upper layer of soil thaws above the permafrost.

Legend:
ALASKA HIGHWAY ————
INSIDE PASSAGE - - - - - - -

nights the howl of a wolf carries for five miles. This is the Alaska of romance and fable.

To the north of the interior province lies the Brooks Range. This northwestern terminus of the Rocky Mountain system extends across Alaska from Canada to the Arctic Ocean. The northernmost trees of North America straggle up its streams and its southern flanks. Today planes cross the range regularly and frequently land within its confines. No longer can the region be classified as unexplored; the eye of the aerial camera has examined every foot of terrain. Yet its physical framework today is unaltered by man from what it was when Vitus Bering discovered Alaska.

In many respects the Brooks Range is different from the Pacific Mountain system to the south. Some of these differences stem from the fact that it seems not to have been as heavily glaciated as the Pacific system. The highest summit in the Brooks Range is below 10,000 feet. Being farther from the North Pacific, this region receives much less precipitation. Spared the consequent intense glacial scouring in many parts, it appears more subdued than does its southern neighbor.

Beyond the northern foothills of the Brooks Range, the arctic coastal plain stretches northward to the ocean. In no sense is this a featureless plain. Although it is almost flat, it is crossed by many rivers, of which the Colville is the most prominent. Close to the range these streams have cut narrow floodplains, lined with low bluffs, into the imperceptibly sloping surface of the plain. Close to the ocean the streams meander helplessly through a maze of sloughs, oxbow lakes and lagoons that are barely above the level of the Arctic Ocean. The sedimentary rocks that underlie the coastal plain have trapped oil, which is now actively being sought.

The entire arctic coastal plain, the Brooks Range and well over half of the interior lowland are underlaid by permafrost. All soil moisture and groundwater are frozen to great depths—sometimes hundreds of feet. In summer the long hours of sunshine raise the temperature enough to melt a surface layer ranging from an inch or two to several feet. This thaw leads to complications.

Seasonal freezing and thawing of the "active layer" subject the surface to alternating expansion and contraction. These forces create a bewildering diversity of stone nets, stripes, ice polygons, frost wedges, icing mounds, pingos and frost-heave features. Building foundations settle unevenly, roads buckle or load up with ice mounds. Nature exacts a high price from those who would live and work in permafrost regions.

This, then, is Alaska's land—a sprawling, diversified frontier; a land of incomparably beautiful alpine peaks, of smoking volcanoes, mighty rivers, tundra-clothed hills, frost-marked plains, warped mountains and ice-scoured coasts. The modern traveler is sorry that Vitus Bering did not see more of the land he discovered. Confronted with even small segments of Alaska's seemingly unlimited store of physical grandeur, he might very well have modified his somber views of 1741.

Steam issues from the caldera of Crater Peak, which last erupted in 1953. The 7575-foot volcano is overshadowed here by Mount Spurr, an 11,070-foot peak two miles away. Both are in the Tordrillo Mountains, west of Anchorage.

271

WILD
WONDERLAND OF
THE NORTH

WILLIS PETERSON

I came from Arizona to Alaska's Wilderness of Denali to search for a truth, for what better way could one reassess life's ambitions than by spending a summer in the Arctic photographing its panoply of moods?

As I drove by an immense overlook I marveled at the contrast of delicate beauty and savage wilderness. Beyond, the Alaska Range grappled for the western horizon. Flecked with snow at their base and fully mantled above, the peaks linked to form a chain of cataclysmic proportions. Shimmering glaciers hung between mountain bastions, finally pouring upon broad valleys. Fingers of dusty green protruded between the ice sheets to burst into a resplendent expanse of tundra. This was a nature photographer's paradise.

Ten days before, I had left Seattle in our heavily laden travel-all with a friend, Frank Hestand, who had come along to help wrestle camera equipment. Though we were still more than a hundred miles from Mount McKinley National Park, this was the Denali Wilderness. I had finally reached a goal I had cherished for years. The Wilderness of Denali embraces far more than Mount McKinley National Park.

When anyone in the park mentions "mountain," he means only Mount McKinley. It is the one phenomenon that every visitor wants to see first, though many are disappointed because it is usually obscured by clouds. Twenty miles is the closest one can approach by road, and perhaps that is just as well. One could not comprehend the sheer massiveness of this towering monolith if one could not compare it with peaks nearby.

But while it honors one of our presidents, the mountain's name does not portray the vastness, the loftiness, the loneliness, the wildness, the remoteness. It cannot even hint at the masterful architecture of vaulted, corniced ice walls hundreds of feet high, the shining glacial sheets cascading down valleys many miles wide, the shielding clouds that constantly generate over their

majestic host, only to dissipate, then re-form.

The Indians, who were so much attuned to their environment, appropriately called the mountain *Denali*, "the High One."

In the predawn light, Denali's towering, icy pillars and massive, snowy summits have an unearthly look of moonglow. As the sun nears the horizon, the colossus takes on a faint pink cast that slowly envelops the mountain's flanks. Finally, striking awe to one's senses, a salmon pink citadel soaring 20,320 feet to the sky reveals itself.

I wrote in my journal . . .

Once more I left at three in the morning to photograph Denali. I'm afraid I have missed the best picture. It is, of course, when the first rays hit her, creating a chiffon-colored dessert of pink massif high in the sky. Today at 3:30 a low layer of stratus is obscuring my mistress. At 4:40 a.m. I still wait patiently to receive her. Now she seems acquiescent. But her chemise of haughtiness and lofty demeanor still conceals her. It is 5:30 and yet I wait. At 6:30 she slowly unveils herself. By 7 a.m. I have seen her. It is 7:45, and, whimsically, her mood changes. It is now 8:30 and she is slowly concealing herself again. At 9 a.m. she is gone.

I am fortunate. This makes the seventh time I have seen Denali come out of seclusion in the weeks I have been in the park.

Not only did clouds obscure Denali that day, but they began to gather in earnest. Frequently, in a matter of moments, fog descended over the ground. Then, just as suddenly, the fog lifted, leaving me in shattering brightness.

It rained the rest of the day, the next and the next. Nothing is so confining and discomforting as having to exist in a damp tent. Even if the rain does not drive through, it seems to penetrate by some strange osmosis.

I walked up to Toklat bar about 9 p.m. on the second day of rain. Up canyon, I studied the cloud fragments as they swirled about the cliffs and promontories of Divide Mountain, filling the glacial valley. Carried by this new onslaught, the mists tumbled over the mountaintops as if caught in an immense, invisible cake mixer and obscured the templed, terraced sheep pastures high above me. Whenever a slight change in temperature occurred, the terraces suddenly reappeared to reveal tiny white dots.

Dall sheep! They were the only visible forms of

life in that wild caldron of churning cloud and cliff. And as I watched, spellbound, another rolling bank of clouds shrouded animal and rock into oblivion.

As I neared camp, where the willows were more than head-high along the strand, above the sound of the storm I heard a heavy tread and snapping brush. My timing couldn't have been better, for the wind and rain snuffed out my scent, and I was able to bypass my first grizzly, a bulging blond shape some fifty feet away in the willows.

Back at the tent I couldn't force the vision of those sheep from my mind. I was determined to climb to them as soon as the weather changed.

It was sunup and 3 a.m. when Frank, Bob Landis (a Wisconsin math teacher turned summer naturalist whom we had met while filming) and I crammed our pack boards with cameras and struck out. By now the sun radiated such dazzling light that it was hard to believe it had been hidden for three days.

The trail to the rams led from the bridge over the East Fork, leaping up a mountain chain which comprises the Sable Mountain area. Much of this country is prime grizzly habitat and therefore off limits to hikers. But it is permissible to explore at either end of the mountains.

We followed a creek bed almost two miles before it disappeared. Then we began to climb, step over step, first on the tundra, then on loose, fractured rock where one step up often resulted in two slipping steps down.

The crest of the divide was elusive; the more I climbed, the farther away the top seemed. And when we finally reached that height, where were the rams? Not exactly where I thought they would be. Still no more than white dots, they were on another pinnacle on a farther ridge. They had moved during the storm.

Down! Down almost to the elevation where we had started. Up! Up another slippery creek bed where loose stones tortured one's ankles. Up and up and up, until I thought my lungs would burst. Each piece of camera equipment seemed to weigh a ton. The last several hundred feet were like a ladder without rungs, so steep the only way to go was up. To attempt to climb down would have been too dangerous.

We had purposely remained in the open, and our quarry was not at all disturbed. I had a vague notion that the rams, stolid and unconcerned at our slow ascent, had taken bets on our questionable arrival.

Only one obstacle remained, and it looked as if it might abort our whole endeavor. A trail led over a 75-degree scree slide, a solid trail but only four to six inches wide, obviously designed by mountain sheep for mountain sheep, not for humans. It followed the inside curve of an old glacial cirque, where it was straight up on one side and practically straight down on the other.

To make matters worse, the storm had washed out two portions of the trail. Don't ask me how we navigated that tightrope of beaten shale, but we did. At the end of the mountain's wall we came out upon the pinnacle where the sheep lay, still watching us intently but as unconcerned as ever.

It was an astounding sight. Fifty-seven rams, huge rams, rams in immaculate white, rams with flaring, golden horns reflecting the sunlight. While a few sentinels watched the valley, most lounged on the carpet of tundra, where myriad species of wild flowers added vivid spots of color to an ethereal landscape.

We moved closer and closer, and still the rams did not regard us with fear. Some lay in shallow beds they had kicked out from the loose shale. Some were surrounded by flowers. Others rested massive heads upon the tundra. A few stared off into space, scrutinizing some faraway form of life only they could see. As they occasionally milled about, I noticed many of the older rams were followed by one or two younger males—a buddy system, as it were, in this exclusive skyline bachelors' club.

Finally we were within 150 feet of the animals. Growth rings on the horns indicated that many were in their seventh to tenth year. I could not really feel that I was there until I squeezed off the first shot on my Hasselblad. By now the sun had quartered around to the west so that the sheep were beginning to be backlighted. They had also become restless.

In twos, in threes and in foursomes, they left to march resolutely down from their stronghold to feed on the tundra slopes below. I sat down, weakened. I still couldn't believe that I had been able to capture the wild spirit, the very essence, of the Far North—the majestic Dall sheep of Alaska.

It was late. It would have been dark almost anywhere else, but this was the arctic summer, and nineteen hours after we had left we crept back

Highest mountain in North America, Mount McKinley towers 20,320 feet in the Alaska Range. "The High One" dominates the country's second largest national park, 3030 square miles of wilderness 250 miles from the Arctic Circle.

into our tent on the Toklat bar in the afterglow of the midnight sun.

There are those who believe Alaska is entirely bleak and cold. In truth, the color pageantry of the wild flowers astounded me, though many of these species grow in the mountains of my own state with what must be less colorful dress.

Pockets of dainty shooting stars were tucked away in the rock walls of canyons. Iceland poppies nodded fragile lemon yellow heads as every gust of wind demanded obeisance. Monkshood, royal blue flowers I had never seen before, stood on slender stalks in boggy areas. In photographing this sedate plant, I sank half to my knees . . . not to mention the legs of my tripod. Lavender blue geraniums sprawled along streamsides, while bright yellow arctic buttercups added a striking contrast. Mountain avens grew in prolific numbers, their blossoms forming rosettes of cream amidst tiny lavender mountain azaleas. In drier locations the ever-prominent fireweed shot magenta wands skyward like solid banks of Roman candles. Where this hardy annual did not thrive, I found its close relative, the dwarf fireweed.

Another day I had worked up the canyon about 2½ miles and had been gone more than ten hours, so I threw the tripod over my shoulder and turned back. But at the edge of the stream where I had made pictures of buttercups less than an hour earlier, I stopped short, barely daring to breathe. Here were the unmistakable paw prints of a giant grizzly. Had the behemoth been watching me? Was he still watching me? He could hardly have missed my scent. And unlike the park bears of Yellowstone—though no bear should be regarded as benign—Denali grizzlies are aloof individuals, intolerant of intruders.

The Alaskan grizzly is, in this country, blond coated and thus easy to see against the green of the tundra. But it is astounding how they can melt into a thicket of willows. These small trees grow in dense stands, and I had been working between two thickets. I had been too quiet, too immersed in my art. The best way out, I decided, was over the canyon side.

In the next few weeks I was able to film this very grizzly as well as the antics of a family of foxes, beaver teaching their kits how to gather food, arctic ground squirrels, moose, the hoary

This closeup of the tundra in Mount McKinley National Park shows the short plants characteristic of the brief arctic summer: gray reindeer moss, the arctic dwarf willow (under two inches high) with reddish leaves, and red lingonberries.

marmot, pikas and caribou. And I often lay back on the tundra to study the birds. Some were old friends. Both the pileolated warbler, with its rakish black cap, and the Gambel's sparrow, wearing a cocky white crown, winter in Arizona.

The wandering tattler was a new species. I often met it in the canyons, where it flitted about constantly. Gulls nested on the glacial bars, and I was startled at first to find them so far from the coast. I must confess that the gray jay made the biggest hit. Its continual poking about and innate curiosity reminded me greatly of my own late profession, that of a press photographer.

By mid-August many of the birds had left. The weather was changing radically, unalterably, hinting the coming of another winter's fury. Arctic ground squirrels, of which there seemed to be countless numbers, had stopped romping. Now their explorations were directed solely to the filling of cheek pouches. Molting ptarmigan were a queer mixture of white, brown and gray.

A side trip to Worthington Glacier near Valdez nearly became our last photographic adventure. We made our way slowly over the ice field by chopping footholds with an axe, until finally we arrived at a sizable crevasse that I wanted to photograph for some ecological studies. We had just set up our equipment at the fissure when the whole glacier seemed to rock. The crevasse creaked and groaned, and a ten- or twenty-ton chunk of ice fell away with a sickening crunch.

Luckily we were perched on the end where the sides came back together. The temperature was only about 40°F. that morning, but I was soaked with perspiration. Later we learned there had been a small earthquake at that precise time.

By now it was September, and the tundra's greens were turning shades of yellow, brown and red. The most strikingly colored plants were the dwarf willows, whose fleshy leaves had become a brilliant crimson. Leaves of the bunchberry had turned another shade of red, while its clusters of red berries glistened in the damp. The tundra presented a fantastic mosaic of autumn.

As I was making pictures of this flamboyant carpet, I thought back over the summer.

It is in the wilderness that one's insignificant being is engulfed by forces of nature never before realized. One has to examine the meaning of existence—that individuals, even civilizations, must abide by truths and laws of nature. In the wilderness, one feels neither unwanted nor wanted, till he proves what he is.

I won't stay away long. I have to go back.

OAHU: THE GATHERING PLACE

STANLEY D. PORTEUS

A visitor to the Hawaiian Islands usually arrives in the middle of the group, or at least a little left of center. He lands on Oahu, which is not the highest, the largest, the youngest, the oldest, the wettest, the first discovered or even the most beautiful island in the group. The first three superlatives belong to the big island of Hawaii, the next three to Kauai, and the last distinction is still, and always will be, in dispute. As regards date of birth, the chief islands should be introduced in this order: Kauai, Oahu, Molokai, Maui and Hawaii, for that is probably how they arose along the great crack in the earth that extends under the ocean far beyond the length of the group.

Personally, I would recommend seeing Oahu slowly. It is like a fine liqueur that must be sipped to be appreciated. Too often visitors are immediately rushed up Nuuanu Valley for a look at the prize view of the island: the Pali. The scene is indeed breathtaking—a wall of mountain so steep that only gray lichens and crevice-clinging ferns can find a foothold, its rock faces robbed of their sternness by sunlit patches between the cloud shadows. Below you is a broken verdurous bowl into which come flooding all the greens and blues and purples of the Pacific Ocean. Yes, it is breathtaking—and satisfying—but then visitors approach other sights with a sense of anticlimax.

There are some scenes on Oahu that you must catch just at the proper moment, like the hedge of night-blooming cereus at Punahou. On opening night it is a wonderful show, with all the floral beauties in their most expensive opera cloaks and adorned with coronets of gold. But the next morning the blooms are withered, and the fat, fleshy

Pacific surf sweeps in at Sunset Beach on the northwest coast of Oahu. Here Hawaiians, who invented the sport of surfing, enjoy some of the most challenging waves in the world: twenty to thirty feet high in January and February.

branches of the cactuslike plants are more suggestive of an assemblage of overfed dowagers. There are some places on Oahu whose beauty is similarly fleeting.

If you continue around the island from the Pali you will miss the "quiet-colored end of evening" at Kaaawa. (Some visitors have wished that a few of these Hawaiian place-names could be disemvoweled; it takes such a long time to say Ka-ah-ah-va.) But if you should be returning toward the Pali in the early evening, you may catch an authentic fragment of the Polynesian past. That is when the shadows of the mountains are laid down over the lagoon, the quiet water edged by the white turmoil of the reef, its reflections broken only by wading Hawaiian women gathering seaweed for the evening meal. There was no hint of this as you passed in the morning, but now at evening there is a contained beauty about the spot.

A little farther along the coast you may capture another fortunate flash of beauty. It is the habit of our clouds to descend at evening and rest in an unbroken bank along the tops of the Koolau Mountains, the shape of which someone has compared to the bottom of an upturned canoe. But there are holes in the hull, one of the widest where the head of Kalihi Valley makes a gap in the range. At times the sun is framed in this space between cloud and mountain as if it were shining through a window. It sends through, hardly a shaft, but a great column of light, dividing the shadows on either hand and pointing seaward until it is diffused in the sunlight offshore. At Iao Valley on Maui you may get this effect quite often, but nowhere else on Oahu except here.

Another place that is at its best in the evening is the stretch of coastal valleys that flank the Waianae Mountains from Kaena to Nanakuli. This is the leeward side of the island and therefore dry and very warm. The valleys, Lualualei and the rest, here represent deep cuts into the substance of the ancient volcanic dome that was the beginning of this island of Oahu. The residual ridges that separate the valleys are composed of bisected flows of red- and chocolate-colored lava, and are cut down very steeply but irregularly, as though they had been chopped out rather than planed down by erosion. Nor was the workman at all careful where the chips flew, for broken boulders

Oahu islanders use an age-old Hawaiian technique to hold captured reef fish in this pond on the island's north coast. Holes in a rock dike allow the high tides to enter from adjacent Kahana Bay, but are too small for the fish to escape.

281

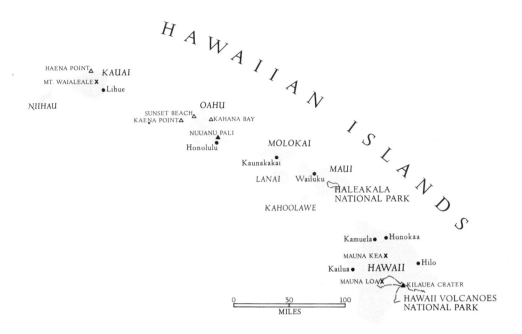

HAWAIIAN ISLANDS

HAENA POINT △ KAUAI
MT. WAIALEALE X
● Lihue

NIIHAU

OAHU
SUNSET BEACH △
KAENA POINT △   △ KAHANA BAY
NUUANU PALI ▲
Honolulu ●

MOLOKAI

Kaunakakai ●

LANAI   Wailuku ●   MAUI
HALEAKALA
NATIONAL PARK

KAHOOLAWE

Kamuela ●   ● Honokaa
MAUNA KEA X
Kailua ●   HAWAII   ● Hilo
MAUNA LOA X   △ KILAUEA CRATER
HAWAII VOLCANOES
NATIONAL PARK

0   50   100
MILES

cover the bottoms of these deep chasms. The only vegetation that can survive the heat and drought is the panini, the prickly pear cactus, some straggly kiawes and sapless lantana. Higher up where nothing grows, the rimrock is so red and forbidding that little imagination is needed to see it again as hot and glowing with internal fires. But here, nightly, the setting sun spreads its palette. The rock walls glow again, but softly; purple shadows fill the canyons, cool breezes stray out of their depths, and the harshness of heat and fiery color is allayed.

There are very many places where beauty will stand and wait for you. It really doesn't matter when you come around the corner and find Kahana—the curving bay, the river resting between the hau thickets, the green mountains at your side, will all be there. Nor does it make much difference when you cross the Waimea bridge and look down on the beach from the bluffs on the other side. At high noon or any other time those long black lava rocks, their backs rounded with a thousand years of ocean buffeting, will still be there, like prehistoric monsters, half-submerged, sleeping on the sand. The contrast between yellow beach and black rock will never fail to surprise you. If you will take time to turn aside, 300 yards upstream will bring you to a little flat strewn with boulders, mossy and fern-covered, all tented over with the spread of monkeypod trees, a temple of shade.

Nearly all Hawaiian traditions center on the sea, and if they could only be recovered, there is no stretch of coast but would have its legend involving every landmark. The people of the islands looked seaward, and the multitude of names descriptive of the moods of the ocean is proof of where their interest lay. They noted the play of sunshine and the constant motion of the sheltered waters near Waialua and named the bay Kaiaka, laughing sea. There was also Kaihili, lashing sea; Kaihoa, friendly sea; Kaiiki, small sea; Kaiki, squirting sea; Kailaa, sacred sea; Kaimakole, red sea; Kaimu, silent sea; Kainamu, growling sea; Kaiehe, murmuring sea; Kaiwiki, quick sea; Kaiolokea, the white rolling sea; and Waikiki, spurting water. There was both truth and poetry in these designations, for, in the old days, the sailor was never permanently home from the sea. He read its storm signals; he knew the places where it was a hungry enemy, a fierce contender. But he knew also where it was quiet or merely murmuring, where his canoe could float lightly, the wavelets gently slapping its koa hull.

Those of us whose recollections go back to the early decades of the twentieth century experience a rude shock upon revisiting Oahu. For where gracefully leaning palms once watched their quiet reflections in the duck ponds and paddy fields, the luxury hotels and apartments of Waikiki now stand. It is understandable—and forgivable, I think—to experience some doubt as to whether these changes really mean worthwhile progress. Fortunately, however, Oahu still possesses many soul-cleansing graces besides the sea.

TERRA INFIRMA

STANLEY D. PORTEUS

This earth is not solid, and Mother Nature can forget all her maternal dignity and kindliness and be just as unpredictable and vindictive as any old harridan. These are some of the lessons that the visitor can learn on Hawaii, the "big island" of the Hawaiian chain. He may even see an island rising out of the sea, for he is coming to a land half of which is built and the other half building. If fortunate, he can watch the process of construction at close hand—the pouring out from cracks on Mauna Loa of millions of tons of molten rock covering thousands of acres. He may realize how infinitely long, in terms of man's experience, the process is, for Mauna Loa has an elevation of 13,680 feet.

Yet this mountain mass is singularly unimpressive when you consider the fact that more than half of its bulk lies beneath the sea.

Naturally, such a steep mass, though buttressed with a mighty weight of water, is none too stable. Part of the island northeast from the volcano of Kilauea is inclined to slip off into the sea. These earth movements are communicated to the ocean by the displacement of untold billions of tons of surface water, which heaps itself up into what we call seismic waves, moving at an unimaginable rate for waves: 300 to 500 miles an hour.

Your first view of Mauna Kea, Hawaii's highest mountain, begins with the 500-foot cliffs that represent its broken seaward edges. You see three zones: the light green of the sugarcane reaching to about 1500 feet elevation, the more somber green of the rain forest running to 9000 feet, and finally the bare, cinder-strewn top of the mountain. Sugar mills are perched just above the edge of the sheer cliffs, in between narrow gulches marked by waterfalls tumbling into the sea. These mills were built in the days of sail, and all their heavy equipment had to be carried ashore—fifteen-ton mill rollers lashed across pairs of rowboats—and then hauled up the cliff face.

However big they may really be, Hawaii's mountains stay in the background—and seldom dominate the scene. Facts and figures usually detract from appearances, but here the reverse is the case. Anywhere else civic pride would have found some means to emblazon those 13,796 feet of elevation on Mauna Kea's sides so that he who runs or rides or buys real estate might read. Tourist literature describes the mountain as standing alone in majesty—but majesty should never stand alone. It needs the comparison of lesser dignitaries to make it impressive. Perhaps what dwarfs its stature is the fact that you are looking up an inclined plane to the mountaintop with no lesser heights between. To appreciate height you must yourself be elevated. So the only realistic views you can get of these Hawaiian altitudes are from the air. When the plane is high enough above the sea to iron out the largest waves to the merest suspicion of wrinkles, you may look away to find Mauna Kea actually towering above you.

All in all, the island of Hawaii succeeds better than any other place on earth in playing down its scenic glories. Even when you leave Hilo for what is proudly advertised as the greatest active crater in the world (the Kilauea, with an area of over four square miles), there is no buildup for the scene itself.

The strip of concrete road unwinds slowly through a tangle of tree ferns, ohias and purple-flowered Brazilian lasiandras. This is locally called a forest, though in Australia or South Africa it would be merely bush, of a particularly pretty and verdant kind. In only one place in thirty miles does the road climb quickly enough to top the forest and give you a view of Mauna Kea in the distance. The experience is rare enough to warrant naming this shoulder of land Mountain View. Otherwise, the sole indication of altitude is the increasing coolness and some change in the vegetation, not so much in the native flora but in the appearance of wild roses, fuchsias and imported trees of the cedar and cypress families that seldom flourish in the lowlands. Still there is no hint of marvels.

Even when, a mile or so past the gates of Hawaii Volcanoes National Park, you roll out onto the edge of the crater, you will find nothing breathtaking. Twenty miles away, Mauna Loa looms, a smooth bank giving absolutely no suggestion of height or grandeur. It offers nothing but a rounded brown expanse with irregular dark blotches here and there, as though some artist had done a clumsy job of camouflage. You may mistake these blotches for cloud shadows except that

283

they do not drift as shadows do. Only when you have crossed similar strips on the road after leaving the park will you recognize them as fields of outpoured lava, miles wide and many miles in length. These are indeed marvels, but marvelously well concealed.

Not even the crater of Kilauea can be accused of blatant overdisplay. To begin with, it is not, to anyone's notion, a mountain at all, but a bulge that has imperceptibly lifted itself to an elevation of 4000 feet. The visitor may be told on good authority that a long distance off toward the sea there is a sharp declivity, but nowhere for miles around the crater is there a slope steep enough to bowl a hoop down. This is a mountaintop without visible means of support. Only your skin tells you that you are up in the air, for even in July and August fires burn on Kilauea hearths, and by sunset people are crowding close to the blaze.

The crater itself is weird rather than wonderful. Halemaumau, where activity centers, is a pit within the pit, a circular funnel 3500 feet in diameter. A winding trail takes you over thirty-foot-deep earthquake cracks lined with ferns, until you reach the lower levels. Then the waves of congealed lava begin to roll confusedly in every direction until they lap against the rubbly cliffs that skirt the main crater for eight miles around. No matter how you try, you cannot describe the scene except in terms of movement, which is most assuredly no longer there. The desert is timeless because nothing indicates change. In Kilauea, time is arrested. All this turmoil is merely held in suspension. These lava waves, glistening black at close view but sooty gray in the distance, once rolled and will roll again. There is no rest, merely immobilization. They heap themselves up without design or order, and so the trail winds between black billows or across ropy outpourings, which record all manner of conflicting pressures.

Light clouds of steam drift across from the west wall or puff out of widely scattered cracks or vents in the crater floor, yet there is little suggestion of imprisoned power. Even Halemaumau is nothing but a great hole in the ground into which, at intervals, avalanches of rock cascade from the crumbling walls. The debris of these rockfalls is scattered untidily over the floor of smooth black lava that has welled up through the bottom at intervals in the past thirty years. There is some fume and smoke rising from a heap of talus hundreds of feet down, but the stage is empty. The whole scene suggests volcanic force about as much

as a teakettle steaming on the kitchen stove resembles a yardful of locomotives all ready to go.

At varying intervals quiescence changes to turbulence. What the scientists call harmonic tremor, a mild volcanic paralysis agitans, sets in around the pit, signifying an upsurge of lava far below; the steam may get thin and blue, marking increased heat. Then, usually very quietly, the black floor opens to reveal a red eye of fire, the initial welling becomes a fountain, a spatter cone is built, and soon the fiery stuff is cascading down the sides, breaking down and melting into its substance the crust of the old flow, forming pools and lakes that glow and congeal, and glow again.

If the eruption is strong, there may soon be a dozen fountains spouting fire, separated by slag heaps between which the molten rivers run. The whole great pit comes alive with rumblings and hissings and tossing of fiery fragments a hundred feet in the air. Thus the caldron may fill for weeks or months, until Kilauea's rusty throat, 1500 feet at its deepest, is ready to brim over into the main crater, or vents open in the mountainsides.

Then the full show for which Halemaumau provided only the dress rehearsals is on. In between these manic episodes, however, the area outside the crater remains quietly beautiful. Lava disintegrates quickly, and watered by the frequent showers that drift across the northeastern slopes of the mountain, great fern and ohia forests blanket the country, masking the old craters. Nothing seems so remote from fire and destruction as one of these green pits with the sun glinting on the tops of the trees and the space filled with the calls of native birds as they search for grubs and insects among the moss-covered trunks of tree ferns. But down at the bottom, well-guarded by tumbled rocks, is a dark lateral tunnel, a smooth black gullet through which there once poured a river of molten stone. Not all these subsidiary craters are hidden, for as you pass along the road you find yourself suddenly looking over the edge of Kilauea Iki, an 800-foot pit suggesting, except for its huge size, an ant lion's trap dug in the sand of the desert. Nor would it take much imagination to believe that a dragon waits at the bottom.

But for all its billowing cauliflower clouds, its terrific blasts, its showers of ash and boulders, the show that Kilauea puts on once in a hundred years

In 1959 a spectacular eruption at Kilauea Iki, in Hawaii Volcanoes National Park, sent a fountain of fiery lava into the sky. Jets of fire soared to 1900 feet, filling the crater with lava 414 feet deep and building a 50-yard-high cone.

or so is nothing but a temper tantrum compared with the hot rage of Mauna Loa, which leaves such utter destruction behind it. Of the great disruptive forces of nature there is nothing that leaves a wake like this. The cyclone may splinter the trees of the forest, the cloudburst may tear away the ground, but here is violence so great that its scars can never, in hundreds of years, be covered. This once-burning river of broken rock across which the Kona road limps is the lava flow of 1868; yet in places it looks as if it might have flowed the year before last. Even with its rage gone cold, it is still terrifying.

Kilauea in size is, of course, nothing but a pimple on the skin of the earth next to the bulk of Mauna Loa, whose base, measured in a straight line, is about seventy miles long. This nearly 14,000-foot mountain is but the visible cap of a vast dome that had already risen 15,000 feet from its lowest levels in the depths of the sea. Mauna Loa also has its summit crater, Mokuaweoweo ("Burning Island"), which can, if it wishes, put on the same kind of performance as Halemaumau. But the weight of this dome compresses within it a core of molten lava agitated by unimaginably mighty accumulations of the gases of combustion. At times, very short intervals in this volcano's millions of years of activity, the inside pressure becomes irresistible and the flank of the mountain cracks open. Then a strange flood of molten stone goes spilling down the slopes toward the sea. If the mountainside is steep, the lava is channeled and it flows like a river; if the slope is gradual, then the lava flow—called *pahoehoe* if smooth, *aa* if a broken clinkerlike mass—feels its way across the surface of older flows, thrusting out tentative "toes" here and there, dividing and reuniting like a stream on a sandy delta. These flows of the Kau desert form one of the most interesting features of the drive around the island.

In spite of periodic ebullitions, however, most of the island is extremely peaceful, and nowhere is this calm more evident than when the lava flows of Mauna Loa are left behind and you approach the quiet slopes of Kona. The road winds along at about 1500 feet, with side roads going down to the shore at such places as Kealakekua Bay where Captain Cook was killed, the city of refuge at Honaunau and the ancient village of Kailua. The forest is all around you and the houses of the coffee farmers dot the clearings, the small green plantations filling the pockets of rich soil between the ancient lava outcrops. The whole place drowses peacefully in the warm sunshine, with the silvered

expanse of the Pacific rising up at the horizon's level to match your elevation.

But this is not all. From eternal sunshine at Kailua you may travel sixty miles farther to Kamuela. For much of the way you are passing across a very ancient tableland with the old lava flows evidenced only by bulges and hillocks covered with bunchgrass. Now, especially when wisps of damp fog curl across the tableland, you have left the tropics and summer behind, and you might be in eastern Oregon during the early autumn. In February with deep snow on Mauna Kea and cold rain squalls sweeping across the bare grassy slopes of the Kohala Mountains (the cattle and horses drifting with their backs to the wind and rain), you have been transported to the high moors of Scotland, or, except for the great elevations, to the Panhandle of Texas.

Then back over the gap and down through the forest to Honokaa and you are in still another world. Here are steep gulches, forest-filled, tumbling down to the sea; spidery trestles carrying water pipes or railroad tracks hanging hundreds of feet in the air; brawling streams; thin, high waterfalls; sugarcane in profusion; and, down below, the dark blue Pacific, no longer sheltered by the bulk of huge mountains but ruffled by whitecaps gleaming under the shadows of the low rain clouds, blown up by the incessant trade winds. It is an entirely different ocean from the one that is stretched out below Kona.

Thus, back again at Hilo you have passed, in circling the big island, through six successive stretches of country, each as different from the rest as though degrees of longitude or latitude lay between. There was first of all the subtropical fern forest from Hilo to Kilauea; the desolate but fascinating volcanic desert from the crater through the wastelands of Kau; the alternating ohia forests and lava flows through South Kona; the coffee-bush and breadfruit belt of Kona itself; the treeless, grassy tundras or moorlands of Kohala and Waimea; and finally the luxuriant river-spaced sugar fields of the Hamakua coast. If you want to go a little distance out of your way, you can see the Kohala district with its wonderful Waipio Valley—a little world in itself. But perhaps six different countries are enough to see in 200 miles of travel.

Near Hilo on the island of Hawaii, Akaka Falls plunges off a 420-foot cliff. The waterfall, framed here by lush ti plants, is on the lower western slopes of 13,796-foot Mauna Kea, a dormant volcano and the highest island peak on earth.

KAUAI: THE GARDEN ISLE

Kauai, nearly circular in shape, is the greenest and fourth largest of the Hawaiian islands.
It is also the only island with navigable rivers. Called the Garden Isle, Kauai has more
native birds, flowers, trees and waterfalls than the other islands in Hawaii. Its lushness is a
result of heavy rains; Mount Waialeale, with an average yearly precipitation of 476 inches, is
the rainiest spot on earth. The 555-square-mile island was the first of the Hawaiian chain
to be visited by outsiders, when the English explorer Capt. James Cook landed on
the southern coast in 1778.

(Below) *Mile-wide Waimea Canyon, cutting through ten miles of western Kauai,
is 2857 feet deep. Long after volcanic action had formed the island, a crack
appeared in the earth and was deepened by erosion to become the canyon.
Its streams are fed by runoff from the slopes of 5080-foot Waialeale near Kauai's
center.* (Right) *Lumahai Beach, near Haena Point, is the most photographed
part of Kauai, which has more beaches than any other Hawaiian island.*

Part VIII

PRESERVING OUR NATURAL HERITAGE

THE WILDERNESS: A NATIONAL TREASURE

ORVILLE L. FREEMAN
AND MICHAEL FROME

Man cannot cast his shadow on the rising of the sun, or halt the flow of the winds, or alter the rhythm of the waves. But he can enrich his humanity with appreciation of the greater world that lies above and beyond his own.

Wilderness is the tangible essence of the greater world placed within our grasp to touch and feel, and to test our sensitivity.

When the Wilderness Act was adopted in 1964, declaring wilderness a valuable national resource in itself, America affirmed faith in its destiny and in the continuousness of its yesterdays and tomorrows. For wilderness always has been, and always will be, part of the search for truth, as well as part of man's desire to know himself and the source of his creation.

In the National Forest System, lands designated for wilderness management and protection as wilderness are still expansive, covering 15.3 million acres. They are located on portions of ninety national forests in twenty-six states, extending from the mountains of New England and the southern Coastal Plains to most regions of the West.

In wilderness no mechanized equipment is permitted (except in emergency and when necessary for administration). Trees are not cut. Virtually all developments except trails are prohibited. The emphasis is on keeping wilderness in its natural state for those who journey beyond civilization. There are exceptions, however, provided for in the legislation for mining, range management and commercial recreational activity. Hunting and fishing are allowed according to state regulations.

Wilderness is an integral part of multiple-use management. It helps in the protection of watersheds, the storage and production of water. It offers refuge and roving room to big animals that might otherwise be lost, including the grizzly bear, mountain lion, mountain goat and elk, as well as deer, fur bearers, birds and small creatures. It furnishes sportsmen opportunities for some of the most challenging hunting on this continent and for fishing in clear, free-flowing streams and lakes carved out of the earth by its own forces.

As a scientific resource, it serves as a living laboratory, a control plot, where the biologist and ecologist can measure the behavior of living things free of human intervention. From such observations have come advancements in medical science, sources of new foods to cultivate and commercial products useful to man.

Wilderness is a many-sided recreational resource. Some come to travel the long trails, others to climb the ancient mountains, to camp in the fullness of night, to exercise the body and stimulate the mind, to contemplate the shape and substance of wild flowers, to follow the arc of the eagle, to luxuriate in solitude, to feel the summons of adventurous times.

In 1964 the United States became the first nation in the long history of civilization to proclaim through legislation a recognition of wilderness as part of its culture and its legacy to the future. The adoption that year of the Wilderness Act, providing for the establishment of a national wilderness preservation system, reinforced the feeling for nature that is deeply rooted in the national conscience.

The wilderness system may in time comprise 150 million acres of wildland—totaling about 10 percent of the entire surface of the country—including portions of national parks, national wildlife refuges and public domain lands, as well as the national forests. These units will continue to be administered by the separate agencies. The system became a reality with the Wilderness Act itself; it designated for inclusion all areas of the national forests previously classified as "wild," "wilderness" or "canoe," areas covering more than 9 million acres.

This act also provides for study over a ten-year period of lands classified as national forest primitive areas under the old regulations, and of all qualified additional areas under jurisdiction of the other two agencies. This act challenges the people. Before additions, deletions or changes are made in the wilderness system, these must be aired and discussed at public hearings and the public must be heard. The Department of Agriculture recently launched a program to study an

Joyce Kilmer Memorial Forest, in western North Carolina's Nantahala National Forest, is a fitting tribute to the poet who wrote "Trees." Clear streams and virgin stands of hemlock, poplar and oak are protected in the 3840-acre preserve.

added 314 undeveloped areas in the national forests covering 10.8 million acres in twenty-eight states as potential future candidates for the National Wilderness Preservation System.

What sort of lands are protected in wilderness?

According to the letter of the law, they must generally appear to have been affected primarily by the forces of nature, with the imprint of man's work substantially unnoticeable. They must have outstanding opportunities for solitude or a primitive and unconfined type of recreation. They may also contain ecological, geological or other features of scientific, educational, scenic or historical value. The wilderness units of the national forests are national documents inscribed in the land. They embrace the range of life communities from desert to brushland, through the alpine to the glacial. Each one tells a different story.

For example:

Bob Marshall Wilderness in Montana includes the Chinese Wall, a fifteen-mile-long escarpment that rises vertically for 1000 feet in sheer cliffs. The spectacular wall is part of the Lewis Overthrust, a major geological feature of the Rocky Mountains. Mountain goats often are spotted on narrow ledges of the cliff face. Covering over 1 million acres of the Flathead and Lewis and Clark national forests, the Bob Marshall Wilderness contains long stretches of wild rivers, a variety of forests, grassy slopes and wild-flower-covered meadows. The wilderness is popular in summer for hiking, trail riding, trout fishing and camping, and in fall for choice hunting. Bob Marshall, for whom it is named, was a vigorous pioneer of national forest wilderness protection and loved this particular area.

Great Gulf Wilderness offers a retreat into solitude and beauty in the heart of the White Mountain National Forest in New Hampshire. The narrow, steep-sided "gulf," with gradual, broadening base, is actually a glacial valley further carved by harsh, tormenting winds. Great Gulf, one of the smaller national forest wildernesses, with 5552 acres, attracts many hikers, who follow the trails from the valley floor at 1700 feet to 5800 feet, near the summit of Mount Washington. The trails pass lovely cascades tumbling downward to the Peabody River, forests of spruce and fir, and alpine flora on the upper reaches. The wilderness forms part of the view from the Mount Washington Auto Road. Visitors to this area are required to obtain wilderness permits.

The High Uintas Primitive Area of eastern Utah covers the major mountain range of the country running along an east-west axis, instead of the usual north-south, and the highest peaks of Utah, rising above 13,000 feet. Over a quarter million acres of the Ashley and Wasatch national forests have been protected and managed as wilderness since 1931. The Uintas, with broad, high basins and purple canyon walls, are noted for hiking and mountain climbing, as well as for fishing. These mountains, as Prof. Walter P. Cottam of the University of Utah has said, are too close to heaven ever to have served as robbers' roosts, too close to winter to make livestock grazing a sustained lucrative business, too poor in mineral wealth to lure the miner, too rugged to shelter weak flesh—either man or beast—for long. The High Uintas are richly endowed in only three basic resource values—water, scientific research, recreation. And if the last two are protected, the first is bound to be protected, too.

Kalmiopsis Wilderness, in the Cascade Mountains of southern Oregon, is a botanist's paradise, devoted to providing sanctuary to a shrub, one of the rarest in the world. The kalmiopsis, somewhat resembling a delicate rhododendron, is a relic of the Tertiary Age and one of the three oldest members of the heath family. It grows among outcrops of weathered rocks, which give a reddish color to the higher peaks. The wilderness covers 168,900 acres of the Siskiyou National Forest and is noteworthy for the variety of flowers. Among the rare and unusual plants are several species of orchids, gentians, the curious darlingtonia and strange members of the lily family.

In such wildlands man himself is the visitor who does not remain.

Until recently, the wilderness areas required little management because they were remote and seldom used. Now, with rising popularity, they must have careful protection to guard against overuse and misuse. Already at some the number of visitors is required to be regulated.

Nevertheless, for all those who enter its portals, for as short as a day, or even for a fleeting hour, wilderness provides a quality of enjoyment and refreshment found nowhere else. One can walk just a hundred yards to feel the unconquered land that once possessed America. Here even invalids can thrill to the rare wonder and beauty. It isn't how much distance one covers, but what he perceives—slowness, indeed, expands the dimensions of time; it encourages one to absorb the fullness of what lies close at hand. So wilderness touches the heart, mind and soul of each individual in a way known only to himself.

BEYOND WHAT THE EYE SEES

FREEMAN TILDEN

The national parks are assuming a larger meaning with every year that passes. More than ever, Americans are visiting their parks not merely for relaxation and physical recreation but with a serious purpose of trying to find their place in a natural world that has drifted further and further from them.

In the early Yellowstone days, the stage drivers dispensed gratis much cheerful misinformation. Some "volunteer guides" turned a few dollars by posing as experts in natural history. What is called interpretation, a service now available in all the national parks, began with some experimental guided trips in Yosemite. From there it grew rapidly in scope until today a park system without this information service is almost as unthinkable as a failure to protect the areas.

If interpretation sounds a bit stuffy, you might call it "getting to the truths that lie behind the appearances." If you want to know the name of that bird or flower, the park naturalist will tell you. But the names are relatively unimportant. How the flower and bird happen to be here, and their interdependence and interaction with all other life in the environment, are what one needs to know to grasp the marvelous order of nature.

Here, in this great outdoor museum, you are in the presence of nature. You do not see it through the eyes of another. If you are in the mood, the slide talk, the campfire gathering, the guided hike on the trail, the self-guided trail with its explanatory labels, the museum and films at the visitor center, the printed folder and booklets are yours for the asking.

Education? Yes, but this program of interpretation is forced on nobody. You can take it or leave it. The other recreative values inherent in the parks remain undiminished. Enjoy yourself as you please, with due regard to the parks and to other people. Boat, swim, fish, romp and suntan as you see fit. If you just wish to lie under a giant sequoia in Kings Canyon Park and spend the day looking up at the sky and meditating, who is to say, considering you and the moment, that that is not the best way you could spend your time? It's what Ralph Waldo Emerson did when he went out to the Mariposa Grove at Yosemite in company with John Muir. The agile John couldn't understand it; he was all for a climb into the High Sierra. But Emerson knew what was good for him.

The aim of interpretation is mindsight. The word is not in the dictionary—yet. It means precisely what Charles Darwin meant when he wrote in his *Voyage of the Beagle* that we must "learn to see with the eye of the mind." Much as we are thrilled by the consummate beauty of the landscapes in the national parks, and satisfying as it is that man should be endowed with the capacity for such emotion, it does not get us far toward that imperative understanding of nature of which Darwin was speaking. And what we see with the eyes may be misleading.

Emotions like compassion can lead us to form absurd judgments. A common illusion is that the wolf that kills and eats the lovely little spotted fawn is a villain. Perhaps you have been so fortunate as to get a picture in Isle Royale Park in Lake Superior of a cow moose standing knee-deep in a pond, browsing on the pondweed. That cow moose and her babies are in constant danger from the twenty-odd wolves that also live on the island. When you know the facts, your picture should have more meaning and therefore be more satisfying to you. If there were no predators on the island—in this case, wolves—the moose population would multiply to the point that the natural browse would not carry the numbers and many would starve.

You may have among your photographs one that you took of an alligator, or a family of them, in the Everglades. By any human appraisal, the alligator is surely not an ingratiating saurian, and it is voracious, a predator on a grand scale. But when you see "with the eye of the mind," you discover that it is also a preserver of life in the glades. When dry times come, it is in the "alligator holes" that many kinds of life take refuge, there to await moisture and renewal. In the natural environment there is neither morality nor immorality as the human concept has meaning. If there is no compassion, there is also no malice. Individual life struggles for survival. That clever little engineer the beaver may change the ecology of the stream valley with its dam, but not to create jobs for itself.

For an example, there is a charming picture taken in Big Bend National Park in Texas: You are looking across the semidesert plain toward the Chisos Mountains that rise wraithlike in the distance, and in the foreground are desert plants —a sotol, a lechuguilla, some species of cactus and the inevitable and tenacious creosote bush. But the picture attains grand meaning when the interpreter tells you something of the harsh discipline of this arid land: the competition of plant life for the meager supply of moisture, the ingenious methods of protection against the desiccating, blistering heat and low humidity. One plant uses a varnish on its leaves; another turns its leaf edges toward the sun; and the ocotillo, when it cannot stand further evaporation, simply drops its leaves and patiently awaits a better time. The animal life likewise adapts to the hard conditions. In the picture all looks bare and unpeopled. But spend a few days in that desert environment and you will be surprised at the activity taking place.

And then there is a picture taken in that wonderful park of land and sea, Acadia National Park on Mount Desert Island in Maine. From Cadillac Mountain you look down upon those islands of Frenchman Bay that were once the tops of hills when the ocean was at a lower level than it is today. The cliffs fall precipitously to the water's edge, so that the buoys of the lobster fishermen are only a stone toss from the shore. Inland are freshwater lakes and ponds, and a long fjord of salt water that nearly cuts the island in half.

But there is something here in Acadia that you can see only with mindsight. All this beauty that surrounds you, all the landscape features that make the island such a vacation gem, are the handiwork of the same craftsman who carved the valley of Yosemite. But here the agent was a continental glacier that something like a million years ago began its slow flow from the north and covered all New England and other states besides. Here where you stand there were 5000 feet of ice—nearly a mile thick—grinding, plowing, sculpturing, plucking. Hard to realize today. But when you learn the story of this colossal invasion from the park interpreters, the area becomes something more than "a pleasuring ground." You have taken your personal step toward understanding nature.

Bryce Canyon National Park is located in southern Utah on a plateau edge eroded by numerous tiny streams and stained various shades of red and orange by rusting iron particles. Indians aptly called these weird formations Men in a Bowl.

UNCLE SAM'S FORGOTTEN LANDS

Few Americans realize they are part owners of some 450 million acres of their nation's deserts, tundras, forests, mountains and rangelands. These are the "forgotten" areas that no settler claimed in the great rush westward. Mostly in eleven western states and Alaska, this acreage amounts to nearly one fifth of the entire country and more than half of all federally owned land. The Department of the Interior's Bureau of Land Management administers these regions separately from state and national forests and parks. Parts of the public lands are leased for grazing, lumbering and mining, but the rest is reserved for everyone to use and enjoy. The bureau has opened hundreds of camping, picnic, historical, fishing, hunting, scenic and nature study areas from Angel Peak, New Mexico, to Nome, Alaska. Every year the bureau increases its recreational facilities, but much of this national heritage will remain as it is—America's untamed out-of-doors.

The twenty-foot tufa towers at the edge of California's Mono Lake were built by mineral-laden spring water. Surprises like Mono Lake, which Mark Twain called "one of the strangest freaks of nature," await those who explore our public lands. Twain accurately reported, "There are no fish in Mono Lake —no frogs, no snakes, no polliwogs—nothing...."

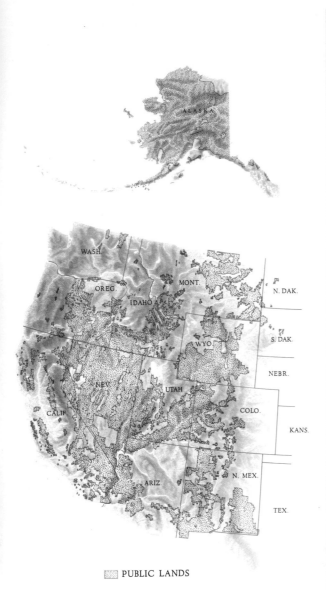

PUBLIC LANDS

Many western towns were deserted when ore veins were depleted or railroads passed them by. Some are still standing on public lands and are easily accessible to visitors. Crumbling walls are among the few remains of Rhyolite, a Nevada ghost town at the north end of the Mojave Desert. One of many mining sites in the mineral-rich Mojave, Rhyolite was named for a common volcanic granite. Three million dollars in gold was mined here within eight years, after a 1904 find. The discoverer, while celebrating his claim, gambled it away for $800. Death Valley lies beyond the low mountains on the horizon.

PRESERVE THE GRANDEUR OF THE LAND

WILLIAM O. DOUGLAS

I have often thought that man's most exciting journey must have been that of Lewis and Clark at the beginning of the last century, up the Missouri and then west over a trackless continent to the Pacific. That was a more telling experience than a trip into outer space, for it was a journey into man's own domain. The prairie grasses of the West stood six feet high; green, rolling hills had blue, snow-flecked mountains as a backdrop. Forests stood in splendor—ponderosa pine, Douglas fir, Sitka spruce, sequoia. Some trees were so large in girth that twenty men holding hands could not encircle them. The abundance of game and fish, the surplus of water, the supply of raw materials, the beauty and serenity of the scene made America the land that man would rather possess than any other in the world. Today America is so interlaced with highways that it is difficult, even in the Pacific Northwest, to get ten miles from a road.

Trees are important for their cellulose, and we need managed forests for lumber and other products. Waterways are useful for disposition of sewage effluent and for generation of electric power. A mountain fastness may have to be invaded for an ore vital to our economy. Valleys and grasslands must be developed to accommodate our steadily growing population. But the planning for wilderness is as essential as the planning for parks and shade trees in our urban centers.

As we pile up in apartments, work in anthill office buildings and hear the roar of subways, autos and trains day after day, we need wilderness for release from the tensions of life. Many people will not crave wilderness adventures. But the opportunities should be left for those great-great-grandsons of ours who turn to the peaks rather than to the playgrounds.

The Virgin River North Fork flows placidly by golden cottonwoods bordering a sheer wall of the Temple of Sinawava in Utah's Zion National Park. The river, weather, growing plants and time carved this twisting 2500-foot-deep canyon.

A river is a "treasure," Mr. Justice Holmes once said. Although a few remain undespoiled, our free-flowing rivers have been largely ruined by sewage and industrial waste. The Potomac, in the environs of Washington, D.C., where John Quincy Adams liked to swim, is now a cesspool. The same story is true across the land. What price a pure, free-flowing Potomac? What price a stream with fast canoe waters, hundreds of swimming holes, picnic grounds beside clean water?

Our seashores also need protection. Cape Cod National Seashore, established in 1966, contains many private homes but preserves the remaining undeveloped acres in perpetuity, preventing uses which might make the area a slum in the twenty-first century. We must do the same in other areas.

Our coast redwoods, tallest trees in the world, make a veritable cathedral of wildness, where all sounds are muted, where man stands humbly before the Creator. We started with nearly 2 million acres of these giants. But at the present rate of cutting the last of the unreserved West Coast redwoods may be gone by 1980.

The views of rivers, bays, rolling hills or ridges have esthetic values far greater than man can create on an easel or shape with his hands. The wilderness is the only area—the ocean apart—where one can escape the crush, din and smoke of civilization. What we need in order to preserve our country's grandeur and beauty is an overall plan —one that takes a whole region, such as the green hills of California or the Potomac Basin, and guarantees that precise areas will be kept as wilderness exhibits forever. Plans to preserve these islands of beauty must be made by constitutional guarantee or otherwise. We need committees of correspondence to coördinate the efforts of diverse groups to keep America beautiful and to retain the few wilderness areas that we have left. We used such committees in the days of our Revolution to bolster the common cause of people everywhere.

The threats to our common cause are everywhere today, too, and the most serious are often made in unobtrusive beginnings under the banner of "progress." Local groups need national assistance, and that means joining hands in an overall effort to keep our land bright and shining. We inherited the loveliest of all continents. We should bequeath it to our grandchildren as a land where the majority is disciplined to respect the values even of a minority. Those values may be esthetic or spiritual, reflecting the principle that beauty is an end in itself, and that man finds relaxation, renewed strength and inspiration in wilderness.

Part IX

A Guide to

ONE HUNDRED SCENIC WONDERS OF AMERICA

HOW TO
USE THIS GUIDE

To encourage you to get out and see the American out-of-doors, the Reader's Digest editors have selected one hundred notable scenic wonders and listed them below by region, beginning with the Northeast. Each entry tells you briefly how to get to the site, what you will see and at what time of year a visit would be most rewarding. Information on accommodations, camping, recreation and guides is also provided. A map of the United States showing the locations of these points of interest and some others as well appears on pages 308–09.

The advice for travelers presented here is necessarily incomplete; there are as many ways to see the country as there are places to see. You can go by car, plane, train or even bicycle. You may visit a Louisiana bayou by dugout canoe, walk along the 2000-mile Appalachian Trail or ride a spotted pony with an original American through his tribal lands. John Steinbeck, in the company of a dog, saw America from a truck; Mark Twain from the pilothouse of a side-wheeler and a careening stagecoach. This guide is meant only as a beginning, a convenient introduction. From here the reader should pick his own parts of America to see and his own way of seeing them.

THE NORTHEAST

BAXTER STATE PARK (*see p. 14*), more than 200,000 acres in area, is the site of Mount Katahdin, which rises 5267 feet above sea level. It is Maine's highest mountain, and it dominates a vast, unspoiled area of lesser peaks, lakes, streams and forests. Indian legend has it that Katahdin was created by a Council of Gods to serve as their sacred meeting place. Baxter Peak, summit of the mountain, is the northern terminus of the Appalachian Trail, a 2000-mile footpath reaching from Mount Katahdin to Georgia. In addition to the scenic qualities of this "forever wild" park, it is richly endowed with animal life, including songbirds rarely found elsewhere in Maine. Few places offer a better chance to observe and photograph moose. Mount Katahdin has two peaks that are over 5000 feet high and another three that top 4000 feet. The literature about this mountain is more extensive than that about any other American mountain. But in addition to the five other mountains over 4000 feet, the park has 36 that are between 1000 and 4000 feet.

BEST WAY TO GET THERE: From Bangor, Maine, take Interstate 95, Maine 157 to Millinocket, and Baxter State Park Road to the South Entrance (about 100 miles). A scenic dirt road winds through the park connecting all three entrances.

BEST TIME TO VISIT: The park season is May 15 to Oct. 15; nights can be cool, even during the summer.
RECREATION: Hiking, swimming, fishing, boating and picnicking.

ACCOMMODATIONS: There are nine campgrounds, two of which are walk-in, and they are open from mid-May to mid-October. Millinocket, about 22 miles from the South Entrance, has motels.

ALLAGASH WILDERNESS WATERWAY is a primitive area northwest of Maine's Baxter State Park. A 92-mile-long corridor through the beautiful forests of northern Maine, it encompasses 200,000 acres. The waterway's many lakes, streams and ponds—especially the swift-flowing Allagash River with its rapids—make a canoe trip a rewarding adventure. This is not a trip for everyone, for the Allagash area lacks a number of creature comforts: There is no public transportation in the waterway; access is limited to a few rough dirt or gravel roads; and camping facilities are primitive. The waterway is divided into two zones. In the inner or "restricted" zone (400 to 800 feet from the high-water mark) camps, timber cutting and construction of any kind are prohibited. In the outer zone, one mile back from the high-water mark, timber harvesting is being carried on under state-approved plans. Registration is required of everyone entering the wilderness area. Some people may want to engage a guide or an experienced canoeist; it is suggested that anyone planning to travel to this

scenic wilderness write for details to the Bureau of Parks and Recreation, Augusta, Maine 04333.

BEST WAYS TO GET THERE: There are several points of access to the Allagash. Perhaps the easiest for many travelers to locate is Baxter State Park (described above). From its entrance continue into the park, turning west six miles after crossing Nesowadnehunk Lake Dam. It is approximately 17 miles from this turnoff to the ranger station at Chamberlain Bridge. Pontoon-equipped planes can also land passengers on certain Allagash waters. The Bureau of Parks and Recreation (see above) has a list of air taxi services. Cars can be rented in Presque Isle (served by plane, bus and train) about 60 miles east.

BEST TIME TO VISIT: Variable weather will be encountered, but cool is the rule. Warm clothing is generally needed.

RECREATION: Canoeing, fishing and hiking.

ACCOMMODATIONS: There are no accommodations in the Allagash Wilderness Waterway. Camping is permitted only at designated sites (most of them provided with tables and fireplaces). A list of registered guides and outfitters for Allagash trips can be obtained from the Bureau of Parks and Recreation (address above).

ACADIA NATIONAL PARK (*see p. 10*), centered on Maine's Mount Desert Island, is a stunning combination of ocean, picturesque coves and teeming tide pools, great headlands, granite mountains and spruce-fringed lakes. Mount Desert Island, Schoodic Peninsula and Isle au Haut were once headlands in a forested plain that untold ages ago sank beneath the sea. The sea continues to gnaw away, and in the fury of a storm great blocks of granite are smashed against the slowly yielding shore. Incredible forces have met here to shape land- and seascapes of remarkable beauty. The best introduction to Acadia is to drive the Park Loop, starting at Sieur de Monts Spring.

BEST WAYS TO GET THERE: Park headquarters at Bar Harbor can be reached from Boston by Interstate 95 (to Bangor), U.S. 1A and Maine 3 (287 miles); from Gorham, N.H., in the White Mountains, follow U.S. 2, Interstate 95, U.S. 1A and Maine 3 (about 200 miles).

BEST TIME TO VISIT: Most visitors to Acadia National Park come during the summer when the naturalist programs and other services are in full operation. But spring and autumn are pleasant and less crowded. The park's roads are closed from December through April.

RECREATION: Hiking, swimming, picnicking, horseback riding, guided nature walks and hikes, mountain climbing, boating, fishing and boat cruises.

ACCOMMODATIONS: Acadia has two developed campgrounds, and the Mount Desert Island towns of Bar Harbor, Northeast Harbor and Southeast Harbor have a number of hotels, inns, motels and cottages. There are also numerous private campgrounds on the island.

THE WHITE MOUNTAINS (*see pp. 16, 20*) of northern New Hampshire comprise one of the most beautiful mountain areas in the northeastern United States. Much of this popular region is in 1100-square-mile White Mountain National Forest, whose most imposing feature is the Presidential Range, an area about eight miles long and two miles wide, where folded beds of rock have been carved and eroded by great continental ice sheets and mountain glaciers. The highest peak is Mount Washington (6288 feet), whose summit can be reached by an auto toll road or by cog railway. Among the area's other attractions are Alpine Garden, with its rare alpine flora; Bigelow Lawn, an area of large, detached rocks

arranged by frost action; numerous cascades and waterfalls; and at least ten glacial cirques, including Tuckerman Ravine (the only true alpine ski area east of the Rockies), Huntington Ravine (a favorite of rock climbers) and the Great Gulf Wilderness. The Appalachian Trail traverses these mountains on its way from Maine to Georgia, and for nearly 20 miles it is above timberline; there are 49 open-front shelters and several huts.

BEST WAYS TO GET THERE: Several highways pass through the White Mountains. Principal highways to the Presidential Range region from the Boston area are Interstate 95, Spalding Turnpike and N.H. 16. This approximately 140-mile-long route leads right to the Mount Washington toll road. Another route from Boston is Interstate 93.

BEST TIME TO VISIT: The White Mountain region is popular all year, but the peak travel season is from spring through fall. Winter (even into spring) is the time for skiers.

RECREATION: Hiking (many hundreds of miles of foot trails, including part of the Appalachian Trail), boating, fishing, swimming, picnicking, mountain climbing, hunting, skiing.

ACCOMMODATIONS: There is camping in the national forest (all of its 20 campgrounds will accommodate trailers) and also in the Franconia Notch and Crawford Notch state parks. Backcountry huts on the trails are spaced a day's hike apart; operated by the Appalachian Mountain Club, they provide hikers with food and lodging. The area has numerous overnight lodging facilities—resort hotels, inns and motels.

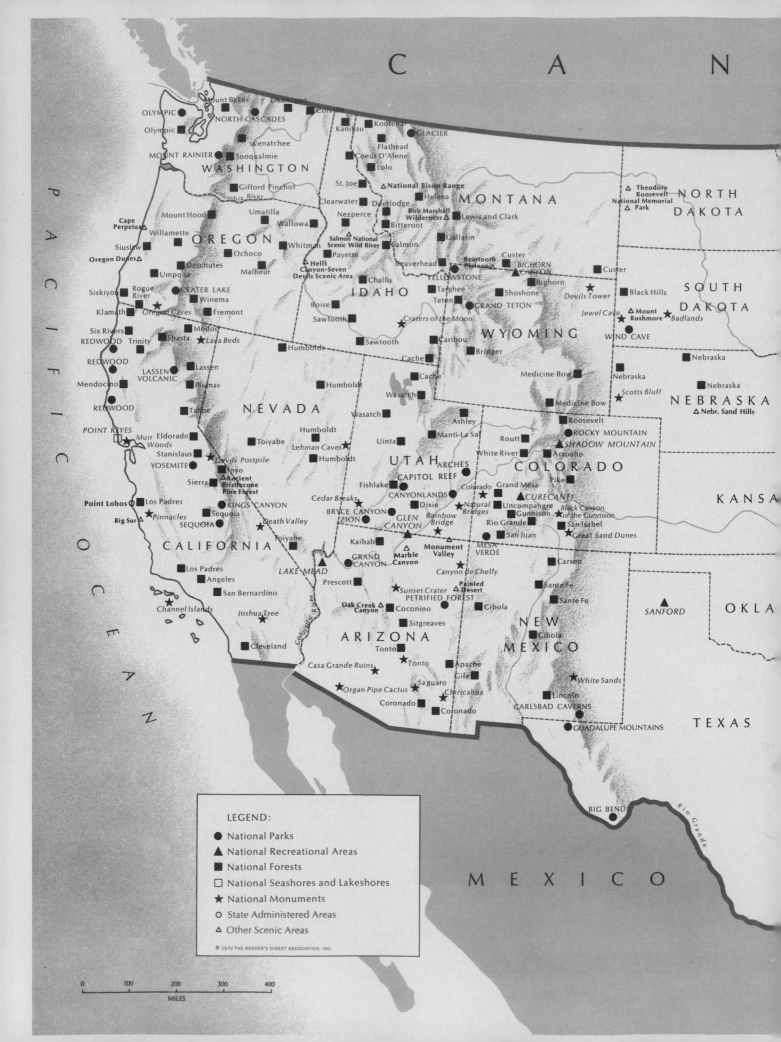

C A N (CANADA)

PACIFIC OCEAN

WASHINGTON
OLYMPIC
Olympic
Mount Baker
NORTH CASCADES
Okanogan
Colville
MOUNT RAINIER
Snoqualmie
Wenatchee
Gifford Pinchot

OREGON
Cape Perpetua
Willamette
Siuslaw
Oregon Dunes
Mount Hood
Umatilla
Wallowa
Deschutes
Ochoco
Whitman
Umpqua
Malheur
Siskiyou
Rogue River
CRATER LAKE
Winema
Klamath
Oregon Caves
Fremont

Columbia River
Kaniksu
Kootenai
GLACIER
Flathead
Coeur D'Alene
Lolo
St. Joe
National Bison Range
Helena
Clearwater
Deerlodge
Nezperce
Bob Marshall Wilderness
Lewis and Clark
Bitterroot
Salmon National Scenic Wild River
Salmon
Gallatin
Hells Canyon-Seven Devils Scenic Area
Payette
Beaverhead
Challis
Beartooth Plateau

MONTANA

Theodore Roosevelt National Memorial Park
NORTH DAKOTA

IDAHO
Boise
Sawtooth
Sawtooth
Humboldt
Targhee
Teton
Caribou
Craters of the Moon
Shoshone
GRAND TETON
Custer
BIGHORN CANYON
Bighorn
YELLOWSTONE
Bridger
Cache
Cache

WYOMING
Devils Tower
Custer
Black Hills

SOUTH DAKOTA
Jewel Cave
Mount Rushmore
Badlands
WIND CAVE
Medicine Bow
Medicine Bow
Nebraska
Nebraska
Scotts Bluff
Nebraska

NEBRASKA
Nebr. Sand Hills

NEVADA
Six Rivers
REDWOOD
Trinity
Shasta
Lava Beds
Medoc
REDWOOD
LASSEN VOLCANIC
Lassen
Mendocino
Plumas
REDWOOD
Tahoe
POINT REYES
Muir Woods
Eldorado
Stanislaus
YOSEMITE
Point Lobos
Big Sur
Pinnacles
Sierra
KINGS CANYON
Sequoia
SEQUOIA
Inyo
Ancient Bristlecone Pine Forest
Toiyabe
Humboldt
Toiyabe
Lehman Caves
Humboldt
Wasatch
Wasatch

UTAH
Uinta
Ashley
Manti-La Sal
ARCHES
CAPITOL REEF
Fishlake
Colorado
CANYONLANDS
Cedar Breaks
Dixie
BRYCE CANYON
ZION
GLEN CANYON
Rainbow Bridge
Natural Bridges
Kaibab
GRAND CANYON
Marble Canyon
Monument Valley
MESA VERDE

White River
Routt
Roosevelt
ROCKY MOUNTAIN
SHADOW MOUNTAIN
Arapaho
Pike
Grand Mesa
CURECANTI
Uncompahgre
Gunnison
Rio Grande
San Juan
Black Canyon of the Gunnison
San Isabel
Great Sand Dunes

COLORADO

KANSAS

CALIFORNIA
Los Padres
Angeles
San Bernardino
Channel Islands
Joshua Tree
LAKE MEAD
Death Valley
Prescott
Cleveland

ARIZONA
Coconino
Sitgreaves
Tonto
Casa Grande Ruins
Organ Pipe Cactus
Coronado
Tonto
Saguaro
Gila
Chiricahua
Coronado
Oak Creek Canyon
Sunset Crater
PETRIFIED FOREST
Painted Desert
Canyon de Chelly
Carson
Cibola
Apache

NEW MEXICO
Cibola
SANFORD
Sante Fe
Sante Fe
White Sands
Lincoln
CARLSBAD CAVERNS
GUADALUPE MOUNTAINS

OKLA

Colorado River

TEXAS
BIG BEND
Rio Grande

MEXICO

LEGEND:
● National Parks
▲ National Recreational Areas
■ National Forests
□ National Seashores and Lakeshores
★ National Monuments
○ State Administered Areas
△ Other Scenic Areas

© 1970 THE READER'S DIGEST ASSOCIATION, INC.

0   100   200   300   400
MILES

A   D   A

Chippewa
Itasca
North Shore Drive
Superior
ISLE ROYALE
Grand Portage
Apostle Islands
Ottawa
Sylvania Recreation Area
PICTURED ROCKS
Hiawatha
NESOTA
MINNESOTA
Chequamegon
Nicolet
WISCONSIN
Kettleson Hogsback
Effigy Mounds
IOWA
Lake Superior
Lake Michigan
Lake Huron
Manistee
Huron
MICH
MISSOURI
Indiana Dunes
INDIANA
ILLINOIS
Hoosier
Hoosier
Shawnee
Clark
Clark
Grove
Mark Twain
Ozark National Scenic Riverways
Ozark
Buffalo River
ARKANSAS
Holly Springs
Ouachita
Ouachita
HOT SPRINGS
St. Francis
Sabine
Angelina
Kisatchie
LOUISIANA
Homochitto
De Soto
Tombigbee
MISS.
Tombigbee
Delta
Bienville
ALABAMA
Conecuh
Talladega
Talladega
Tuskegee
Apalachicola
GULF OF MEXICO
Mississippi River
Pascagoula River
Pearl River
Ohio River
KENTUCKY
MAMMOTH CAVE
Daniel Boone
Cherokee
TENNESSEE
Russell Cave
Chattahoochee
William B. Bankhead
Natural Bridge
Cherokee
Nantahala
GREAT SMOKY MOUNTAINS
Blue Ridge Parkway
Pisgah
Sumter
Oconee
Francis Marion
Savannah River
GEORGIA
Okefenokee Swamp
Osceola
Ocala
FLA.
EVERGLADES
The Florida Keys
OHIO
Wayne
Wayne
Hocking Hills State Park
WEST VIRGINIA
Monongahela
George Washington
Jefferson
Jefferson
SHENANDOAH
Chesapeake and Ohio Canal
PENNSYLVANIA
Allegheny
Lake Erie
Lake Ontario
Niagara Falls
Finger Lakes
NEW YORK
Adirondacks
Hudson River
DELAWARE WATER GAP
NEW JERSEY
Pine Barrens
M.D.
Trussum Pond
DEL.
ASSATEAGUE ISLAND
VIRGINIA
NORTH CAROLINA
Uwharrie
Croatan
CAPE HATTERAS
CAPE LOOKOUT
SOUTH CAROLINA
Sumter
S.C. Sea Islands
VT
N.H.
White Mountain
Green Mountain
MASS.
CAPE COD
Litchfield Co.
CONN.
R.I.
Great Swamp
Boscobel
FIRE ISLAND
MAINE
Allagash Wilderness Waterway
Baxter State Park
ACADIA
ATLANTIC OCEAN

ALASKA
MOUNT McKINLEY
Chugach
Katmai
Chugach
Glacier Bay
Mendenhall Glacier
Tongass
0 100 200 300
MILES

Waimea Canyon
HAWAII
HALEAKALA
HAWAII VOLCANOES
0 50 100
MILES

PUERTO RICO
Caribbean
VIRGIN ISLANDS
VIRGIN ISLANDS
Buck Island Reef
0 30 60
MILES

THE GREEN MOUNTAINS (*see p. 22*), a range of the ancient Appalachians, form a rugged backbone down the center of Vermont from its Canadian border south to the Massachusetts line. This is a magnificently scenic region of granite peaks, dense forests, shimmering lakes, cool streams and beautiful valleys. Mount Mansfield, in the state forest of that name, is Vermont's highest peak (4393 feet); the profile is noted for its resemblance to a human face. A toll road (winding and with sharp curves) runs to the summit; from there the visitor is greeted by splendid panoramas of the surrounding country. The Mount Mansfield area is immensely popular as a winter sports center. Green Mountain National Forest, containing about 365 square miles in central and southern Vermont, offers innumerable opportunities for outdoor recreation. The well-marked Long Trail, which follows the crest of the main range for 255 miles, is popular with hikers for its marvelous views. Though this wilderness footpath is rugged, it may be followed safely by inexperienced hikers—for its full distance or for short walks from one of the east-west highways that cross the mountains. Eighty miles of the Long Trail are in the national forest.

BEST WAYS TO GET THERE: Many roads lead to the Green Mountain region. Major north-south highways are U.S. 7 and Interstate 91/U.S. 5. East-west roads include Vt. 9 (Molly Stark Trail), U.S. 4 and Interstate 89/U.S. 2.

BEST TIME TO VISIT: The first spring thaws mark the start of the maple-sugaring season, and apple trees begin to flower in mid-May. The land is green and the climate comfortable during the summer; the brilliant-colored fall foliage attracts many visitors, and the snowy winters are a lure for skiers.

RECREATION: In the Green Mountains and surrounding areas there are opportunities for hiking, fishing, hunting, horseback riding, picnicking, swimming, boating and winter sports.

ACCOMMODATIONS: Green Mountain National Forest has several developed campgrounds (which can take trailers up to 15 feet), and many of the state areas also have campgrounds. Shelters from lean-tos to cabins are placed every few miles on the Long Trail. The towns and villages of this area have a wide selection of overnight lodgings.

THE CAPE COD PENINSULA (*see p. 29*) extends like a giant flexed arm some 70 miles east from the Massachusetts mainland into the Atlantic Ocean. Most of the eastern end of the Cape, in which a national seashore is located, remains in private hands, but four sections of the seashore are open to the public: The Province Lands Area (4400 acres), at the tip of Cape Cod, contains several miles of some of the most spectacular dunes along the Atlantic. Some move dramatically over the area, smothering entire forests in their paths; others have been stabilized by vegetation. Just off Race Point Road is Ocean View Overlook, and the "Hook of the Cape" commands a panorama across Province-town into Cape Cod Bay. There are guided walks into the beech forest and pond area. In the Pilgrim Heights Area (1700 acres) pitch-pine forests dot portions of the high ground. A self-guided nature trail leads along bearberry- and heath-covered slopes into a large kettle formed by melting glacial ice, and follows through azalea- and blueberry-dominated vegetation on the bottom. Another trail leads down the south slope to a spring believed to have been the one first used on the Cape by the Pilgrims. The Marconi Station Area consists of 1800 acres along the ocean in South Wellfleet. Overlooks along the high cliffs provide stunning views of Great Beach and the ocean. A swamp crowded with white cedar, rare in this area, is accessible by trail. The Nauset Area is divided into three small sections: Great Beach, which is on the ocean side (known to Cape Cod res-idents as the backside) and usually offers excellent surf fishing; the Salt Pond visitor center; and a self-guided trail into a red-maple swamp.

BEST WAY TO GET THERE: U.S. 6 is the principal route to the national seashore area. Provincetown can also be reached by airplane or bus.

BEST TIME TO VISIT: Summer is the peak travel season on the Cape, but spring and fall can also be enjoyable.

RECREATION: There are hiking, boating, swimming, fishing, hunting, beach-buggy tours, bicycle trails in the National Seashore, bridle paths in the Province Lands area, and guided walks in season.

ACCOMMODATIONS: The seashore has no facilities for camping or overnight lodging, but hotels, motels and campground accommodations are available in nearby towns.

THE ADIRONDACK PARK (*see p. 40*) of New York extends from Lake Champlain west to the valley of the Black River, and north from the Mohawk Valley to the farming areas that border the St. Lawrence River and neighboring Quebec. The Adirondack Forest Preserve, which encompasses nearly all of this magnificent region, covers 8000 square miles, about half of which is owned by the state. The forest preserve has two natural divisions: The Mountain Belt, about 40 miles at its greatest width and occupying the eastern and southern parts, runs southwest from Lake Champlain. It is a wild area of rugged mountains that belong to one of the oldest known strata of the earth's crust; four separate ranges parallel one another through the entire belt. Mount Marcy, at 5344 feet New York's highest point, heads the list of 42 Adirondack peaks that rise more than 4000 feet above sea level. The second division—the Lake Region— stretches westward from the base of the main Adirondack range to the forest's borders, a distance of about 50 miles. It has hundreds of picturesque lakes and ponds. Some bodies of water are so closely connected that trips of 100 miles can be made in guide boats or canoes with only short portages.

BEST WAYS TO GET THERE: The numerous gateways to the Adirondack Forest Preserve are accessible by at least one (if not all) of the following: automobile, bus, rail or airplane.

BEST TIME TO VISIT: The Adirondacks may be visited at all seasons. Much will depend on what sort of outdoor activity (or what degree of solitude) the visitor is seeking.

RECREATION: The range of activities is tremendous: hiking (more than 700 miles of marked trails), picnicking, boating (sail and motor, rowboats and canoes), hunting, fishing, golf and tennis, swimming, water skiing, horseback riding and a variety of winter sports (such as skiing, ice skating and tobogganing).

ACCOMMODATIONS: Within the state lands of the forest preserve there are 40 public campsites and innumerable lean-tos along the hiking trails, plus 48 state-owned islands in Lake George that are available for camping. The many communities within the overall boundaries of the forest preserve provide a great selection of private camps, resorts, hotels, motels, cottages, cabins, lodges, inns and dude ranches.

THE FINGER LAKES area of central New York is noted for its scenic beauty and recreational opportunities. The six

major lakes are roughly parallel and extend in a generally north-to-south direction; they were created by glacial action. Seneca, with a maximum depth of 618 feet, is one of the deepest lakes east of the Rocky Mountains. Much of its shoreline is carved from precipitous ledge rock, and its clear waters, born in giant springs, are known to have frozen only a half-dozen times. At Seneca's south end is Watkins Glen State Park. Here a spectacular gorge drops about 700 feet in two miles; it contains fascinating rock formations, grottoes and 18 waterfalls, most impressive of which is Rainbow Falls. Longest of the Finger Lakes is Cayuga, measuring 38.3 miles. Most of its shoreline drops off rather abruptly into deep water, but the north and south ends have conspicuous shoals. Beautiful Taughannock Falls (in a state park on Cayuga's west shore, about 18 miles north of Ithaca) has a 215-foot drop. The imposing bluff at Y-shaped Keuka affords a view of a dozen lakes and seven surrounding counties. Skaneateles, easternmost and most crystalline of these narrow, sparkling lakes, serves as a source of water for Syracuse and is a particularly fertile fishing ground. Canandaigua and Owasco are equally as lovely and accessible as their sister lakes.

BEST WAYS TO GET THERE: Many fine roads lead to the Finger Lakes region. Among them are the New York State Thruway (Interstate 87 and Interstate 90), Interstate 81, N.Y. 17 and U.S. 20.

BEST TIME TO VISIT: The most popular time is from spring into fall, with summer as the peak travel season.

RECREATION: There are numerous public and privately operated recreational facilities. Among the opportunities in the area's state parks are hiking, boating (using your own or a rented boat), swimming, fishing, golf and picnicking.

ACCOMMODATIONS: Most of the area's state parks have cabins and tent and trailer sites. (For information, write the Finger Lakes State Park and Recreation Commission, Taughannock Falls State Park, R.D. #3, Trumansburg, N.Y. 14886.) Elsewhere in the region there are numerous lodging facilities.

THE NIAGARA FRONTIER (see p. 45) has as its major attraction majestic Niagara Falls. With almost 6 million visitors a year, this mighty cataract is the most popular of the world's great natural wonders. Although the water from the Niagara River that roars over the 1075-foot-wide American Falls is less than 10 percent of the total flow (most of it plunges into the gorge over the huge cataract of Canada's Horseshoe Falls), the amount is impressive— from 3.6 to 4.5 million gallons of water a minute. Two massive rock slides at the American Falls in 1931 and 1954 piled up rocks at the base to such a degree that the full 167-foot drop was diminished in some spots to half that distance—the cataract threatened to turn into a series of cascades. As a result, during the latter half of 1969, visitors had the unique experience of seeing the dry rock channel and bare face of the falls on the American side. The United States, with Canada's concurrence, had diverted the river to determine how to preserve the falls. They were able to lower the water level of the pool below the falls, achieving a drop of 182 feet. Visitors could once more walk to within a few feet of the falls' foaming crest or take the Cave of the Winds trip to a point directly in front of the falls at their base. Other ways to see the falls are from an observation tower on the American or Canadian side—or on a boat ride that provides an exciting view from the river below them. Incidentally, a visit to Niagara should also include the Great Gorge and Whirlpool Rapids, farther down the Niagara River.

BEST WAYS TO GET THERE: The Niagara Falls area can be reached by superhighway, bus, plane or railroad. The New York State Thruway is a direct route for motorists.

BEST TIME TO VISIT: The falls are a year-round attraction, although some of the special ways of seeing them, such as the Cave of the Winds trip and the *Maid of the Mist* boat ride (both late May to early October), are seasonal.

RECREATION: State parks in the Niagara Frontier region offer opportunities for hiking (trails into the gorge at Whirlpool and Devils Hole state parks), boating, fishing, swimming (in Lake Ontario) and picnicking.

ACCOMMODATIONS: A variety of motel and hotel accommodations are to be found on both sides of the border. The nearest state camping area (tent and trailer sites) is at Four Mile Creek Annex to Fort Niagara (some 16 miles north of the falls).

THE SOUTH

ASSATEAGUE ISLAND NATIONAL SEASHORE (*see p. 64*) is a 37-mile-long barrier island off the Delmarva Peninsula. About a third of it is in Virginia; the rest is in Maryland. The alignment and topography of the island's seaward side are constantly changed by the buffeting of the elements. The sea- and wind-built dunes form a barrier protecting Assateague's low-lying mass from violent storms. The dunes themselves are fragile and unstable, anchored by grasses tolerant of salt spray but vulnerable to human feet. Beyond the dunes, pines and shrubs have taken a firm hold to create a substantial plant cover. Here dwell deer, foxes, rabbits, raccoons and birds usually associated with mainland forests and meadows. Most notable of the island's four-footed inhabitants are its wild ponies. No one knows where their forebears came from, although legend has it that they were survivors of the wreck of a Spanish galleon. The Virginia section of Assateague consists mostly of Chincoteague National Wildlife Refuge. The Maryland portion (which is comparatively new except for the 688 acres of already established Assateague State Park) is being developed to assure a balance between maximum recreational use and conservation of the island's natural beauty. The land north of the state park will remain in its primitive state; that between the park and the wildlife refuge will be the principal recreation area.

BEST WAYS TO GET THERE: At present no road connects the Virginia and Maryland sections, but there are bridges from the mainland to each end of the island. To reach the Virginia section use U.S. 13 and Va. 175. For the Maryland section (national seashore headquarters and the state park) take U.S. 50 and Md. 611, or U.S. 113, Md. 376 and Md. 611. Norfolk, Va., is less than 100 miles away, and Washington, D.C., is about 165 miles distant.

BEST TIME TO VISIT: From spring through autumn.

RECREATION: A National Park Service-managed day-use area at the Virginia tip of Assateague has fishing and protected beaches for swimming; the wildlife refuge has a nature trail for hiking. In the Maryland section, there are protected areas for swimming in both the national seashore and state park areas. With permits, oversand vehicles may use portions of the beaches administered by the National Park Service. Land north of the state park is currently not available for public use.

ACCOMMODATIONS: The state park has a modern year-round campground, and primitive camping is permitted in the Maryland section from mid-April through October. Canoe-in and hike-in backcountry campsites are available on a reservation basis. Ocean City, Md., a few miles to the north, has motels and campgrounds. The Virginia section has no camping facilities, but there are accommodations on Chincoteague Island, which has a fishing village flavor.

MAMMOTH CAVE (*see p. 72*) in Kentucky was not fully established as a national park until 1941, but its beauty and variety have drawn visitors from all over the world for nearly 200 years. Conditions leading to the formation of caves in this region have been traced back 300 million years, when Kentucky lay under a shallow inland sea. More than 180 miles of the cave's underground passages have so far been explored. Several tours take visitors through the many rooms and corridors to view incredible deposits of travertine stalagmites and stalactites, columns, draperies and flowstone. In the drier parts of the cave, formations of white gypsum can be seen in soft, delicate shapes: flowerlike petals, rosettes and fibrous masses resembling cotton. Tours range from the 1½-hour Frozen Niagara Trip to the 4½-hour excursion through the vast system of "halls" and "rooms."

Mammoth Cave tends to be damp and cool (54° F. all year), so dress accordingly. Rubber-soled walking shoes are recommended.

BEST WAYS TO GET THERE: Mammoth Cave is 100 miles south of Louisville, Ky., via Interstate 65 and Ky. 70. It is the same distance north of Nashville, Tenn., via Interstate 65 and Ky. 255.

BEST TIME TO VISIT: The cave temperature is constant at all seasons. But for those who want to enjoy the surface features of the park—beautiful hardwood forests, fine displays of wild flowers and an interesting variety of wildlife—spring is the beginning of the flower display. Summer can be hot and sultry; the park bursts into color in autumn; and winter, though often freezing, can also be pleasant.

RECREATION: Hiking (the park has a number of winding surface trails), fishing, picnicking, camping and a concession-operated scenic boat trip.

ACCOMMODATIONS: Mammoth Cave has a motor hotel with motel, lodge, hotel, cottage and cabin accommodations and a developed campground. Several adjacent towns have motels.

SHENANDOAH NATIONAL PARK is a 300-square-mile section of northwestern Virginia sitting astride the Blue Ridge Mountains. Though it is probably best known for its Skyline Drive, which threads a winding course along the scenic Blue Ridge summit, Shenandoah has more than magnificent panoramas. Between the drive and the park's eastern and western boundaries are miles of ridges and valleys, gentle hills and hollows, all laced with waterfalls and sparkling streams; and wild gardens of vines, shrubs and flowering plants. The drive itself has 75 parking overlooks along its 105 miles, presenting vistas of the Piedmont to the east and the Shenandoah Valley to the west.

BEST WAYS TO GET THERE: The Skyline Drive leads directly into the Blue Ridge Parkway at its southern end; its northern terminus is Front Royal, Va., at the junction of U.S. 340, Va. 55 and U.S. 522. East-west roads crossing the drive are U.S. 211 and U.S. 33.

BEST TIME TO VISIT: The Skyline Drive is open all year except when the weather makes driving conditions hazardous. The park's camping season is usually from May to October, but Big Meadows campground is open all year.

RECREATION: Naturalist-conducted field trips, hiking, horseback riding, mountain climbing, fishing and picnicking.

ACCOMMODATIONS: Shenandoah has four family campgrounds and one for youth groups. The ARA-Virginia Sky-Line Co., Inc. (Box 727, Luray, Va. 22835) operates lodges and cabins at Skyland, Big Meadows (open in winter) and Lewis Mountain. Several towns within an easy drive have motels.

THE OUTER BANKS (*see p. 78*) are a series of barrier islands stretching for about 120 miles along the North Carolina coast. Forty-five square miles of this beautiful beach land—from Whalebone Junction to Ocracoke Inlet—are preserved in the first national seashore, Cape Hatteras. On this long strip of islands the sea and the winds have contended with the land for countless years, continually reshaping shore and landscape. Natural attractions, in addition to the miles of beaches and dunes, ocean surf and the quieter waters of Pamlico Sound, include wild flowers that grow profusely in the humid climate, and more than 300 species of birds. There is a wide variety of sport fishing in the waters around the beaches. The Outer Banks are also rich in historical lore—from tales of the New World's first English settlement on Roanoke Island to the Wright brothers' first heavier-than-air flight at Kill Devil Hills (Bodie Island) in 1903.

BEST WAYS TO GET THERE: From the Norfolk area (to the north) it is approximately 85 miles to Whalebone Junction, at the northern end of Cape Hatteras National Seashore, via Va. 168, N.C. 34 and U.S. 158. The western approach is via U.S. 64 or U.S. 264. The national seashore can also be reached by ferry. There is daily service all year from Cedar Island, N.C., to Ocracoke, the southernmost island. (Cedar Island is about 75 miles east of Jacksonville, N.C., via N.C. 24 and U.S. 70.) A good road runs the length of the national seashore except at Hatteras Inlet where there is a free daytime ferry.

BEST TIME TO VISIT: Summer has cool evenings and sunny days. Hurricanes occur infrequently, usually in August or September; should one be forecast, visitors are warned. High humidity and strong northerly winds make winter seem much colder than it is.

RECREATION: Activities in the national seashore include fishing (the season extends from mid-April to mid-November), beachcombing, hiking, boating, sailing, swimming, bird watching and interpretive programs. Pea Island National Wildlife Refuge is within the boundaries of the national seashore.

ACCOMMODATIONS: Three campgrounds are open year round, and two others during the summer season. There are motels and commercial campgrounds in villages on the barrier islands and just north of the national seashore.

THE GREAT SMOKY MOUNTAINS (*see p. 80*), which straddle the North Carolina–Tennessee border, form a majestic climax to the Appalachian Highlands. With outlines softened by a lush

forest mantle, the mountains stretch away to remote horizons in sweeping troughs and mighty billows. Shrouding the mountains is the smokelike mist—a deep blue haze—that gives them their name. Some 800 square miles of this wilderness (about half in Tennessee and half in North Carolina), much of it virtually unspoiled, lie within the boundary of the Great Smoky Mountains National Park. Many peaks rise above 6000 feet, but this elevation is not high enough to escape the enveloping forests. A great diversity of trees, shrubs, herbs and other plants are fed by the fertile land and nourished by heavy rainfall and rushing streams. There are a number of scenic drives, but the most rewarding sights are to be found along the more than 650 miles of woodland foot and horse trails. Connecting this park with Virginia's Shenandoah National Park (described above) is the 469-mile-long Blue Ridge Parkway (*see p. 76*), a beautiful drive along the mountain crests of the southern Appalachians. Many overlooks make it a rich motoring experience.

BEST WAYS TO GET THERE: Good highways lead to the Great Smoky Mountains National Park from all directions. Certainly the most picturesque road from the northeast is the Blue Ridge Parkway. From the Gatlinburg, Tenn., entrance U.S. 441 crosses the park.

BEST TIME TO VISIT: Spring weather can begin as early as January or as late as

March, and March through May can be variable. Warm days and cool nights prevail from June through August. Clear days, cool nights and autumn foliage (which reaches its color peak in late October) make the fall a popular time. Winter is an unpredictable season. The Blue Ridge Parkway is most heavily traveled during the summer and autumn—and less crowded in the spring. The road may be closed at times during the winter, particularly in January and February, and some high sections both east and west of Asheville, N.C., may be shut down by icing until as late as Apr. 15.

RECREATION: The Great Smoky Mountains National Park offers many recreational opportunities, among which are hiking (with both conducted and self-guided walks), horseback riding (including pack trips), guided tours, mountain climbing and fishing. The Blue Ridge Parkway is more than just a scenic drive, for along it or within a short distance are hiking (including naturalist-guided walks) and horse trails, picnic areas and swimming, and there is hunting and swimming in adjoining national forests.

ACCOMMODATIONS: The national park has eight modern campgrounds and a number of primitive camping areas; cities and towns outside the park have many hotels and motels. The Blue Ridge Parkway has nine campgrounds; overnight facilities are at Doughton Park, Peaks of Otter Lodge and Pisgah Inn, with housekeeping cabins at Rocky Knob. In addition, there are many motels in communities near the parkway.

CHATTAHOOCHEE NATIONAL FOREST, in northeastern Georgia, extends over nearly 700,000 acres of land rich in scenic attractions. Rising abruptly from the Piedmont foothills, it sweeps over the Blue Ridge like a giant wave, sloping to the north after crossing the crest. One of its major attractions is Brasstown Bald Mountain, which rises 4784 feet above sea level, the highest point in Georgia. Also in this Blue Ridge Mountain setting is Anna Ruby Falls, one of the forest's eight designated scenic areas; its most notable feature is twin waterfalls with drops approaching 80 and 150 feet. A half-mile foot trail to the falls winds along a cascading creek strewn with large boulders. The flowering shrubs and trees—laurel, rhododendron, wild

azalea, dogwood and tulip—add to the unspoiled beauty of the region.

BEST WAYS TO GET THERE: A number of roads lead into and through various parts of Chattahoochee National Forest. If driving from Great Smoky Moun-

tains National Park (described above), take U.S. 441, U.S. 76, Ga. 75 and Ga. 66 to reach Brasstown Bald. For the Anna Ruby Scenic Area, continue south on Ga. 75 to County 56 (this area is about 87 miles north of Atlanta).

BEST TIME TO VISIT: The most popular period begins in early April and ends in November, when fall colors fade at last.

RECREATION: Facilities in the 200-acre Anna Ruby Scenic Area are limited to picnicking sites, but throughout the rest of this vast forest, which has 38 developed recreational areas, there are fishing (800 miles of trout streams), horseback riding, hiking, swimming and hunting.

ACCOMMODATIONS: The forest has 27 campgrounds, and rental cabins are available from the concessionaire at Lake Winfield Scott (reservations required). Several towns within the national forest boundary or near it have motels.

OKEFENOKEE SWAMP (*see p. 88*), one of the most primitive swamps in the United States, is located in southeastern Georgia and northeastern Florida. About four fifths of this remarkable 412,000-acre region of water, woods

and wildlife is occupied by the Okefenokee National Wildlife Refuge. The deposit of peat (up to 20 feet thick) that covers much of the swamp floor is so unstable in some areas that stamping the surface can actually cause trees nearby to tremble. The swamp dwellers —alligator, bear, raccoon, otter and such water-loving birds as the egret, ibis, wood duck and anhinga—follow their way of life without interference by man. About 60,000 acres of Okefenokee are prairie or open marsh, and here in spring aquatic flowers spread a varicolored carpet. Okefenokee's main outlet is the Suwannee River (made famous by Stephen Foster's song). The privately owned Okefenokee Swamp Park adjoins the north side of Okefenokee Refuge—from which point visitors can take guided boat tours along winding watercourses through the swamp's most beautiful cypress forest and through typical Okefenokee prairie. Visitors can follow the Suwannee Canal into the heart of the swamp to an area that offers some of the nation's finest freshwater sport fishing. Stephen Foster State Park is at the West Entrance.

BEST WAYS TO GET THERE: Okefenokee Swamp Park is about eight miles south of Waycross, Ga. (Waycross is 256 miles southeast of Atlanta), just off U.S. 1/23. Stephen Foster State Park

may be reached by leaving U.S. 441 about a half mile southeast of Fargo, Ga., and following Ga. 177 northeastward for about 15 miles.

BEST TIME TO VISIT: Okefenokee is far enough south to be visited all year.

RECREATION: Boating, including guided tours (some waterways and the Suwannee Canal are open to visitors who have their own or rented boats, but licensed guides are required in some areas); picnicking.

ACCOMMODATIONS: The only facilities in Okefenokee are cabins at the state park. Several nearby towns have motels.

EVERGLADES NATIONAL PARK

(see p. 91) in southern Florida was established in 1947 to protect a complex of unique plant and animal communities from threatened destruction. Some of its animals—crocodiles, manatees, roseate spoonbills, reddish egrets, ibises and bald eagles—are rare or unseen elsewhere in the country. From the visitor center just west of Homestead a 38-mile paved road runs through the southern part of the park to Flamingo, and short spur roads lead from it to major points of interest. Royal Palm Hammock, on Paradise Key, is an area noted for its rich variety of tropical plants and animal life and as the start of the famous Anhinga and Gumbo Limbo nature trails. Flamingo serves as a base for exploratory trips into the vast wilderness of Whitewater Bay and the hundreds of miles of winding mangrove-lined rivers and lakes, the channels and keys of Florida Bay, the Gulf of Mexico and the mangrove coast with its tropical beaches. The Western Water Gateway (Everglades City), at the northwestern extremity of Everglades, is the boater's entrance to the waters of the Ten Thousand Islands and the Gulf Coast; privately operated sight-seeing boat tours leave from the Gulf Coast Ranger Station here. And off the Tamiami Trail (U.S. 41) a 15-mile Shark Valley tram ride (free) leads into the northern part of the park—a different wilderness.

BEST WAYS TO GET THERE: From Miami it is approximately 40 miles to the main entrance via U.S. 1 and Fla. 27. To bypass Miami, take the Homestead extension of the Florida Turnpike to Florida City, then Fla. 27. To reach Shark Valley or Everglades City, take U.S. 41.

BEST TIME TO VISIT: Everglades National Park is an all-year attraction.

RECREATION: Hiking (self-guided trails and ranger-naturalist-conducted walks), houseboating, sight-seeing boat tours, picnicking, fresh- and saltwater fishing (this area is a sport fisherman's mecca).

ACCOMMODATIONS: Campgrounds have been developed at Flamingo and Lone Pine Key, and camping is permitted on the beaches and at designated locations in the backcountry. Houseboats can be rented at Flamingo; for information and reservations, write Everglades Park Catering, Inc., Flamingo, Fla. 33030. This company also operates the lodge at Flamingo (reservations should be made well in advance). Park facilities at the town of Everglades are not completed, but motels are available. Homestead, east of the main entrance, also has motels.

THE FLORIDA KEYS

THE FLORIDA KEYS are a magnificent chain of almost 1000 coral and limestone islands that sweep in a great arc southwest and then west from the Florida mainland and come within 90 miles of Cuba. Their offshore shallows and reefs are treacherous to mariners. Off the northern part of the upper keys, the shallow waters to this day harbor much of the only living coral reefs along the coast of North America (now protected in John Pennekamp Coral Reef State Park). The noted painter-naturalist John James Audubon spent seven months in 1831–32 exploring and sketching the birds and plants of the keys. The birdlife is varied, abundant and exotic, while the surrounding emerald waters are a home for more than 600 varieties of fish. The most unusual animal is the elusive Key deer, a delicate miniature species that reaches a height of only 20 inches at maturity. About 400 Key deer now live on the 6697-acre National Key Deer Refuge,

north of Key West; fewer than 50 of these lovely animals remained when the refuge was established in 1954. Such trees as the Key lime (Key lime pie is famous), gumbo limbo, wild cinnamon, tamarind, mahogany and several types of palm are among the many subtropical plant species to be found. Threading the principal keys is the toll-free Overseas Highway (U.S. 1), which in its island-hopping path from the Florida mainland to Key West, southernmost city in the United States, crosses 42 bridges over the sea.

BEST WAY TO GET THERE: It is 159 miles from Miami to Key West via U.S. 1.

BEST TIME TO VISIT: The average year-round temperature of the keys is 77.2° F. During the winter the range is 65°–75° F.; during the summer it is 78°–89° F. and the humidity is low.

RECREATION: Boating, fishing (many sportsmen consider the waters of the keys to be the finest fishing grounds in the world), skin and scuba diving, water skiing, beachcombing, shell collecting, picnicking, glass-bottomed-boat tours, tennis and golf.

ACCOMMODATIONS: Several of the islands have motels, but probably the greatest concentration is at Key West.

THE MIDWEST AND THE GREAT PLAINS

SYLVANIA RECREATION AREA lies within Ottawa National Forest, which is on the Upper Peninsula of Michigan at its Wisconsin border. The woods and waters of Sylvania total more than 30 square miles; its heart is a nearly virgin tract of 14,300 acres of land and 4000 acres of water in over 30 lakes—a unique reminder of the magnificent, unspoiled north woods of earlier years. The tranquil beauty of Sylvania comes from its dense hardwood forests of maple, birch, mountain ash and pine, which provide a habitat for white-tailed deer, black bear, ruffed grouse and woodcock. The sparkling lake waters abound in bass, northern and walleyed pike, trout and various species of panfish; waterfowl are numerous during migration. Motor vehicles and motorboats are restricted in Sylvania, but it is a haven for canoeists. A visitor center, just outside the area at the junction of U.S. 2 and U.S. 45, was opened in the summer of 1969. Additional recreational facilities are being developed in this area, which has been available to the public only since 1966.

BEST WAYS TO GET THERE: The visitor center is at the junction of U.S. 45 and U.S. 2; entry to the recreation area is via U.S. 2, County Road 535 and Forest Service roads 346 and 16. It is 78 miles south of Houghton, Mich. (see Isle Royale National Park, described below), where cars may be rented.

BEST TIME TO VISIT: Sylvania is open year round. Summers are moderate and pleasant, with cool nights. The swimming season is mid-June to mid-August. Winter arrives by mid-November; snow may last into early April.

RECREATION: Major activities are boating, fishing, swimming, hunting and picnicking.

ACCOMMODATIONS: Eighty-eight wilderness-type camping units are available. Motels are located in nearby Wisconsin and Michigan communities.

PICTURED ROCKS NATIONAL LAKESHORE (*see p. 129*), on the coast of Michigan's Upper Peninsula, was established late in 1966 because of its superlative scenic attributes. Along a 15-mile stretch of Lake Superior shoreline lies the Pictured Rocks escarpment—multicolored sandstone cliffs that rise as much as 200 feet above the lake, with thunder caves,

arches, columns and promontories, most of which are visible only from a boat (privately operated cruises run daily in summer from Munising). Grand Sable Dunes and Banks were formed by glacial and wind activity in the eastern part of the lakeshore. Grand Sable Banks is the exposed part of an old bay-mouth bar extending five miles along the present shore and rising to 275 feet above the lake at a sharp an-

gle. Perched on top of the banks are Grand Sable Dunes, which rise an additional 85 feet and cover a five-square-mile area. Much of the inland portion of the lakeshore is densely forested, and spring flowers and autumn foliage are spectacular. Common throughout the area are inland lakes, ponds, streams, waterfalls and bogs. Munising Falls drops 50 feet over the sandstone bluff into a large natural amphitheater; at the base of the bluff it is possible to walk behind the falls without getting wet. A great variety of mammals and birds can be found in this region.

BEST WAY TO GET THERE: Munising, the entry point, is about 127 miles east of Houghton, Mich., via U.S. 41 and Mich 28. Houghton is served by bus and airline and has car rental service.

BEST TIME TO VISIT: Late spring to early fall.

RECREATION: Full development of recreational facilities may not be completed until the mid-1970s. But hiking (on established trails or Twelve-Mile Beach), fishing, boating, picnicking and hunting opportunities exist now.

ACCOMMODATIONS: Camping is limited to three primitive campsites, but eventually extensive campground facilities will be provided. There are motels in Munising.

ISLE ROYALE NATIONAL PARK, the largest island in Lake Superior, is one of the few readily accessible wilderness regions of the conterminous United States. This roadless archipelago of unspoiled forests, glacial lakes and streams, scenic shores and waterscapes can be reached by boat or by floatplane from mainland Minnesota or Michigan's Upper Peninsula. The island's soil cover is shallow—from a few inches to a few feet—but it is sufficient to support magnificent evergreen and hardwood forests and other vegetation, including several hundred species of wild flowers. The only animals living on Isle Royale are descendants of those that could swim, float or fly from the nearest mainland (15 miles is the closest point) or cross the ice bridge that sometimes links the island with Canada. This population includes a number of mammals, from moose to red squirrels, and more than 200 kinds of birds. The main island (about 45 miles long and some 9 miles across at its widest point), a number of small adjacent islands and the offshore waters within the authorized park

boundary cover more than 840 square miles.

BEST WAYS TO GET THERE: Ferries leave from Grand Portage, Minn., and Houghton and Copper Harbor, Mich., and there is a seaplane service from Houghton. A passenger boat circumnavigates the island, making stops. Houghton is reached by airline, and both Grand Portage and Houghton, by bus.

BEST TIME TO VISIT: Isle Royale National Park is open from about May 15 to Oct. 20, but ferry service does not begin until mid-June. Midsummer temperatures rarely exceed 80° F.; evenings are usually cool.

RECREATION: Boating (Rock Harbor Lodge has docks and a marina, open late June to Labor Day), hiking (more than 120 miles of foot trails), boat tours, canoeing, fishing (both lake and stream) and picnicking. Swimming is not recommended because the waters of Lake Superior are extremely cold. The numerous shipwrecks in the area can be explored by skin-diving enthusiasts, but a permit is required.

ACCOMMODATIONS: Isle Royale has 22 lakeside and trailside campgrounds. Overnight lodging facilities at Rock Harbor Lodge consist of motel-type rooms and housekeeping cottages. The lodge is open June 20 to Labor Day, and reservations are required (for information and rates, write National Park Concessions, Houghton, Mich. 49931, during the season; before June 15 the address is Mammoth Cave, Ky. 42259).

THE NORTH SHORE DRIVE (U.S. 61) parallels Lake Superior between Duluth and Grand Portage in Minnesota's Arrowhead region and provides one of the most scenic rides in the country. Its attraction is the quiet beauty of northland woods and lakes. About 150 miles of this route are in the United States (it continues almost 500 miles farther, in Canada), passing by or through seven state parks—and also through part of Superior National Forest, which embraces nearly 4800 square miles of northeastern Minnesota. More than a million acres, one third of this national forest, have been set aside as a perpetual wilderness called the Boundary Waters Canoe Area. Extending nearly 200 miles along the Minnesota-Ontario border, this region is a unique combination of primeval forests and numberless lakes, streams and islands. It offers a remarkable and exciting vacation opportunity for the adventuresome; travel through this serene wilderness is only by canoe (or other portable watercraft) and portage, for permanent roads are not allowed here. On the North Shore Drive near the Canadian border is Grand Portage Na-

tional Monument, which preserves and memorializes a once-vital link on the principal route into the Northwest interior. The Grand Portage wilderness is still much as it was during the fur-trade era. The town of Grand Portage is an access point for travel to Isle Royale National Park, Mich. (described above).
BEST WAYS TO GET THERE: Duluth, Minn., is the starting point for the North Shore Drive. The Boundary Waters Canoe Area is accessible by road from Ely, Grand Marais, Isabella, Tofte and Crane Lake. (If contemplating this trip, contact the Forest Supervisor, Superior National Forest, Duluth, Minn.) Duluth is reached by airline, rail and bus, and rental cars are available there. Grand Portage National Monument is at the northern end of U.S. 61, some 150 miles from Duluth.
BEST TIME TO VISIT: Late spring to mid-October is the pleasantest time of year in this northern area.
RECREATION: The North Shore Drive region offers almost limitless opportunities for outdoor activities: picnicking, hiking, skiing, hunting, fishing, swimming and boating (including canoeing).
ACCOMMODATIONS: Along the North Shore Drive there are a number of communities with motels, and some state parks have campgrounds. The Boundary Waters Canoe Area has no developed campgrounds (permanent facilities cannot be constructed in a wilderness area),

but more than 1600 wilderness campsites are available for public use.

PIPESTONE NATIONAL MONUMENT in southwestern Minnesota is the site of a unique quarry—immortalized by Longfellow in "The Song of Hiawatha"—which for at least three centuries has supplied the red stone for a large proportion of the highly valued ceremonial pipes used by Plains Indians. To the Indians this stone was an object of reverence, and the area from which it came was traditionally held in awe. These pipestone deposits, lying between thick layers of an ancient formation known as Sioux quartzite, are reserved by federal law for Indians, who are allowed to quarry them under special permits issued by the National Park Service. In addition to the vast quarry the monument has other striking geological features—such as the **Three Maidens,** the **Oracle,** Lightning-Struck Rock, Leaping Rock and Winnewissa Falls. Pipestone lies in an area of great natural beauty, with virgin prairie grassland, flowering plants and birds.
BEST WAY TO GET THERE: The monument is reached by Minn. 23, Minn. 30 and U.S. 75. Nearby Sioux Falls, N. Dak., has rental cars and air taxis.
BEST TIME TO VISIT: The monument and its visitor center are open all year; spring, summer and autumn are the most popular seasons.

RECREATION: Hiking (a fascinating ¾-mile walk along the Circle Trail passes most of the major points of interest).
ACCOMMODATIONS: The monument has

no camping facilities, but the town of Pipestone, just a mile away, has motels.

OZARK NATIONAL SCENIC RIVERWAYS is the first area to be so designated and made part of the

national park system. It is essentially an elongated park, embracing wild, free-flowing rivers and strips of land on either side to assure preservation of their immediate surroundings. Located in the Ozark Mountains of southeastern Missouri, this scenic riverways contains a unique collection of streams and rivers, caves and sinks, plants and animals. It includes about 134 lineal miles of the mostly unspoiled, unpolluted Current and Jacks Fork rivers, the shores of which abound in tall, rocky bluffs. This area is renowned for large, clear, cold springs. Big Spring flows at an average rate of 276 million gallons of water a day. Numerous water-eroded caves are scattered throughout the riverways. More than three fourths of the area is covered with forest, and 1500 different kinds of plants are found here. Birdlife is abundant; the forest sustains a substantial animal community; and 93 species of fish have been recorded in the Current and Jacks Fork. Visitor centers are Powder Mill at Owl's Bend on the Current River, and the Red Mill at Alley Spring on the Jacks Fork.
BEST WAYS TO GET THERE: The riverways administrative headquarters is at Van Buren, Mo., 48 miles northwest of Poplar Bluff on U.S. 60. Both Owl's Bend and Alley Spring are on Mo. 106.
BEST TIME TO VISIT: Spring is short, with crisp, clear days. Summer is hot, with occasional extremes bringing uncomfortably high humidity (the air is

usually cooler in the hills). Autumn is pleasant; winter is cold but frequently sunny.

RECREATION: The major attractions are canoeing and float trips, but activities include swimming, fishing, hiking, picnicking, guided walks and cave tours. Demonstrations are given in making sorghum, whiskey and boat paddles, and in corn milling and blacksmithing. There are also one-room schoolhouse sessions and special programs of Ozark music and turkey calling. Program schedules are posted in the centers.

ACCOMMODATIONS: Campgrounds are located at various points along the rivers; major ones are at Akers, Pulltite, Round Spring and Big Spring on the Current River, and Alley Spring on the Jacks Fork. There is a camping fee in summer. Rental cabins are available at Big Spring from April through October. Motels are found at Van Buren and other nearby communities.

BADLANDS NATIONAL MONUMENT in South Dakota, in its nearly 382 square miles, includes some of the most rugged and spectacular examples

of the erosive effects of weather to be found anywhere: remarkable sawtoothed ridges, pinnacles, steep-walled canyons, gullies, pyramids and knobs. Colors range from those of the tinted cliffs to distinctive gray or whitish layers. Several tens of millions of years ago this was a broad marshy plain, a home for many mammals now extinct that have left their bones. As the ages passed, streams deposited layer after layer of sediment and volcanic dust

blown in from the west. The climate changed, the land became drier, and grasslands replaced the swamps and marshes. Water, wind, heat and frost carved this land and continue to do so; few landmarks remain for many generations. A section of several acres may suddenly slump into a gully, or a scenic feature may be eliminated overnight by one of the region's infrequent cloudbursts.

BEST WAY TO GET THERE: From Rapid City to the Cedar Pass visitor center, take Interstate 90 east and U.S. 16 A.

BEST TIME TO VISIT: Badlands is open all year, but the most popular seasons are summer, spring and autumn. The annual precipitation in the region is about 15 inches.

RECREATION: Guided tours, hiking (there are self-guided trails) and picnicking.

ACCOMMODATIONS: The monument's all-year campground is near the visitor center, and cabins are available at Cedar Pass Lodge. Some communities near the entrances have motels.

THE BLACK HILLS (*see p. 150*) region of western South Dakota and eastern Wyoming is noted for its magnificent scenery, its recreational facilities and its associations with some of the legendary characters of the Old West such as Calamity Jane and Wild Bill Hickok. About 100 miles long and 60 miles wide, most of the area now lies within the boundaries of Black Hills National Forest, Wind Cave National Park and Custer State Park. The Black Hills are believed to be an eroded mountain range; 7242-foot Harney Peak, northeast of Custer, is the highest mountain in North America east of the Rockies. The region's natural wonders include lakes, streams, waterfalls, mountains and canyons, plains and valleys, buttes and mesas, some notable caves and stunning examples of surface erosion. The most awesome man-made feature in the Black Hills is the colossal sculptures carved on Mount Rushmore, a national monument southeast of Rapid City, S. Dak.—the heads of four great U.S. Presidents: Washington, Jefferson, Lincoln and Theodore Roosevelt. If their full figures had been carved, they would be 465 feet tall.

BEST WAYS TO GET THERE: Interstate 90 skirts the Black Hills on the north and east, and several highways penetrate the region. Rental cars and air taxis are available in Rapid City (25 miles from

the memorial), which is served by major airlines and bus lines.

BEST TIME TO VISIT: Most of the Black Hills region is enjoyable all year, but best from spring through autumn. Try to see the sculpture in morning light.

RECREATION: There are outstanding recreational opportunities, particularly in the federal or state-administered lands: hiking, picnicking, fishing, hunting, horseback riding, mountain climbing, swimming, skiing and guided tours. For information on Black Hills National Forest write: Forest Supervisor, Forest Service Office Building, Custer, S. Dak. 57730.

ACCOMMODATIONS: Black Hills National Forest has several hundred campsites, and there are numerous others in this region's state parks and recreation areas. Several Black Hills communities have motels and lodges.

WIND CAVE NATIONAL PARK, on the southeastern flank of the Black Hills region of South Dakota, preserves not only a distinctive type of limestone cavern but also a prime and beautiful segment of the original prairie grassland. From spring until the first frosts of autumn, the region presents a frequently changing display of wild flowers. The park is a sanctuary for many species of

wildlife that were characteristic of the Great Plains and Rocky Mountains before the white man came. Wind Cave itself is a series of fascinating subterranean passages and rooms, some lined with colorful calcite crystal formations. Cave trips lasting an hour or more are conducted year round. Since the cave temperature hovers around 50° F, a sweater or jacket and slacks are recommended wear for all who enter, as well as a pair of stout walking shoes. The strong air currents that blow in and out of the cave—depending on whether the outside atmospheric pressure is higher or lower than that inside the cave—gave rise to its name.

BEST WAYS TO GET THERE: Wind Cave is about 20 miles southeast of Custer, S. Dak., via U.S. 385, which runs through the western part of the park. From Mount Rushmore (described above), some 24 miles southwest of Rapid City, take U.S. 16A (inquire locally about trailer restrictions on part of this route), S. Dak. 87 and U.S. 385 (45 miles).

BEST TIME TO VISIT: The popular seasons at the park are spring, summer and fall. The climate is relatively dry, but thunderstorms and hailstorms may occur during the summer; windy days are frequent during the spring.

RECREATION: In addition to drives through the park and the cave trip, there is an enjoyable 1¼-mile-long (round trip) self-guided nature trail that leads to the summit of Rankin Ridge.

ACCOMMODATIONS: The campground, open mid-May to mid-September, is on a first-come, first-served basis; it has no utility connections for trailers. Custer and Hot Springs (12 miles south via U.S. 385) have motels.

THEODORE ROOSEVELT NATIONAL MEMORIAL PARK (*see p. 154*) is in the Badlands of North Dakota. Brig. Gen. Alfred Sully, who campaigned against the Sioux in the 1860s, described the region as "grand, dismal and majestic . . . at sunset it looked exactly like the ruins of an ancient city." The park is in three separate units: North, South and the Elkhorn Ranch Site (part of the land owned and worked by Theodore Roosevelt, who first came here in 1883). Both the North and South units are spectacularly scenic; few badlands have such colorful and intricate topography as these along the Little Missouri River. Wind and water have cut away the plains into an infinity of hills and ridges, buttes and mesas, gullies and gorges, ravines and valleys, which blend into the distance like a great in-rolling surf. This maze of forms is filled with color: the grays and buffs of sand and clay beds, bands of black coal veins and arrays of yellows, reds and purples. Sometimes the lignite beds catch fire from lightning or other natural causes and burn for years (one such burning vein can be seen in the South Unit). Some mammals are found in abundance; the region has a great variety of birdlife and is by no means void of vegetation.

BEST WAYS TO GET THERE: The larger South Unit is on Interstate 94 near Belfield and some 130 miles west of Bismarck, N. Dak. Entrance to the North Unit is on U.S. 85 between Belfield and Williston, N. Dak. Rental cars are available in Bismarck and Williston, both of which are served by air and bus lines.

BEST TIME TO VISIT: From spring to fall.

RECREATION: Guided tours, hiking, picnicking and open-range horseback riding.

ACCOMMODATIONS: Campgrounds with facilities for trailers as well as tents exist in both the North and South units, but there are no utility connections for trailers. Overnight lodgings are available in nearby towns.

THE ROCKY MOUNTAINS

ROCKY MOUNTAIN NATIONAL PARK, northwest of Boulder, Colo., comprises 263,880 acres of incredible natural splendor. This is one of the most fascinating parts of the Front Range of the Rocky Mountains; within park limits are 61 named peaks between 10,000 and 14,255 feet. In addition to steep mountains, there are alpine lakes, glacier-gouged valleys, rugged gorges and vast areas of alpine tundra—yet this park is one of America's most accessible tall-mountain areas. The 50-mile Trail Ridge Road, the highest continuous auto road in the United States (reaching an elevation of 12,183 feet), links the east and west sides of the park and provides sweeping views of mountains, forests and open meadows. At nearly every point on this and other park roads are open vistas—ideal for sightseeing from a car. A short drive to Bear Lake takes visitors to the very base of the east face of the Front Range, which rises abruptly above the lake. Auto sight-seeing is extremely popular in the park, but those who venture out on foot will see much more—many of the walks along the 300 miles of trails are short and easy, and all will be found immensely rewarding.

BEST WAYS TO GET THERE: From Colorado Springs (134 miles) or Denver (65 miles) take Interstate 25/U.S. 87 and the Denver-Boulder Turnpike (U.S. 36) to Lyons, from which there are two approaches: Colo. 7, highly scenic and with access to campgrounds at Wild Basin and Longs Peak, or U.S. 36 and Colo. 66, a route 16 miles shorter. U.S. 34 passes through the park, but is partly closed during winter. Buses run from Denver, Granby and Greeley.

BEST TIME TO VISIT: Although the spectacular Trail Ridge Road is closed from late October to May, there is something to do and see in Rocky Mountain National Park at any season.

RECREATION: Guided tours, hiking, picnicking, horseback riding, mountain climbing, fishing and winter sports (including ice skating). Shadow Mountain National Recreation Area (also administered by the National Park Service), just outside the park's southwestern (Grand Lake) entrance, offers guided tours, hiking, picnicking, horseback riding and fishing, plus hunting, skiing, boating and other water sports.

ACCOMMODATIONS: There are five campgrounds in the national park and five in the recreation area. Trailers can be accommodated at all but the Longs Peak Campground, but there are no utility connections. Campsites are available on the basis of first-come, first-served, and they usually fill up early in the morning. Neither area has overnight lodging facilities, but such surrounding communities as Estes Park, Grand Lake and Granby have a wide selection of motels, cottages, lodges, ranches and hotels.

GREAT SAND DUNES NATIONAL MONUMENT (*see p. 162*) lies in the broad San Luis Valley of south-central Colorado. The dune formations in this 56-square-mile area are among the tallest and largest in the world. For thousands of years southwesterly winds have funneled sands into an arid basin, where they are trapped by the eastern and northeastern base of the Sangre de Cristo Mountains. At the eastern edge of the valley, dunes are piled to heights of nearly 700 feet. Much of the sand came originally from the volcanic San Juan Mountains, which form the valley's western flank. Unending winds constantly alter and shape these spectacularly beautiful dunes. Day-to-day changes can be seen in the lacelike patterns of ripples that stretch across every ridge and trough. Despite the seemingly inhospitable nature of this desert, vegetation has taken root in protected depressions, and small mammals and birds abound along the southeast edge of the dunes area (more than 150 species of birds have been observed).

BEST WAY TO GET THERE: From Colorado Springs (167 miles) or Pueblo, Colo. (127 miles), take Interstate 25, U.S. 160 and Colo. 150.

BEST TIME TO VISIT: Great Sand Dunes Monument and its visitor center are open all year, and the weather is rarely unfavorable.

RECREATION: Hiking (there are no trails on the dunes—a walk to the top and return takes about three hours, and early morning or late afternoon is preferred, for the sands are often extremely hot), picnicking and, in summer, naturalist-conducted walks to the dunes. In addition, the Montville Nature Trail offers a self-guided half-hour stroll through a small valley.

ACCOMMODATIONS: The monument campground is north of the visitor center. There are motels in Alamosa, 35 miles away.

THE BLACK CANYON OF THE GUNNISON NATIONAL MONUMENT,

an area of 21 square miles, protects the deepest, most awesome part of a spectacular gash in the earth—the result of some 2 million years of abrasive action by the waters of western Colorado's Gunnison River. This is one of the world's wildest canyons, and at its deepest part—about ten miles long—the depth ranges from 1730 to 2425 feet, while the width narrows to 1300 feet at the rim and to as little as 40 feet at the base. A view into the gorge from one

of the overlook points is an overwhelming experience. The lichen-covered, black-stained walls of the canyon, which inspired its name, are shadowed much of the day, standing in somber contrast to the rich vegetation on the surface. Rim drives with overlooks and foot trails to the canyon reveal the scenic splendor of this national monument. There is a gravel road to the canyon's north rim and a gravel rim drive, but the south rim is more accessible, as the roads are paved.

BEST WAYS TO GET THERE: The route from Grand Junction is U.S. 50 and Colo. 347. From Colorado Springs (236 miles) it is Colo. 115, U.S. 50 and Colo. 347.

BEST TIME TO VISIT: May to October is the most popular season. Campground programs are held from mid-May to Labor Day, but Park Service rangers are on duty only in summer months.

RECREATION: Hiking and picnicking are the only recreational activities in the monument, unless you are willing to make the arduous trek to the canyon floor for fishing. However, immediately east of the monument is Curecanti Recreation Area, part of the national park system, where there are facilities for hiking, hunting, fishing, boating and other water sports.

ACCOMMODATIONS: There is a campground on each rim, but no overnight lodging in the monument. Curecanti also has a campground, and there are motels in nearby Montrose.

COLORADO NATIONAL MONUMENT is a part of the Uncompahgre Highland, a tremendous upwarp in the earth's crust in western Colorado,

which occurred at about the time the Rocky Mountains were being created. Great rock displacements cracked the crust to form a ten-mile-long fault. Today three to four miles of this fault form a conspicuous escarpment, hundreds of feet high, that edges the monument on the northeast and constitutes a spectacular scenic delight. Persistent erosion has cut and continues to shape a landscape of massive ramparts, sheer-walled canyons, open caves and delicately carved monoliths and spires visible from observation points along 22-mile Rim Rock Drive. To the north and northeast the Book Cliffs form the skyline and mark the north side of Grand Valley. Looming to the east is a basalt-capped plateau, Grand Mesa.

BEST WAYS TO GET THERE: Follow Business 70 through Grand Junction for the East Entrance, or exit Interstate 70 at Fruita for the West Entrance.

BEST TIME TO VISIT: The monument is open all year, but the period from April to September is the most propitious. The region's total rainfall is only 11 inches, and wild flowers dot the landscapes in early spring and late summer.

RECREATION: Picnicking and hiking. Window Rock and Coke Ovens self-guided trails provide short, enjoyable walks along the canyon rims; Liberty Cap and Monument Canyon trails are somewhat longer and more strenuous.

ACCOMMODATIONS: The Saddlehorn Campground, near the West Entrance, is open year round. The Grand Junction area has campgrounds and motels.

DEVILS TOWER, a huge monolith standing conspicuously against the sky in northeastern Wyoming, became in 1906 the heart of the first attraction in the nation to be set aside as a national monument, with an area of two square miles. It is a colossal stump-shaped, compact cluster of rock columns that rises 865 feet above its forested base and 1280 feet above the nearby Belle Fourche River. This imposing formation, tallest of its type in the United States, measures 1000 feet across at its base and 275 feet across at the top. In the ever-changing light, the symmetrical, curiously fluted form of Devils Tower assumes many shapes and colors —and it can be readily seen why the monolith played an important role in Indian legends. The Sioux related that the flutings were left by the claws of a giant grizzly trying to reach men on the top. The monument is a natural botanical exhibit of plant succession, for here can be witnessed every step in the process toward establishment of a forest—from bare rock to ma-

ture ponderosa pines. Prairie dogs are the most frequently seen native mammals, and about a half mile west of the entrance is a thriving prairie dog "town."

BEST WAYS TO GET THERE: From Casper, Wyo., take Interstate 25, Wyo. 387 and Wyo. 59, Interstate 90 and U.S. 14. From Wind Cave National Park, South Dakota (see above), it is 137 miles via U.S. 385, U.S. 16, U.S. 14 and Wyo. 24.
BEST TIME TO VISIT: Devils Tower National Monument is open all year. Summer days are generally sunny, but when the warm sun sets, a sweater will be needed.

RECREATION: Picnicking, hiking (a 1¼-mile-long self-guided nature trail, Tower Trail, encircles Devils Tower; it is about an hour's walk). The monolith can be scaled (several hundred skilled climbers have done so), but it is a strenuous and exhausting climb, and permission must first be granted by the monument superintendent.
ACCOMMODATIONS: The Devils Tower Campground is adaptable for both trailer and tent camping; site reservations are not available. There is a cabin camp just off the monument road, and motels in Hulett, Sundance and Gillette, Wyo.

BIGHORN CANYON NATIONAL RECREATION AREA, east of Yellowstone and the Beartooth country, extends from southern Montana into northern Wyoming. Included in its 140,459 acres is a 71-mile-long mountain-bordered reservoir, behind Yellowtail Dam spanning the Bighorn River. Its lower 47 miles lie within a rugged, steep-walled canyon hundreds of feet deep, cut through the Pryor and Bighorn mountain ranges. Colorful cliffs along the canyon contain fossils and exposed rocks that span more than half a billion years. The recreation area abounds in a great array of plants (from dwarf juniper forests to dense stands of spruce) and animals (from mammals like black bear, elk, beaver and mink to game birds such as grouse, chukar partridge and pheasant).
BEST WAYS TO GET THERE: The Bighorn Canyon Visitor Center, at the southern end of the area, is at the junction of U.S. 310 and U.S. 14A, near Lovell, Wyo. To reach the northern visitor center at Yellowtail Dam from Billings, Mont., take Interstate 90 and Mont. 313. At Lodge Grass, Mont., 50 miles north of Sheridan, Wyo., there is a shortcut to Yellowtail Dam that saves about 35 miles, but as part of this road is gravel, drivers should inquire locally as to its condition before attempting this route.
BEST TIME TO VISIT: Bighorn Canyon Recreation Area is open all year, but the normal visiting season is mid-April to late October. This region has little rainfall, low humidity and plenty of summer sunshine. There are frequent temperature fluctuations in spring and summer.
RECREATION: The Bighorn Canyon Area is still being developed; when everything is completed, water-related activities will be the basic recreational attrac-

tion. Present facilities include launching ramps, docking, and a boat and fishing supplies center. But even today activities in the Bighorn area include many forms of outdoor recreation: hunting and fishing in designated areas, boating, swimming, hiking and picnicking.
ACCOMMODATIONS: Camping areas have been developed at Afterbay in the northern part and at Barry's Landing, Horseshoe Bend and Kane Bridge (all accessible from the south). Trailers cannot be driven to Barry's Landing. Lovell, Wyo., and Hardin and Fort Smith, Mont., have overnight lodging.

YELLOWSTONE NATIONAL PARK (*see p. 168*) is the first (1872), largest (more than 3400 square miles) and best-known in the nation's national park system—and it embraces about the most diversified assortment of scenic splendors. Most of the park lies in northwestern Wyoming, but its boundaries extend into Montana and Idaho. Its central part is essentially a broad, elevated volcanic plateau, with an average elevation of about 7500 feet. The highest peaks and ridges of mountains

surrounding this tableland on the south, east, north and northwest rise from 2000 to 4000 feet above it. Yellowstone is known primarily for its thermal wonderland of thousands of hot springs and geysers, steam and gas vents, highly colored boiling pools and violently churning mud volcanoes. Its unrivaled geysers are world-renowned for size, power and variety of action. The major thermal areas can be reached easily on the park's Grand Loop Road. The spectacular hues of the Grand Canyon of the Yellowstone and its upper and lower falls can be enjoyed from numerous viewpoints along the road or from the extensive system of trails along the canyon rim. Yellowstone Lake provides one of the easiest means of access to the wilderness area in the park's southeastern corner. And the wildlife display in Yellowstone is unsurpassed in the United States for those with time to seek it out.

BEST WAYS TO GET THERE: Among the several routes to Yellowstone's five entrances are U.S. 89, U.S. 212, U.S. 16 and U.S. 191.

BEST TIME TO VISIT: The park's main travel season is from mid-June to mid-September. But 60 miles of park road—from Gardiner at the North Entrance to Cooke City, east of the Northeast Entrance—are open throughout the year.

RECREATION: Hiking (trails, reaching all parts of Yellowstone, vary from casual walks to those requiring more skill and stamina), guided horseback trips, boating (boats, launches and rowboats may be rented at several places on Yellowstone Lake), picnicking, guided tours, stagecoach outings and fishing (no-fee license required).

ACCOMMODATIONS: Yellowstone has three hotels, motel-type cottages and a number of cabins throughout the park. Reservations are required during the main season (for information, write Yellowstone Park Co., Yellowstone National Park, Wyo. 82190). Campgrounds (including a trailer park with utilities) are open from about June 1 to Sept. 15 (a few may open earlier) on a first-come, first-served basis.

GRAND TETON NATIONAL PARK (*see p. 174*), south of Yellowstone, encompasses the most beautiful stretch of the glacier-carved Teton Range in Wyoming: lofty, majestic peaks—blue-gray pyramids of 2½-billion-year-old rock; wild canyons; extensive forests of pine, fir, spruce, cottonwood and aspen; the broad basin called Jackson Hole, a floral valley in bloom from early spring to late autumn; the twisting course of the Snake River; and valley lakes that mirror nearby mountains whose summits rise with sheer slopes a mile or more above them. Grand Teton is also a wildlife sanctuary. Among the larger mammals that can be seen are pronghorn, bighorn, mule deer, elk and moose; even the rare trumpeter swan is one of the more than 200 species of birds that have been recorded in the park. Many of the finest scenic offerings can be viewed only from the well-marked trails that penetrate into deep canyons, follow cascading streams, unexpectedly pass jewellike lakes and eventually lead to high alpine meadows. Hikers can travel on their own or join a naturalist-conducted walk.

BEST WAYS TO GET THERE: Several highways reach Grand Teton, and Rockefeller Parkway traverses the park north-south. Frontier Airlines has service to Jackson Hole (near the South Entrance) where there are rental cars. There are bus connections from Idaho Falls and Rock Springs, and from Jackson Lake Lodge in the park to Yellowstone.

BEST TIME TO VISIT: Grand Teton National Park is open all year, but early June to Labor Day, when most accommodations and services within the park are available, is the preferred travel season. However, with the advent of modern oversnow vehicles, it is now possible to visit many sections of Grand Teton in winter and enjoy its spectacular landscapes.

RECREATION: Hiking, picnicking, mountain climbing, bus and boat tours, horseback riding, float trips on the Snake River, fishing, boating, water skiing and winter sports such as ski touring and snowshoeing.

ACCOMMODATIONS: There are six campgrounds (they are usually filled by noon or earlier during the summer; advance reservations are not accepted); all except Jenny Lake permit trailers, but the concessionaire-operated trailer village at Colter Bay is the only one with utility connections. For overnight stays there are lodges, cabins and cottages (advance reservations are advised), plus a number of motels near the park.

BEARTOOTH PLATEAU, an area of wild mountain grandeur, is located in the Gallatin and Custer national forests of Montana and the Shoshone National Forest of Wyoming. The average elevation is high, with many peaks approaching or exceeding 12,000 feet. Two of the features of the area are Grasshopper Glacier, a unique natural phenomenon by which countless millions of migrating grasshoppers were frozen in the ice of a forming glacier (Goose Lake Road, passable with four-wheel drive, leads to within two miles of the glacier—the rest must be hiked), and Granite Peak, at 12,799 feet the highest point in Montana. Its almost vertical north face looms 3000 feet over a lake at its foot,

and a glacier clings to its side above the lake. Breathtaking views will reward those who travel the 66 miles of 11,000-foot-high U.S. 212 from Cooke City, outside Yellowstone's Northeast Entrance, to Red Lodge, Mont. There are hundreds of lakes, flower-filled mountain meadows, hanging valleys, alpine plateaus, white-water cascades, glacial moraines, snowcapped peaks, great forests—and pink snow, the color of which comes from microscopic plants growing on the surface.

BEST WAY TO GET THERE: A road map of Beartooth country, outlining the points of interest along U.S. 212, can be obtained from the Forest Service office at Cooke City, Mont., or the Red Lodge Ranger Station near Red Lodge, Mont. Cars can be rented at Billings, Mont., served by air, rail and bus.

BEST TIME TO VISIT: The months from mid-June to October are ideal for a trip along this highway or for treks into wilderness areas. At other times the road may be closed by snow. The weather tends to be cool at these elevations, often cold and windy, so jackets or warm sweaters should be handy.

RECREATION: Beartooth country and other sections of these national forests provide innumerable opportunities for recreation: hiking, picnicking, horseback riding, fishing, boating, rockhounding, hunting and skiing. Near Red Lodge a double chair lift (operating only during the ski season) rises vertically more than 2000 feet to the top of Grizzly Peak.

ACCOMMODATIONS: There are a number of motels, lodges and dude ranches in the Red Lodge and Cooke City areas; the 60-mile stretch of land in between is back country. Sections of the national forests north and south of U.S. 212 have 12 campgrounds, most of which can accommodate trailers.

THE BOB MARSHALL WILDERNESS, in the Flathead and the Lewis and Clark national forests of Montana, was named for a founder of the Wilderness Society. This wild and rugged country, abounding with big game, comprises 949,356 acres of surging rivers, majestic mountains, glaciated canyons and valleys, clear streams and lakes, open grassy slopes and floral meadows, and a great variety of forest cover. One of the outstanding features of this wilderness is the Chinese Wall, a 15-mile-long

escarpment that rises 1000 feet in sheer cliffs, on the ledges of which mountain goats can usually be seen. Here also are countless jagged peaks of the Swan, South Fork, Continental Divide and Teton mountain ranges. Old Indian game trails are still in evidence, as are Indian paintings in red, yellow and purple on many rock walls and cliffs.

BEST WAYS TO GET THERE: Several ranger stations convenient to the wilderness are within a day's drive of Yellowstone National Park (described above). From Helena, Mont. (about 150 miles northwest of Yellowstone), take Interstate 15 and U.S. 287 to reach ranger stations at Augusta and Choteau; for the Lincoln and Seeley Lake stations, take Mont. 200 and 209. The station at Spotted Bear is reached by a road leading off U.S. 2 near Hungry Horse.

BEST TIME TO VISIT: The wilderness can be entered at any time of the year, but persons planning a trip there may find it most enjoyable from late spring to autumn. Travel assistance may be obtained in advance from the Forest Supervisor at Lewis and Clark National Forest, Federal Bldg., Great Falls, Mont. 59401, or Flathead National Forest, 290 N. Main, Kalispell, Mont. 59901.

RECREATION: Hunting and fishing (Montana licenses required), hiking, horseback riding, ski touring, snowshoeing, mountain climbing. Information on licensed commercial outfitters and guides is available from the Montana Fish and Game Dept., Helena, Mont. 59601, or from a local forest ranger.

ACCOMMODATIONS: Camping is permitted anywhere, except for a few sites occupied by commercial outfitters and guides under special-use permits; there are suggested sites but no developed campgrounds. There are motels in Choteau and Augusta, two of the main access points to the wilderness.

GLACIER NATIONAL PARK (*see p. 180*) in northwestern Montana contains nearly 1600 square miles of the most superb mountain scenery in North America: precipitous peaks and sharp-edged ridges girdled with densely forested valleys. Nestled in the higher peaks are several dozen glaciers and more than 200 sparkling lakes. Streams that start here flow north to Hudson Bay, south and east to the Gulf of Mexico and west to the Pacific. Wildlife abounds in Glacier—most of the important mammals native to the United States find a home in its forests and alpine gardens; many species of birds also thrive in these surroundings. Brilliant floral displays, for which the park is noted, reach their colorful peak in early July. Nearly every section of Glacier can be reached by foot, for there are 700 miles of wilderness trails; for motorists the Going-to-the-

Sun Road is one of the world's outstanding scenic routes. In connecting the east (St. Mary) and West Glacier entrances to the park, the road crosses the Continental Divide through Logan Pass. Immediately north of Glacier, in Canada's Alberta Province, is Waterton Lakes National Park; although separately administered, the two parks jointly comprise the Waterton-Glacier International Peace Park. The picturesque Chief Mountain Road links them.

BEST WAYS TO GET THERE: By car, take U.S. 2 or 89. Several airlines go to Great Falls or Kalispell, Mont. Both buses and Amtrak stop at East Glacier and West Glacier. But for travel within the park, arrange to have a car.

BEST TIME TO VISIT: The main travel season in Glacier National Park is from about mid-June to mid-September (the Going-to-the-Sun Road is usually closed by snow from mid-October to June).

RECREATION: Guided tours, hiking, horseback riding, mountain climbing, boating, fishing (all fishing must conform to park regulations, but no license is required) and other water sports.

ACCOMMODATIONS: The park has 18 campgrounds (which are often full during July and August); nearly all have trailer space, but none has utility connections. For overnight lodging there are hotels, motels and lodges in the park. Advance reservations, which are advised, can be made by writing Glacier Park, Inc., at East Glacier Park, Mont. 59434, from May 15 through Sept. 15, and during the rest of the year at 735 East Fort Lowell, Tucson, Ariz. 85719. There are also motels in towns immediately adjacent to the park.

CRATERS OF THE MOON, at the base of the Pioneer Mountains in south-central Idaho, is one of the most amazing landscapes in America, and the best part of this extraordinary volcanic region has been set aside in an 83-square-mile national monument. Vast lava fields are pocked with cinder cones, forming large central basins that in some respects resemble the craters seen on the moon. Lava that geologists believe erupted here over the course of many thousands of years ceased to flow only about 1600 years ago. The floods of molten rock destroyed all vegetation in their path and left a barren, sterile land. Today over 200 species of plants are native to this seemingly desolate area, and animals, too, now find a home here. A seven-mile loop drive and side roads leading from it offer views of some of these volcanic landscapes, while foot trails lead to others. Points of interest include the lava tubes of the Cave Area and Big Cinder Butte, one of the largest purely basaltic cinder cones in the world.

BEST WAYS TO GET THERE: From Salmon, Idaho, take U.S. 93 and 93A/

26/20(159 miles). From West Yellowstone take U.S. 20 (about 190 miles). From Idaho Falls take U.S. 20 (about 80 miles). Idaho Falls is served by bus and airline and has rental cars.

BEST TIME TO VISIT: The park and visitor's center are open all year, but snow may temporarily close the loop drive at times during the winter. Spring wildflower displays in the cinder gardens are spectacular.

RECREATION: Guided tours, hiking and picnicking.

ACCOMMODATIONS: The monument campground is open from about Apr. 15 to Oct. 15; campsites cannot be reserved. There are no regular overnight lodging facilities. Idaho's popular Sun Valley area is only some 65 miles west of the monument.

THE SALMON RIVER in central Idaho is guarded by precipitous cliffs and canyon walls, and surrounded by stately forests and rugged beauty. In their ramblings this untamed river and its North, South and Middle forks meander through six national forests. Traveling the Salmon River, even today, is a challenge to high adventure. For 135 miles the Middle Fork plunges northeast between granite walls to join the main Salmon. This mighty fork (now designated a national scenic wild river)

is passable only by float boat. Few trails enter its backcountry, nor are motor vehicles or motorboats allowed. Marked trails to many parts of the national forests can be used by the wilderness traveler, but nearly 2 million forest acres have been set aside as wilderness or primitive areas with neither trails nor permanent structures.

BEST WAYS TO GET THERE: A few county roads meander into the forests from Salmon and Challis and other points along U.S. 93. Air taxis fly into primitive areas from Salmon, Challis and Boise.

BEST TIME TO VISIT: These national forests can be enjoyed at any season, but summer is the only time when scheduled river trips can be made. The Lost Trail Pass Visitor Center in Salmon National Forest is open June to October.

RECREATION: Fishing and hunting opportunities are outstanding. There are also hiking, boating, river trips, pack trips, swimming, picnicking and winter sports. For detailed information on national forest recreation facilities and on commercial operators of pack, guide and boat services, write the Forest Supervisor at one of the following addresses in Idaho: Boise National Forest, 210 Main St., Boise 83702; Challis National Forest, Challis 83226; Salmon National Forest, Salmon 83467; Nezperce National Forest, Grangeville 83530; Payette National Forest, McCall 83638; or Idaho Outfitters and Guides Association, P.O. Box 95, Boise 83701.

ACCOMMODATIONS: Each national forest has a number of campgrounds. In addition there are motels in several communities in this area.

HELL'S CANYON—SEVEN DEVILS SCENIC AREA is located in the Pay-

ette and Nezperce national forests of Idaho bordering on the Wallowa-Whitman National Forest of Oregon. It is a land of bold contrasts, an awesome monument to the forces of nature, a place as forbidding as it is beautiful.

The Snake River, which divides Oregon and Idaho, flows through what is commonly called Hell's Canyon, the deepest gorge in North America. In its most spectacular 26-mile stretch, the gorge reaches depths greater than a mile. The west side of the canyon is formed by the ridge between the Imnaha River and the Snake, which varies in elevation along its crest from 6000 to 6896 feet above sea level. On the canyon's east side, the Seven Devils Mountains in Idaho rise more than 8000 feet above the river. Both sides of the canyon slope precipitously to the water's edge. Until recently, only the most adventuresome explorers have dared to wander far into this magnificent country. Now, however, multipurpose roads and a trail system are being built to permit all types of forest recreation, including sightseeing.

BEST WAY TO GET THERE: Access to the scenic area, with the best views of Hell's Canyon, is afforded by a graded county road from Council, Idaho (on U.S. 95), which winds 38 miles to Cuprum, then 15 miles farther to the canyon rim. Near Riggins, farther north on U.S. 95, another access road leads to the Seven Devils area. New approach roads into the area are planned.

Mont., take U.S. 12, Idaho 13 and U.S. 95.

BEST TIME TO VISIT: Until more and better access roads are completed, most visitors will want to make this trip in the fair-weather period between spring and fall.

RECREATION: Long-range Forest Service plans for the scenic area include 256 miles of trails, 12 boating sites, 28 observation points and 55 campgrounds and picnic sites. Family jet-boat tours of the canyon may be arranged with a licensed outfitter. Because of progress being made, tourists planning to visit this area should first check with a forest supervisor at one of the following: Nezperce National Forest, Grangeville, Idaho 83530; Payette National Forest, McCall, Idaho 83638; or Wallowa-Whitman National Forest, Baker, Oreg. 97403.

ACCOMMODATIONS: A forest supervisor should also be consulted regarding campgrounds available at the time of your visit. At present there are motels at McCall, Council, Bambridge and Weiser, but as this area grows in popularity, more will probably be opened.

THE SOUTHWEST

PADRE ISLAND (*see p. 190*) extends some 113 miles along the Gulf coast of Texas, from Corpus Christi south almost to the Mexican border. Ranging in width from a few hundred yards to about three miles and separated from the mainland by a shallow lagoon with a maximum width of ten miles, Padre Island has been termed "a textbook example of a barrier island, built by wave action and crowned by wind-formed dunes." Padre Island National Seashore protects about 68 miles of the undeveloped central portion. The island is subject to constant change wrought by prevailing winds and strong tides of the Gulf of Mexico. The dunes shift under these pressures, and vegetation fights for survival. Yet the plant and animal life here is remarkable. There are flowering shrubs and vines, and stands of sturdy grass; more than 350 species of birds find a home here or pass through; mammals include coyotes and gophers; turtles and earless lizards are numbered among the reptiles; and the waters teem with aquatic life. Hikers can roam in most areas, but motor-

ists must stay on the main roads or the beach corridor. Four-wheel drive is essential beyond the first few miles.

BEST WAY TO GET THERE: National seashore headquarters is on Tex. 358 in Corpus Christi, just before the Kennedy Causeway to the island. The Queen Isabel Causeway connects Port Isabel, Tex., with the southern end, but because of a sea channel that cuts through the island, it is not possible to drive from one end to the other, even with a four-wheel-drive car.

BEST TIME TO VISIT: Padre Island is an all-year area, but short periods of cold weather may occur in winter.

RECREATION: Swimming (be careful of Portuguese man-of-war jellyfish that sometimes float in the surf and wash ashore), game fishing in the lagoon (Laguna Madre) and the ocean (a Texas license is required), beach driving (with the precautions previously noted), hiking, surfing, boating.

ACCOMMODATIONS: There is limited camping in the national seashore's Malquite Beach development; camping elsewhere along the beach is permitted, but campers must supply their own water and do without other conveniences. Trailers are permitted as far as a regular car can drive; there is a trailer park at each end of the island—at Nueces County Park in the north and at Cameron County Park in the south. Motels and services are also found at both ends of the island, as well as in Corpus Christi and Port Isabel and along approach highways near the shore.

BIG BEND NATIONAL PARK (*see p. 194*), 708,221 acres in southwestern Texas, has as its southern boundary the great arc of the Rio Grande, and the land here more closely resembles that of northern Mexico than that of the United States. Big Bend has spectacular scenery—great expanses of desert, colorful, deep canyons, rugged mountains that rise abruptly into the sky from arid plateaus—and a wide range of plant and animal communities to match the terrain. The five automobile tour routes in this park—the last large wilderness area in Texas—and foot and horseback trails lead to awesome gorges and up to sweeping panoramic views of the park and of a large area of Texas (and even more of nearby Mexico). The Chisos Mountains rise to 7800 feet.

BEST WAYS TO GET THERE: The only way to the park is by car, and there are

only three paved approaches: U.S. 385 from Marathon to the North Entrance; Tex. 118 from Alpine to the West Entrance; and Tex. 170 (the "Camino del Rio") from Presidio to the West Entrance. Rental cars are available in Alpine (78 miles from the park), which can be reached by train or bus.

BEST TIME TO VISIT: Spring in the park is a long season, with a succession of desert blooms beginning in February and reaching the mountain heights in May (some desert plants flower all year). The temperature in the desert and river valley may stay around 100° F. during midsummer days, but in the mountains it averages 85° F. and nights are cool. The fall is usually sunny and warm; in winter the mountain regions can be cold, but the lowlands remain comfortably warm. The rainy season usually lasts from July through September.

RECREATION: Hiking, horseback riding (the 14-mile horseback trip to the South Rim and back is considered a real adventure), pack trips, guided tours, boating, fishing.

ACCOMMODATIONS: There is camping at The Basin (which is at an elevation of 5400 feet) and at Rio Grande Village; small trailer parks at Rio Grande Village and Panther Junction (consult a park ranger before trying to take a trailer up to The Basin); and overnight accommodations at Chisos Mountains Lodge. Reservations at the lodge are advised; write National Park Concessions, Inc., Big Bend National Park, Tex. 79834.

CARLSBAD CAVERNS NATIONAL PARK (*see p. 198*), containing the largest known underground caves in the world, is in the foothills of the Guadalupe Mountains in southeastern New Mexico. These magnificent limestone caverns came into being eons ago when the area was a barrier reef of an inland extension of the sea. When the water table lowered, air entered eroded subterranean cavities, which became enlarged as rock masses weakened and fell. And as mineral-laden water continued to percolate into the rooms, they became adorned with incredible formations—curtains of cave onyx, delicate, translucent draperies of stone, and stalagmites, both massive and graceful, that rise from the cave floors, sometimes meeting descending stalactites. Connecting chambers open to the public include the Green Lake Room, King's

Palace, Queen's Chamber, Papoose Room and the aptly named Big Room (1800 by 1100 feet, with a ceiling 255 feet high at one point). One of the most unusual events to be experienced at Carlsbad is the flight of bats (which may number well in the thousands) from the caverns' natural entrance; this occurs at dusk each day, from late spring to autumn.

BEST WAYS TO GET THERE: The entrance to Carlsbad Caverns is on U.S. 180/62 about 20 miles south of the city of Carlsbad and 185 miles east of El Paso, Tex. It is 290 miles from Big Bend (described above). Buses go to the park from Carlsbad and El Paso. Both cities are reached by bus and airline and have air taxi and car rental services.

BEST TIME TO VISIT: Because Carlsbad Caverns lie beneath the earth, with a year-round temperature of 56° F., there is no special season for tourists (but bring a sweater, warm wrap or jacket and good walking shoes to use on your tour at any time of the year). As noted above, however, the bat flights are a seasonal event.

RECREATION: There are two tours of the caverns: The Walk-In Tour is a rather strenuous 3-mile, 3½-hour trip; the return is by high-speed elevator. The Big Room Tour duplicates only the last part of the longer tour; it follows a comparatively easy 1¼-mile walk around the Big Room, and the trip down and back to the surface is by elevator. For hikers a self-guided nature trail near the natural entrance will acquaint them with the unusual plants that have adapted themselves to the harsh life of the desert.

ACCOMMODATIONS: Carlsbad Caverns National Park has no facilities for overnight lodging or for camping. There are motels in nearby towns.

WHITE SANDS NATIONAL MONUMENT, in south-central New Mexico, protects the most magnificent section of the largest gypsum desert in the world. Except for some plants that have managed to take root here against seemingly insurmountable odds, this is an austere world of white—vast undulating dunes of glistening white gypsum sands, where even some of the animals, darker in other habitats, have taken on a light protective coloration that blends into the background. The dunes of White Sands are always changing, growing and shifting. Vegetation has succeeded in stabilizing some of the fringe dunes;

in others it struggles to keep from being buried. All the active dunes are slowly inching their way to the northeast under the persistent pressure of prevailing winds, and in some places even man has lost the battle, for occasionally a section of the Heart of Sands Loop Drive into the monument has had to be rerouted. As its name indicates, this scenic route, a 16-mile round trip from the visitor center, leads motorists on a fascinating drive to the very heart of the dunes.

BEST WAYS TO GET THERE: The park entrance is on U.S. 70/82, between Alamogordo (15 miles) and Las Cruces (54 miles). Rental cars are available in both cities.

BEST TIME TO VISIT: This remarkable attraction can be visited at any time. There are seasonal rains, but during much of the year the weather is sunny.

RECREATION: Dune climbing (from turnout points along the loop drive), picnicking (picnic areas are near the end of the drive) and in summer naturalist-conducted walks and illustrated programs on White Sands' history and ecology.

ACCOMMODATIONS: The nearest public campgrounds are at Aguirre Springs (30 miles to the west) and in the Lincoln

National Forest, east of Alamogordo. There are commercial campgrounds and motels in Las Cruces and Alamogordo.

CHIRICAHUA NATIONAL MONUMENT, in southeastern Arizona, is a 17-square-mile area of nature-carved rock fantasies. The extensive volcanic activity that was common in this region millions of years ago left a series of volcanic rock deposits of varying thick-

nesses. Then the earth thrust up, tilting and shaping rock masses into mountains. Subsequent eons of erosion (still a slow but ceaseless process in the monument) and undercutting left a weirdly sculptured spectacle—pinnacles, stone likenesses of huge beasts and men, and other bizarre shapes.

Lying at elevations of from 5160 to 7365 feet, Chiricahua is a green oasis that rises abruptly from the surrounding desert, and its range of plant and animal life is remarkable. A paved mountain road, Massai Point Drive, runs up Bonita Canyon to a point affording extensive views of the monument and the valleys lying to the east and west.

BEST WAY TO GET THERE: To reach the Chiricahua National Monument entrance from White Sands (described above) use U.S. 82/70, Interstate 10, Ariz. 186 (from Willcox) and Ariz. 181 (286 miles). Rental cars are available in Tucson (served by major air, bus and rail lines), about 100 miles west.

BEST TIME TO VISIT: Moderate temperatures are the general rule throughout the year—from a mean daily temperature of 40° F. in January to 74° F. in July. Most of the average annual precipitation of 18 inches falls during July and August.

RECREATION: There are several hiking trails in the monument—from the self-guided Foothills Forest Trail (an easy 15- to 20-minute walk) to the Heart of Rocks Trail, an interesting four- to five-hour trip. Horseback riding is permitted (most trails in the monument are open to riders), also picnicking (bring your own charcoal if you plan on cooking) at a designated area in the campground.

ACCOMMODATIONS: The only campground is in Bonita Canyon, half a mile from monument headquarters; trailers up to 22 feet can be accommodated, but no facilities for them, such as electrical hookups, are provided. There are motels in such relatively nearby towns as Willcox (35 miles from Chiricahua).

SAGUARO NATIONAL MONUMENT

is named for a stately cactus that may grow to 50 feet tall and live to be 200 years old. The two-section monument, lying on either side of Tucson, Ariz., encompasses remarkable forests of these giant succulents, unique to the Sonoran desert of southern Arizona and northwestern Mexico. From the visitor center at the larger Rincon Mountain Section, the desert sweeps east to the mountains; as the land rises, several other major plant communities gradually take over. Leading from various points along the nine-mile Cactus Forest Loop Drive are short trails well marked for easy identification of the desert's impressive plant life. The western, or Tucson Mountain Section, has a vast but younger stand of saguaros. In addition to this forest there are some plants and animals not to be found in the Rincon Mountain Section. Well-kept dirt roads lead to hiking trails, picnic sites, scenic overlooks and other points of interest.

BEST WAYS TO GET THERE: Rincon Mountain Section (about 16 miles east of Tucson): Take Speedway Boulevard, Kolb Road, Broadway and Old Spanish Trail. Tucson Mountain Section: Drive west from Tucson on Speedway Boulevard, then on Kinney Road (15 miles). There is no public transportation.

BEST TIME TO VISIT: The creamy white saguaro blossom (state flower of Arizona) is in bloom in May and early June. The rainy season lasts from December through March, but local thunderstorms may also occur from July through September. Average temperatures in July usually range from 94° F. in the Cactus Forest to 68° F. on the mountaintops.

RECREATION: Picnicking, horseback riding and hiking are the chief activities. Trails range from short self-guided nature walks to more strenuous treks to the tops of mountains.

ACCOMMODATIONS: Plan on staying in or near Tucson, for there are no facilities for camping or lodging in either section of Saguaro National Monument.

ORGAN PIPE CACTUS NATIONAL MONUMENT,

a 330,874-acre tract in the Mexican border region of southwestern Arizona, was named for a spectacular species of cactus rarely found in the United States. Protected and preserved within the monument are the rare animals and plants and unusual landscapes of a portion of the Sonoran desert. It is a starkly beautiful land of rough mountains, rugged canyons, vast outwash plains, creosote-bush flats and dry washes. There are two exceptionally scenic loop drives from the visitor center: One winds 21 miles into the Ajo Mountains; the other extends 51 miles around the Puerto Blanco Mountains and along the Mexican border (at least half a day should be allowed for this longer drive). Of historic interest are campsite remains of prehistoric cultures going back 12,000 years.

BEST WAYS TO GET THERE: The monument is 140 miles south of Phoenix via U.S. 80 and Ariz. 85. It is 142 miles west of Tucson via Ariz. 86 and Ariz. 85.

BEST TIME TO VISIT: The winter climate is usually warm and sunny, with infrequent light rains. Temperatures at night can drop below freezing, and occasionally there may be chill winds from December to March. The skies stay clear and the temperatures become progressively hotter from April through June. The next three months (when temperatures of 95° to 105° F. are common) are humid, and half of the annual 8½-inch rainfall occurs in the form of violent thunderstorms during these months. It can be windy at any time, but duststorms are rare in this region.

RECREATION: Picnicking, hiking. (There are several marked trails, including the one-mile Desert View Nature Trail. Cross-country hiking is possible at almost any point, but visitors planning such off-track walks are asked to consult with a National Park Service ranger.)

ACCOMMODATIONS: Camping is permitted only in the designated campground south of the visitor center. There are a few motels in nearby towns.

THE PAINTED DESERT

of Arizona sweeps in a great crescent from the

Grand Canyon (in the Marble Canyon region) southeast along the Little Colorado River and east to Petrified Forest National Park. The desert's impressive vistas of vividly tinted plateaus, mesas and buttes are among the West's most fascinating scenic wonders. The Petrified Forest, a 94,000-acre national park that protects much of this strange and colorful land, contains a world-famed array of petrified logs that sparkle with jasper and agate, carnelian and onyx. In some sections the earth is literally paved with shattered remnants of these ancient turned-to-stone trees—many-hued chips and pieces that reveal every detail of the original living tree. (Visitors are advised that federal law strictly prohibits the removal of even the smallest sliver of petrified wood from the national park.) The visitor center is in the northern part of the park (off Interstate 40). From there a road leads to several points offering marvelous views of the Painted Desert, and then runs 25 miles south through Rainbow Forest, which contains extensive deposits of fossil wood. There is a fine museum at the southern entrance. **BEST WAYS TO GET THERE:** The park is about 250 miles from Phoenix and 69 miles from Gallup, N. Mex. The Rainbow Forest Entrance, the southern access, is on U.S. 180. The Painted Desert Entrance in the north is on Interstate 40. Westbound travelers on Interstate 40 can tour the park and exit in the south on U.S. 180, which joins Interstate 40 in Holbrook, 19 miles west. **BEST TIME TO VISIT:** Summer days can be warm, and sudden thunderstorms are not unusual. Cold, snowy days are frequent during the winter. Strong winds may be expected at any season. **RECREATION:** There are established hiking trails in both sections of the Petrified Forest National Park; most are in the southern half. Picnicking is permitted only at Chinde Point, overlooking the Painted Desert, and in Rainbow Forest.

ACCOMMODATIONS: No camping is permitted in the park, but there are motels in nearby towns.

OAK CREEK CANYON, in Coconino National Forest, Arizona, is an area whose vividly colored sandstones and limestones have been shaped by wind and water into unusual forms of superlative beauty. In its upper reaches the

canyon is deep, narrow and steep-walled, typified by the Oak Creek Natural Area, which includes the rugged West Fork. Here Zane Grey wrote his novel *Call of the Canyon.* At the mouth of the canyon, around Sedona, a variety of rock formations, including Cathedral Rock, Courthouse Butte and Bell Rock, attract thousands of sight-

seers and photographers all year round. Vegetation in the 75,000-acre area varies from semidesert plant life to the ponderosa pine and Douglas fir of higher elevations.

BEST WAYS TO GET THERE: Oak Creek Canyon is about 15 miles south of Flagstaff, Ariz., on U.S. 89A. From Phoenix (about 118 miles south) take Interstate 17, Ariz. 179 and U.S. 89A. Both Flagstaff and Phoenix have rental cars. **BEST TIME TO VISIT:** This is a year-round attraction.

RECREATION: Oak Creek Canyon and Coconino National Forest are among the most popular recreation areas in Arizona. Picnicking, hiking, horseback riding, fishing, swimming and hunting are some of the opportunities offered here. **ACCOMMODATIONS:** The Oak Creek area has five Forest Service campgrounds; two of them accommodate trailers. For open dates, contact the Sedona Ranger District, P.O. Box 300, Sedona, Ariz. 86336. There are overnight accommodations (a resort, cabins and cottages) in the immediate vicinity, and motels in Sedona and Flagstaff.

SUNSET CRATER NATIONAL MONUMENT, northeast of Flagstaff, Ariz., was named for the colorful cinders that blanket its crest and give its summit the appearance of being continually bathed in the glowing colors of a desert sunset. A little more than 900 years ago the last volcanic activity in this region took place. When the eruption had subsided, a 1000-foot-high cinder cone had come into being, with rough flows of lava at its base. Except for the trees and other vegetation that have successfully taken hold on its slopes, Sunset Crater is believed to look almost the same now as it did right after the eruption.

BEST WAY TO GET THERE: From Flagstaff it is 15 miles (via U.S. 89) to the monument road and 2 miles from there to the visitor center. The road loops across the lava flow and north about 18 miles to another visitor center at nearby Wupatki National Monument, site of one of the area's most important prehistoric Indian villages. Buses, planes and trains go to Flagstaff, where visitors may rent cars or arrange bus or aerial tours.

BEST TIME TO VISIT: Although Sunset Crater and its visitor center are open all year, they may be closed for short periods by winter snows.

RECREATION: Hiking along Lava Flow

Nature Trail (the trail to the top of the crater is now closed), or through the Wupatki ruins. Bring heavy shoes. **ACCOMMODATIONS:** The Bonito Campground near the Sunset Crater visitor

center has 44 sites and is open April through October. There are other campgrounds nearby and motels in Flagstaff.

THE GRAND CANYON (*see p. 206*) of the Colorado River, some 217 miles long and 4 to 18 miles wide, is one of the most spectacular natural wonders of the world. Most of this overwhelmingly beautiful scenic attraction is protected in the 1.2 million acre Grand Canyon National Park in northwestern Arizona. The park now includes parts of the Lake Mead National Recreation Area, the primitive Tuweep area (formerly the Grand Canyon National Monument) and the Marble Canyon (formerly a national monument). The Grand Canyon is the "prize geological source book in the world," for the exposed base rock is part of the earth's original crust, while the rocks layered above it are our most nearly complete record of the eras of geological time. *The South Rim:* Leading from Grand Canyon Village is the eight-mile West Rim Drive, which passes a number of superlative lookouts. This trip should be planned so you can arrive about dusk at Hopi Point, famous for its sunsets. The 25-mile-long East Rim Drive from the village leads to Desert View. Many visitors feel that Lipan Point, on the way, offers the best view of the canyon. *The North Rim:* Across the mile-deep chasm, 214 miles by road, is the higher North Rim, unfortunately passed up by many visitors to the South Rim. Among its great attractions is the drive to Cape Royal (22 miles from Grand Canyon Lodge by paved road), which offers superb views of the canyon and eastward to the Painted Desert. Point Imperial provides equally magnificent scenes. *The Tuweep area:* In this remote section Toroweap Point offers a view of the canyon found nowhere else—straight down the sheer rock walls to the Colorado River a dizzying 3000 feet below. *The Marble Canyon:* Extending northward to the southern boundary of Glen Canyon, this 50-mile-long preserve contains little more than the river and its canyon walls. But these are certainly spectacular. The sheer red sandstone and white limestone walls rise up to 3000 feet above the rushing Colorado, and vast alcoves in these soaring walls enhance their beauty.

BEST WAYS TO GET THERE: The South Rim is reached via U.S. 180 and Ariz. 64. There are scheduled flights from Phoenix and Las Vegas to Grand Canyon Airport (seven miles from the village), and buses from Flagstaff and Williams. Rental cars are available in Grand Canyon Village, and in summer there is a free shuttle bus on the South and West Rims. The North Rim is accessible via Ariz. 67 (closed in winter). In summer there are bus tours to the North Rim from Cedar City, Utah; also,

Grand Canyon Airlines has daily flights across the canyon. Toroweap Point can be reached in good weather by a 70-mile stretch of mostly graded road leading off U.S. 89A at Fredonia, Ariz. The town of Marble Canyon is on U.S. 89A, about 5 miles from Lees Ferry, Ariz.,

34 miles from Page, Ariz. and 86 miles from the North Rim. About the only way to see Marble Canyon is by boat from Lees Ferry. Flagstaff, Cedar City and Page have rental cars; the first two also have air taxis.

BEST TIME TO VISIT: The South Rim is for all seasons, but a winterlike cold snap sometimes occurs in spring, and July and August are known for frequent thunderstorms. Autumn is comparatively short. The first snowfall may come as early as October or November, but from then until April daytime temperatures range in the 40s and 50s, dropping to below freezing at night. On the North Rim, where elevations are 800 to 1800 feet higher than the South Rim, the weather is generally cooler and precipitation is greater. More than 200 inches of snow may fall during the winter, when the North Rim is closed, and thunderstorms may be severe during the summer. But colorful spring flowers are in bloom by early May, and the North Rim can be comfortably enjoyed until about mid-October. Summer is the best season for both Toroweap Point and the Marble Canyon.

RECREATION: Opportunities at the South Rim include picnicking, visits to the museums, horseback trips, hiking on self-guided trails and (far more strenuous) down into the canyon. In addition there are adventurous muleback trips into the canyon: the trip to Tonto Plateau, 3200 feet below the rim, takes seven hours; the trip all the way down to the Colorado takes even longer. Trekking to the Phantom Ranch, on the canyon floor, is an exciting two-day outing, and the return is by a different, but equally scenic trail. (Early reservations are mandatory for the May to October season; for the mule trips children under 12 or adults weighing more than 200 pounds cannot be accommodated.) The North Rim offers self-guided and ranger-naturalist-led hikes, fishing (an Arizona license is required), horseback trips and muleback trips down the North Kaibab Trail to the canyon floor (as exciting as those from the South Rim). The Kaibab Trail takes hikers into the canyon, across the river by bridge and up the other side. A minimum of three persons is required for each trip. Most river-running trips begin at Lees Ferry, taking passengers through the Marble Canyon and the Grand Canyon, and lasting several days. For a list of boat concessionaires write to: Superintendent, Grand Can-

yon National Park, Grand Canyon, Arizona 86023. Reserve far ahead.

ACCOMMODATIONS: The South Rim has campgrounds in the village and at Desert View, as well as in specially designated areas at the bottom of the can-

yon. A trailer village, not far from the visitor center, has utility hookups. Overnight accommodations include a motel, a hotel and two lodges. Early reservations are essential for any of these facilities. (For rates and reservations write Trans World Airlines Services, P.O. Box 400, Cedar City, Utah 84720; in summer contact them at North Rim, Ariz. 86022.) Tent sites cannot be reserved in the park's campgrounds, and stays are limited to seven days. Back country expeditions require a permit. For visitors to Marble Canyon, the campground at nearby Lees Ferry (in the Glen Canyon National Recreation Area) is convenient. It has 56 sites with water, restrooms and picnic tables. There are motels at Page and at Jacob Lake, 41 miles west. Near Toroweap Point there is a small campground, but without water or supplies of any sort.

MONUMENT VALLEY (*see p. 212*), in the Navaho Tribal Park, lies in northeastern Arizona and southeastern Utah; most of its 30,000 acres, however, are in Arizona. This region of the Colorado Plateau is an incredible land, twisted and carved by millions of years of geologic processes. At one time it lay under primeval seas; then ages of subsequent upheavals, great volcanic action and the inexorable forces of wind, water and sun slowly shaped the valley into the spectacle that it is today. Jutting from its red floor is an amazing array of marvelously eroded rock forms—cathedral-like spires, isolated mesas and buttes, beautifully sculptured sandstone arches. All visitors are asked to respect the fact that they are on lands belonging to the Navaho (the tribal park is part of the much larger Navaho Indian Reservation), and while here they must not photograph Navaho without their permission or enter their dwellings (hogans) without a guide and interpreter (who will obtain the necessary permission). A self-guided motor tour along the valley floor (approximately 14 miles) touches many of the scenic highlights. Commercial tours are available in Mexican Hat and Goulding's Trading Post, Utah, and in Kayenta, Ariz. **BEST WAYS TO GET THERE:** From Flagstaff, Ariz. (167 miles), or Sunset Crater National Monument (described above —151 miles), take U.S. 89 and U.S. 160 to Kayenta, then U.S. 163. To approach from the north, also take U.S. 163. Kayenta and Mexican Hat, starting points for tours, may be reached by bus. **BEST TIME TO VISIT:** Monument Valley is open all year, but May and October are usually the ideal months. Brief but severe thunderstorms occur in June, July and August—motorists are advised to use caution after such storms. **RECREATION:** Hiking and picnicking (bring your own wood or charcoal if planning to cook—firewood is scarce). **ACCOMMODATIONS:** Camping is permitted in the tribal park, but bring water and fuel. There are lodgings at Kayenta, Goulding's Trading Post and Mexican Hat; advance reservations are recommended.

GLEN CANYON NATIONAL RECREATION AREA has 186-mile-long Lake Powell at the heart of its nearly 1.2 million acres of magnificent scenery and extensive recreational facilities. Impounded by Glen Canyon Dam in northern Arizona (one of the highest dams in the world), the lake lies mostly in southern Utah, and its canyon-indented shoreline measures 1800 miles. There are roads into several interesting areas of this rugged terrain. But the best way to enjoy it and to explore its scores of spectacularly colored, fjordlike side canyons—narrow and crooked, and often shadowed by soaring vertical red sandstone walls and overhanging cliffs—is from a boat on Lake Powell's blue-green waters. Rainbow Bridge National Monument, which lies near the southern border of Utah and is now

part of the Glen Canyon Recreation Area, was once accessible only on horseback or by foot over a dirt road from Arizona. Today this huge, symmetrical arch can be reached by a 50-mile boat trip from either Wahweap or Halls Crossing to a landing that is an easy one-mile hike away. Rainbow Bridge is quickly spotted; it is made of salmon pink sandstone and soars 309 feet above a stream bed.

BEST WAYS TO GET THERE: Recreation area headquarters at Wahweap, Ariz., can be reached from the Grand Canyon South Rim (described above) via Ariz. 64 and U.S. 89 (about 145 miles) or from the North Rim via U.S. 89A and U.S. 89 (about 131 miles). Page, Ariz., four miles from Wahweap, can be reached by air or bus and has rental cars. From Mexican Hat, Utah, at the northern end of Monument Valley (see above), take Utah 261 and Utah 95 to Hite, the northernmost park ranger station and boat-launching facility in the area (90 miles). Utah 95 is particularly scenic west of Natural Bridges National Monument. **BEST TIME TO VISIT:** Roads and waterways in Lake Powell are open all year. Temperatures at Wahweap may occasionally reach a low of zero in winter and a high of 106° F. in summer. **RECREATION:** Water sports dominate the recreational activities. There are concessionaire-operated boat rentals at Wahweap, Lees Ferry (on the Colorado below the dam), Halls Crossing and Hite; boating and camping supplies can also be obtained at Bullfrog and Rainbow Bridge Landing. In addition there are boat tours, water skiing, swimming and fishing. Other activities are hiking and hunting.

ACCOMMODATIONS: Glen Canyon has several campgrounds, trailer parks, marinas and a motel. Page, Ariz., only a couple of miles from Wahweap, also has motels and lodges.

ZION NATIONAL PARK extends over 230 square miles of the incredibly scenic canyon and mesa country of southwestern Utah. Here massive forces of nature—erosion, volcanic activity and earth upheavals—have shaped this dramatically colored land of sandstone, shale and limestone into awesome patterns. Entry from the south brings visitors into renowned Zion Canyon, and on the drive up the canyon (a 12-mile round trip) some of Zion's spectacular shapes are revealed. Motorists using the East Entrance travel a road that is considered a great engineering feat; it includes passage through Zion–Mount Carmel Tunnel (more than a mile long), in which at three points windows have been cut through the mountain wall to give brief views of the canyon below. Trails in the park are almost as famous as its outstanding scenery; one of the most popular is the mile-long footpath from the Temple of Sinawava past the Hanging Gardens of Zion to the beginning of the Narrows. Another goes to Weeping Rock, where springs form "tears" that drip down the cliff. A 5.2-mile spur road from Interstate 15 leads into the less-visited northwestern section of the park; from here visitors can view expanses of the Escalante Desert to the north.

BEST WAYS TO GET THERE: Zion is about 121 miles from Grand Canyon and 158 miles from Las Vegas. From U.S. 89, which passes east of the park, take Utah 15 to the park entrances. From Interstate 15, west of the park, take Utah 15 or 17. TWA has summer bus tours from nearby Cedar City, which is served by airlines. Rental cars are available. **BEST TIME TO VISIT:** Zion is open all year. Winter temperatures range from a maximum average of 60° F. to average lows of 15° F. Snow may occasionally fall from December to March, but it usually doesn't last on the canyon floor. Summer afternoon temperatures usually exceed 100° and thunderstorms are common, but September and October provide excellent hiking weather. **RECREATION:** Hiking (the ten major trails in Zion range from simple to strenuous and cover all the outstanding points of interest), guided walks, and guided horseback trips. Fishing

(permitted with a Utah license) is poor.
ACCOMMODATIONS: Both South and Watchman campgrounds are open in summer, and one or the other is open all year; there are facilities for campers and trailers, but no utility hookups. Zion Lodge (within the park) is open from May through early October. For a summer visit, early reservations should be made with the Utah Parks Division of TWA Services, Cedar City, Utah, 84720. Near the South Entrance are motels and a commercial campground.

CEDAR BREAKS NATIONAL MONUMENT,

covering nearly ten square miles, is a huge multicolored amphitheater carved by erosion into a part of the Wasatch formation known as Pink Cliffs. During the past 13 million years the earth has been slowly forced up to its present elevation of more than 10,000 feet. The erosive force of wind, water and frost has dissolved softer parts of the rock, leaving spires and ridges of innumerable fantastic shapes. The amphitheater, still being scooped out by nature, is surrounded by flowering meadows and majestic stands of trees. Numerous birds and animals populate the area. The monument's name came from the early settlers' word for badlands—"breaks"—and the erroneous identification as cedars of the junipers growing near the base of the cliffs. The five-mile Rim Drive rambles through forests and meadows; adjacent to the road are a number of panoramic viewpoints of the breaks and of Utah's high country. The wild-flower display, which begins here as soon as the snow melts, reaches its peak during July and early August.

BEST WAYS TO GET THERE: Cedar Breaks is about 70 miles from Zion National Park (described above). From the South Entrance, take Utah 15, Interstate 15 to Cedar City, then east on Utah 14; if exiting from the east, take Utah 15 and U.S. 89 to Long Valley Junction, then west on Utah 14. There are bus tours from Cedar City (only a few miles away and served by scheduled airlines); rental cars are available.

BEST TIME TO VISIT: The monument travel season is from early June to late October, depending on the weather.

RECREATION: Hiking (several trails are maintained, but none of them leads to the bottom of the amphitheater) and picnicking. Visitors accustomed to lower altitudes are advised to take it easy if they experience shortness of breath.

ACCOMMODATIONS: There are no overnight accommodations within the monument. There is a campground, which is open from mid-June to mid-September, and motels are to be found in several neighboring communities.

BRYCE CANYON NATIONAL PARK

encompasses in its 60 square miles of scenic southern Utah one of the most colorful erosional forms in the world. A spectator standing on the rim of Paunsaugunt Plateau—the Pink Cliffs of Bryce Canyon—sees before and below him "a city of stone: cathedrals, spires and windowed walls, structures of countless shapes and sizes delicately tinted in shades of pink and red and orange, and softened further by grays and whites and creams—all sculptured by the never-lagging forces of erosion." Located along the 20-mile rim of the plateau are 12 horseshoe-shaped natural amphitheaters, each presenting its own spectacular show. The rim road extends all the way south to Rainbow Point, but the lower 14 miles are closed during the winter. There are foot trails along much of the canyon rim and more strenuous paths to various levels below the rim. (Visitors unused to high elevations should take a more leisurely pace than they would at a lower altitude.)

BEST WAYS TO GET THERE: The entrance to Bryce Canyon is about 57 miles east of Cedar Breaks National Monument (described above) via Utah 14, U.S. 89 and Utah 12. From Zion National Park (described above) via the East Entrance take Utah 15, U.S. 89 and Utah 12 (86 miles). There are bus tours (operated by TWA Services, Inc.) from Cedar City to Bryce Canyon from early June to early September. Cedar City, which is served by scheduled airlines, has both rental cars and air taxis. Private planes can use Bryce Canyon airport, just four miles north of the park.

BEST TIME TO VISIT: Bryce Canyon is open all year. Days are warm and nights are cool from April to November (during the summer occasional thunderstorms occur). From November through March it is cold on the plateau, but the days are almost always enjoyably bright and crisp.

RECREATION: Hiking, which calls for sturdy walking shoes and a certain amount of energy (hiking can be with Ranger-guided tours or on one's own), picnicking, and (from mid-May into October) guided horseback tours, tram rides and evening programs. Winter ac-

tivities include skiing and snowshoeing. Snowshoes are available at the park.

ACCOMMODATIONS: There are two campgrounds within the park for tents and trailers. Campsites are available from early May to November, depending upon weather conditions; reservations are not accepted. The Bryce Canyon Lodge is open from early May to early October; reservations may be made by calling toll-free 1-800-634-6951. There are also motels near the park.

CAPITOL REEF NATIONAL PARK,

241,671 acres, in Utah northeast of Bryce Canyon National Park, contains the Waterpocket Fold, which extends from north to south (about 100 miles) and strikes downward from west to east. This incredibly sharp tilt of the earth's crust, which took shape millions of years ago, is exposed as a high cliff of brilliantly tinted rock layers. Nature—in the form of wind and water—has carved the great cliff into a fantasy of towers, domes and pinnacles that rise imposingly from the surrounding desert floor; the name of the park is derived from the white dome-shaped rocks that cap the cliffs. All presently developed roads in Capitol Reef offer views of the highly colored, deeply eroded cliffs; colors appear most intense in early morning and late afternoon. From the visitor center a road runs south to and beyond Capitol Gorge. One of its spurs leads to Grand Wash, which is within easy walking distance through the Narrows—where walls that rise sheer for 1000 feet are only 16 feet apart at their base. Included in the northern end of the park is Cathedral Valley, where spectacular reddish-brown monoliths, many of them freestanding, rise from 400 to 700 feet. Many of the rocks bear Indian picture writing.

BEST WAYS TO GET THERE: Two routes lead from Bryce Canyon (described above) to Capitol Reef: The longer, fully paved route (total: 125 miles) is via Utah 12, U.S. 89, Utah 22, Utah 62 and Utah 24. The alternate route is via Utah 22, gravel for about 40 miles, but about 30 miles shorter. The park entrance is on Utah 24, which connects with several highways.

BEST TIME TO VISIT: Except for occasional short periods when heavy rain or snow may close its roads, the large park is open all year. Midsummer daytime temperatures are in the 80° to 90° F. range, with normally cool nights. Spring and fall are mild; from the latter part of December through January it is usually cold.

RECREATION: Hiking (most of the trails are easy), guided tours, picnicking.

ACCOMMODATIONS: A guest ranch located inside the park is reached by the scenic drive. There are motels in Bicknell, a few miles west of the entrance. Within the park, Capitol Reef Lodge also has overnight accommodations with utility hookups for trailers. The campground is just south of the visitor center.

ARCHES NATIONAL PARK (*see p. 216*), in Utah's red-rock country not far from Canyonlands National Park, more than doubled in size in January 1969 when a presidential proclamation added nearly 49,000 acres to it. Here the earth's crust warped upward many millions of years ago. The crest of this huge fold sank in, forming what are now Salt and Cache valleys. Erosion along fractures of the fold produced thin fins of soft sandstone, which weathering in subsequent ages has carved into the continent's greatest concentration of natural stone arches (almost 90 have been discovered here to date),

windows, spires and pinnacles. Arches National Park encompasses the Salt and Cache valleys, as well as such striking formations as the Marching Men and the huge fins in Herdina Park. The roads in the park, most of them paved, lead visitors to within walking distance of many of its spectacular sights, such as those in Courthouse Towers, the Windows and Devils Garden sections, the Delicate Arch and the Fiery Furnace. Animal life includes birds, deer, coyotes and foxes.

BEST WAY TO GET THERE: The entrance to Arches is about 140 miles east

of Capitol Reef National Park on U.S. 163, near Moab. Moab is served by air and bus and has rental cars.

BEST TIME TO VISIT: Arches is open all year, but the most popular season is from mid-April to mid-October. From May to August, wild flowers blanket moist places in the park, particularly in Salt Valley.

RECREATION: Guided tours, hiking and picnicking.

ACCOMMODATIONS: The park campground for tents and trailers is located in the Devils Garden section. The nearest restaurants and lodgings are at Moab, five miles south of the entrance.

CANYONLANDS NATIONAL PARK (*see p. 218*), newest of Utah's national parks, is a thrilling and indescribably diverse geological wonderland of wide plains, intricately twisting canyons, high, bold mesas and crenelated buttes, strikingly beautiful arches, spires, needles and countless other strangely sculptured forms. The Colorado River is its primary shaper. Joining it here is the Green River, and together, at their confluence, they form one of the wildest rivers on this continent. The action of these powerful streams has divided Canyonlands into two districts. Island in the Sky, the upper district, is a vast plateau ringed by sheer cliffs and joined to the main land mass to its north only by a 40-foot-wide neck of land. It serves as a superb vantage point for viewing some of the park's wonders—such as Monument Basin, with its concentration of huge sculptured fins and standing rocks, and the geologically unique features of Upheaval Dome. The Needles, Canyonlands' lower district, includes peaceful parks circled by bristling jumbles of fantastic pinnacles; the quickly changing scenery of Elephant Canyon, climaxed at its head by Druid Arch; and many other equally remarkable attractions. Most of the roads in the upper district are open to regular passenger cars, but much of the Needles calls for four-wheel-drive vehicles. In fact, such vehicles are the preferred means of transportation within Canyonlands at this stage of its development.

BEST WAYS TO GET THERE: To get to the Island in the Sky district of Canyonlands from Arches National Park (described above), drive two miles south on U.S. 163, then take Utah 279. The Needles district is reached by taking U.S. 163 south from Moab or north from

Mexican Hat to an unnumbered road that leads west into the park. Both approaches are by graded dirt roads that, though slippery when wet, are regularly used by drivers of ordinary passenger cars.

BEST TIME TO VISIT: Elevations in the park climb from 3600 to almost 7000

feet, and temperatures may vary from a high of 100° F. in summer to a low of −20° F. in winter. This is a dry country with an average annual precipitation of five to nine inches—mostly in the form of late-summer thunderstorms and winter snows.

RECREATION: Experienced professional guides offer tours by four-wheel-drive vehicles, pack trips into Canyonlands and boat trips through the canyons of the Green and Colorado rivers. There are picnic areas and hiking trails.

ACCOMMODATIONS: Canyonlands has camping areas, but at present there are no overnight lodging facilities. Motels are available at Monticello and Moab.

NATURAL BRIDGES NATIONAL MONUMENT, the center of a region of brilliant cliffs, twisting canyons, sandstone pinnacles and graceful arches, is in an isolated part of southeastern Utah. Its most impressive attractions are three outstanding natural bridges. Symmetrical Sipapu Bridge is the largest—222 feet high with a span of 268 feet—and its abutments are now far enough from the stream bed so that the river that created it no longer has any erosive effect. Bulky Kachina Bridge is geologically young; flood waters in White Canyon are still cutting away at the opening under the span. Owachomo Bridge, smallest of the three, is in a late phase of its life, and river erosion no longer is a problem—only rain, frost and blowing sand. A nine-mile paved scenic drive circles the monument, and short trails from it lead to the bridges; the road has a number of scenic overlooks. Mule deer, bobcats, coyotes and cougars are present but will not necessarily be seen. What can be seen are prehistoric ruins in plenty.

BEST WAYS TO GET THERE: The route from the Needles district of Canyonlands (described above) is U.S. 163 and Utah 95. If driving from Mexican Hat, Utah, in Monument Valley (described above), take Utah 261 and Utah 95. Utah 261 is a dirt road with steep grades, best avoided during and after rainstorms. Utah 95 and roads within the monument are paved.

BEST TIME TO VISIT: Natural Bridges is open year round, except when winter snows or heavy rains block the roads. The most enjoyable season is from late April to November.

RECREATION: Walks on the hiking trails and picnicking are the only recreational activities.

ACCOMMODATIONS: Natural Bridges Campground is near the visitor center. The nearest motel accommodations are at Blanding and Mexican Hat.

LAKE MEAD NATIONAL RECREATION AREA, the first such area in the United States, straddles the border between Nevada and Arizona. Within its 3000 square miles, where elevations range from 517 to 6990 feet, are two lakes: 67-mile-long Mohave and 115-mile-long Mead (in capacity the largest man-made lake in the U.S.). In addition there are stretches of fascinating desert country, deep, colorful canyons and lofty tablelands—regions to be explored on foot, by car and by boat. The recreation area begins south of Lake Mohave; it extends north and then east to include Lake Mead (which covers part of the Colorado's old course), and adjoins Grand Canyon National Park. For some of the best views of the Colorado, the Grand Wash Cliffs and Gregg's Basin on Lake Mead, leave the Kingman Highway (U.S. 93) 50 miles southeast of Hoover Dam. A mostly paved road leads about 50 miles northward to Pierce Ferry and passes through one of the largest forests of Joshua trees (actually a treelike species of yucca) in the Southwest.

BEST WAYS TO GET THERE: The visitor center is on U.S. 93, near Boulder City and 10 miles from Las Vegas. Las Vegas has a commercial airport and rental cars. Private planes can land at Boulder City and North Las Vegas, and there are landing strips within the recreation area.

BEST TIME TO VISIT: Lake Mead is an all-year area, but most visitors come here during the summer months. The National Park Service reports that even during July and August, when daytime temperatures may rise above 100° F., the heat is not oppressive because of low humidity; from late September through December, and from early February through late May, the weather is delightful. Temperatures during the winter can sometimes be low, particularly during the mornings and evenings, so warm clothing is required if you plan to visit during that season.

RECREATION: Fishing (a Nevada or Ari-

zona license is required; both if you fish from a boat), swimming, boat cruises on Lake Mead, boating (there are a number of launching ramps, and boats can be rented, chartered or purchased from several concessionaires), water skiing, skin diving, hiking, tours through Hoover and Davis dams, and picnicking. Motorists can also arrange an auto tape tour of shore roads.

ACCOMMODATIONS: The Lake Mead Recreation Area has seven developed campgrounds and eight trailer courts. There are motels in Boulder City, Las

Vegas, Overton and Searchlight, Nev., and in Bullhead City and Kingman, Ariz.

THE PACIFIC WEST

DEATH VALLEY NATIONAL MONUMENT (*see p. 228*) lies partly in Nevada but mostly in California. Here, on the rocky slopes of the Amargosa and Panamint ranges and on the floor of the valley, plants and animals have had to adapt to the harsh environment of the desert—or face certain extinction. Furnace Creek is one of the main areas of interest and the best starting point for trips to the southern part of the monument. Stovepipe Wells is the most convenient point from which to explore the northern half. Miles of roads enable visitors to reach numerous places of great interest in the nearly 140-mile-long desert valley and the mountains surrounding it. Included in the monument is the lowest dry land in North America, 282 feet below sea level. Visitors to Death Valley are warned that driving off established roads is not permitted.

BEST WAYS TO GET THERE: From Boulder City, Nev. (see Lake Mead National Recreation Area, described above), to Death Valley headquarters at Furnace Creek (about 162 miles) take U.S. 95, Nev. 29, Calif. 127 and Calif. 190. From Barstow, Calif. (180 miles), to Furnace Creek take Interstate 15, Calif. 127 and Calif. 190. A commercial busline runs from Las Vegas to Death Valley from Oct. 15 to May 1. There is also limited air service.

BEST TIME TO VISIT: The long, intensely hot summer (May through October) invites only the hardy and venturesome. Many spurs from the valley's main road are closed for that period. Winter is the recommended season for a safe and comfortable visit.

RECREATION: Hiking, horseback riding, mountain climbing and guided tours.

ACCOMMODATIONS: An inn and a ranch are located at Furnace Creek, and a hotel at Stovepipe Wells, but their services are limited from May through October. The National Park Service maintains nine campgrounds, three of them in the Furnace Creek area.

YOSEMITE NATIONAL PARK (*see p. 232*) includes some of the most superb sections of Yosemite Valley and the High Sierra. With elevations from 2000 to more than 13,000 feet, this park has been called a "geological wonderland with sculptured peaks and domes; waterfalls tumbling from hanging valleys down the faces of shining granite cliffs; groves of giant sequoias and extensive forests of pine, fir and oak; wild flowers in alpine meadows; hundreds of species of birds and mammals; and scenic drives and trails to areas of high-country grandeur with sparkling, glacial lakes." Visitors (who are urged to stop at the information center in Yosemite Valley before starting their tour) should not limit themselves to the best-known attractions of the valley, which covers only 7 of Yosemite's 1189 square miles. Now much of the splendor of the high country is accessible to motorists over many miles of primary and secondary roads and to hikers on more than 700 miles of trails.

BEST WAYS TO GET THERE: The park entrances may be reached by Calif. routes 41, 140 or 120. Tioga Pass Road (Calif. 120) crosses east-west through the park and offers an outstanding introduction to it. But inexperienced drivers, or those who feel uneasy on steep and winding mountain roads, should forgo this adventure. (Tioga Road is closed during winter.) Daily bus service is available between Yosemite Valley and Merced (year-round) and Fresno (summer only), both of which are served by airlines, Amtrak and transcontinental buses. There is also summer bus service to and from Modesto. Guided car tours of the park are offered.

BEST TIME TO VISIT: Yosemite is open all year, but some points of interest are closed in winter; for the average visitor the spring, summer and fall seasons are probably best. The spectacular waterfalls in Yosemite Valley are at their peak in May and June; after mid-July and through early autumn (when the snow runoff has ended), some of them may completely dry up.

RECREATION: Hiking, riding, pack trips, rock climbing (only for the experienced), scenic drives, fishing (a California license is a must), picnicking, swimming (there are pools at several of the lodging units), naturalist-guided walks, a full-scale naturalist program in summer, and winter skiing.

ACCOMMODATIONS: There are 19 campgrounds but only 3 are open all year. Several accept trailers but there are no utility connections. Visitors with trailers should make inquiries at their entry point. Group campsites must be reserved in advance. Also, overnight lodging is available in facilities that range from fine hotels to simple cabins and tents. Reservations should be made as far in advance as possible at all hotels, lodges and cabins operated by the Yosemite Park and Curry Co. For information and reservations, write them at Yosemite National Park, Calif. 95389.

SEQUOIA NATIONAL PARK (see p. 235), the better-known neighbor of Kings Canyon National Park (described below), can claim the distinction of having within its boundaries the tallest mountain in the conterminous United States—14,495-foot Mount Whitney. In addition to its Sierra Nevada peaks and its awesome, unspoiled beauty, the park is notable for its groves of giant sequoia, or Sierra redwood—trees that are unique for their age and their massiveness. The greatest of them, the 3500-year-old General Sherman Tree, 274 feet high, with a circumference of nearly 103 feet, is in Sequoia's Giant Forest. Generals Highway, the main road through the park, affords motorists a highly scenic 46-mile drive from the Ash Mountain Entrance in the south through the Giant Forest and on to General Grant Grove; roads branching from it lead to other attractions or pass within a short hiking distance of them. But the greatest scenic thrills await those who take the hike or ride along the more than 900 miles of trails that penetrate the mountain wilderness.

BEST WAYS TO GET THERE: Visitors coming from points south should take Calif. 198 from Visalia. From Fresno take Calif. 180. From mid-May into September there is bus service between the park and Fresno, connecting with bus, train and air terminals. There are overnight motor coach tours from Fresno.

BEST TIME TO VISIT: Sequoia National Park, including Generals' Highway, which passes through it, is open the year round, but most visitors will prefer the summer.

RECREATION: Naturalist-guided walks through the Giant Forest and to important points of interest are conducted during the summer; they are usually half a day or less in duration. Other available activities include hiking, riding, pack trips, fishing (almost every lake and stream has trout—brook, brown, golden and rainbow; a license is required), mountain climbing and winter sports.

ACCOMMODATIONS: The park has a motel, a lodge and a camp with some cottages and cabins, usually open late May to October. There are many campsites and three trailer camps, but without hookups for water or electricity. Motel accommodations are nearby.

KINGS CANYON NATIONAL PARK (see p. 235), east of Fresno, Calif., embraces in its 460,000 acres some of the most splendid mountain wilderness country in the United States. Two vast canyons of the Kings River and crests of the High Sierra are dominant features of the park. In Kings Canyon itself the granite walls rise steeply to peak a mile or more above the valley floor. There are many miles of trails for exploring this primitive land of deep canyons, granite domes, sparkling lakes and rivers, waterfalls, vast meadows and varied animal life. General Grant Grove, a part of this park yet separate from it, contains superb examples of giant sequoias, the world's largest trees. The General Grant Tree, standing 267 feet high, has a circumference of nearly 108 feet. Kings Canyon National Park and its southern neighbor, Sequoia National Park, are jointly administered.

BEST WAYS TO GET THERE: Generals Highway, the main route in Sequoia, leads to the General Grant Grove section. To get to the main part of the park, continue in a northerly direction on Calif. 180 (through Sequoia National Forest), which ends at Copper Creek, about six miles beyond the ranger station at Cedar Grove. For other ways to reach the park, see those offered for its neighbor, Sequoia National Park (described above).

BEST TIME TO VISIT: General Grant Grove is open all year, but snowfall usually obstructs access to the main body of the park from October until spring.

RECREATION: Hiking (including carefully laid-out nature trails in General Grant Grove), guided tours, horseback riding (including pack trips), mountain climbing, fishing and winter sports.

ACCOMMODATIONS: Kings Canyon has two lodges and some housekeeping cabins. There are two trailer camps and hundreds of campsites. For information and reservations, write Sequoia and Kings Canyon Hospitality Service, Sequoia National Park, Calif. 93262.

THE ANCIENT BRISTLECONE PINE FOREST, high on the wind-

swept, rock-strewn slopes of California's White Mountains, stands in the heart of Inyo National Forest. Here grow the world's oldest known living things—bristlecone pines. Clinging to life in an inhospitable, arid environment on shallow limestone soil, some of these incredibly gnarled and weathered trees are over 4000 years old. The most an-

cient are clustered at 10,000 feet, in an area known as Schulman Grove. From there a two-mile hike leads to Methuselah Walk, where the world's oldest living tree can be seen. Methuselah, grotesquely beautiful, is more than 4600 years old. It has lived 1000 years longer than the oldest known sequoia. Higher up, at 11,000 feet (an approximately 12-mile drive north from Schulman Grove), is the Patriarch, the largest known bristlecone pine, in a setting suggestive of a moonscape. Although it takes a day to reach and see these ancient specimens, the trip is well worth the effort. There are also spectacular panoramic views—of White Mountain Peak and of the eastern escarpment of the High Sierra, including Palisade Glacier, the southernmost glacier in the United States—from the higher elevations along the road.

BEST WAY TO GET THERE: Take U.S. 395 to Big Pine (15 miles south of Bishop in the valley separating the two sections of Inyo National Forest), then Calif. 168 to Cedar Flat Entrance Station. Bristlecone Road (paved) leads from there to Schulman Grove. Other, poorer roads penetrate the Botanical Area.

BEST TIME TO VISIT: The Ancient Bristlecone Pine Forest area is normally open from June 1 to Oct. 30; the weather is usually at its best in July and August (the wild flowers are particularly colorful in August). Much can be seen on a one-day trip, but a longer

stay affords visitors many new areas to explore each day.

RECREATION: Hiking, picnicking and rock-hounding (small pieces can be taken as souvenirs with a permit). The Inyo National Forest (which extends north into Nevada) has high-mountain fishing, areas for winter sports, swimming and boating.

ACCOMMODATIONS: There is an improved campground on the road to Schulman Grove and there are numerous campgrounds and resorts within the boundaries of Inyo National Forest. Both Bishop and Big Pine have motels.

DEVILS POSTPILE NATIONAL MONUMENT lies at an elevation of 7600 feet in the magnificent forest and lake country southeast of Yosemite Park. Dominating this 800-acre tract is an extraordinary 900-foot-long, 200-foot-high formation of symmetrical blue-gray-bronze basaltic columns, some of which, rising more than 60 feet above their base, fit closely together like the pipes of a giant organ. Worn smooth by glacial action, the Postpile is a remnant of a basaltic lava flow that took place at least 915,000 years ago. As the hot lava cooled, it shrank to form small plates separated by cracks, in much the same way that mud on the bottom of a drying pond forms a cracked surface as the soil shrinks toward many centers. Each plate became the top of a column.

Two miles down the river trail, where the Middle Fork of the San Joaquin River makes a sheer plunge of 140 feet

into a deep green pool surrounded by an enchanting wild garden, is Rainbow Fall. Evidences of volcanic activity are several bubbling hot springs and the samples of pumice (porous volcanic rock that will float in water) found in the northern part of the monument.

BEST WAYS TO GET THERE: From Bishop in the south or from Calif. 120 out of Yosemite National Park (described above) take U.S. 395 to Calif. 203, the spur road leading to the Postpile—a 10½-mile drive on a paved road, then 7 miles of unpaved road from Minaret Summit to the monument. The spur road is 39 miles from Bishop and 26 miles from the junction of Tioga Pass Road (Calif. 120) and U.S. 395.

BEST TIME TO VISIT: Summer and early fall are the best seasons.

RECREATION: Hiking (Devils Postpile is one of the key points on the John Muir Trail between Yosemite and Sequoia national parks), fishing (a state license is required) and picnicking.

ACCOMMODATIONS: There is a campground near the ranger station, open from about June 15 to Oct. 1, with a small fee per night. Red Meadows, two miles from the campground, has cabins, a lodge, and a store, and also saddle and pack animals. A lodge and an inn are at Mammoth Lakes on the spur road.

PINNACLES NATIONAL MONUMENT contains the last remnants of an ancient volcano, carved into fantastic pinnacles and spires by rain, wind, heat and frost. This cluster of spiked peaks, from 500 to 1200 feet in height—a result of millions of years of relentless erosion and change—is a startling contrast to the gentle contours of the surrounding country. And thriving on the rugged slopes is a dense, bushy growth called chaparral (sometimes referred to as a pygmy forest because the shrubs simulate trees in shape and form), which serves as the habitat for a fascinating community of plants and animals. Two major earth faults—Chalone Creek Fault on the east and Pinnacles Fault on the west—have developed on either side of the lava-formed domelike volcano, believed to have once towered 8000 feet over this spectacularly eroded area. These faults are considered to be splinters of the great San Andreas Fault, which lies six miles east of the monument. The formation of pinnacles and the deepening of canyons are still continuing processes here.

BEST WAYS TO GET THERE: The route

from Fresno is Calif. 41 and Calif. 198 to Calif. 25, then north on Calif. 25 to the spur road to the visitor center at Bear Gulch (about 150 miles). From San Francisco it is about 112 miles to the spur road via U.S. 101 and Calif. 25. Fresno and San Francisco offer air taxi and car rental services.

BEST TIME TO VISIT: Pinnacles National Monument can be visited in any season. One of the most enjoyable times is spring, when the hills are mantled with new vegetation and sprinkled with a multitude of colorful wild flowers. In summer grassy slopes turn golden brown under daytime temperatures that occasionally reach 100° F.

RECREATION: Hiking is the main activity; marked trails, including High Peaks, Chalone Creek, Rim, Balconies and Moses Spring (a keyed, self-guided nature trail), reward hikers with caves, watered canyons and sweeping panoramas of the entire Pinnacles National Monument.

ACCOMMODATIONS: There are two campsites for trailer and tent camping, and motels in nearby towns.

BIG SUR (*see p. 238*) is an almost legendary mountain coastal region of California in Monterey County. Stretching southward for about 50 miles from the Monterey-Carmel area, it is remarkably unspoiled—not only because it is away from the mainstream of traffic, but because its residents have fought to keep it that way. Perched above the coast is a section of the state's first designated Scenic Highway, Calif. 1, a two-lane road that dazzles visitors with matchless views of the wild beauty of this rugged Pacific coastline at al-

most every dip and turn. Bold headlands drop precipitously to meet the pounding surf, while rising abruptly east of the highway is the Santa Lucia Range and its forested wilderness, most of which is part of Los Padres National Forest. Calif. 1 winds through 18 miles of the national forest where it pushes down to meet the sea, while in other sections the forest lands begin east of the highway.

BEST WAYS TO GET THERE: Monterey, which could serve as the start or finish of a Big Sur trip, is about 130 miles south of San Francisco, 143 miles west of Fresno and 136 miles north of San Luis Obispo. Less experienced drivers may find it more comfortable to make this drive from south to north.

BEST TIME TO VISIT: Summer generally is the best time for a tour of this region; don't try it on a foggy day, however.

RECREATION: There are several state parks with magnificent scenery along the coast, including Point Lobos State Reserve (notable for the Monterey cypress), Andrew Molera State Park (with beach access), Pfeiffer Big Sur State Park (with hiking, swimming, fishing) and Julia Pfeiffer Burns State Park (where a waterfall spills directly into the ocean). There are also five all-year camping areas (Kirk Creek, Mill Creek, Plaskett Creek, Sand Dollar and Willow Creek) along or near the ocean in Los Padres National Forest, with facilities for fishing and picnicking.

ACCOMMODATIONS: Pfeiffer Big Sur State Park offers a lodge, cabins and restaurant. Camping is permitted there and at Kirk Creek and Plaskett Creek. The town of Big Sur and the Monterey Peninsula towns have accommodations.

POINT REYES NATIONAL SEASHORE preserves a fascinating part of California's scenic coastal region, only an hour's drive northwest of San Francisco. The peninsula's many habitats, ranging from dense forests to open coastlands, provide living space for more than 300 species of birds, 72 species of mammals and a great variety of plants. Geologically, it is not a true peninsula but an island separated from the mainland by the San Andreas Fault. (During the 1906 earthquake the peninsula moved northward along this fault; between 15 and 20 feet of offset were recorded in some places.) As a result the rocks on that part of the peninsula lying west of the fault differ completely from those on the mainland

to the east. Much of the land within park boundaries is still in private ownership, but the public Bear Valley Area has more than 50 miles of trails winding through wild-flower meadows and forests to the sea or up to the heights of Inverness Ridge.

BEST WAY TO GET THERE: From San Francisco take the Golden Gate Bridge and Calif. 1 to Olema (about 47 miles). A spur road from there, the Sir Francis Drake Highway, leads to the Point Reyes National Seashore headquarters and the beach areas.

BEST TIME TO VISIT: Point Reyes' ocean beaches are often foggy and windy enough to make warm clothing welcome. Throughout the summer these beaches have more days of fog than of sunshine, but spring and autumn can be mild and pleasant. The country east of Inverness Ridge, accessible by hiking trails, is free of summer fog, but it has heavy rains in winter and spring. The spring flower season lasts from February to late July.

RECREATION: Tours, beach walks and nature hikes and talks are offered in summer by the Park Service staff. There are a number of self-guided hiking trails, and horseback riding is permitted on all trails except Bear Valley, the most popular one, during weekends and holidays. In addition, the Bear Valley and Coast trails are suitable for bicycling. Beach picnics, surf fishing and swimming can also be enjoyed. (There is no swimming at Point Reyes Beach, however; the pounding surf is too dangerous.)

ACCOMMODATIONS: The Bear Valley Area has three walk-in campgrounds, and there are motel facilities in nearby towns, in addition to San Francisco's hotels and motels.

REDWOOD NATIONAL PARK (*see p. 243*), created in October 1968, is the culmination of a decades-long fight to save from cutting some of the most impressive old growths and virgin stands of primeval coast redwoods—the tallest living trees on earth. Commonly reaching more than 300 feet in height (one has been found that stands taller than 367 feet), some of today's mature individual redwoods have been growing 2000 years or more. At one time redwoods were widely distributed across this continent and even in western Europe, but now they are unique to the coastal regions of northern California and southernmost Oregon. A cathedrallike redwood grove is an inspiring spectacle. Several already existing

redwoods state parks (Jedediah Smith, Del Norte Coast and Prairie Creek), as well as 40 miles of scenic Pacific coastline, are also part of this new national park.

BEST WAYS TO GET THERE: The park is accessible via U.S. 101 south from Crescent City and north from Eureka and Arkata, or via U.S. 199 from the east and Grants Pass, Oreg., by private car or scheduled bus service. Local airlines connect Eureka-Arkata with Crescent City, which is served by scheduled airlines. Rental cars are also available.
BEST TIME TO VISIT: Temperatures here

are generally moderate throughout the year. Most of the rainfall occurs between November and March. At other times heavy coastal fogs extend into the redwood forests during the night and early morning.
RECREATION: Hiking is a principal activity, and the incorporated state park areas have facilities for swimming, fishing (a California license is necessary) and picnicking. Boating is also popular in certain waters.
ACCOMMODATIONS: Camping sites are available in state park areas and several private campgrounds. There are no overnight accommodations in Redwood National Park, but there are motels in nearby towns along the coast.

LASSEN VOLCANIC NATIONAL PARK preserves the site of the last active volcano in the conterminous United States. The impressive, now-dormant 10,457-foot Lassen Peak—the largest plug-dome volcano in the world—evolved from a vent on the side of a larger extinct volcano. Lava forced up through that vent created the peak but in doing so plugged its source, and for a long time Lassen slumbered. But on May 30, 1914, the mountain exploded, and eruptions continued intermittently for more than seven years. In addition to presenting awesome views of the devastated region from Lassen Park Road or from some of the 150 miles of foot trails, the park has vast areas of scenic wonders including forests, wild-flower meadows, clear lakes and streams, boiling mud pots and hot springs—and is unusually endowed with animal- and bird-life.
BEST WAYS TO GET THERE: Lassen can be reached by car on Calif. 89 from the north or south, and on Calif. 36 and 44 from the east or west. There is daily bus service (except on Sundays and holidays) from Red Bluff and Susanville to Mineral, the park headquarters. Nearest commercial airports are Chico and Redding; Redding is a train stop.
BEST TIME TO VISIT: Although Lassen is a center for winter sports, summer is the best time for general touring.
RECREATION: There are well-marked hiking trails, fishing (required California licenses can be obtained in the park), riding, boating (except motorboats) and picnicking. Winter sports include cross-country and downhill skiing and ice skating.
ACCOMMODATIONS: Within the park overnight accommodations are available

at Drakesbad Guest Ranch from July 1 to Labor Day. There are also four camping areas, with space for trailers. There are motels in towns within a few miles of the park entrances.

LAVA BEDS NATIONAL MONUMENT is in northern California not far south of the Oregon boundary. Here,

ages ago, a number of erupting volcanoes spewed forth great rivers of molten basaltic rock on the lands below. As the flow cooled and hardened, it formed one of the continent's most rugged and fascinating landscapes and created a series of caves, or lava tubes. Nearly 300 of them have so far been discovered at Lava Beds; 17 of them can be reached from the Cave Loop Road, which begins at monument headquarters. Despite the volcanic devastation, the plant life is remarkably colorful, and there are about 40 species of mammals and 200 of birds. California bighorn sheep have been reintroduced and can be observed along Gillem's Bluff. An interesting historic sidelight is that Lava Beds was the principal scene of a clash between whites and Indians, the Modoc War of 1872–73. There are also prehistoric rock inscriptions.
BEST WAYS TO GET THERE: From Manzanita Lake, in Lassen Volcanic National Park (described above), it is about 145 miles to Lava Beds' Southeast Entrance. From Klamath Falls, Oreg., it is 41 miles to the Northeast Entrance. Access to the monument is over roads leading off Calif. 139. One can fly to Klamath Falls and rent a car.
BEST TIME TO VISIT: Summer is preferred; snow is possible in most months.
RECREATION: Hiking (electric lanterns for cave visits are available at monument headquarters) and picnicking.

ACCOMMODATIONS: Lava Beds has an improved campground, but the nearest lodgings, food and vehicle services are in Tulelake, Calif., 30 miles north of monument headquarters.

CRATER LAKE (*see p. 250*), dominant feature of a unique national park in south-central Oregon, is a body of incredibly blue water occupying a basin believed to have resulted from the collapse within itself of the volcanic cone of Mount Mazama. Encircled by multicolored lava walls, Crater Lake is the deepest lake in the United States—1932 feet. Except for Pumice Desert (north of the lake), the once-devastated volcanic landscape is softened by wild-flower meadows and green forests, which give shelter to a variety of mammals and birds. The 35-mile Rim Drive around the remarkably transparent waters of the lake offers magnificent vistas from a number of observation points. Not to be missed are short spur roads to the Pinnacles and to Cloudcap. Wizard Island, a volcano within a volcano in the western part of the lake, can be reached by park launch.

BEST WAYS TO GET THERE: Roads to the park's South Entrance (46 miles north of Klamath Falls) and to the West Entrance (69 miles from Medford) are open year-round. Access to the North Entrance (92 miles south of Bend and 125 miles below Eugene) and Rim Drive are closed most of the year because of snow. There is bus service between the park and Klamath Falls in summer. One can reach Medford and Klamath Falls by air or transcontinental bus, and Klamath Falls by rail.

BEST TIME TO VISIT: Although there are no accommodations in the park from late September to early June, and it is snow-covered for eight months of the year, the National Park Service considers Crater Lake to be a four-season attraction, with each season offering a different spectacle. July and August weather is like that in the spring at lower altitudes. The North Entrance usually is open from mid-June (the Rim Drive from early July) until the first heavy snow.

RECREATION: There are a number of short hiking trails, including a self-guided nature trail; guided walking trips, launches and buses are scheduled daily in season. Horseback riding (on the Pacific Crest Trail), skiing, fishing and picnicking are also possible.

ACCOMMODATIONS: Campgrounds usu-ally are open July to October, depending on snow. There is a fee and no reservations are taken; also, there are no utility connections for trailers. For information and reservations at the lodge and cabins in Rim Village (open from mid-June to mid-September) write Crater Lake Lodge, Inc., Crater Lake, Oreg. 97604. There are other accommodations a short drive from the park.

OREGON CAVES NATIONAL MONUMENT, described by the poet Joaquin Miller as "The Marble Halls of Oregon," lies in the southwestern part of the state. The cavern's numerous galleries contain remarkable examples of nature's subterranean handiwork. Over untold ages water seeping from the cavern roof has left deposits of calcium carbonate that have formed shapes

ranging from exquisite to bizarre. And stalactites have slowly descended from vaulted domes while stalagmites have inched upward, in some cases to join and form floor-to-ceiling pillars.

BEST WAYS TO GET THERE: From Grants Pass, Oreg. (49 miles), or from Crescent City, Calif. (77 miles), take U.S. 199, then Oreg. 46. Because parking space is limited, it is recommended that during the summer season you plan to arrive in the morning.

BEST TIME TO VISIT: Surface temperatures have little meaning—in the cave the temperature is always about 45° F.

RECREATION: The cave tour is the principal visitor activity at this national monument. Proper clothing, including a jacket and walking shoes, should be worn. (Children under six are not admitted to the cave, but supervised child care is available for a fee.) There are also areas for hunting and fishing.

ACCOMMODATIONS: Lodge rooms and cottages (open from near the end of May to about Sept. 10) are located close to the cave entrance. Grayback Campground in Siskiyou National Forest, on Oreg. 46 just eight miles west, has tent, trailer and picnic sites. A second Forest Service area, the Cave Creek Campground, is four miles from the monument on Oreg. 46, and has tent and picnic sites only. There are motels in several towns within 70 miles.

THE OREGON DUNES, a unique region not far south of Cape Perpetua (see description below), start at Sea Lion Caves and run down the coast to Coos Bay, a distance of over 50 miles. The dune area extends inland from 1½ to 2 miles; most of it is within the boundaries of Siuslaw National Forest. The Umpqua Dunes Scenic Area, the southernmost part, has been set aside to preserve in nearly natural condition 2760 acres of the most outstanding of these formations. The dunes rise from sea level at the shoreline to a height of over 300 feet, and their crests provide panoramic views of the extensive dune sheet and the Pacific Ocean. Winds from the sea may change their height as much as six to eight feet in a single storm. Ancient stabilized dunes that exist within the shifting dune sheet have blocked the passage of many coastal streams, creating numerous freshwater lakes that add to the dune area's scenic value.

BEST WAYS TO GET THERE: To reach the Umpqua Dunes Scenic Area from Grants Pass, Oreg., take Interstate 5, U.S. 99, Oreg. 42 and U.S. 101 (155 miles). From Coos Bay, Oreg. (served by airline and bus and offering car rental service), take U.S. 101.

BEST TIME TO VISIT: The weather here is similar to that at Cape Perpetua (described below).

RECREATION: Hunting, picnicking, hiking, boating, swimming, and stream, lake and ocean fishing.

ACCOMMODATIONS: Along this 50-mile coastal stretch a number of state and Forest Service camping areas have accommodations for both tents and trailers. There are also motels.

CAPE PERPETUA, in Siuslaw National Forest, offers spectacular panoramas of the Pacific and the Oregon coast from vantage points nearly 800 feet above the ocean. Here the visitor can discover the fascinating marine life of the tide pools, walk the outstanding trails of the Restless Waters, the Whispering Spruce and Cape Cove, or take a 22-mile self-guided auto tour beginning at the Devil's Churn and winding through this scenic region's beautiful coastal valleys and forests.

BEST WAYS TO GET THERE: The cape is about 33 miles south of Newport and about 65 miles north of Coos Bay on U.S. 101, the Coastal Highway. Coos Bay is reached by bus and airline and offers car rental service.

BEST TIME TO VISIT: Weather on the Oregon coast can be capricious. Summer days may be windy (beach hikers should have a jacket or windbreaker) and frequently foggy, while winter can bring a hurricane-force storm on one day and clear, calm and sunny weather on the next.

RECREATION: In addition to the hiking trails noted above, the Cape Perpetua Recreation Area has guided nature walks and numerous sites for picnicking, fishing, boating, scuba diving and swimming; hunting is also permitted in nearby parts of the national forest.

ACCOMMODATIONS: There are 42 camping units in the recreation area; another

Siuslaw National Forest camp at Tillicum Beach, a few miles north, has seven camping units and room for 39 trailers. There are also a number of motels along or near the ocean both north and south of Cape Perpetua.

THE COLUMBIA RIVER east of Portland, Oreg., is particularly impressive in the Columbia Gorge area, a region of outstanding beauty and rare geologic phenomena that was created when the Columbia cut its way through the Cascades. Here basalt cliffs rise almost perpendicularly hundreds of feet above both the Washington and Oregon sides of the river. Surging over these precipitous cliffs are many spectacular waterfalls, the most outstanding of which is Multnomah Falls in Mount

Hood National Forest (see description below); its drop of 620 feet makes it one of the highest waterfalls in the United States. Beyond the cliffs are densely forested mountains that rise abruptly to heights of 4000 to 5000 feet above sea level. Crown Point, at the western end of the gorge, affords one of the finest views of this scenic area.

BEST WAYS TO GET THERE: Fine highways parallel both shores of the Columbia River, but the notable waterfalls and especially scenic viewpoints are on the Oregon side. Access from Portland is via U.S. 30/Interstate 80N, and the round trip can be made in a day. Twelve miles east of Portland one can leave the superhighway for an alternate scenic route. The north bank route goes through Vancouver, Wash., and east via Wash. 14. Portland, served by major transportation lines, has rental cars.

BEST TIME TO VISIT: The Columbia Gorge is a year-round area, but for those visiting it primarily for its natural attractions, summer and early fall are the best seasons.

RECREATION: A number of state parks are in the vicinity of the river in the 50-mile stretch between the start of the scenic route and the town of Hood River. There are numerous trails and facilities for swimming, fishing and boating.

ACCOMMODATIONS: Portland has many hotels and motels, and there are motels in such river towns as Hood River and The Dalles. Some of the parks have camping areas.

MOUNT HOOD NATIONAL FOREST, sweeping from the Columbia River south to Mount Jefferson and from the foothills near Portland to the eastern plateau country of Oregon, covers more than 1.1 million acres that are rich in scenic splendor. Mount Hood, peaking at 11,235 feet, is the state's highest elevation; fumaroles high on its perpetually snow-clad summit still spew forth steam and gas, indicating that this ancient volcano is not yet extinct. Waterfalls, mountain streams and lakes, hot springs, flower-laden alpine meadows and forested slopes and valleys all contribute to the beauty of this section of the Cascades. Several winter sports areas are in the vicinity.

BEST WAY TO GET THERE: For the highly scenic Mount Hood Loop Highway trip (probably the best way to become acquainted with this area's attractions), take U.S. 26 from Portland to the forest boundary at Zigzag. Continue to Oreg. 35, leading north to the Columbia Gorge area at Hood River. For those not planning a stay in the forest, this journey can be combined with the Columbia Gorge trip described above. Fascinating side roads from the loop highway include those leading up to

Timberline Lodge and Cloud Cap Saddle.

BEST TIME TO VISIT: There are numerous facilities for visitors to Mount Hood in any season, but for those primarily interested in a scenic trip, summer and early fall would be the best seasons.

RECREATION: The extensive facilities for

recreation in Mount Hood National Forest include excellent areas for skiing, boating and other water sports, fishing, hunting, hiking, picnicking and horseback riding.

ACCOMMODATIONS: Mount Hood National Forest has more than 100 campsites, 33 of which will accommodate trailers. Timberline Lodge, at 6000 feet on the south slope of Mount Hood, is a famous year-round resort. (For accommodations outside the forest, see the Columbia River description above.)

MOUNT RAINIER NATIONAL PARK (*see p. 254*), about 58 miles southeast of Tacoma, Wash., is dominated by one of the most impressive landmarks of the Northwest—the mountain that gave the park its name. The towering, glacier-clad, dormant volcanic peak of Mount Rainier stands in stark contrast to the flower-blanketed alpine meadows and majestic forests of its lower slopes. More than 140 miles of roads within the park provide motorists with a wide variety of views of the spectacular mountain scenery.

BEST WAYS TO GET THERE: From Tacoma to the park headquarters at Longmire it is 70 miles via Wash. 7 and Wash. 706. There is also daily bus service (late June to mid-September) from Seattle and Tacoma.

BEST TIME TO VISIT: Mount Rainier often is obscured by fog or clouds, but from July 1 to mid-September (and frequently well into October, when fall colors reach their peak) some warm, clear weather can be expected.

RECREATION: The park has more than 300 miles of well-marked trails, ranging from 15-minute walks over self-guided nature trails to 90-mile-long Wonderland Trail, which circles the entire mountain. There is some fishing, but late in the season it is limited by the cold of the glacial streams and lakes. Mountain climbing is for the hardy only; professional guide service, instruction and rental equipment can be obtained at the Paradise visitor center. Winter sports are featured from early December to early May.

ACCOMMODATIONS: Hotels within the park are National Park Inn at Longmire (early May until mid-October) and Paradise Inn (late June to Labor Day); write to Mount Ranier National Park Hospitality Service, 4820 South Washington, Tacoma, Wash. 98409, for rates and reservations. There are six main campgrounds and three smaller, more primitive ones. Trailers are admitted, but campsites cannot be reserved. Campgrounds are closed in winter except for a small one at Sunshine Point.

OLYMPIC NATIONAL PARK (*see p. 258*), occupying the center and the western edge of Washington's Olympic Peninsula, is a unique wilderness of rugged mountains, extraordinary coniferous rain forests, varied wildlife, glaciers, streams, lakes, abundant wild flowers and unspoiled Pacific seascapes. The rain forests, among the major attractions in the park, can be seen in the lowlands of the west slope (in the valleys of the Hoh, Quinault and Queets rivers). Several spur roads enter the park, and Hurricane Ridge, in the north, offers superb mountain views. The Pacific Coast Area (*see p. 261*), a 50-mile-long strip that is part of but separate from the main park, is notable as one of the most primitive coastlines remaining in the conterminous United States.

BEST WAY TO GET THERE: To Winslow by ferry from downtown Seattle; then take Wash. 305 and Wash. 104 to U.S. 101, which circles the Olympic Peninsula and runs through part of the park's Pacific Coast Area and along Lake Crescent in the north. The best park entry is the Port Angeles Visitor Center.

BEST TIME TO VISIT: Olympic National Park is open all year, but the best weather is in the summer and early fall. Most of the high-country roads are snowfree by June and the trails by July. Summers are generally cool and sunny in the Northwest, so plan your wardrobe accordingly; some wet-weather clothing may come in handy.

RECREATION: There are numerous and varied trails, and maps and trail guides are available. No license is required for the fine fishing in the park's streams and lakes, but check park headquarters or ranger stations for seasons. Horses and guides are available in Port Angeles and Forks. There are numerous designated picnic areas.

ACCOMMODATIONS: Campgrounds are located throughout Olympic National Park, some of which will accept trailers; reservations are not available. A concessionaire-operated trailer village (now open all year) is on the north shore of Lake Crescent. For information on the park's cabins and lodges, write the Park Superintendent, 600 East Park Avenue, Port Angeles, Wash. 98362. Motel facilities are available in towns outside the park.

NORTH CASCADES NATIONAL PARK, established by Congress in October 1968, has been described as encompassing "an area of alpine scenery unmatched in the United States . . ." and as "the most breathtakingly beautiful and spectacular mountain scenery in the contiguous 48 states." In setting aside this remarkable region of Washington as a park, Congress also created the Ross Lake National Recreation Area and the Lake Chelan National Recreation Area on its southeastern boundary. The park, thus divided into north and south sections, encompasses 505,000 acres.

BEST WAYS TO GET THERE: Driving south from Bellingham (about 75 miles) or north from the Seattle-Tacoma area (less than 150 miles), take Interstate 5 and Wash. 20. The latter is the North Cascades Highway, which leads into the Ross Lake Area and then dips southeast toward the Lake Chelan Area.

Access to the southern tip of Lake Chelan is via U.S. 2 and U.S. 97.

BEST TIME TO VISIT: The climate varies considerably from the wet, frequently foggy regions on the park's west side to the semiarid Stehekin Valley in the southeast. As with other northwestern areas, summer is considered the best time to visit.

RECREATION: The Ross Lake National Recreation Area offers camping (with sites accessible from the highway), picnicking, fishing, boating and hiking. There are self-guided nature trails to points of interest, evening campfire programs and exhibits that enhance one's enjoyment of the magnificent mountains, forest-carpeted valleys, cirques and glaciers. A 55-mile trip by boat or float plane up the length of Lake Chelan brings visitors to Stehekin, within the Lake Chelan Area, where similar activities are offered.

ACCOMMODATIONS: Lodging, food, gasoline and other basic supplies and services are available from the early spring through late fall within both of the recreation areas. Many services are available year-round in Stehekin.

ALASKA, HAWAII AND THE CARIBBEAN

MOUNT McKINLEY NATIONAL PARK (*see p. 272*) embraces more than 3000 square miles of a huge subarctic Alaskan wilderness. Towering over this starkly beautiful land—just 250 miles south of the Arctic Circle— is 20,320-foot Mount McKinley, the highest mountain in North America. The topography varies from lofty peaks to lowlands and stream valleys; there is a similar variety of plant and animal communities. A single terminal road, normally open from about June 1 to Sept. 10, passes an ever-changing panorama of rugged mountain scenery, forests, colorful tundra and rivers as it penetrates the park interior. In addition to moose and grizzly bears, Mount McKinley has two species of mammals unique in the national park system— Dall sheep and barren-ground caribou (which are frequently seen near the road in numbers varying from one to several hundred and even thousands, particularly during the migrating season in late June and early July). The 132 species of birds that have so far been identified in the park vary in size from the tiny kinglet to the large, soaring golden eagle. White and black spruce, interspersed with quaking aspen, white birch and balsam poplar, constitute the bulk of the forest, but most of the park lies above timberline.

BEST WAYS TO GET THERE: The park entrance is 235 miles from Anchorage via the Glen Highway (Alaska 1) and Alaska 3, and 123 miles from Fairbanks via Alaska 3, a divided highway completed in 1972. There is scheduled air service to Anchorage and Fairbanks, where cars can be rented and chartered air tours arranged. In summer the Alaska Railroad has daily passenger service, with vistadome cars, from Anchorage (seven hours) and from Fairbanks (four hours).

BEST TIME TO VISIT: June and July are the preferred months; unfortunately this is also the favorite season for mosquitoes (be sure to bring insect repellent). "Cool, wet and windy" basically describes the park's summer weather, but there is much variation, so go prepared for moderately warm, sunny weather as well.

RECREATION: Hiking, guided tours, mountain climbing and fishing.

ACCOMMODATIONS: Seven campgrounds are located along the park road from the hotel area to Wonder Lake. (There are no utility outlets for trailers, and no food or gasoline is available. Campers should bring warm clothing, good sleeping bags and a kerosine- or gas-burning camp stove. Some type of waterproof shelter is imperative, as rainy days and nights are frequent. McKinley Park Hotel offers lodging and meals on the European plan. Camp Denali, a small resort just north of Wonder Lake, outside the park, also provides accommodations and meals.

KATMAI NATIONAL MONUMENT,

on the Alaska Peninsula, is remote from civilization, a vast, wild landscape that offers remarkable scenery and a memorable wilderness experience. Its 4362 square miles of northern frontier land include the site of a tremendous volcanic eruption; some magnificent wild animals, specifically the Alaska brown bear; a series of large, beautiful lakes north of the volcanic area; and gemlike islets off the seacoast. On June 6, 1912, at the present site of Novarupta Volcano, a thunderous blast spewed forth masses of pumice and rock fragments. Within minutes 2½ cubic miles of white-hot ash were expelled, trees were snapped off and carbonized by scorching wind, and more than 40 square miles of valley floor were buried to depths as great as 700 feet. The hot gases and steam rising through countless holes and cracks in the earth—they are called fumaroles—caused this ash-buried region to be named Valley of the Ten Thousand Smokes. At or about the same time the entire top of Mount Katmai, six miles to the east, collapsed, creating a chasm almost three miles long and two miles wide. This was one of the biggest volcanic eruptions in history, but not one human life is known to have been lost. Now all but a few of the fumaroles are extinct, but the valley is still a place of absorbing interest— for its deposits of varicolored volcanic rock and its hardy pioneer plants struggling to reestablish a cover over the bare ground. Other areas of Katmai have a healthy and varied plant life which provides food, protection and breeding ground for many kinds of birds and mammals.

BEST WAY TO GET THERE: Katmai is accessible only by air. Package air tours

are available from Anchorage to three camps at the monument. Anchorage can be reached by highway and by scheduled airline service.

BEST TIME TO VISIT: Air tours to the monument are scheduled from June 1 to Labor Day.

RECREATION: Four-wheel-drive bus tours, float-plane tours, hiking, boating (including boat rentals) and fishing.

ACCOMMODATIONS: The concessionaire-operated accommodations in Katmai are Brooks Lodge, Grosvenor Camp, and Kulik Lodge, all with cabins, bathhouses, and modern lodges. There is a National Park Service campground at Brooks River, but visitors can camp anywhere once they receive a fire permit.

MENDENHALL GLACIER, in North Tongass National Forest, Alaska, is one of the largest glaciers in the world accessible by road. Its massive face of deeply crevassed ice is almost 1½ miles wide and between 100 and 200 feet high; the glacier fills the valley for nearly 12 miles. This spectacular ice

341

mass is receding northeast at the rate of a little less than 50 feet a year; the ice now seen on the face is about 200 years old. As the glacier slowly moves and shifts, great icebergs detach from its face and plunge into Mendenhall Lake, which has been formed by the glacier's melt. From the lake, the Mendenhall River winds through a ten-square-mile glacial flat toward its outlet in one of the many coves on southeast Alaska's Inland Passage. Mendenhall Glacier has its source in the great Juneau Ice Cap, a vast, permanent snowfield covering the entire mountain divide for almost 80 miles between Juneau and Skagway. Across Mendenhall Lake from the glacier a circular visitor center affords an all-weather view of the glacier face; visitors may learn about glaciation from exhibits and from Forest Service naturalists and may follow a self-guided trail to observe glaciation effects at first hand.

BEST WAY TO GET THERE: The visitor center is accessible by highway from Juneau (13 miles). Juneau is reached by highway (Alaska 7) and by airlines. **BEST TIME TO VISIT:** Although Mendenhall Glacier is an all-year attraction, most visitors come during the summer. **RECREATION:** Hiking, picnicking and over 106 remote fishing, hunting and camping sites in the Tongass National Forest. **ACCOMMODATIONS:** Mendenhall Campground, located on the west shore of the lake, contains camping and trailer units. The nearest overnight lodging is at Juneau, where there are hotels, inns and lodges.

GLACIER BAY NATIONAL MONUMENT, extending over 4381 square miles in southeastern Alaska, is an incredible region of ice-capped mountains, active tidal glaciers, deep fjords, remarkably lush forests and an abundant assortment of wildlife. The glaciers offer a spectacular show of geologic forces in action. As water undermines the ice fronts, great blocks up to 200 feet high break off and crash into the sea, creating tremendous waves and filling the narrow inlets with massive icebergs. Muir and Johns Hopkins glaciers discharge such great volumes of ice that it is seldom safe to approach their cliffs closer than two miles. The mountains of the Fairweather Range are as impressive as the glaciers. The highest peak is 15,320-foot Mount Fairweather, and several other summits ex-

ceed 10,000 feet. Glacier Bay and its many fjords are a result of erosion by glacial quarrying and abrasion, plus thundering glacier-caused landslides. The bay itself was little more than a dent in the shoreline when Capt. George Vancouver sailed past in 1794. Since then, however, the glaciers have receded more rapidly than anywhere else in the world. Today few glaciers extend to the sea, and all stages of plant succession are strikingly illustrated in the monument. Alaska brown bears, black bears and the rare glacier, or "blue," bears may sometimes be observed quite close to the glacier fronts as well as in the more developed plant communities. Mountain goats are abundant, and Sitka deer inhabit the forests near the mouth of Glacier Bay and the ocean coast. Numerous streams are filled with spawning salmon in late summer and early autumn, and Dolly Varden and cutthroat trout live in many of the crystal-clear lakes and streams.

BEST WAYS TO GET THERE: Travel to the Glacier Bay National Monument is limited to boats and planes. Flying time from Juneau to monument headquarters is about 30 minutes, via scheduled airline or chartered plane. By boat the distance is about 100 miles. In order to see a representative part of the area, visitors by private or chartered boat should plan to spend at least two days. **BEST TIME TO VISIT:** Mid-June to mid-September is the main travel season. Summer temperatures seldom exceed 72° F. **RECREATION:** Guided tours, hiking, mountain climbing, fishing and boating. (Private boaters should not attempt to navigate Glacier Bay without appropriate charts, tide tables and local knowledge. Floating ice is a special hazard.) **ACCOMMODATIONS:** Glacier Bay Lodge at Bartlett Cove (monument headquarters) is open from late May to mid-September; there is also a campground. The monument's several hundred miles of shoreline and its many islands provide unlimited camping opportunities. Be prepared, however, for cool, damp, weather.

HALEAKALA, "The House of the Sun," a dormant volcano on Hawaii's Maui Island, has one of the largest and most colorful "craters" on earth, its sides streaked with red, yellow, gray and black. (Actually this huge depression is an erosional scar, and not a true volcanic crater.) Millions of years ago

a subterranean disturbance created a volcano 18,000 feet below the ocean's surface. Repeated eruptions over the ages spread layer upon layer of lava until the volcano head emerged from the sea to become the island of Maui, finally towering thousands of feet above the Pacific. Haleakala National Park, covering some 34 square miles, includes the 10,023-foot volcano with its 7-mile-long and 2½-mile-wide cone-studded

water-carved "crater," forests, exotic plants and birds, and the seven Oheo Pools of Kipahulu. The summit crater was once revered as the haunt of Maui, a demigod who, legend says, snared the sun's rays until the sun promised to cross the sky more slowly. Among the plants is the rare silversword; when mature it develops a huge cluster of 100 to 500 yellow and reddish purple flower heads, each consisting of hundreds of florets. Native birds that may be seen are the iiwi, whose bright scarlet body and black wings and tail make it one of the most beautiful of all Hawaiian birds; the rare nene, or Hawaiian goose (recently reintroduced); the scarlet, white and black apapane and the speedy, bright green and yellow amakihi. Most of the other birds, however, and all mammals but one (a small brown bat) have been introduced by man and have unfortunately upset the island's natural balance.

BEST WAY TO GET THERE: It is 26 miles to park headquarters from Kahului Airport (served from Hilo and Honolulu), via Hawaii routes 37, 377 and 378.

BEST TIME TO VISIT: Weather varies considerably; summers are generally dry and moderately warm, but there are occasional cool, windy days. Afternoons are best for observing and photographing the crater, mornings for viewing neighboring islands and western Maui.

RECREATION: Hiking (the crater has 30 miles of well-marked trails—permits are required—and there are several shorter walks), horseback riding (there are guided trips into the crater).

ACCOMMODATIONS: Haleakala National Park has four primitive campgrounds, two of them in the crater wilderness. There are three cabins that accommodate 12 persons each and can be reached only on foot or horseback. Maui, however, has a number of lodging facilities: resort hotels and apartments, motels, cottages and beach clubs.

HAWAII VOLCANOES NATIONAL PARK (see p. 283), embracing one of the most active volcanic areas on earth, is on the island of Hawaii—largest in the chain that comprises our only island state. The park's famous summits are 13,680-foot Mauna Loa and, 9000 feet below, Kilauea. Both volcanoes are young, geologically, for their growth keeps well ahead of the persistent

agents of erosion. Since man has watched it, Mauna Loa has been intermittently active, with periods of quiet ranging from a few months to more than a decade. One of the most voluminous flows in its recorded history began on June 1, 1950, and lasted for 23 days.

The highly fluid lava, liberated through a fissure 13 miles long, reached the sea in less than three hours. Kilauea's most spectacular eruption began on Nov. 15, 1959, when lava fountains played from a rift along the side of Kilauea Iki Crater. One of the fountains reached 1900 feet—by far the highest fountain of molten lava ever measured in Hawaii and probably in the world. The best introduction to the park is the 11-mile Crater Rim Drive. It passes lush jungle with incredible giant tree ferns, raw craters and great areas of volcanic devastation; along the road are scenic overlooks and trails to points of special interest. One of the features off Mauna Loa Strip Road, west of the visitor center on Kilauea, is a bird park with a self-guided nature trail entering open forest with many varieties of native trees. Another spectacular motor route is Hilini Pali (cliff) Road. The very scenic Chain of Craters Road was severely damaged by a spectacular 23-hour eruption of Kilauea in June 1969, but it had already been closed because of eruptions earlier in the year.

BEST WAYS TO GET THERE: There are scheduled flights from Honolulu to Hilo and Kailua-Kona several times daily (Hilo is 30 miles from park headquarters; Kailua-Kona, 96 miles). Unscheduled ship transportation is also available. Taxis meet all planes and ships, and cars can be rented in either city.

BEST TIME TO VISIT: Seasons in this semitropical climate are not pronounced, but summer tends to have the best weather. As Kilauea Volcano is 4000 feet above sea level, the weather can be cool at any time. Be sure to bring a raincoat—rainfall at park headquarters averages 100 inches a year.

RECREATION: Guided tours, hiking, mountain climbing and fishing. The main trails in the park range from simple walks that take a quarter of an hour to an all-day hike on the Crater Rim Trail. The climb up Mauna Loa is a three-day trip.

ACCOMMODATIONS: Hawaii Volcanoes National Park has several developed campgrounds and two semi-equipped overnight cabins for those who climb Mauna Loa—one at 10,000 feet and one at the summit. Volcano House is a concessionaire-operated hotel on the rim of Kilauea Crater and is open all year. There are numerous lodging facilities—hotels, apartments, inns and motels—in Hilo and Kailua-Kona.

WAIMEA CANYON (see p. 288) is on Kauai, Hawaii's "Garden Isle." Kauai was the first of the Hawaiian chain to be free of volcanic activity and is believed to have been the first to be settled. The lack of volcanic activity has given nature time to turn Kauai's lava into rich soil and the island into a verdant wonderland. At the center of Kauai is Mount Waialeale—reputed to be the wettest spot on earth, with a

concentration of rainfall that may reach up to 60 *feet* a year. The erosive power of this immense amount of water is particularly evident in unforgettable Waimea Canyon, which developed from a fault in the earth's crust west of Waialeale. The paved Kokee Road (Hawaii 55) makes the precipitous climb up to and along the rim of the canyon, to Kalalau Lookout. There are spectacular views from here of the beautiful Kalalau Valley and, to the south and 4000 feet below, the Pacific Ocean. On the way up to Kalalau, at the 3400-foot level, is Canyon Lookout, which offers the best views of this long, multihued canyon. Kokee State Park, between Canyon and Kalalau lookouts, is a rugged and primitive section of Kauai, with a number of hiking trails. Captain Cook landed at Waimea in 1778.

BEST WAYS TO GET THERE: Scheduled air service runs from Honolulu to Lihue, county seat of Kauai (the flight takes about 25 minutes). Jetfoil service (waterborne) is also available. The Waimea Canyon section can be visited by guided bus or helicopter tour, and automobiles may be rented right at the airport.

BEST TIME TO VISIT: There is not much seasonal variation in temperature, but visitors should be prepared for the cooler weather they may experience several thousand feet above sea level; rain gear should be taken.

RECREATION: Hiking, picnicking, fishing, hunting and shell collecting are to be enjoyed in the two state parks.

ACCOMMODATIONS: Kokee State Park has a campground; elsewhere on Kauai there are a number of resort hotels, many of them on or near the island's beaches.

CARIBBEAN NATIONAL FOREST is

the largest natural tropical forest in Puerto Rico and the only tropical unit in the vast national forest system. About half of the nearly 58,000 acres within its boundaries are Forest Service lands. The most remarkable feature of this region is the luxuriant rain forest, which occupies the lower elevations. The crowns of tropical hardwoods are vine-clad, while every trunk or branch supports fascinating air plants (epiphytes), including many pineapplelike bromeliads with their red-orange spikes. Beneath the tall trees are smaller species, which rise out of a blanket of flowers, herbs, mosses and ferns (some of which grow 30 feet high). Of the more than 50 species of birds in the national forest, most remarkable is the rare blue, red and green Puerto Rico parrot. The forest contains 240 native trees, which vary with the topography—from tropical hardwoods indigenous to the humid rain forest to sierra palms at high elevations. The highest point in the rain forest, El Yunque, is 3493 feet above sea level.

BEST WAY TO GET THERE: Caribbean National Forest is about 25 miles east of San Juan via P.R. 3 and P.R. 191. Rental cars are available in San Juan, and there are tours from the city.

BEST TIME TO VISIT: The forest is an all-year attraction. Temperatures range in the 70s and 80s; storms are usually comparatively brief. Visitors to the rain forest should be prepared for the moisture. Shelters are available along the trails and in the picnic areas.

RECREATION: Caribbean National Forest offers facilities for picnicking and swimming. There are a number of hiking trails, including those that lead to the observation towers on El Yunque, the Pinnacles and Mount Britton.

ACCOMMODATIONS: The national forest has no camping or overnight facilities.

Nearby El Verde has a hostelry, and San Juan has a variety of accommodations.

VIRGIN ISLANDS NATIONAL PARK is on St. John, smallest and

least populated of the main American Virgin Islands. Nearly two thirds of its land mass and much of the colorful offshore waters are set aside as our only national park in the West Indies. Here visitors can experience a marine adventure on an underwater nature trail and enjoy breathtaking seascapes and long, stretching views of rocky coastlines, crescent-shaped bays and gleaming white beaches that contrast with the ever-changing blue-green waters. St. John is famous for white coral beaches, scenic mountain roads, walking trails, quiet coves and the magnificent coral gardens that fringe the island.

BEST WAYS TO GET THERE: Most visitors to St. John start from the nearby island of St. Thomas, from which the national park can be reached by boat or airboat to Cruz Bay. Here taxi tours can be arranged and jeeps rented (reservations should be made far in advance). Also popular are all-day, all-inclusive tours that originate in St. Thomas.

BEST TIME TO VISIT: St. John has an equable, mildly tropical climate. The temperature varies only slightly between winter and summer; lowest on record is 61° F., highest is 98° F., and the year's average is 79° F. Rainfall averages about 40 inches a year, mostly in brief night showers.

RECREATION: Swimming, snorkeling (equipment can be rented at Trunk and Cinnamon bays, and guided snorkel trips are conducted weekly), scuba div-

ing (equipment can be rented and serviced on both St. John and St. Thomas), numerous hiking trails (including a guided trip into Reef Bay Valley to see ancient petroglyphs) and nature walks, sail- and powerboat trips and horseback riding.

ACCOMMODATIONS: Cinnamon Bay Campground has tent sites (complete camping equipment can be rented here) and furnished beach cottages. Cottage and campground reservations *must* be made well in advance. Write to: The Concessioner, Cinnamon Bay Camp, St. John, V.I. 00830. Accommodations outside the park are available at Cruz Bay, Caneel Bay and Lille Maho.

BUCK ISLAND NATIONAL MONU-MENT is only a tiny dot in the Carib-

bean, just six miles from Christiansted in St. Croix (largest of the U.S. Virgin Islands). At the eastern end of Buck Island is a truly magnificent barrier reef—and one of the finest marine gardens in the entire Caribbean area. The seaward front of this barrier reef, which is immediately below the surface of the Caribbean just a few hundred yards offshore, is a solid wall of staghorn and elkhorn coral. The reef extends like a giant horseshoe around the land mass (the island is only a mile long and a third of a mile wide), fencing off the incredibly clear emerald waters of the lagoon. Snorkeling is the only way to follow the marked underwater trail through this submarine world of brightly colored tropical fishes, coral grottoes and swaying sea fans, and most boats that bring visitors here from St. Croix furnish the necessary equipment. The uninhabited island itself is a rookery for majestic frigate (man-o'-war) birds and pelicans; green turtles lay their eggs on the beaches. Beautiful Turtle Beach occupies Buck Island's southwestern shoreline.

BEST WAYS TO GET THERE: St. Croix, about 40 miles south of St. Thomas, is served by several scheduled airlines. Trips by boat to Buck Island can be arranged from there.

BEST TIME TO VISIT: The semitropical climate of this area makes Buck Island a year-round attraction.

RECREATION: Snorkeling, picnicking (visitors must bring their own lunch, although many boats furnish refreshments), swimming and hiking.

ACCOMMODATIONS: Buck Island has no camping or overnight lodging facilities.

INDEX

ILLUSTRATION CREDITS

"PART" PHOTOGRAPHS: 8–9: (Acadia National Park) Grant Heilman. 58–59: (Cypress trees) Photo-Library. 108–09: (Illinois landscape) John H. Gerard. 156–57: (Glacier National Park) Helen Cruickshank. 188–89: (Spider Rock, Canyon de Chelly) Debs Metzong. 226–27: (Olympic National Park) Bob Clemenz. 264–65: (Pololu Valley, Hawaii) David Muench. 290–91: (Sierra Blanca, New Mexico) Dick Kent. ALL OTHER PHOTOGRAPHS: 10–11: Don Renner/Photo Trends. 14–15: Arthur Griffin. 17, 18: Dick Smith. 20–21: Laurence R. Lowry/Rapho Guillumette. 22–23: Dick Smith. 24–25: Grant Haist. 26–27: Bullaty-Lomeo. 30–31: E. R. Degginger. 33: Ned Barnard. 35: Frank Eck. 36–37: Ned Barnard. 38–39: E. R. Degginger. 40–43: Eliot Porter. 44: Charles E. Rotkin. 46–47: Jack Zehrt. 48–49: Kenneth P. Sneider. 51: Ned Barnard. 54, 57: Walter Chandoha. 61: William H. Amos. 62–63: H. H. Harvey. 64, 65: M. E. Warren/Photo Researchers. 66–67: Raymond L. Nelson. 70–71: Walter S. Terhune, U.S. Forest Service. 74–75: National Park Concessions. 76–77: Jack Zehrt. 78–79: Peter Sanchez. 80–81: Eliot Porter. 83: Marjorie Pickens. 86–87: Ernest Ferguson/Photo Arts. 89: Kirtley-Perkins. 92–95: James A. Kern. 96: William D. Griffin. 98: Alabama Bureau of Publicity and Information. 102–03: Ross E. Hutchins. 104: Dennis J. Cipnic. 105: (top) Dennis J. Cipnic; (bottom) E. R. Degginger. 107: Kenneth L. Smith. 110–11: Dan Morrill/Stock Photo Finders. 114–15, 117: Irvin L. Oakes. 118–19: Allan Roberts. 120–21: E. R. Degginger. 122: James Stanfield/Black Star. 124–25: Ken Dequaine. 127: Larry West/Full Moon Studio. 129: National Park Service. 130–31: Laurence R. Lowry/Rapho Guillumette. 135: Tom Burgess. 136–37: Jack Zehrt. 138–39: Paul Lefebvre. 142–43: E. R. Degginger. 146–47: Grant Heilman. 149: Jack Zehrt. 150–51: E. R. Degginger. 152–53: Durward L. Allen. 154–55: Wilford L. Miller. 158–60: David Muench. 162–63: Jack Zehrt. 164–65, 167: David Muench. 168–69: Jack Zehrt. 171–73: Bob Clemenz. 174–75: David Muench. 176–77: Helen Cruickshank. 180–81: B. B. Jones. 182–83, 185, 186: B. E. Norton. 190–91: George F. Tuley. 192: National Park Service. 194–95: Jack Zehrt. 198: Josef Muench. 199: Dick Kent. 200–02: David Muench. 205: E. R. Degginger. 208–10, 213: David Muench. 214–15: Josef Muench. 216–17: David Muench. 218–19: Hildegard Hamilton. 221, 222: Bill Ratcliffe. 224, 225: David Muench. 228–30, 232–33, 236: David Muench. 238–41: Dennis Brokaw. 242, 245: David Muench. 246–47: Jack Zehrt. 250–51: David Muench. 252–53: Ray Atkeson. 255: Kenneth W. Fink. 256: William C. Bullard. 258–59: Dennis Brokaw. 262–63: Ned Barnard. 266–67: Robert W. Young/Lenstours. 268–69: Willis Peterson. 270: Steve McCutcheon. 274–75: Bob and Ira Spring. 276: Floyd Norgaard/Lenstours. 278–81: Jack Zehrt. 285: Robert W. Carpenter. 286, 288, 289: David Muench. 293: J. E. Coufal. 296–97: E. R. Degginger. 298–99: Ray Atkeson. 300–02: David Muench.

PICTURE EDITOR: Robert J. Woodward.   MAPS: James Alexander; John Ballantine.   DRAWINGS: John Pimlott.

351

ACKNOWLEDGMENTS

The quotation on the opening page of this book is from *This Is the American Earth* by Ansel Adams and Nancy Newhall, © 1960, The Sierra Club.

THE NATURAL LOOK OF NEW ENGLAND, by Louise Dickinson Rich, cond. from *The Natural World of Louise Dickinson Rich,* © 1962, Louise Dickinson Rich; reprinted by permission of Dodd, Mead & Company, Inc. A NOTCH IN NEW HAMPSHIRE, by Freeman Tilden, as "Franconia Notch State Park" in *The State Parks;* reprinted by permission of Alfred A. Knopf, Inc., publishers. THE WEATHERED PEAKS OF VERMONT, by Rockwell Stephens, as "The Green Mountains" in *Vermont Life,* © 1967, Vermont Life magazine, pub. by the Vermont Development Dept. AMERICA'S PRICELESS SEASHORE, by Don Wharton, from *National Wildlife,* © 1966 and pub. by The National Wildlife Federation. BEWITCHED BY THE GREAT SWAMP, by Robert C. Frederiksen, from the Providence *Sunday Journal,* © 1967 and pub. by Providence Journal Co. CONNECTICUT'S PASTORAL PERIMETER, by Joel Lieber, as "Pastoral Perimeter" in *Travel* magazine, © 1964 and pub. by Travel Magazine, Inc. WALKING IN THE ALLEGHENY FOREST, by Edwin L. Peterson, cond. from *Penn's Woods West,* © 1958 and pub. by The University of Pittsburgh Press. THE WEALTH OF JERSEY'S "BARRENS," by John T. Cunningham, from *Audubon* magazine, © 1966 and pub. by The National Audubon Society, Inc. DELAWARE'S WILD LANDS, by Willard T. Johns, as "They're Saving Delaware's Wild Lands" in *National Wildlife,* © 1968 and pub. by The National Wildlife Federation, Inc. TOWPATH ALONG THE POTOMAC, by William O. Douglas, cond. from *My Wilderness, East to Katahdin,* © 1961, William O. Douglas, pub. by Doubleday & Co., Inc.; reprinted by permission of William Morris Agency, Inc. SENTINEL IN THE FOREST, by Maurice Brooks, cond. from *The Appalachians,* © 1965, Maurice Brooks, pub. by Houghton Mifflin Co. NATURE'S UNDERGROUND CATHEDRAL, by Bill Surface, cond. from *Travel* magazine, © 1969 and pub. by Travel Magazine, Inc. OUR FIRST NATIONAL SEASHORE, by Don Wharton, cond. from *Today's Living,* © 1960 and pub. by New York Herald Tribune, Inc. THE GREAT SMOKIES, by George Laycock, from *National Wildlife,* © 1963 and pub. by The National Wildlife Federation, Inc. SOUTH CAROLINA'S SEA ISLANDS, by Eugene B. Sloan, as "Coast Toast: South Carolina's Sea Islands" in *Travel* magazine, © 1961 and pub. by Travel Magazine, Inc. INTO THE RIVER OF GRASS, by Roger Tory Peterson and James Fisher, cond. from *Wild America,* © 1955, Roger T. Peterson, pub. by Houghton Mifflin Co. SCENIC PARADISE IN ALABAMA, by John Goodrum, as "Alabama's Mountain Lakes" in *Travel* magazine, © 1969 and pub. by Travel Magazine, Inc. ISLAND OF ADVENTURE, by Ross E. Hutchins, cond. from the book, © 1968, Ross E. Hutchins; reprinted by permission of Dodd, Mead & Company, Inc. FLOATING THE BUFFALO RIVER, by Bern Keating, cond. from *Ford Times,* © 1969 and pub. by Ford Motor Company. OUR GLORIOUS GREAT LAKES, by Noel Mostert, cond. from *Holiday,* © 1968 and pub. by The Curtis Pub. Co. FANTASY IN SANDSTONE, by Freeman Tilden, as "Hocking State Park" in *The State Parks;* reprinted by permission of Alfred A. Knopf, Inc., publishers. ILLINOIS: HEARTLAND OF AMERICA, by Donald Culross Peattie, as "My Favorite State" in *New York Times Magazine,* © 1959, The New York Times Co.; reprinted by permission of Noel R. Peattie and his agent, James Brown Associates, Inc. WISCONSIN'S TWENTY-THREE APOSTLES, by Howard Mead, as "The Apostle Islands" in *Wisconsin Tales and Trails,* © 1967 and pub. by Wisconsin Tales and Trails, Inc. HIAWATHA COUNTRY, by Gene Caesar, as "Michigan's Upper Peninsula" in *Holiday,* © 1965 and pub. by The Curtis Pub. Co. THE SOURCE OF THE MISSISSIPPI, by Willard Price, cond. from *Rivers I Have Known,* © 1965, Willard Price, pub. by The John Day Company, Inc. THE GLACIERS' GIFT TO IOWA, by R. V. Cassill, as "The Lakes of Iowa" in *Holiday,* © 1966 and pub. by

The Curtis Pub. Co.; reprinted by permission of Robert Lantz-Candida Donadio Literary Agency, Inc. UNPREDICTABLE OKLAHOMA, by Angie Debo, cond. from *Oklahoma: Foot-Loose and Fancy-Free,* © 1949 and pub. by The University of Oklahoma Press. HIGHROAD UNDER THE BIG SKY, by Thayne Smith and Clelland Cole, as "Prairie Parkway" in *Kansas!* pub. by the Kansas Department of Economic Development. NEBRASKA'S GREEN SEA OF DUNES, by Edwin Way Teale, cond. from *Journey Into Summer,* © 1960, Edwin Way Teale; reprinted by permission of Dodd, Mead & Company, Inc. THE BLACK HILLS, by Badger Clark, cond. from the book, edited by Roderick Peattie, © 1952, The Vanguard Press, Inc.; reprinted by permission of The Vanguard Press Inc. THE ROCKIES AND THE GREAT DIVIDE, by David Lavender, cond. from *The Rockies,* © 1968, David Lavender; reprinted by permission of Harper & Row, Publishers. THE YELLOWSTONE NOBODY KNOWS, by Erwin A. Bauer, from *National Wildlife,* © 1966 and pub. by The National Wildlife Federation. MONTANA'S MISSION MOUNTAINS, by Helen Gere Cruickshank, as "A Summer of Riches" in *Audubon* magazine, © 1966 and pub. by The National Audubon Society. IDAHO: "SUN IN THE MOUNTAINS," excerpted from *Idaho: A Guide in Word and Picture* (American Guide Series), © 1937, 1950, Oxford University Press, Inc.; reprinted by permission of the publisher. TEXAS' TREASURE ISLAND, by William M. Hall, as "The Many Faces of Padre Island" in *American Forests* magazine, © 1966 and pub. by The American Forestry Assn. MY SOUTHWEST, by Jack Schaefer, from *Holiday,* © 1959, Jack Schaefer; reprinted by permission of Harold Matson Company, Inc. UTAH'S POCKET SAHARA, by Joseph Wood Krutch, as "Coral Dunes" in *Audubon* magazine, © 1968 and pub. by The National Audubon Society. CALIFORNIA'S MAJESTIC SEQUOIAS, by Stewart L. Udall, as "Sequoia and Kings' Canyon" in *National Parks of America,* © 1966 and pub. by Country Beautiful Foundation, Inc. OUR IMMORTAL REDWOODS, by Donald Culross Peattie, cond. from *Frontiers* magazine, © 1945, The Academy of Natural Sciences of Philadelphia. SNOWCAPPED RULER OF THE REALM, by Robert Walkinshaw, cond. from *On Puget Sound,* © 1929, G. P. Putnam's Sons, renewed 1957, Robert B. Walkinshaw, pub. by G. P. Putnam's Sons. THE AWESOME OLYMPIC RAIN FOREST, by Ruth Kirk, as "The Rain Forest" in *Audubon* magazine, © 1966 and pub. by The National Audubon Society, Inc.; reprinted by permission of The University of Washington Press. WASHINGTON'S WILD AND ROCKY SHORE, by William O. Douglas, cond. from *My Wilderness, the Pacific West,* © 1960, William O. Douglas, pub. by Doubleday & Co., Inc.; reprinted by permission of William Morris Agency, Inc. THE LANDSCAPES OF ALASKA, by Thomas M. Griffiths, as "The Landscapes of Far Alaska" in *Natural History* magazine, © 1960 and pub. by The American Museum of Natural History. WILD WONDERLAND OF THE NORTH, by Willis Peterson, as "Denali Interlude" in *Audubon* magazine, © 1967 and pub. by The National Audubon Society. OAHU: THE GATHERING PLACE and TERRA INFIRMA, by Stanley D. Porteus, cond. from *Calabashes and Kings,* © 1945, Stanley D. Porteus, pub. by Pacific Books. THE WILDERNESS: A NATIONAL TREASURE, by Orville L. Freeman and Michael Frome, cond. from *The National Forests of America,* © 1968, Country Beautiful Foundation, Inc., pub. by permission of G. P. Putnam's Sons. BEYOND WHAT THE EYE SEES, by Freeman Tilden, from *Travel and Camera,* © 1969 and pub. by U.S. Camera Publishing Corp. PRESERVE THE GRANDEUR OF THE LAND, by William O. Douglas, cond. from *Ladies' Home Journal,* © 1964 and pub. by The Curtis Pub. Co.

The editors of Reader's Digest are deeply indebted to the many people in the state and federal agencies (particularly the National Park Service and the United States Forest Service) whose cooperation made this book possible.